Procopius

THE TRANSFORMATION OF THE CLASSICAL HERITAGE

Peter Brown, General Editor

I

Art and Ceremony in Late Antiquity
by Sabine G. MacCormack

II

Synesius of Cyrene: Philosopher-Bishop
by Jay Bregman

III

Theodosian Empresses: Women and Imperial Dominion
in Late Antiquity
by Kenneth G. Holum

IV

John Chrysostom and the Jews: Rhetoric and Reality
in the Late Fourth Century
by Robert L. Wilken

V

Biography in Late Antiquity: A Quest
for the Holy Man
by Patricia Cox

VI

Pachomius: The Making of a Community
In Fourth-Century Egypt
by Philip Rousseau

VII

Change in Byzantine Culture in the Eleventh
and Twelfth Centuries
by A.P. Kazhdan and Ann Wharton Epstein

VIII

Leadership and Community in Late Antique Gaul
by Raymond Van Dam

IX

Homer the Theologian: Neoplatonist Allegorical
Reading and the Growth of the Epic Tradition
by Robert Lamberton

X

Procopius and the Sixth Century
by Averil Cameron

XI

Guardians of the Language
The Grammarian and Society in Late Antiquity
by R.A. Kaster

PROCOPIUS

and the sixth century

Averil Cameron

University of California Press
Berkeley and Los Angeles

University of California Press, Berkeley and Los Angeles

Library of Congress Cataloging in Publication Data

Cameron, Averil.
Procopius and the sixth century.

Bibliography: p.
1. Procopius, of Caesarea. 2. Byzantine Empire—
Intellectual life. 3. Byzantine Empire—History—
Justinian I, 527-565—Historiography. I. Title.
DF505.7.P7C35   1984   907′.2024   84-28020
ISBN 0-520-05517-9

Printed and bound in Great Britain

For

ARNALDO MOMIGLIANO

Contents

Preface

This book has been a long time in gestation. It owed its inception to a suggestion by Hugh Lloyd-Jones, too readily taken up by me in the belief that a book on Procopius would not be too difficult a task for one who had after all used Procopius constantly and thought she knew him. But he proved not to be easily cracked, and the book which has resulted, after many hold-ups of another sort, is very different from the one originally envisaged. While nearly all existing work on Procopius has concentrated on how reliable he is, how much 'fact' can be extracted, the problem that interested me most was how to deal with his three apparently very different works without resorting to psychological speculation or becoming too embroiled in circular arguments about dating. Procopius has attracted many admirers for the wrong reasons. Some of these misconceptions need to be corrected and the works seen for what they are before we can begin to use them.

I was much helped by a year's leave from King's College in 1977/78 spent at the Institute for Advanced Studies, Princeton, and by a short stay as a Summer Fellow at Dumbarton Oaks in 1981. Otherwise my thanks are due above all to the many friends and colleagues who have shared with me the results of their own work so that I could make this book as indicative of current trends as possible in the many fields on which Procopius' work touches. I am especially grateful to T.S. Brown, P.J. Casey, Maria Cesa, Brian Croke, James Crow, Geoffrey de Ste. Croix, Alanna Emmett, Michael Maas, Philip Mayerson, John Nandris, Andrew Poulter, Roger Scott, John Smedley, Edward Thompson, Yoram Tsafrir, Everett Wheeler, L.M. Whitby and Ian Wood. Arnaldo Momigliano read the typescript when it was still in a crude form; he will forgive me for my perversity in not following all his suggestions. To mark his seventy-fifth year I dedicate this book to him with affection and gratitude to a teacher and a friend.

London
1 January 1984

A.M.C.

Introduction

Procopius of Caesarea has always enjoyed a lively reputation. He was recognised immediately as a major historian. Rediscovered after the eclipse of letters in the seventh and eighth centuries, he was a main source for Theophanes' *Chronicle*. In modern times he has been known since the fifteenth century, and he provided the basis for the favourable view of Justinian held by the early modern jurists. With the discovery of the *Secret History* in the Vatican Library in 1623, he became the centre of controversy: how could one and the same man have written the admired *History of the Wars* and this scurrilous pamphlet? There were many who denied the possibility, but serious nineteenth-century studies, with the excellent critical edition by J. Haury (1905-13), established the uniformity of style between the *Wars*, the *Secret History* and the *Buildings*. J.B. Bury, who had previously denied Procopian authorship of the *Secret History*, was forced to change his view. Since then there has been a mounting bibliography of studies on individual passages or particular problems, but remarkably little overall discussion. Yet Procopius is the main (often the only) source for Justinian's wars. He is the major writer of the period, and that on a voluminous scale. There is no way to understand Justinian's reign, or Justinian himself, without understanding Procopius first, and the main historians of the period, Bury and Stein, not to mention Gibbon, found that they had to produce an analysis of Procopius' work for themselves. A.H.M. Jones, typically, took a more astringent view, but used Procopius just as much.

So there is no dispute about the stature of Procopius. Yet since Dahn in 1865 there has been no substantial book in any language that deals with all the main aspects of Procopius' work: only the encyclopaedic Pauly-Wissowa article by B. Rubin (1957). Much more seriously, the greater part of the work that has been done, especially where it is work of interpretation, has been focussed in the wrong direction. This book attempts both to provide the general study that is so much needed and to lay down the foundation for a different and more realistic way of interpreting Procopius. So much more needs to be done in this period, as well as for Procopius' own work (critical editions of other works, a lexicon for Procopius) that much will for now have to remain sketchy and even impressionistic. But the most pressing problem, as I see it, is that of methodology – how to read Procopius. If that at least is tackled, the rest

can follow later. We are in a field here which is still remarkably unknown
by comparison with most periods of ancient history – some may find it
difficult to realise quite how unknown it is. Procopius is our main guide.
If we get him wrong, we have not much chance of going any further.

There are two main ways in which Procopius has been misunderstood,
first in terms of the relation between his three works, and secondly in
relation to sixth-century society and culture. That is why this book is
titled *Procopius and the Sixth Century*. It tries both to explain the works
by taking them as a unified system and to place this system within a
comprehensible, and therefore explicable, contemporary context. It
makes Procopius seem more easily graspable as a writer at the expense of
making him less unique, and certainly less comfortably 'classical'.

That was the first error, and it still persists – to start from the *Wars*,
which is cast in the familiar mould of classical Greek historiography, and
to seize on Procopius as an old friend in a strange world, the world of
Justinian, church councils, S. Sophia, Theodora. But this approach
causes awful problems with the *Secret History* and the *Buildings*, which
appear far from classical; indeed a large part of the literature is taken up
by attempts to explain the relationship between the three. An extra
dimension of difficulty is added by the problems of dating the works.
There is also the fact that Procopius is so often our only source: how
should his 'evidence' be judged? Not merely 'Is he accurate?' but also
'How can we get round the difficulty that so much essential source
material is filtered through one writer?' Most studies have only asked the
first of these questions. Procopius is commonly regarded as a highly
objective writer, so that the only real problem has seemed to be how to
reconcile statements made in the *Secret History* with statements made
in the *Wars*, on the assumption that if a way could be found Procopius
would hold no more difficulties. The first priority, then, is to find a way
round this dilemma, to explain the relation between the works without
resorting to a crude developmental or psychological view (for we know
next to nothing about Procopius except what can be got from his own
works). The first step towards this explanation will be a detailed
demonstration that, however superficially different, Procopius' works all
exhibit an overall coherence; the *Secret History* is not so undisciplined,
the *Buildings* not so 'insincere' and, above all, the *Wars* not so splendidly
objective and rational as they appear in most modern books. Only then
shall we be able to use Procopius with real understanding. Much of this
book, therefore, is devoted to a fairly detailed analysis of the structure
and articulation of the three works. And because the *Wars* has always
been so privileged over the other two for its supposed classicism, I have
chosen to begin that analysis from the *Secret History* and the *Buildings*,
and only then to work backwards to the *Wars*.

But that leaves the second problem – how to relate Procopius to his
background. While the *Wars* seemed so securely classical in style, this

was hardly a difficulty that arose, especially if the *Secret History* and *Buildings* could be explained in terms of the personal psychology of Procopius. A less idealised view of the *Wars*, however, carries the obligation of placing the other two works not only in the context of Procopius' own life and work (where the argument is circular anyway) but also in their proper social and intellectual setting, in other words of seeing Procopius as a recognisable product of the reign of Justinian, not as some kind of classical throwback. Two chapters therefore are devoted to drawing comparisons between Procopius and other contemporary writers, with the intention of showing how closely he belongs with them, not how different he is from them. But here again we are on treacherous ground, for critical study of some of these writers is only just beginning, and serious overall studies of sixth-century literature in its social context are sadly lacking. It is not yet possible to do more than map out the territory, to try to get out some guidelines for a general view. This book aims to do just that – to find a way of dealing with Procopius, and then to locate his works within a thick context. Much more study of individual authors will be needed, and much more work on Procopius himself, but eventually perhaps we can begin to write a fuller history of Justinian that makes sense of all the different aspects of the reign and does not resort, or resorts less, to unfounded assumptions.

There are many good reasons why it might now be propitious to make this attempt, but the main one is the exciting way in which the study of late antiquity has opened up in recent years. In particular the *Buildings* finds a new urgency in the light of the growth of interest in the archeology of this period; we can now begin to read it in a way that was simply not possible until recently. But the increasing interest in the literature and history of late antiquity for its own sake means, I hope, that the high value placed on Procopius for his 'classical' manner of writing ought to be a thing of the past. From being an author scrutinised for his 'evidence' but studied for himself only by a few, he should surely by now be fitted into the general background of Greek literature in the sixth century, a process that is long overdue.

It would be difficult to exaggerate his importance simply as the writer most responsible for shaping our whole idea of Justinian. Yet if it now seems as though the *Buildings* seriously magnifies the actual extent and importance of the Justinianic building programme, perhaps the *Wars* has led us to place a wholly unwarranted emphasis on the 'reconquest'. Accepting Procopius' formulation, it is tempting, though not necessarily correct, to see the reign largely in terms of a hoped-for restoration of the Roman past. But this is to see it through the eyes of a conservative and a traditionalist for whom change is always an evil. All three of the works, the *Wars* included, present their subject matter only through the filter of Procopius' own views, and he is a highly artful reporter. The Justinian we get from Procopius is Procopius' Justinian, and the wars are Procopius' wars. This book tries to ask how the material is filtered; what are the methods and the typical ploys which Procopius follows, and what influences him as he arranges and selects his material? Why does he include some things and not others, and what kind of critical judgment does he bring to bear?

Procopius is such an important author for the period that he must be rescued from the specialised audience by which he has been largely appreciated in the past and be made more accessible. This is especially necessary since the difficulty of reading a group of texts of this kind also raises the most basic problems of signification, while most previous readings of Procopius have been of the naive kind that has as its main objective the digging out of nuggets of believable information. At this stage both the artfulness of Procopius and the cultural values that his work embodies need to be emphasised. Reporter though he is, in much of the *Wars* at least, he is not and cannot be the straightforward recorder of objective 'truth'. These are the problems which underlly my treatment of his work, and which make him a writer of interest over and above the factual information that he may or may not provide. In the hope, therefore, of making this book accessible to students, western medievalists and non-specialists who may be interested in the wider problems, I have avoided or at least translated Greek; for similar reasons I have chosen to refer to the works by English titles. Thus *Secret History* rather than *Anecdota*, and *Buildings* rather than *De Aedificiis*. It is a little more complicated with the *Wars*, of which there are eight books collectively known as the *Wars* (*Bella*), and commonly therefore numbered I-VIII. Of these I-VII were finished and published together, VIII later. But they also break up into geographical divisions, by field of conflict, and are often referred to in this way. Thus *Wars* I-II = *Persian Wars* I-II; *Wars* III-IV = *Vandal Wars* I-II and *Wars* IV-VIII = *Gothic Wars* I-IV. Since (following Procopius) I have treated the eastern, African and Italian sections separately, I have found it clearer in general to use the terms *Persian Wars, Vandal Wars* and so on. It has to be remembered, however, that *Gothic Wars* IV (*Wars* VIII) was added after the rest, and includes material relevant to all fronts, i.e. it brings up to date to the time of writing (AD 553/4) what has happened everywhere since *Wars* I-VII were finished in 550/1. When it is a matter of making clear this relationship, therefore, it is better to write of it as *Wars* VIII. It is essential for the understanding of Procopius to have a clear idea of the relation of the works as texts, and for this the English titles probably help, in contrast to the Latin abbreviations commonly used.

Modern scholarship on Procopius began with Felix Dahn's *Prokopius von Cäsarea* of 1865 but received its greatest advance with the critical edition and companion publications by J. Haury (1891, 1896, Teubner edition 1905-13, rev. G. Wirth, 1962-4). Many of the discussions of Procopius came not in works specifically devoted to him but in general histories: Gibbon's *Decline and Fall*, with a notable section on Procopius, Bury's *Later Roman Empire* (1889 and 1923, with change of position on the *Secret History* in the later version), Stein's *Histoire du Bas-Empire* II (1949). More recently, the major work is that of B. Rubin in his monumental Paul-Wissowa article (1957, published Stuttgart 1954 as a separate item, from which I cite it), and in his unfinished *Das Zeitalter Iustinians* I (1960). The Pauly-Wissowa article includes commentaries on all the works, which, though incomplete are none the less a useful starting point: Rubin's main fault is his belief that everything about Procopius is to be explained in terms of his relation to Belisarius. Apart from the useful articles by O. Veh (1950-2), the modest book by J.A.S. Evans (1972) and the work of Z.V. Udal'cova on early Byzantine historians in general (1974, in Russian), there is no other general work on Procopius, though there is a mass of periodical literature of varying quality (mention may be made of the basic work on the *Buildings* by G. Downey and the two recent articles by Maria Cesa). There are, however, a number of more general works on the period which inevitably cover Procopius, among them Robert Browning's *Justinian and Theodora* (1971), P.N. Ure's lively *Justinian and his Age* (1951) and J.W. Barker's *Justinian and the Later Roman Empire* (1966). In addition there is a mass of popular work focussing on either Belisarius (Robert Graves's *Count Belisarius* is the best by far of the modern ones, but there was a huge output of drama based on Belisarius in the seventeenth century and later – see Conclusion), or nowadays more commonly Theodora (see Chapter 5 below), of which the titles alone suggest the kind of appeal Procopius has tended to have. Clearly a critical study of Procopius' work in itself is needed, especially one that is open to newer approaches in historical method (for example, Patlagean 1977), the more so since there has been in recent years both a new willingness to regard late antiquity as a period worth studying in its own right and, side by side with this development, a new interest by archeologists in working on early Byzantine sites which makes Procopius' *Buildings* a text of crucial importance. Since the standard work on the reign of Justinian, with the exception of A.H.M. Jones's *Later Roman Empire*, remains E. Stein's *Histoire du Bas-Empire* II, published posthumously by J.R. Palanque in 1949, there is also need of a major history of the period on a large scale. For that there is much groundwork to be done in all areas of scholarship. But the work of Procopius is a cornerstone, and must be tackled first.

PART I

CHAPTER ONE

Procopius: the Problem

With the works of Procopius of Caesarea we encounter in an acute form
the problem of the dominance of a single author for the history of an
important period. The *Wars, Secret History* and *Buildings* of Procopius
not only represent the main historical source for the reign of Justinian
(AD 527-65), but frequently constitute the only source. As Thucydides
does for the Peloponnesian War, or Tacitus for the early Empire, so
Procopius provides the filter through which we must view the reign of
Justinian. He is the major Greek historian of Late Antiquity,
perhaps even of Byzantium as a whole, and the proper understanding of
his works is crucial to many issues, not least that of the transition from
the ancient to the medieval world. He is both a traditional writer and a
product of his age. But his works have usually been considered so sharply
different that the problem of finding an explanation for these differences
has preoccupied the secondary literature. Most often it has been resolved
by the simple means of taking the more obviously classicising *Wars* as
basic (and preferable), and then somehow explaining away the notorious
Secret History and the unpalatable *Buildings*. Such an approach has
been a too familiar one in the field of Byzantine literature.[1] In Procopius'
case, there have been two main strategies – either to deny him authorship
of the *Secret History* altogether (the most extreme, and now discredited
view) or more commonly to explain the differences in terms of his
psychology, his responses to changing personal and political circumstances. The trouble with the latter approach, however, is that the dating
of the *Buildings*, and on some views also the *Secret History*, is not
absolutely secure, so that the argument can only be circular. The object
of this book is to find a way round this difficulty and to approach the
'classicism' of Procopius by placing his work firmly in a contemporary
context. As he is by far the most important author for the period, a
proper understanding of his work must be a starting point for a

---

[1] See Kazhdan and Cutler 1982, 454f on the visual arts; the same applies to literature.
There is no comprehensive book on Procopius, and the inflated Pauly-Wissowa entry by B.
Rubin (1957, previously published separately, 1954) remains the standard guide. See too
Evans 1972 (introductory); Veh 1950-52; Udal'cova 1974; Stein 1949, 709ff.; Bury 1923, II,
417ff. and in his edition of Gibbon, IV, 513ff.

history of the sixth century and for Late Antiquity in general.

Since we must of course discuss the evidence for the date and purpose of Procopius' three works, it will not be possible to avoid altogether the question of his personal views and their development. Indeed it will occupy a major place, especially in the discussion of the *Wars*, too often assumed to be monolithically uniform. Nevertheless the first way forward must be to take the three works together and to look first at their underlying likenesses; to give more weight to the 'minor' works, the *Secret History* and the *Buildings*, and to get away from the automatic privileging of the *Wars* on grounds of classicism. That is why the two shorter works are here treated first, in what may seem a paradoxical arrangement. When they have had their say, the *Wars* can speak for itself. The result will be to present a more homogeneous and a more Byzantine Procopius, in the sense that he will seem more closely related to his own culture and less of a stray from classical historiography who happened occasionally to reveal his Byzantine origins in an unfortunate lapse.

Surprisingly, there has not been the number of serious studies of Procopius that one would have expected. On the contrary, his work has been taken so much for granted that modern histories of the period still tend to paraphrase large sections of the *Wars*.[2] He is, after all, the major source of basic information.[3] But although a great many studies exist on individual problems, most begin from the kind of assumptions about the three works which I have already indicated. Thus a prevailing view of Procopius emphasises his supposed 'rationalism', and has inevitable difficulty in explaining the *Secret History*, with its virulent personal attacks, its sexual explicitness and its straightforward acceptance of the demonic nature of Justinian and Theodora.[4] The textual history of the work provided a way out of the dilemma, however, for the *Secret History* was not known until the seventeenth century, and it was relatively easy for scholars accustomed to draw from Procopius' other works confirmation of their favourable estimate of Justinian as Catholic lawgiver to deny that he could be the author of this newly discovered scandal sheet.[5] No one today would maintain that Procopius did not write the *Secret History* (though it is only in modern times that the case for Procopian authorship has been fully set out),[6] but the traces of those early attitudes can still clearly be seen in modern works. Thus most authors regard the relation between the *Wars*, the *Buildings* and the

---

[2] E.g. Bury 1923, II, passim, and indeed the majority of books on Justinian.
[3] For standard recent accounts of the reign see Stein 1949; Jones 1964. Bury 1923, II, is still often useful, despite n. 2 above.
[4] For the latter, see *SH* 12.14f.
[5] Mazzarino 1966, 102ff.
[6] See Dahn 1865; Rubin 1954, 252 and especially Haury 1890/91 and 1934.

Secret History as a primary problem;[7] it is still usually posed, moreover, in terms of the contrast between the classicising *Wars* and the other two works, and solved in terms of Procopius' supposed intentions or psychology. But now with more study of sixth-century literature such standard assumptions as that of the superiority of classicising history to 'popular' chronicles are being questioned,[8] and it is certainly time to apply these newer perceptions to the central body of work basic to sixth-century Byzantine political history – that of Procopius.

Clearly it is necessary to set out my understanding of the facts, such as can be known, of Procopius' life and writing career.[9] The evidence, which is meagre, comes mostly from his own works.

He tells us himself, for instance, that he was a native of Caesarea in Palestine,[10] a Hellenic foundation famous for its library, whose core was provided by the books of Origen, organised by Pamphilus, the mentor of the church historian Eusebius, bishop of Caesarea in the reign of Constantine.[11] The functioning of Caesarea as an intellectual centre was at its height in the fourth century, when its schools attracted Gregory of Nazianzus and when Libanius remarked on the high pay of its teachers.[12] There is much less evidence for the sixth century, but it continued as a centre of education and perhaps functioned as a feeder for the law schools of Beirut.[13] Choricius of Gaza in his funeral oration for the great rhetor Procopius reveals that Caesarea succeeded in capturing him for a time, only to lose him to his yearning for his native Gaza.[14] Certainly our Procopius would have had access there to a rich intellectual tradition. Caesarea was a cosmopolitan city with a mixed population of Christians and Jews. There were many Samaritans too, and Procopius could write with authority and experience of the Samaritan revolts and their harsh suppression, especially in AD 529.[15] He wrote, therefore, as a provincial, and as a native of an area and a city which knew what religious division and persecution meant in practice; it is not surprising, then, if in his writings he condemned Justinian's policies towards religious minorities.

[7] For example, Evans 1972. Compare Gibbon, ed. Bury, IV, 210f.: 'Procopius successively composed the *history*, the *panegyric* and the *satire* of his own times ... such base inconsistency must doubtless sully the reputation, and detract from the credit, of Procopius.'

[8] E.g. Beck 1965; Patlagean 1968; Averil Cameron 1979 (= 1981, XVIII).

[9] For full documentation see *PLRE* III s.v. and see Fatouros 1980.

[10] *Persian Wars* I.1.1; *SH* 11.25.

[11] Levine 1975; Downey 1975; Ringel 1975. Caesarea is one of the key sites where recent excavation is making possible a much clearer view of urbanism in the early Byzantine period. The synagogue was in use in the sixth century (Levine 1975, 40f.; Hohlfelder, 1982), and there is evidence of continued use of the main harbour and of an archive/library complex south of the Crusader city.

[12] Libanius, *Or.* 31.92 (Foerster, II, pp. 143-4); see Schemmel 1925.

[13] Zach. Rhet., *Vie de Sévère*, 26 (*PO* II.98).

[14] Choricius, *Or.* VIII (7), p. 113 Foerster.

[15] *SH* 1. 24f.; *Buildings* V.7.

In so doing, however, he was one of the very small number of Christians in the Late Empire who did explicitly condemn religious persecution as such.[16] Such a reaction to official policy does not however imply, as many have thought, that Procopius was not a Christian.[17] Interestingly enough, it was shared by Agathias, the continuator of the *Wars*, who held conventional Christian views on other matters.[18] Nor does it mean that Procopius shared modern liberal ideas: on the contrary, most of his attitudes were totally reactionary, as we shall see. It probably had much to do with early first-hand experience in Caesarea of the ruthless treatment of dissenters, which may have done much to shape Procopius' later attitudes. Felix Dahn in the nineteenth century sought to explain Procopius' alienation from the official line by supposing that he was born a Jew;[19] he was surely wrong, though in the context of the social composition of Caesarea it is not so unlikely a suggestion as it may appear. Later in life, during the writing of the *Wars*, Procopius had several occasions to feel personally threatened by imperial persecution, especially in AD 528/9 and 546, years which saw attacks on suspicious pagan and heretic intellectuals, doctors and lawyers in Constantinople – just the sort of class that Procopius represented.[20]

In fact Procopius probably came from the Christian upper classes of Caesarea. The name is common enough, and little can be deduced from it;[21] of Procopius' family we know nothing, but that he came of the landowning provincial upper classes is likely from the political attitudes manifested especially in the *Secret History*, where one of the main themes is that of the exhaustion of this class by the fiscal and other demands of the government. The legal training which Procopius evidently had was a common entry for sons of such families into the administration. It led John the Lydian into a post in the Praetorian Prefecture[22] and Agathias from obscure Myrina to legal practice in Constantinople.[23] Whether Procopius studied at Gaza, as has been claimed,[24] is extremely doubtful, since there is no direct evidence for the idea and nothing to make the hypothesis necessary. It follows that we

[16] Below, pp. 119f.
[17] Below, Chapter 7.
[18] *Hist.* I.7; Averil Cameron 1970, 110.
[19] Dahn 1865, 193; but see Veh 1950/51.
[20] See Lemerle 1971, 68ff.
[21] Rubin 1954. 13-23; *PLRE* III s.v.; Procopii in the sixth century: Zacos and Veglery 1972, nos. 478-81, 683. For the tomb of a Procopia at Caesarea, see Ringel 1975, 138.
[22] Below, p. 243.
[23] *Hist.* III.1; Averil Cameron 1970, 1-11. Procopius' legal training (doubted by Dahn and Haury) – Veh 1950/51, 5.
[24] Downey 1958a, 314; 1960, 156; 1963, 112, followed by Evans 1972, 31f. The idea is based on no more than an assumed connection between Procopius as an imitator of Thucydides and Gaza as a centre of Thucydidean studies, for which see Downey 1958a, 314 n. 76. Haury 1896, 11ff., argues for the identification of the historian with a pupil of Choricius of the same name, and suggests that Procopius was born at Gaza.

cannot appeal to the intellectual background of Gaza as an explanation of Procopius' attitudes.[25] Nevertheless his social and geographical origins do account for many of his interests and his limitations. Thus his education will have been the standard secular education of the day, based on imitation of the classical authors and on the study of rhetoric.[26] There is little to suggest serious study of philosophy. If we are right about his social origins, he can be seen to share the prejudices of the traditional élite.[27] His interests lay in preserving traditional ways against the encroachment of autocracy. But he totally supported Byzantine imperialism as a revived ideal. It was not the ideal of reconquest or its military basis to which he objected but its realisation by Justinian. In this he was followed by Agathias, who lacked Procopius' military experience but shared his approval of the end and disapproval of the means.[28] Procopius was not a philosophic historian; his critique was directed against personalities and particular policies, not general principles. He wrote according to the values of the class from which he came. Indeed the kind of history he wrote – secular, classicising history, concentrating on the military and political events of his own day and of which he often had personal experience, could only be written by one of his class, and it was natural that it should be revived in his generation, during which that class was under fatal pressure from a strong centralised government and after which its end was sealed along with that of the late antique cities which it supported. It is no accident that the histories of Procopius' successors, from Agathias to Theophylact Simocatta under Heraclius, increasingly show the breakdown of the old demarcation lines and the effective end of classicising history for many generations.

Procopius' background and the influence of his education may also have made it difficult for him to handle the increasing Christianisation of the state, which underlay most other issues, though we should not forget that the Gaza authors, for example, and many others too, could combine Christianity with high classical culture. The key lay in separation. Paul the Silentiary wrote excellent classicising epigrams, even highly erotic ones, but kept his Christianity for more suitable contexts. Similarly Procopius' self-imposed limitations of subject matter caused him to exalt military narrative above all else, and to interpret personal ambition, court intrigue and 'greed' as proper subjects for political analysis. They led him equally to omit altogether many of the major religious and social issues that actually determined governmental action, and to disregard, most of the time,[29] the day-to-day impact of Christianity on the lives of

[25] Evans 1972, 126f. (despite Evans 1971, 98, n. 30).
[26] For élite education in the sixth century see Averil Cameron 1979 (= 1981, XVIII), 27.
[27] See especially Udal'cova 1972 and 1974.
[28] *Hist.* V.14.
[29] But see Chapter 7 below.

the majority. He may have intended to treat such matters elsewhere. But in the *Wars* these limitations were not conducive to a high level of political and historical analysis. On the contrary, secular historiography in the classical manner could no longer be adequate for a world in which the very issues had changed. This above all posed the serious and basic problems of resolution which account for the oppositions in Procopius' three works. It is thus less Procopius' psychology than the failure of a certain sort of traditionalism in the sixth century to cope with the contradictions and tensions of contemporary life that explains the juxtaposition of opposites in his work. This would change,[30] but in the first half of Justinian's reign the tensions in culture and society were at their height.

From AD 527 Procopius was at the side of the general Belisarius as his assessor (legal adviser and secretary), and he seems to have spent the rest of his life either on campaign with Belisarius or in Constantinople. He was certainly an eye-witness there of the plague in AD 542, after Belisarius had been replaced and had returned to the capital from Italy.[31] His interest in events, like his personal career, was bound up in the fortunes of Belisarius. Thus much of the *Wars* is taken up with the early, successful years; after 540 his enthusiasm waned, probably in disappointment at Belisarius' failure to come out openly against Justinian when he was offered the crown in Italy.[32] The final success there was won not by Belisarius but by the eunuch Narses, and he left that narrative for another to record.[33] The writing of much of the *Wars* must have been done in the 540s, and a good deal depended on notes or diaries taken in the early years. Books I-VII were complete by AD 550, and Book VIII, which was finished in 554, merely brought things up to date. Overall, then, the *Wars* belongs to the earlier part of the reign of Justinian, and should have been in the main a success story. But the eclipse of Belisarius after his recall in 548 aroused complex feelings in Procopius. The later part of the *Wars*, especially *Gothic Wars* III, vividly catalogues the increasing disillusion with which he viewed Belisarius' more recent role, and the transfer of his admiration to others, notably the ill-fated Germanus. Thus even the *Wars* was bound to be an equivocal work, and it does not take much analysis to see that this is so. The mood changes in the course of the work from joyful excitement and enthusiasm to a worldly and critical resignation. In the final book the real hero is the Gothic Totila, a reversal that would have been unthinkable when Procopius began writing.

Since Haury, most scholars have accepted the argument that the

---

[30] Averil Cameron 1979 (= 1981, XVIII), 24f.

[31] *Persian Wars* II.22.9.

[32] *Gothic Wars* II.29.18. The best discussion of the composition of the *Wars* is still that in Haury 1890/91, but see also Bury 1923, II, 420 and *PLRE* III s.v. Procopius.

[33] See Averil Cameron 1970, 30ff.

Secret History belongs to AD 550, the very year of the publication of *Wars* I-VII.[34] At first sight that seems impossible, but once the disillusion of the *Wars* has been noticed the connection is easy to explain. The references in the *Secret History* to a period of thirty-two years of rule for Justinian[35] must lead us either to 558-9 (from AD 527, Justinian's accession), or to 550 (from 518, counting Justinian as ruling during the reign of his uncle Justin I).[36] But there is no secure reference in the work to the later period, and the earlier date is far preferable in view of the intimate connection between the *Secret History* and the *Wars*, for which the former work claims to be giving the 'true' explanations.[37] Its whole aim was to say what could not be said in the *Wars*,[38] that is, to be a secret companion volume. There would be little point unless the subject matter was still topical, and little point in dwelling for so long on Theodora, who was recently dead in 550, but past history by 559. Indeed, by 559, Justinian's reign was coming to an end, and the atmosphere was fraught with different problems. The aged Belisarius was drawn from retirement in 559 to lead the desperate resistance against the Huns.[39] This was not the moment for a scathing attack entirely focussed on the young Belisarius and his wife Antonina, and the imperial couple in the heyday of reconquest.[40] It was now of no relevance to describe the dead empress as a demon in human form; her memory was now sanctified into pious observance,[41] whereas in 550 Procopius may well have wished to counteract the eulogies produced at her death.

It is best, then, to place the completion of the *Secret History* in its present form in 550, contemporaneous with *Wars* I-VII, and followed a few years later by *Wars* VIII. We must assume that the *Secret History* indeed remained secret; as Procopius says in his introduction, it was too dangerous to make public. The *Buildings* was a different matter altogether, a public work of the first order, conceivably even commissioned by the emperor. Again there are problems of dating, this time more serious ones. The work – a panegyric on Justinian's building activity throughout the empire, but omitting Italy – is usually placed either in AD 554/5[42] or in 559/60, the latter mainly on the grounds of a

[34] Haury 1891, 10f.; 1896, 37f.; Bury 1923, II, 422; Stein 1949, 720; Veh 1950/51, 9; Rubin 1954, 81. For 559/60 however, see Evans 1972, 45-46 with Evans 1969.

[35] *SH* 18.33; 23.1; 24.29, 33. For bibliography on this point see Evans 1969, n. 1. Procopius constantly dates Justinian's real rule from the beginning of the reign of Justin I: see too *Vandal Wars* I.9.5; *Buildings* I. 3.3; 4.29.

[36] But see further on the composition of the *Secret History* Veh 1951/52, 31ff. and Chapter 4 below.

[37] *SH* I.1f. and below, Chapter 4. For an argument for the later date see also Scott forthcoming (b).

[38] *SH* I.2-3.

[39] Agathias, *Hist.* V.15f. – a vivid, if rhetorical, account of an extreme crisis.

[40] *SH*, chapters 1-5.

[41] E.g. in 558, *De Caer*. I, pp. 497-8 Bonn.

[42] Stein 1949, Appendix V, p. 837.

reference to the great bridge over the Sangarios river (still standing) which according to Theophanes was only now begun.[43] The disadvantage of the latter view, however, is that it must explain why Procopius passes over in total silence the collapse of the dome of S. Sophia in 558 (though he describes the church in great detail) as well as the Samaritan revolt in 555 and the defection of the Tzani in 557.[44] It is true that the formal arguments for 554/5 are arguments *ex silentio*, as against the direct testimony of Theophanes. But the earlier date accords far better on all grounds with Procopius' work. It is hard to assume (and it would have been untypical of Procopius) that he could have passed blandly over an event of such devastating psychological significance for the Justinianic programme as the collapse of the dome of S. Sophia. A panegyrist writing in 559/60 might, one supposes, have thought it best to ignore this inconvenient fact; but the rebuilding started almost at once, and called forth a major and very different kind of panegyric in its own right – the long *ekphrasis* by Paul the Silentiary.[45] Thus for Procopius in 559/60 omission of the collapse would have meant deliberately shutting his eyes to the real fact of rebuilding then actually going on; and to concentrate in those circumstances on the original foundation at such great length, as he actually does, would have seemed perverse. Again, Procopius' work is a celebration of imperial glory, relevant enough in 554 when Italy had just been finally won, and when a good part of the ambitious building programme in Africa had been carried out,[46] but very out of place in 559 when the darkness of plots and disillusion was settling round the aged Justinian.[47] The panegyric that Paul actually produced for the re-dedication in 563 was of a quite different kind, very much more religious in tone, and conscious of a background of trouble and difficulty. An optimistic work like Procopius' *Buildings* was not in place in the late 550s. Were we to place it there, indeed, it would stand alone: the years from 550 on otherwise show a remarkable silencing of the outpouring of

[43] Theophanes, p. 234 de Boor. For the later dating, see Bury 1923, II, 428; Downey 1947, 182-3. Haury 1891, 27-8, argued for Book I only (which includes the description of S. Sophia) having been written before 558 and the rest in 559/60. I am grateful to Dr Michael Whitby for letting me see a forthcoming paper in which he argues again for the later date. Veh 1952/53, 15 supposes that the *Buildings* was under way simultaneously with the *Wars* and only Bk. V added later (in 554).

[44] S. Sophia: *Buildings* I.1.20-77 (below, Chapter 6); Samaritans: V.7.16 (presented as peaceable Christians); Tzani: III.6.6 (reformed characters who had given up their old brigandage). In the case of the Samaritans, Procopius does mention their past revolts, which in the context would make total silence about the 555 one after the event particularly remarkable.

[45] Ed. Friedländer 1912 and now the subject of an Edinburgh Ph.D. thesis by J.M. Whitby (1983)..

[46] See below, Chapter 10; Pringle 1981, 121ff. (a detailed analysis of the *Buildings* in the light of other datable archeological and other evidence for Justinian's building in Africa); Averil Cameron 1982, 34f.

[47] Theophanes, pp.234ff. de Boor.

panegyric and glorification that had marked the early part of the reign, and it is noticeable that the extant epigrams of the *Cycle* poets, many of whom clearly belong in Justinian's reign, do not make the glories of Justinian a central theme.[48] By 560 there was certainly a need for the mobilisation of public opinion, but it would be to a different end, no longer emphasising imperial glory but the harmony of God and emperor. Only a year before, Justinian had celebrated his 'victory' over the Bulgars with a Byzantine *adventus* with religious overtones, very far from the Roman pageant of the Vandal triumph,[49] and the *ekphrasis* of Paul, delivered as part of the Epiphany services, commemorated the majestic but tired figure of an emperor drawing near the close of a long reign. As the *Secret History* turns its pitiless gaze on an imperial couple and their servants in the full vigour of active life, so the *Buildings* best fits a time when the drama of reconquest was still alive. As the *Secret History* fits closely with the *Wars*, so the *Buildings* fits with the *Secret History*.[50] Indeed it is not impossible that Procopius had the *Buildings* already in mind when he wrote the *Secret History*.[51] Nor should such an idea seem surprising, for panegyric was the bread and butter of any writer of the period and certainly did not evoke the problem of 'sincerity' ascribed to it by modern scholars. Even without an imperial commission (and Justinian was keen to enlist available literary talent),[52] a work such as the *Buildings* would have been an obvious next step for Procopius. Furthermore, we shall see that it allowed him to express certain attitudes with which he wholly concurred, for his criticism in the *Secret History*, as in the *Wars*, was a critique of means and of personalities coexisting with an acceptance of the basic assumptions of the Justinianic régime. The three works of Procopius, therefore, represent different sides of the reality of Justinian and of Procopius' perception of it; in this régime freedom of speech was denied,[53] and it was unlikely that a writer could express himself fully in any single type of work. Procopius had to write three apparently very different works to find his full expression.

It is not essential for our thesis – though it is obviously helpful to it – that the three works should be close in date, and the formal dating arguments for the *Buildings* in particular are not in themselves

---

[48] Averil and Alan Cameron, 1966, 23 – though naturally, the *Cycle* having been put together in honour of Justin II, poems in praise of Justinian might have been weeded out. The dating to the reign of Justin II still holds good, despite Baldwin 1977, 1980c; see Averil Cameron 1980, 537. For the silence that seems to fall after 550 see Scott 1980.

[49] Vandal triumph: *Vandal Wars* II.9, see below, Chapter 10. Justinian's entry: *De Caer.* I, 497-8 Bonn.

[50] *SH* 18.38; cf. *Buildings* II.7. See Rubin 1954, 298; Veh 1953, 15. *Persian Wars* II.12.29 on Edessa does not necessarily imply the *Buildings*.

[51] As argued by Rubin and Veh; but the text at *SH* 18.38 is uncertain.

[52] He tried with John the Lydian (*De Mag.* III.28).

[53] See the remarks of Honoré 1978, 28f., in the course of a lively assessment of Justinian as seen by a Roman lawyer.

conclusive. There is another consideration that has seemed to support the late dating – the identification of Procopius the historian by John of Nikiu, the late seventh-century chronicler of the Arab conquest of Egypt (not a reliable source for Constantinople in the sixth century) with a patrician and prefect, perhaps then the prefect of that name in 562 known from Theophanes.[54] But the fame of Procopius in his own day and later was great, and the historians who followed him and used his work do not hint at this identification; they refer to him merely as *rhêtôr*.[55] It may be tempting to assume that the city prefecture was a reward for the writing of the *Buildings*,[56] but it is more likely that the assumption of identity in John of Nikiu is in fact a simple error. In fact the prefect of 562 presided over the investigation of conspiracy against Justinian in which Belisarius himself was accused and subsequently disgraced. It would be ironic if this was indeed Procopius the historian.

All in all, the *Secret History* and the *Buildings* are both more easily explicable if they are assigned an early date. If that is correct, Procopius wrote nothing, or at least nothing that survives, after 554. Indeed, whether or not the *Buildings* is actually unfinished (the omission of Italy is hard to explain otherwise), it is surely unrevised,[57] and we shall see that the *Secret History* too is far from being a well-finished work. It could well be, therefore, that Procopius died in or soon after 554. That is the most economical hypothesis. If he lived beyond that date, or if he did in fact write the *Secret History* and the *Buildings* c. 560, he wrote looking backwards to the first half of the reign and without a discernible sense of connection with contemporary events. Such a procedure would be strikingly out of keeping with the known characteristics of Procopius in the *Wars*.

It is certainly one of Procopius' chief claims to a high reputation as a historian that he had personal knowledge of so much of what he describes. Many modern studies of individual passages or aspects of his work have devoted themselves to detecting the extent of this personal knowledge.[58] Increasingly, however, it seems that even when he was describing places and events at which he was present himself he could

[54] John of Nikiu, *Chronicle*, trans. Charles, p. 92; Theophanes, p. 238 de Boor.

[55] Agathias, *Hist.*, pref., 22, 32; II.19; IV.15, 26, 29, 30; Evagrius, *HE* IV.12, 19; V.24; Suda s.v. Menander, fr. 27, calls him *dikêgoros*.

[56] For the title *illustris* (cf. *Suda* s.v.) see Stein 1949, 712. It was a lesser title than would have been held by a prefect of the city. Procopius might have been rewarded with the honorary illustrissimate on retirement; he would then have become a senator (*PLRE* III, s.v.). Stein supposed that this comparatively lowly honour might have contributed to Procopius' disillusion with the régime when he wrote *Wars* VIII, on the assumption (because the *Suda* does not know of the *Buildings*) that Procopius received it after *Wars* I-VII.

[57] See Downey 1947 and Chapter 6 below. *Secret History*: Veh 1951/52, 31ff. and below, Chapter 4.

[58] E.g. Beševliev 1970; Hannestad 1960; Downey 1938, 1953a and many more. Such studies make up the majority of the bibliography on Procopius.

distort for reasons of political or personal bias, or even simply get things wrong; and this happens not just in the *Secret History* and the *Buildings*, where traditionally he has been accorded more licence, but also in the *Wars*.[59] It is no news, admittedly, that the ethnographical and antiquarian sections in the *Wars* are often defective;[60] but in the narrative parts too, Procopius can be seen to be shaping and selecting his material in a highly self-conscious way, or simply lapsing into vagueness, or finally varying considerably in the quality of his record according to the date of writing. Despite his credentials as an eye-witness reporter, we can rarely check where he got his information, since he usually does not tell us. No doubt he used his own early diaries, and possibly sometimes official reports, as perhaps for the Persian sack of Antioch in AD 540.[61] But generally his is the only surviving account, and we often cannot check by external references that he had good information or that he recorded it objectively. So there is much less reason for privileging the *Wars* than has usually been supposed. All Procopius' evidence, not just the *Secret History* and the *Buildings*, needs to be carefully evaluated, even the parts where he does seem to be drawing on official documentation to which he had access through his military role. It is easy and tempting to use Procopius' data as a starting point, as so often happens with the material in the *Buildings*, where he seems to provide the hard facts against which archeological evidence can be matched. But here too the pitfalls of such an assumption are becoming more and more obvious.[62] We often have little idea of how extensively he travelled in the provinces which he did visit, and there may be a great difference between the value of remarks made about the hinterland and those about the cities and battle-sites. Finally, of course, the value of Procopius as an eye-witness, through which he saw himself as writing contemporary history in the manner of Thucydides, is the most deceptive aspect of all; it depends totally on his own subjective impressions, the quality of his observation, what he thought important and the purpose to which he put the information he collected. There is no such thing as completely objective reporting and we certainly shall not find anything like it in the work of Procopius.

Only part of his movements can in fact be traced. We know neither the date of his birth nor his precise whereabouts before AD 527, when he was

[59] See e.g. Downey 1953a on Antioch; Croke and Crow 1983 on Dara; Mayerson 1978 on Sinai (but see below, Chapter 6).

[60] See now Goffart 1980 for a vigorous attack on Procopius' credibility (below, Chapter 12).

[61] Downey 1961, 539.

[62] For some cautionary remarks see Averil Cameron 1982, 31ff., and for a recent example of research showing how misleading Procopius can be, Cherf 1982. The central aim of the *Buildings* is to convey an impression that Justinian was a great builder – so obvious a panegyrical theme that we ought to have been suspicious of it even before the evidence against it was pointed out (for which see Chapter 6 below, and on the Balkans, p. 219f.).

chosen as *symboulos* (assessor) of Belisarius, who was then *dux* of Mesopotamia.[63] From then on he was with the Roman troops in the east until 531, and described the battle that took place near the fortress of Dara as an eye-witness.[64] After that he returned with Belisarius to Constantinople, but went out with him again on the great expedition against Vandal Africa in 533; while the fleet waited in Sicily he met an old friend from Caesarea.[65] He was present at the Byzantine landing, and entered Carthage with the victorious troops.[66] It is not clear whether he stayed in Africa when Belisarius returned to Constantinople, but he was in Carthage in 536 during the great mutiny, and fled with Solomon to Misua and thence to Belisarius in Syracuse.[67] We next meet him in Italy, between 536 and 540, years which he describes in great detail, having been sent after the first siege of Rome to Naples in charge of supplies for the army, and then again with Belisarius at the siege of Auximum in 539.[68] In the spring of 540 he was with the Byzantine troops as they entered Ravenna.[69] At this point he probably left Italy for Constantinople, where he was certainly present in 542 when the plague struck the city.[70] From now on he seems mostly to have stayed in the capital, and he may have been forced to leave Belisarius' service when the emperor turned against him.[71] He did not return to Italy with him in 544, though the detail of the narrative of the Italian war in the years 546/7 has suggested that he was there at that time.[72] From now on, we have no more direct statements from Procopius himself about his movements and can only draw conclusions from the dating of the works themselves. Haury constructed an elaborate hypothesis based on his dating of the *Buildings* to 560 and his identification of Stephen, the governor of Palestine killed during the Samaritan revolt in 555, with Procopius' father, according to which the *Buildings* was a kind of thank-offering to Justinian for his prompt action in quelling the revolt;[73] but this fantasy does not explain why in that case he did not mention the revolt itself in the work. It is far easier to accept the earlier dating. Further, the unfinished appearance of the *Buildings* makes one suspicious of the idea

---

[63] *Persian Wars* I.1.3; 12.24.

[64] I.13f.; *Buildings* II.1.4f. He did not however have personal knowledge of the restoration of Dara, though he describes it in detail (Croke and Crow 1983).

[65] *Vandal Wars* I.14.7f.

[66] Caput Vada: *Vandal Wars* I.14.17; entry to Carthage: ibid., 21.6.

[67] *Vandal Wars* II.14.39-41; see Rubin 1954, 24.

[68] *Gothic Wars* II.23.23ff.

[69] II.29.32; other signs of autopsy: 17.10; 20.22.

[70] *Persian Wars* II.22.9.

[71] *SH* 4.15. For the possibility that he went to the Persian front with Belisarius in 542, see below, Chapter 9 and *PLRE* III s.v.

[72] Haury 1891, 8f. Bury 1923, II, 419, supposes that after 540 he was continuously in Constantinople; see Rubin 1954, 26-7.

[73] Haury 1895, 25f., 45; see, however, Bury 1923, II, 420 n. 1.

that Procopius could have been appointed *praefectus urbi* in 562 as a mark of imperial gratitude; more likely he died before bringing the work to completion, just has he failed to fulfil promises of further writings made in the *Secret History*.[74] In fact we have no firm knowledge of Procopius after about 555, on the early dating of the minor works. He had thrown in his lot very closely with that of Belisarius since his early youth. Up to the early 540s his loyalty was maintained, but in the war narrative of the years from 544 on he is increasingly critical; the disappointment and disillusion with Belisarius which was to erupt into the bitterness of the *Secret History* was already building up.[75] But there is no sign that Procopius was taken up by any other of Justinian's generals, and certainly not by Narses who replaced Belisarius to win the final victories in Italy.[76]

The biography of Procopius, then, though uncertain in places, is important to us in the sense that it shows how some portions of the narrative in the *Wars* and of the 'extra details' in the *Secret History* are indeed based on personal experience, whereas others were probably composed totally in Constantinople where Procopius' sources of information were much less certain. The scale of the narrative varies quite dramatically according to whether he was present himself at the action or not. He records fully, for instance, the events of the Vandal war and the early Gothic campaigns, where he was not only present but deeply involved and excited. But it is quite different with Belisarius' second Italian expedition, where he was probably not present. On the other hand, his account of the second Persian expedition is oddly brief and one-sided, even though he may have been there.[77] So there is no fixed and easy rule.

It is much more questionable, however, whether a study of Procopius' biography can help to resolve the apparent differences between the *Wars* and the minor works, particularly, of course, if we accept the earlier dating for both the *Secret History* and the *Buildings*. Moreover, a developmental view of Procopius' works was made possible only by accepting datings which are at best far from well established, and then indulging in an unacceptable degree of speculation. A better way forward, and a way of avoiding these traps, is to look at the three works together as forming a whole, with less emphasis on their supposed differences; and some progress has been made in this direction, after the crude reaction of seventeenth-century scholars to the discovery of the *Secret History*, and

[74] *SH* I.14; 11.33; 26.18, suggesting, however surprisingly, that Procopius meant to write an ecclesiastical history.
[75] See below, Chapter 11.
[76] Narses' appointment: *Gothic Wars* IV.21.6f. Busta Gallorum – IV.29f. The story was in fact continued by Agathias, but not for another twenty years.
[77] Below, p. 163.

their denial of its authenticity.[78] Similarly, the *Buildings* is coming into its own with the growing interest in Byzantine archeology and urban history.[79] Of course there are enormous differences between the three works. But together they constitute a body of material that forms a composite whole and in which there are certain clearly distinguishable recurring themes and modes of expression.

The relation of the *Wars* and the *Secret History*, where the problem of Procopius' work has seemed at its most acute, in fact reveals these links very clearly. At every point the *Secret History* proclaims its relation to the *Wars*. It claims to be by the same author, who announces that he is from Caesarea[80] and gives as his purpose that of revealing the 'true reasons' for what was narrated in the *Wars*.[81] That is, the *Secret History* is to be a commentary on the *Wars*, but one which could not be made generally known for fear of reprisals against the author and his family.[82] Several times it explicitly refers back to the *Wars*,[83] and the greater part does go over ground already covered there. But as well as pointing back to *Wars* I-VII, it also points forward to the *Buildings*.[84] The style is so consistent with these other works, and the authorial idiosyncrasies so noticeable (the elaborate and theorising opening, its way of calling Constantinople by the anachronistic name Byzantium, its classicising vocabulary, its characteristic passages about divine vengeance and the role of fortune),[85] that the authorship cannot be doubted. As in the case of Eusebius' *Life of Constantine*, [86] it was doubted only because of a false assessment of Procopius and a too limited view of an author's capacity.[87] That the *Secret History* was not read in Byzantium, so far as we can tell, before the tenth century,[88] is not at all surprising in view of Procopius' own words in its introduction. It was a serious, dangerous and subversive

[78] Haury 1896, 36; see n. 5. Bury 1889, I, 355 and 359f. denied that Procopius wrote the *Secret History* ('It is ... almost impossible to believe that Procopius, the author of the *Historiai*, would ever have used the exaggerated language in which the author of the *Secret History* pours out the vials of his wrath upon Justinian') but later changed his mind (Bury 1923, II, 420ff.) after Haury's work on the subject.

[79] See Veh 1977; Crow and Croke 1983, with R. Hodges and D. Whitehouse, *Mahomed, Charlemagne and the Origins of Europe* (London, 1983).

[80] *Persian Wars* I.1.1; *SH* 11.25.

[81] *SH* I.1.1f.

[82] Ibid.

[83] See below, Chapter 4.

[84] Above, n. 51, with the reservation there expressed.

[85] Chapter 4 below. And most striking of all, its high degree of conformity with the other works in the matter of prose rhythm: Dewing 1910; de Groot 1918; Kumaniecki 1927.

[86] See e.g. Drake 1976, 8; cf. 134 n. 31 on the willingness of scholars now to re-evaluate Eusebius in the light of the *Life*.

[87] See Bury 1923, II, 426 ('the only reason for doubting the genuineness of the libel was the presumption that the political views in the two works were irreconcilable').

[88] It has been argued that Evagrius might have known the *Secret History* (Rubin 1953, 456; cf. Tricca 1915), but the case is still unproven and the latest writer on Evagrius is sceptical (Allen 1981, 10).

work, as he well knew, and would have earned him, if discovered in the repressive official circles of Justinian's régime, exactly the penalties he names. Only a generation later the monophysite *Church History* of John of Ephesus had to be smuggled out in sections by John's friends from his prison in Constantinople.[89] Like Procopius, John found himself both the recipient of imperial favour and an outspoken opponent of the official line.[90] But unlike Procopius he did not manage to escape severe reprisals. We cannot, then, evade the issue by denying that Procopius wrote the *Secret History*; nor is it wholly satisfactory to explain away his three seemingly divergent works by appealing to his personal life and psychological development (though we shall find that some development can indeed be traced). A different approach is needed.

There is however an alternative way out which needs to be considered first, and that is the explanation in terms of genre. Procopius was a highly self-conscious writer who imposed artificially severe restraints on himself by adopting so classicising a literary form.[91] In many ways this presented him with extra problems, and in my view it prevented him from achieving in the *Wars* a wholly satisfactory analysis of contemporary events. As we have seen already, he seems to have decided that there was room for political history and ecclesiastical history but that the two could not be combined. In the case of the *Buildings* and the *Secret History*, he was concerned with panegyric and invective respectively, and it will be clear that each of these works, like the *Wars*, has been influenced quite deeply by literary demands. Procopius was very far from being an unselfconscious writer whose work can be taken at face value. A main task, therefore, is to come to terms with these literary features in his work, and to try to decide how much weight should be attached to them.[92] Nevertheless, even when due attention has been paid to these real differences between the three works, I shall argue that they are superficial rather than basic to Procopius' thought. In all three, beneath these superficial differences lie the same fundamental themes, the same thinking, the same preoccupations. Given the formal demands of genre, these preoccupations are expressed in the same manner and with the same linguistic tools. Procopius may, in the *Wars*, have tried to write classicising history, but he belonged completely to the sixth century. He is not the intellectual outsider or classical survival that so many have mistakenly thought him, and which has led them into great but unnecessary problems with the *Buildings* and the *Secret History*. Once we have perceived this simple fact much else will fall into place, and it is in order to demonstrate its truth and bring out its consequences

[89] *HE* II.50.
[90] See Averil Cameron 1977, 11ff.
[91] See especially pp. 34ff. below.
[92] See below, Chapter 3.

that I have chosen to begin the central section of this book with the 'minor' works and not with the *Wars*. For it is the *Wars* that most needs a re-examination, and that can best be done through an understanding of the shorter works. Before that, however, it will be necessary to locate Procopius' work in relation to other sixth-century literature in Byzantium, and to come to terms in a preliminary way with the problem of his 'classicism'.

CHAPTER TWO

Procopius and the Crisis of Sixth-Century Literature

Though it is impossible to judge Procopius' works except in relation to the writing of his own day, this approach has been sadly lacking in most modern discussions. We must now therefore try to see what the intellectual and literary background was against which Procopius wrote.

Probably the first impression given by the literature of the reign of Justinian is one of variety and contradiction. The writers of the day differ profoundly in the style and level of their writing as well as in the attitudes they express. Thus we have high-level history, 'low'-level works of piety and all shades in between. Yet even to use these terms is to import premature judicial attitudes. Not surprisingly, modern reactions to such variety have often gone wrong, and in ways not dissimilar to the modern assessments of Procopius himself.

One such view, held by many scholars, tends to see the reign, or at least its earlier stages, as marked by a sense of revival and restoration, a feeling which underlay and therefore influenced not only political events and policies, such as that of reconquest, but also the intellectual and artistic spheres. Justinian's own phraseology in the preambles to his laws certainly encourages such an impression, and the terminology of restoration is strikingly applied to Justinian by Procopius' contemporary, John the Lydian:

> The emperor's excellence is so great that institutions that have come to ruin in the past are eagerly awaiting a rebirth by his intervention.[1]

Thus in a situation in which a number of writers did indeed choose to display their excellent classical training in traditional literary genres where they could show off their knowledge of Greek or even Latin

---

[1] *De Mag.* II.5.3; cf. III.55, 71; II.28. Preambles to the *Novels*: see especially *Novels* 24-31, all from the years 535-6. It is clear that the theme of restoration was strongly pursued in contemporary debate: see Michael Maas, *Innovation and Restoration in Justinianic Constantinople* (PhD thesis, Berkeley, 1982); Ladner 1959; *Buildings* I.1.6f. Of course the extent to which Justinian's laws reflect his own language is an open one, but see below, p. 255.

authors, it is tempting to suppose that a régime conscious of an aim of 'restoration' was exercising a kind of patronage of the arts, and that this artistic classicism is a main characteristic of the period.[2] Procopius' *Wars* would then be a prime example of it, and an interpretation of the *Wars* laying most emphasis on its 'classicism' would inevitably follow. A similar view has been very influential in the interpretation of Justinianic art.[3] It has been tempting and easy to see the reign as marking a 'revival', and to label undated objects of fine workmanship as 'Justinianic' on this basis.[4] Certainly Justinian represented his rule in terms of a restoration of the glorious past. He had himself shown as Achilles, as Procopius tells us.[5] Yet there are difficulties with the idea of artistic classicism as a clearly defined characteristic of the period. Take for example the work of the *Cycle* poets, writers of classicising Greek epigrams later collected by Agathias Scholasticus into an ensemble known as the *Cycle* and dedicated to the emperor.[6] Many of these poets were imperial functionaries;[7] one was Paul the Silentiary, who wrote the official poem for the re-dedication of S. Sophia in January 563.[8] Their learning is quite remarkable. Yet their work does not prove Justinianic patronage, for the dedicatee was certainly in fact Justin II, Justinian's nephew and successor.[9] They do, obviously, tell us about contemporary taste. Yet this turning to Hellenistic epigram might represent a deliberate avoidance of more serious themes. The case of Procopius' *Wars* shows just how difficult it was to deal within a classical frame with a political reality that was very different. In general, Justinianic policy had two faces. The codification of the law, for instance, could seem like a return to the Roman past, were it not accompanied by autocratic and innovatory legislation on Justinian's own part.[10] The concept of a Justinianic revival in the visual arts is as shaky, when it comes to assigning individual works

[2] Downey 1940, 1958b; Mathew 1963, 62ff. See Mango 1975, Brown 1971, 176f.

[3] Kitzinger 1958, 1977; see Averil Cameron 1975 (= 1981, VI) for discussion, and for the problems of such a conception, Shelton 1981, 66, 68 n. 27.

[4] For the idea of a Justinianic revival, see Kitzinger 1977, 98. A typical example is the idea of the Sinai Pantokrator, dated by Weitzmann on these grounds to the age of Justinian (Weitzmann 1976, B1, cf. Weitzmann (ed.), 1979, 528), but by Kitzinger to '*c*. 700' (Kitzinger 1977, 120).

[5] Justinian's statue: *Buildings* I.2.7-12; see Downey 1940, Gantar 1962 (the latter arguing that Procopius' treatment is deliberately ironic).

[6] *AP* IV.3 (dedication); see Averil Cameron 1970, 12ff., Alan Cameron (forthcoming).

[7] See e.g. Madden 1977; Alan Cameron 1976, 1977; Baldwin 1979.

[8] Chapter 1, n. 45. For Paul's epigrams and his learning in general, Cameron and Cameron 1966, 17f.; Day 1958, 50ff.

[9] Above, p. 11.

[10] See Honoré 1978, ch. 1. In the main, Procopius' view was that Justinian's laws demonstrated 'meddling' (see below, pp. 61, cf. 255f.), but he puts the official case at *Buildings* I.1.10. Modern views of Justinian as legislator differ as widely, from hostility (Honoré) to reverence (Gerostorgios, 1982), but have moved away from the admiring respect of the early jurists (who did not know the *Secret History*) to a more balanced view; see Archi 1970; Biondi 1936, 1966, and see below.

to it, as such ideas are in other periods, while in the case of literature Justinian seems to have been singularly unfortunate in his attempts to find writers to celebrate his régime; we do not know whether John the Lydian ever wrote the history of the Persian wars that the emperor wanted.[11] Paradoxically, more of the official side of things comes out in the unclassical *Chronicle* of Malalas than in formal works.[12] To approach the *Wars*, therefore, with the assumption that it emanated from a general classical revival supported by imperial patronage is to start from unwarranted premises.

Indeed we may now be less ready to see Justinian as a patron of the liberal arts and more to see him as a repressive autocrat.[13] It was Justinian who burnt books,[14] Justinian who arrested intellectuals,[15] Justinian who closed the Academy at Athens and ended the consulship, an even older institution.[16] While the reign saw surprising accomplishment in élite circles, it also saw a diminution in the circulation of learned books. The reconquest of Italy, for instance, saw no cultural revival; on the contrary, many of the educated Roman aristocracy had migrated to the east and were now replaced by military personnel.[17] When Cassiodorus returned to Italy, he went to secluded Vivarium, where, though he did insist on the copying of secular works, they were seen strictly as a preparation for 'divine' learning.[18] Similarly, in Byzantine Africa, there had been secular learning displayed under Vandal rule and in the first days of reconquest, but Corippus, the last African to write a secular poem in the classical manner, left to find a career in Constantinople.[19] There seems to have been no attempt after this to promote the production or circulation of secular literary works; all the energies of the imperial government went instead towards ecclesiastical matters, and it was here that literary production was stimulated.[20] The

---

[11] *De Mag.* III.28.

[12] Scott 1981.

[13] Honoré 1978 compares him with Stalin. Cf. Mango 1980, 135 ('if university life at the end of the fifth century was beginning to resemble that of Nazi Germany, worse was to come').

[14] Malalas, p. 491 Bonn (AD 562).

[15] Ibid., p. 449 (529); see Lemerle 1971, 68ff.; Stein 1949, 370ff.; Cavallo 1978, 211f. Constantelos 1964-5 is slight, while Downey 1958 and others, e.g. Gerostergios 1982, seek to defend Justinian.

[16] Malalas, p. 451 Bonn. It does not seem likely, despite Alan Cameron 1969, that the Academy could have survived the law of 529 as an organised institution, even if individual teachers continued to write: see Blumenthal 1978, Wilson 1983, 37f. The last ordinary consul held office in 541. For the reasons for the cessation of the office (which had much to do with increasing autocracy and Justinian's fear of rivals), see Cameron and Schauer 1982.

[17] See Cavallo 1978, 228. This article, which sees the reign as representing a state of intellectual crisis (p. 235), marks a distinct advance on previous work. For Italians in Constantinople, see below, Chapter 11.

[18] O'Donnell 1979, though see *JRS* 71 (1981), 181-6; further, p. 194f. below.

[19] See Averil Cameron 1982, 1983; Clover 1982.

[20] See Averil Cameron 1980 (= 1981, VIII).

writers of Byzantine Africa are typically ecclesiastics, and the effect of
Byzantine reconquest in this province seems to have been to damp down
if not extinguish the literary culture which had flourished even under the
Vandals.

Zonaras, writing at the end of the Byzantine period, did not see
Justinian as a patron of culture. Quite the opposite: he ascribed the
closure of schools, or rather, the denial of funds payable to teachers, to
the emperor's need for money for church building. His word for the
resulting situation when the schools of the empire thus declined was –
tellingly – 'ignorance' (*agroikia*).[21] In fact Justinian's measures against
teachers began before he embarked on his church building programme,
which in Zonaras' view followed on from his first major project, the
rebuilding of S. Sophia after the Nika revolt of 532. As early as 529 he
forbade the pagan teachers of the Athenian Academy to continue
teaching.[22] But this was less a specific measure against the Academy
than part of a general reduction of higher education in the cities of the
empire,[23] and one of a series of measures directed against pagan
intellectuals. Thus laws were passed forbidding them to teach,[24] and
later there were pogroms and book burning.[25] These policies succeeded in
their aim: in 529 the Athenian philosophers went on a romantic quest to
Persia, and some of them continued writing within the empire after their
return,[26] but the Academy itself remained effectively closed, as
archeology seems to confirm.[27] Whether the motives for Justinian's harsh
measures against education were fiscal or religious, they had serious and
lasting effects in hastening the decline of classical learning and replacing
it with more acceptable and less subversive forms of writing.[28] Such
measures, however, aroused violent opposition in intellectual quarters.
Even the laconic statements of Malalas about the persecution of
suspected pagans reveal that their numbers were not negligible, and we
can assume that the term 'pagan' was a convenient label for subversives.
Christians who had themselves made an accommodation between their
classical culture and their religion also disapproved of the government's
repression.[29] This was a deeply tense and divided society in which it was

[21] Zonaras XIV.6.31-2.
[22] Malalas, p. 451 Bonn.
[23] See *Secret History* 26.1-2; Zonaras, loc. cit.
[24] *CJ* I.5.18.4; 11.10.2 (528-29); see Honoré 1978, 14-15.
[25] See Cavallo 1978, 212.
[26] Agathias, *Hist*. II.30ff.; on Simplicius and the rest after 529, see Blumenthal 1978,
377ff., arguing against the view of Alan Cameron 1969, 22f. that Simplicius returned to
Athens (see too Lynch 1972, 167 and especially Sorabji 1983, 199f.).
[27] N. 16 above. For discussion of the evidence see Blumenthal 1978, 375ff., with Frantz
1975, 36f.; Frantz 1965; Thompson 1959.
[28] See Averil Cameron 1979 (= 1981, XVIII), 27ff., with further bibliography,
emphasising the serious effects of these purges as a contributory factor to the development
towards a more conformist culture.
[29] Agathias himself sympathised with the Athenian philosophers.

hard to tread the right path and equally hard to assess imperial attitudes objectively, and this division is reflected in modern judgments, when against the conception of the liberal Justinian, patron of the arts, we set that of an emperor who conducted 'an offensive against every cultural manifestation that could be seen as dissent'.[30]

The use of classical models, therefore, still an inevitable result of the secular education of most of the élite, and thus something from which they could free themselves only with difficulty, could be a sensitive issue. It was easily tolerated in some genres, such as the classical epigram on personal themes, and in the visual arts it survived in such uncontroversial areas as that of silverware for a considerable time yet.[31] But in serious works of history or political thought it was far less easy to deploy successfully. Any notion of Justinianic classicism as a simple or unified phenomenon must be rejected. The concept has no explanatory force; on the contrary, it must itself be explained.

In more general terms the reign of Justinian was characterised by deep oppositions. It opened with a revolt in which fifty thousand people are said to have been killed by government troops in the heart of the capital. This incident, in which the troops were led by Procopius' hero, Belisarius, demonstrated the ruthlessness of the imperial government and its readiness to take strong measures (whatever embroideries Procopius may have about the emperor's indecisiveness) while the very readiness of the crowds in 532 to join in wholesale rioting must be a demonstration of extreme social tension.[32] The crisis of power which Justinian resolved by the most drastic and ruthless means inevitably showed itself in literature, and the apparent contradictions in the works of Procopius, which generations of scholars have found so puzzling, are simply the manifestations of that crisis;[33] it would be surprising if it were otherwise. The problems went very deep and had much to do with the changing role of cities and the increasing difficulty of maintaining the fiscal and administrative system inherited from the Late Empire. Justinian's policies of reconquest, conceived as revitalisation, in fact proved a death-blow to that system. It was inevitable that the tensions of a society under such pressure should somehow be reflected in its literature, and particularly that a representative like Procopius of the conservative property-owning classes who were hardest hit by the centralist fiscal policies of the government would find that he could not

[30] Cavallo 1978, 212.

[31] See Kitzinger 1977, 109 ('an era notable for its interest in the Graeco-Roman past'); Cruikshank Dodd 1961.

[32] Rather than mere sporting hooliganism that had got out of hand (Alan Cameron 1976, 278ff. and generally) – a view that naturally appealed to Procopius himself (below, pp. 144f.). The catalogue of faction riots in Justinian's reign recorded by the chroniclers, often resulting in much bloodshed, does not suggest that the Nika revolt was as unique as it appears from Procopius. The government's reaction to the rioting was severely repressive.

[33] For a similar view, see Cavallo 1978, 236.

express himself fully in public works of literature. Thus the tensions of classicism were only part of a wider context of problems of expression.

Another construct of modern scholarship is the Justinian of the lawyers. According to this view, his achievement has to be seen in the long term. He is both the codifier of Roman law and the transmitter of Catholic orthodoxy to the western Middle Ages, the defender of centralised government and the rule of law.[34] Today such a view is much less attractive,[35] for obvious reasons, and Byzantinists too are less likely then formerly to idealise the reign of Justinian,[36] though western medievalists by contrast still tend to emphasise the continuity of Byzantine development and make the period an important component of it. Naturally the *Secret History* was a great embarrassment to those whose thought had been formulated very much on the basis of the legal work of Justinian. Strangely enough, however, Procopius gives very little attention to this side of Justinian's activity even in the *Wars*,[37] and can be – if we care to look – almost as critical of Justinian there as in the *Secret History*. Nevertheless, like the classicising view of Justinian, the idealising view of his influence as lawgiver retains its appeal.[38]

Faced with these different views, and with the great differences which seem to lie between the various literary productions of the period, modern scholars have usually resorted to the procedure of preferring one sort over the other. Generally this means that the classicising works are privileged, while the 'unclassical' are downgraded by the derogatory term 'popular'. Thus the *Secret History* causes difficulty, since it seems to have 'popular' features. We must therefore consider what, if anything, there is in this distinction of 'élite' (i.e. educated, serious, worthy of consideration) and 'popular' (everything else), since at first sight there seems to be something here for the interpretation of Procopius and especially the relation between his three works.[39] We shall see that 'élite' is a more useful term than 'popular', since it can denote the highly-wrought products of the educated minority, to whom Procopius certainly belonged, but that 'popular' elements, besides being hard to identify in themselves, also figure in 'élite' writing. Thus again the sharp distinction between the *Wars* and the *Secret History*, at least, is undercut. All Procopius' works are élite works, and all, in a sense, have

[34] N. 10 above, with Alisavatos 1913 and Schindler 1966. For Justinian as conservative and classicising, see Stein 1949, 276; Barker 1966, 172f. and as the fount of order, Ullmann 1966, 132f.; Downey 1968.

[35] The Justinian of the lawyers: Mazzarino 1966, 104. Modern reactions: Honoré 1978, ch. 1; Biondi 1936, 183f.

[36] For a critical view see Mango 1980, in particular emphasising the extent of urban (and therefore cultural) collapse in the seventh century.

[37] See below, p. 228.

[38] Gerostergios 1982 is an extreme example.

[39] The distinction is implicit in Udal'cova 1972 and 1974, for instance, and basic to nearly all discussions of Byzantine literature.

their 'popular' side too, though it would be better to avoid the word altogether. To some degree Procopius' work is already showing the breakdown in genre divisions which we can see in the writing of the next generations, though the external features of his work still conform to traditional types. At least we shall see that we should avoid the simple assumption that the *Wars*, as a classicising work of the first order, is thereby somehow uniquely important and reliable. For the Soviet historians, on the contrary, the *Wars* is the product of an aristocratic (and thereby decadent) élite, while the *Secret History* speaks with the voice of popular protest – an equally over-simple view.[40]

In the reign of Justinian the aim of high style still held good for many types of literature. On this basis, all three of Procopius' works are élite works, for all three are written in the same classicising Greek, difficult to acquire and difficult for a sixth-century Byzantine to read.[41] The choice of this pure, classicising Greek was an indication of the author's qualifications and of his intentions; it also imposed constraints upon him. The imitation of classical authors was an integral part of the whole process. It is essential to realise, then, that the *Secret History*, just as much as the *Wars* and the *Buildings*, is written in the same artificial manner.[42] We cannot privilege the *Wars* over the other two on grounds of high style or seriousness of composition. Equally, none of the three works can be assumed to represent Procopius' 'real' views, for all are highly artificial, if in different ways. Thus the *Secret History* is assigned in the *Suda* to the formal genre of *psogos* (inventive) and *kômôdia* (satire),[43] while the *Buildings* belongs to the most artificial of all classical genres to modern taste, that of panegyric.[44] The *Wars*, finally, is no heartfelt outpouring of Procopius' real opinions, but a carefully composed literary work in a distinct late antique historiographical tradition, with its own rules and conventions.[45] Not only did this tradition dictate style, but also the type of content that could be permitted in a secular history. We must remember that the *Wars* is as much shaped by its genre as the other works are by theirs; all are élitist, minority works and all three must be given equal weight.

To turn from the élite to the popular. It seems doubtful whether the concept of 'popular' literature can be of much help to us, if it means that

[40] See too Udal'cova 1965 (Malalas as 'popular'); for a different view, see Scott 1981, Beck 1965, Averil Cameron 1979 (= 1981, XVIII), especially 24ff.

[41] See Browning 1978, 1983.

[42] Rubin 1954, 258; see below, Chapter 4.

[43] S.v. Procopius.

[44] On panegyric in late antiquity see MacCormack 1974 and 1981, focussing on imperial panegyric and ceremonial. There is sad need for discussion of the implication for late antique culture of the domination of panegyric.

[45] For an introduction to this tradition see Cameron and Cameron 1964; Blockley 1981, with Blockley 1975 (Ammianus); Scavone 1970 (Zosimus); Udal'cova 1968 (Theophylact), 1972 (more general); Averil Cameron 1979 (= 1981, XVIII), 24ff.

élite literature did not share any of its features, or that its practitioners or its readers were not members of the élite. Take for instance the *Chronicle* of John Malalas, a world chronicle extending from Adam to the latter years of Justinian. It is written in a simple and unpretentious Greek and makes no attempt at critical history; indeed it is full of crass errors. The closing section has an Antiochene emphasis taken to represent the availability of material from the author's native town, and the work as a whole is often supposed to have been designed for the 'man in the street', thus a perfect example of 'popular' literature.[46] Yet it is not impossible that it is the work of the Antiochene John Scholasticus, patriarch of Constantinople from 565 to 577 and a sophisticated theologian.[47] He was one of the most influential men in the empire at the time of Justinian's death and in the reign of his successor, a central member of the élite, therefore. Further, it seems that the chronicle drew on sources of official information,[48] so that it is unlikely that it was some kind of spontaneous, 'popular' production; yet we know nothing of its destined audience. One thing we can say, however, is that the ninth-century chronicler Theophanes drew heavily on both Malalas and Procopius without feeling any awkwardness about combining them. Nor is Malalas' work popular just because it is Christian, in contrast to the secular *Wars*; ecclesiastical and secular works were now coming closer together, so that the church historian Evagrius, for instance, found no difficulty in basing himself on Procopius.[49] It seems rather as though the taste of the élite itself is changing in this period, that what once may have seemed inadmissable can now be tolerated. In particular, we cannot make the simple equation of 'popular' and Christian. What, for example, of Romanos, the most famous composer of Christian poetry in the period?[50] His material and the style of his *kontakia* (liturgical hymns) are very far from classical, and there is a sense in which they may seem popular, both because they were indeed accessible to many through their liturgical performance and because they actually use folk motifs, as did the more commonplace sermons which the people heard.[51] But in their complexity and technical subtlety they are as accomplished and élitist as anything in secular literature. Some of them, indeed, even deal with imperial panegyrical themes and thus enter the world of high literature.[52] A better word than 'popular', then, is 'unclassical'. It is true that different, unclassical and indeed usually specifically Christian literary forms begin during this

[46] Udal'cova 1965 and often.
[47] See Hunger 1978, I, 319f.; Haury 1900; on John Scholasticus, Beck 1959, 422f. This old controversy cannot be resolved while the available editions of Byzantine texts remain so bad, but a new edition and new translation of Malalas are expected.
[48] Scott 1981.
[49] Allen 1981, 171ff.
[50] See Grosdidier de Matons 1977; Trypanis 1968.
[51] Dramatic homilies: MacCormack 1982, 298f.
[52] See Topping 1977, 1978 and below, pp. 254f.

period to oust the familiar classical genres. But their appeal is not solely to the masses; it is to all sections of society, high and low alike, and their success is an indicator of the process which Justinian did so much to encourage, the replacement of a culture based still in élite circles on classical models by one based firmly on a unitary Christian world-view.[53] By the reign of Heraclius this change was virtually complete, and the years of difficulty that followed almost cut off classical culture altogether until its revival in the ninth century.[54] Procopius, in an obvious sense, represents those who were resistant to this change, which was perfectly apparent to them; yet, I shall argue, he was not impervious to it and already shows in his work some of the traits found in the non-classicising authors of his time.

One such was Cosmas Indicopleustes ('India-returned'), a flat-earther, who wrote his *Christian Topography* not merely without pretension to formal literary canons, but even in direct opposition to them.[55] His work set forth an alternative view of the world and man's relation to God – alternative not only to pagan philosophy but also specifically to the current Alexandrian synthesis of Aristotelianism and Christianity. Cosmas' work is professedly polemical in purpose, but its linguistic vulgarisms and its curious mélange of travelogue, theology and geography, scarred by historical howlers and absurd stories, earned it the condemnation of Photius as well as of most moderns.[56] However, it would be premature to dismiss the work, odd though it is, as a popular and ignorant compilation.[57] It is certainly diffuse and anecdotal, with 'plus de couleur que de volume'.[58] But for all its faults when judged by élite standards, it belongs in a well-defined nexus of intellectual controversy and to the very years when Procopius was working on the *Wars* and planning the *Secret History*. Most of it was written in 547-9, when the Three Chapters dispute was at its height and when Facundus of Hermiane had set off in haste from Africa for Constantinople and was busily composing his *Defence of the Three Chapters*.[59] These were the real issues of the day, though they are deliberately ignored by Procopius. Cosmas wrote as a Nestorian, a follower of the Theodore of Mopsuestia now condemned by Justinian, and although his work was mainly directed against John Philoponus and the Alexandrians, who were strongly opposed to Theodore's teachings, its thrust had a wider significance in terms of current imperial policy. Further, Cosmas was

[53] As argued in Averil Cameron 1979 (= 1981, XVIII).
[54] Mango 1980, ch. 6; Wilson 1983, ch. 3. The decline had much to do with the break in continuity of urban life, and the consequent adverse effects on the provision of advanced education, but the change had begun already in the sixth century.
[55] See Wolska 1962, with remarks in MacCormack 1982.
[56] Photius, *Bibl.*, I, cod. 36 (ed. Henry, I.21).
[57] See also Hunger 1978, I, 520f.
[58] Wolska 1962, 30-1.
[59] See Averil Cameron 1982, 45ff.

indebted to the same Mar Aba of Nisibis whose teachings were presented to the Greek world at this time in a curious pamphlet by Justinian's African quaestor, Junillus, another contact of the African bishops and a man, oddly enough, viciously attacked by Procopius.[60] It does less than justice, then, to dismiss even the *Christian Topography* of Cosmas as a popular work. It may not have conformed to Photius' literary requirements, but it was nevertheless a serious work, deeply engaged in current disputes. It is not so much a difference of level as one of perspective: Procopius did not think the Three Chapters affair relevant to his kind of history, while Cosmas did not think that matters of real life and of the first religious importance had to be dressed up in classical guise. As he explains, 'it is not fine phrases the Christian requires but right notions',[61] and he was undeterred by the fact that he had not received a secular education and a training in rhetoric;[62] as he engagingly puts it, he had acquired much knowledge by his own efforts, when time permitted. It is too easy a way out, then, to condemn Cosmas for his strange ideas.[63] In fact he was expressing a point of view held by many, and not only by the ignorant. The disputes underlying Cosmas's work were still a live issue when Agathias wrote his *History* in the 570s, and while it is of course true that Cosmas represents both the opposition view and the reactionary view, it would not be unfair to argue that his preoccupations were as central, if not more central, to contemporary society, than were those of Procopius.

In a real sense, Procopius' work is distinguished from other contemporary literature not so much by its level as by the limitation of its range of interest. Above all, Procopius distanced himself from the issues that were predominant in the years which he covered by his refusal to include ecclesiastical history, whereas Cosmas, so often and easily condemned, was involved in the very heart of the controversy. Taken alone, Procopius gives us a very one-sided impression of life in the mid-sixth century and his evidence is partial in both senses of the world.

Some of the reason for the common mistakes in approaching Procopius' work lies in a simple neglect of other important sixth-century texts. One such, to take an almost random example, is the *Life* of the patriarch Eutychius of Constantinople by his disciple Eustratius.[64] Though not written until after Eutychius' death in 582 it has much to say on his appointment to the patriarchate just before the Fifth Ecumenical Council of 553, that is, just when the Three Chapters affair was reaching

---

[60] *SH* 20.17.; below, p. 231. Junillus' work: *PL* 68.15-42; see further Honoré 1978, 237ff; Guillaumont 1969/70. For Philoponus see Sorabji 1983, e.g. 198f., 268f.

[61] *Christian Topography*, prologue 2 (trans. McCrindle).

[62] Ibid., II.1.

[63] So Winstedt 1909, 7 ('apparently the first and one hopes the only person to collect and develop into a system the strange cosmographical ideas hinted at in early theologians').

[64] *PG* 86.2, 2273-2389.

its culmination in the brutal methods adopted at the Council. The *Life* is a work of a different kind, it may seem, from Procopius', yet it too is written with high stylistic and literary pretensions, and it is absolutely central to the crucial years when Procopus' works were being produced. Passages of the *Life* read like imperial panegyric – as valid a panegyrical style as the *Buildings,* and reminiscent of the similarly political tone of some of Romanos' *kontakia* – and Eutychius himself was clearly pushed into the patriarchal seat by Justinian as a suitably docile president of the Council.[65] That is what political life was like under Justinian, but it is an aspect which Procopius does not deal with directly in the *Wars* and only hints at in the *Secret History.* Yet this *Life* was certainly an élite work too. It was delivered before the Emperor Maurice; its subject matter is political and often concerns the imperial family; it is composed in an elaborately rhetorical style. Its audience would be the same as for Procopius' *Wars* or Agathias' *Histories* which continued the *Wars* in the 570s. There was not one audience in the highest circles of Constantinople for hagiography and another for secular works, however much Procopius might lead us to think so.

The next chapter will explore the problem of the relation of style and content in Procopius' works, what it means that he chose to be a classicising author. For we cannot move on to discuss individual passages until the general issues have been faced. But first, some unclassical elements in the *Wars.* When seen against the context that I have been describing, it would be surprising if we could not also find in his work traces of the attitudes and preoccupations of less 'classicising' works, whatever their intellectual level. At this point we may concentrate on just two features which seem untypical of a true classicising history – the resort to the miraculous and the interest in holy men.

First, then, the resort to the miraculous, which is commonly to be found even in the *Wars* in default of explanation in human terms, and this despite Procopius' widespread reputation for 'rationalism'.[66] Often he will resort for an explanation of events to the concept of 'fortune', in the manner of so many classical historians, or even to the idea of the jealousy of God (*phthonos*), ever ready to destroy good luck.[67] At other times he will confess his own bewilderment coupled with his conviction that all must be for the best; a notable example of this is his famous description of the plague in Constantinople in AD 542.[68] But often too he

---

[65] I hope to produce with Dr Anna Crabbe a translation and commentary on this important text.

[66] See Averil Cameron 1966 (= 1981, I). The approach of this paper could now be improved, but the conclusion is reinforced by the wider argument of this book. See especially Chapter 7 below.

[67] *Gothic Wars* II.8.1; cf. the notion of the 'game' which Tyche plays with men (ibid. IV.33.24, for the motif, Dodds 1965, 10f.). On fortune in Procopius see Elferink 1967 and art. cit. (n. 66) with p. 477 on *phthonos*.

[68] *Persian Wars* II.22.2, cf. 10.4 (the sack of Antioch); *Gothic Wars* I.3.6.

simply admits and accepts a miraculous explanation of events. In the *Buildings*, of course, he writes openly in the mode of orthodox Christianity, and can therefore easily attribute Justinian's choice of architects for S. Sophia, for instance, to divine inspiration.[69] But in the *Wars* too he resorts to the same kind of explanation. Thus he says that the sack of Antioch by Chosroes in AD 540 was preceded by a sign which the inhabitants should have recognised (but did not), for the military standards spontaneously turned from west to east and back again.[70] Again, when Marcian the future emperor was taken prisoner by the Vandals, an eagle hovered over his head,[71] while at Apamea during the Persian war an exposition of the city's relic of the True Cross was marked by a miraculous flame hovering over it, and the city was duly saved.[72] In Italy a local interpreted an omen to mean that a eunuch would destroy the ruler of Rome; people laughed at such an absurd idea, but the prophecy came to pass in the appointment of Narses.[73] Of course classical historiography too had a tradition of prodigies, but Procopius' are clearly Christian miracles. He accepts the Apamea story, for instance, without hesitation, and this and other similar instances show that any paganising tinge, as in the passages about the jealousy of God or fortune, is purely superficial. Such incidents as the Apamea story come very close to the explanatory framework of hagiography or ecclesiastical history, as do the references to holy men – James, for instance, the holy man of Amida whose saintliness was such that a band of lawless Huns who wanted to shoot him found their bows transfixed in their hands.[74] Procopius shows not the slightest qualms about this story, even though he puts it in the same chapter as one of his most self-conscious references to monks.[75] There is also Symeon at Amida, simply described as a 'holy man'.[76] Especially in the *Persian Wars*, bishops like Megas of Beroea, Candidus of Sergiopolis and Thomas of Apamea are the natural leaders of their cities in negotiations with the Persians. Procopius makes no attempt to dissociate himself from this articulation of contemporary urban life. Instead, he comments of Candidus that it was right that he should have been tortured, kept under guard and never released by Chosroes because he had reneged on his agreement and therefore should no longer be a priest.[77]

Against these instances are the many places where Procopius seems to be trying hard to pretend that Christianity was strange to him and his

---

[69] *Buildings* I.1.25.
[70] *Persian Wars* II.10.1. See further below, p. 114f.
[71] *Vandal Wars* I.4.9.
[72] *Persian Wars* II.11.14f.
[73] *Gothic Wars* IV.21.17.
[74] *Persian Wars* I.7.5f.
[75] Ibid. 22. They were 'keeping some annual festival to God on that day'.
[76] *Persian Wars* I.9.18.
[77] Ibid. II.20.16.

readers – quite impossible at this date[78] – and those where he invokes the pagan Tyche. How are we to deal with the discrepancy? Again, the wrong side of Procopius and the wrong passages have been emphasised.[79] We should regard as primary indicators the passages cited above, not the 'unfamiliar' references to Christianity or the musings about Tyche. Of course Procopius had difficulties in reconciling his conception of secular classicising historiography with his Christian subject matter, and it is hardly surprising if he failed to come up with a consistent answer. It was not just a matter of 'insincerity' or the demands of Christian panegyric that made the author of the *Wars* able to write in the *Buildings* of Justinian as if he were divinely inspired, or describe the churches of Constantinople in such a way that 'the contemporary growth of the cult of the Virgin is a notable feature of the treatise'.[80] Similarly, it is not at all surprising that the admirer of James of Amida should seriously see Justinian and Theodora as demons and suppose that the emperor levitated at night and was to be seen in the palace without his head.[81] Procopius gives his own assent ('to me and to most of us ...') and then appeals to authority – stories told by Justinian's mother, by men of 'pure souls' who were with the emperor late at night in the palace,[82] a 'certain monk, very dear to God', the lovers of Theodora, 'most of the people'.[83] Far from being so unworthy of Procopius as to be quite incredible, the whole passage illustrates perfectly his acceptance of the miraculous and the supernatural as an adequate replacement for historical analysis, an acceptance which he shared with other writers of late antiquity both ecclesiastical and secular.[84] Thus the supposedly 'rational' Procopius in fact differs little from the authors of hagiography and 'popular' literature. That this should be so stems from a change in society, whereby a far greater place was allowed to religion and its representatives such as holy men, whether Christian or pagan. History and chronicle differ therefore not in their 'level', but in their form and choice of focus;[85] there is much in them that is shared. An élite writer like Procopius can have popular features, if by popular is meant a shared acceptance of the irrational, the miraculous and the supernatural.

[78] Below, Chapter 3, and see Cameron and Cameron 1964; Averil Cameron 1965.

[79] Downey 1949 tries to reconcile the inconsistent passages, but this is to miss the point.

[80] Downey 1953, 724.

[81] *SH* 12.14f.

[82] Presumably clergy and monks.

[83] *SH* 12.18-19, 20f., 24, 38; 13.1. It is not that we should insist on Procopius' own belief (the careful verification and authentication underlines the fact that these stories play a functional role in the work, whatever their objective 'truth'), but that we should recognise that there is nothing *a priori* unlikely in supposing that Procopius did believe them and take them perfectly seriously.

[84] See the interesting remarks of Gabba 1981, 61f.; Cracco Ruggini 1981, 166f.; 1979. There is little to choose here between Procopius and the church historians.

[85] For Patlagean 1968 they represent different points in a continuum.

Appeal to this kind of explanation is not confined, however, to the lower échelons of society; it pervades the élite at the highest level. Once recognised, this helps us to see sixth-century society more positively. It underlies, for instance, the universal, not merely the 'popular', appeal of icons and relics.[86] It explains why there could never be a classical renaissance in the fullest sense and why Procopius found difficulty in harmonising his three works, and even in making the *Wars* internally consistent. All this should be a warning not to be content with the surface of Procopius' work, with its seductively classical appearance. For beneath that surface is a set of assumptions much more closely in line with those of the rest of his society than his classicism might suggest, and which lead him to appeal for verification to a very unclassical kind of authority.

[86] Averil Cameron 1979 (= 1981, XVIII), 18ff. and Brown 1981. Icons as evidence of 'popular' religion: Kitzinger 1954.

CHAPTER THREE

The Discourse of Procopius

Even the best modern surveys of Procopius' work are riddled with judgments based on only a selection of the total evidence.[1] Thus we are told that he was exceptional for his freedom of thought and his outspokenness, an opinion which has the corollary that he must be defended from charges of gross flattery in the *Buildings* and assumed not to be serious when in the *Secret History* he presents Justinian and Theodora as demons in human form.[2] Thus we are given an author not only detached from his literary context, but not even seen from the perspective of the totality of his own writings. It is simply assumed that it is possible, without further discussion, to select from his work the part that is to be considered historically credible, and to discard the rest.

Yet in trying to approach the problem by another route we immediately encounter formidable obstacles. For Procopius himself has placed an extra barrier between himself and us – that of literary style. One of the most prominent features of his writing, as of so much Byzantine literature, is the imitation (*mimêsis*) of the classical authors.[3] Such imitation was effectively dictated by the educational system of the Roman empire, where stress was laid exclusively on a backward-looking study and reworking of a fixed canon of the classics, with low value being attached to originality. It could at times be taken to absurd lengths.[4] But

[1] For example, Stein 1949, 720, assuming that the *Secret History* is 'un livre unique dans son genre', full of 'facéties grossières' (721).

[2] On the *Buildings*: 'the conscious dignity of independence was subdued by the hopes and fears of a slave; and the secretary of Belisarius laboured for pardon and reward in the six books of the Imperial *Edifices*' (Gibbon, ed. Bury, IV, 210-11). But Gibbon recognised the value of both the secondary works. Bury was equally scathing about Procopius' motives in composing the *Buildings* ('there can be no doubt that Procopius wrote it ironically', ibid., Appendix, 515). For Udal'cova 1974, chiefly interested in Procopius as critic, the *Buildings* is a work to be passed over as quickly as possible.

[3] See Hunger 1969-70. I have written on this topic in relation to Procopius (Averil Cameron 1964 (= 1981, II), but for a better discussion of the process see Adshead 1983. Imitation was a necessary technique in the laborious writing of high style Greek, apart from its wider implications. For the whole problem of differing stylistic levels in Byzantine prose see Ševčenko 1981.

[4] Many examples of what not to do are to be found in Lucian's treatise 'How to write history'. Historians were especially given to seeking a classical dress for their work, especially for battles, sieges and other purple passages, and Procopius was only following in a long tradition.

not even the best or most serious writers could dispense with it
altogether, if they aimed at an educated audience and wrote on
traditional themes such as political history. Procopius was, if nothing
else, an ambitious writer, and followed this general trend more
successfully than most. He thus interposes an extra layer of artificiality
between himself and the reader. Furthermore, this classicism goes much
deeper than the superficial adoption of vocabulary and phraseology from
an author like Thucydides. It meant, for Procopius, the taking over of a
whole conception of historiography with its attendant modes of thought.
For the style of writing adopted in the *Wars* carried with it restrictions on
content as well as positive injunctions; it imposed rules of language,
prescriptions for the organisation and type of material to be included,
even assumptions about appropriate authorial comments. How then to
disinter a 'real Procopius' from all this superstructure? Not, certainly,
just by pointing out genuine contemporary knowledge in this or that
digression, or by arguing that the incident so amazingly close to one in
Thucydides could have actually happened,[5] for that too is to suppose
that there is a Procopius separate from what he has chosen to write, and
whom we can grasp if only we look closely enough. We must instead
acknowledge that there is no separation between the author's thought
and its expression. The one is formed by the other. Only in part does
Procopius consciously choose to write in a classicising style; much more,
it is part of him and part of his conception of history, which he would not
have been able to write otherwise. So the understanding of the classicism
of Procopius is not a simple matter of peeling off an external layer. The
phenomenon goes far deeper and is much more pervasive, right to the
heart of Procopius' work.

Most important of all, it formed all three of his works, not merely the
Wars. In particular, work on the *Secret History* in recent years has
demonstrated the unity of his writings, in language, vocabulary, modes
of thought.[6] As if to underline this for us, Procopius introduces constant
cross-references from one work to another,[7] pointing out that they must
be read together, that one must not be separated from the rest. As the
Wars is full of 'classical' features such as ethnographical digressions, so
the *Secret History* too begins with an elaborately rhetorical preface and

[5] Most of the older work on the subject of Procopius' imitation of Herodotus and
Thucydides is at this kind of level: see bibliography cited in my art. cit., (n. 3), especially
Braun 1885, 1894 and the discussion of Haury, 1896, 1ff. Soyter 1951 is still defending
Procopius against charges of falsification, i.e. the importation of whole incidents from the
classical authors. For Procopius' plague description (also defended by Soyter) see below.

[6] Above, p. 16; see Bury 1923, II, 424.

[7] Ibid., 422f. and see Haury 1890/91, 21. One of the most striking is between the openings
of *SH* and *Wars* VIII. Similarly the *Buildings* frequently refers to the *Wars*. For a list of
criticisms in the *Wars* that parallel the *Secret History* see Bruckner 1896, 51-2, and for
cross-references see below, Chapter 4 n. 12 (*Secret History*) and *Buildings* I.1.6, 20; 10.2-3;
II.1.4; 10.10; III.1.12; V.1.6; VI.1.8; 5.6; 6.9.

introduces quotations from Aristophanes and Homer even where Procopius' attack on Justinian and Theodora is at its most violent.[8] That same Aristophanean vocabulary recurs in the *Buildings*, applied to S. Sophia.[9] It is an easy way out to dismiss this and similar usages as irony[10] – but that is to beg the question of intention again. Better for the moment to concentrate on the linguistic system which Procopius has evolved in his three works, leaving aside until later their different purposes, and to note also the highly mimetic quality of the preface to the *Buildings*, where material is drawn less from rhetorical panegyric than (as with the other works) from historians moralising about history and truth.[11] Of course in three works of such different superficial intent there will be differences, including linguistic differences; the pool is not exactly the same for each. But, remarkably, they all – even the *Secret History* – observe strict and idiosyncratic rules of prose rhythm,[12] perhaps the most surprising indicator of their essential unity. And all alike – again, even the *Secret History* – follow the rules of linguistic exclusion from high style,[13] whereby certain common words and phrases are either avoided altogether or used only with a clumsy periphrasis. Not only that: there are even near-identical passages in the three works.[14] Again there will naturally be small differences: explanations for Christian terms (thought to be insufficiently 'classical') appear more often in the *Wars* than in the *Buildings*, which is a more overtly Christian work. Yet they are far from absent either from the *Buildings* or from the *Secret History*, and all three works also avoid or apologise for technical terms and Latinisms in the same clumsy way.[15] In the religious sphere, especially, this makes it extremely difficult to decide what Procopius 'really' thought. Take his use of the abstract 'the divine' for God, often thought either to be a

[8] For the preface, see below, p. 50. For Aristophanes, *SH* 13.11 (*Clouds* 620), 13.3 (*Knights* 692); Hunger 1969-70, 30. On the language of chs. 13-14, see below, p. 58, and for further allusions to Aristophanes, Rubin 1954, 34.

[9] *Buildings* I.1.61 (the mind's reaction to S. Sophia); the passage is translated in Mango 1972, 73f. More likely the present usage is merely indicative of the uniformity of the texture of Procopius' prose.

[10] See though Gantar 1962 on *Buildings* I.2.7f.

[11] Procopius relies heavily on Diodorus: see Lieberich 1900, 4ff.

[12] Chapter 1 above, n. 85. Procopius follows an unusual pattern (see too Averil Cameron 1970, 68f.) but he does so uniformly.

[13] By pretending not to know standard expressions which happen to be unclassical or otherwise offensive to purists: see Cameron and Cameron 1964 (= 1981, III); Averil Cameron 1966 (= 1981, I). There is a list of such usages in Procopius at Averil Cameron 1970, Appendix J.

[14] Procopius' whole style of writing is self-referential, and the effect is enhanced by the limitation of his vocabulary (below, Chapter 13).

[15] When he does not go in for periphrases, he will do his best simply to vary the expressions he uses, so as not to keep on using the same standard term. The technique was so standard in high-level Byzantine prose that the *Strategikon* of Maurice expects its readers to pick up the point at once when it states without fuss that there will be no fancy rhetoric, for such would be out of place in a plain military treatise (preface, 3).

Herodotean imitation or else a sign of theism;[16] neither is predicated of
Justinian, though the emperor too constantly uses such terms in the
Novels. Again, the references to Fortune (Tyche), which figure so large in
modern studies both of Procopius and of the ecclesiastical historians,[17]
are much less indicative of Procopius' views on historical causation than
of the inherited language of classicising writers, part of a whole from
which individual words of phrases should not be isolated. It is difficult in
principle, then, to know which words or phrases to stress, on where to lay
the weight of our explanation; further, such apparently key words and
concepts like Fortune lose some of their persuasiveness in this role when
we see that Procopius will equally 'explain' even the most familiar
expressions. Thus while it might seem reasonable that he should explain
the name 'S. Sophia' in a formal work such as the *Wars*, it is far less
appropriate when he does so in the *Buildings*, a work devoted to just this
subject matter, and moreover just before a very lengthy description of the
church.[18] This 'mania for periphrasis'[19] is to us an awkward feature of
Procopius' work, though there was nothing new or individual about it. It
makes it particularly difficult to decide what if anything can be taken at
face value. But for our present purposes it is a major indicator, with the
extraordinary care for prose rhythm, of the unity of Procopius' three
works as parts of one system.

The texture of Procopius' writing displays classical imitation at many
different levels, from the purely linguistic, the use of a classicising Greek
far removed from daily speech in the sixth century,[20] to the adoption of
specific incidents or events from classical works, and the deeper influence
on his work of a whole conception of formal writing, comprising not only
selection and arrangement but also the stance of the historian himself to
his subject. Part and parcel of his adoption of the traditional classicising
style of historiography is his concentration in the *Wars* on military
events, his inclusion of 'digressions', his focus on personalities and his
feeling of obligation to investigate 'causes' (where he is actually the least
successful). All these aspects will be discussed in later chapters. The
same reasons led to his omission of nearly all ecclesiastical matter from
the main narrative of the *Wars* – again an approach which he simply
inherited from the earlier tradition but which in this age he was unlikely
to be able to achieve with complete rigour. In fact the *Secret History* (like
some individual passages in the *Wars*) shows that ecclesiastical policies
were at the heart of his critique of Justinian. If he seriously intended to
write a separate ecclesiastical history, [21] the very need for such a rigid

[16] Dahn 1865, 181 ('Theismus'); Teuffel 1971, 222 ('deistisch'); Veh 1952, 21 ('Hellenic')
etc. In fact *to theion* and *to kreitton* are both terms frequently used by Christian writers.
[17] For example, Chesnut 1973, 1975.
[18] *Buildings* I.1.21; cf. *Vandal Wars* I.6.26 (virtually the same).
[19] Hunger 1978, I, 298.
[20] Browning 1978.
[21] *SH* 1.14; 11.33; 26.18; *Wars* VIII.25.13.

separation is an admission of the difficulties which the classicising tradition laid upon him, as of the limitation of the types of material and comment which he could admit to the *Wars*. It is not that the *Secret History* and the *Buildings* are essentially different from or at odds with the *Wars*, but rather that a different emphasis is possible. But we should not assume that Procopius' 'real' opinions are easily detectable. Instead, his opinions are inseparable from the whole complex of his classicism. That is not to say, however, that there will not be tensions in certain areas. In particular, the 'causes' admitted in the *Wars* are likely to be formally limited to acceptably classical notions of historical causation (hence the prominence of Fortune). But in many places Procopius actually relies on a miraculous explanation, or a statement of unswerving belief in divine providence, as he does most conspicuously when he writes of the sack of Antioch, or the plague, even though he had Thucydides' famous plague description very much in mind.[22] Naturally, his discourse is complex, and he has not been well served by modern scholarship which has tried to take away its complexity. Once the complexity is admitted it is much easier to do without either the psychological or the simple developmental explanation of the three works, and to place them together, all three showing – admittedly in differing degrees and different ways – the same complex discourse.

Prominent in Procopius' literary influences is of course Thucydides, as the prologue to the first book of the *Wars* spells out.[23] Procopius picks out the importance of the eye-witness account, as shown by Thucydides, and he follows Thucydides again when he goes on to discuss the differences between modern and ancient military technology, as Thucydides had done in his own preface.[24] This debt is shown at every turn in the *Wars*, not merely the *Gothic Wars*, where Procopius uses the Thucydidean dating formulae explicitly, but throughout, especially in speeches and battle-scenes. But the prologue also evokes Herodotus and Polybius, the former with the familiar justification for history, that great events should not go unsung (note the Herodotean *exitêla*),[25] and the latter with the appeal to impartiality.[26] In the prefaces to the other two works Polybius is far more to the fore, together with Diodorus,[27] and it is clear that Arrian was also an important source.[28] The *Wars* is self-consciously

---

[22] Below, pp. 40f.

[23] The chief discussions are Braun 1885; Bruckner and Haury, both 1896; see too Duwe 1885. Haury as usual is the most sensible.

[24] *Persian Wars* I.1.16; Thuc. I.5.3f, 10. 4f 13.3. Cesa 1981, 397f. sees in this discussion prominently placed in the opening chapter of the *Wars*, a deliberate avoidance of the ideological justification of Justinianic reconquest; for other suggestions, see p. 397 n. 33. But an intelligent paper by Ann Kuttner more plausibly links it both to Thucydides and to Procopius' overall conception of war as *technê* (cf. *Gothic Wars* IV.11.27f.).

[25] I.2.2; Herod. I.2, intro.

[26] I.1.5; Polyb. I.14.5.

[27] See Lieberich 1900, 1-6.

[28] P. 216f. below.

Thucydidean, while being at the same time a mixture of a political history and a work largely concerned with geography; the long opening sections and frequent geographical digressions sit uncomfortably with the military narrative, and Procopius was undoubtedly influenced by later writers who had taken a less restricted view of what to include than had Thucydides. Nevertheless, Procopius deliberately evokes Thucydides, and his own military experience and intense political involvement placed him in an unusually close relation to his model. He found it natural to follow the pattern of diplomatic passages, emphasis on foreign affairs, speeches, military set-pieces and so on, so that his narrative has a distinctly Thucydidean look overall. He also locates his subject in relation to the classical past in a more general way, rather than to recent and more realistic examples.[29] There had been many centuries of use and re-use of Thucydides before Procopius; not surprisingly, therefore, his conception of history is something of a composite.[30] The geographical spread of Justinian's wars meant that Procopius was writing about a wider world than Thucydides, with resultant adaptations of the method. But to this wider frame he applied the traditional constraints and limitations of a mode of history inherited – at whatever remove – from Thucydides. Procopius' vision saw Justinian and the wars of reconquest through the eyes of Greek historiography.

We need not suppose that Procopius' Thucydidean conception of history was owed to a close reading of Thucydides himself in order to accept the validity of the description. He could hardly have avoided the influence in any case, for the famous passages had gone through such a working and reworking in all the intervening centuries of rhetorical education that no educated Greek could have failed to know them; they were simply part of his consciousness. It is clear, for example, that Choricius of Gaza imitated Thucydides in the same way as Procopius and that he often used the same model passages.[31] In the general texture of his prose Procopius constantly incorporates individual phrases from Thucydides (and Herodotus), many of which are uninteresting in themselves and important only for their contribution to its general flavour.[32] For an author following the élite cultural pattern of writing in

[29] Alexander – *Persian Wars* I.10.9; Cyrus – II.2.14, *Buildings* I.1.12f., referring to Xenophon's *Cyropaedia*.

[30] There is also of course much of Herodotus in Procopius' work (see Braun 1894), especially in the discursive treatment, the digressions and the wide geographical scope; this too has gone through the filter of many centuries and many intermediaries (Xenophon, Arrian). But Procopius is more self-consciously a follower of Thucydides, as his subject matter and his own situation dictated. See further below, pp. 134f. and Cesa 1982.

[31] See Haury 1896, 11f. On knowledge of Thucydides at Gaza see Downey 1958a, 314, n. 76; there is no reason however why Procopius should not have studied Thucydides at Caesarea.

[32] See Braun etc. (n. 23), and for convenience, Averil Cameron 1964 (= 1981, II), 49. Procopius' language is a tissue of words and phrases from both writers, far more so than with Agathias, who also imitated both authors but was more of a stylist himself.

high style, a close study of classical exemplars was essential, and there were no doubt actual handbooks to help, which would account for the frequency with which certain words and phrases were taken up.[33] We can assess the laborious nature of this writing process from the remarkable consistency with which Procopius kept up his favoured rhythmical sentence endings throughout the three works. Undoubtedly the Thucydidean influence at this linguistic level was very strong. It has often been pointed out, moreover, that Procopius seems to have taken whole episodes from Herodotus and Thucydides, on the strength of which he has been accused of importing sheer fiction into his own history.[34] But as with the vocabulary and phraseology, this is part of a centuries-old tradition in certain sorts of history-writing. There was nothing new about what Procopius did. Moreover, the charge of direct plagiarism is anachronistic. Procopius – like his predecessors – was taking advantage of the continuity of ancient warfare, especially siege warfare, over many centuries, to give his work the required classical tinge.[35] It was all part of the expected technique to evoke a well-known passage or incident in one's own narrative, and there could be many gradations between plagiarism and gentle evocation.[36] The point is that it would have been difficult to describe some of these events and incidents in classicising language *without* evoking famous passages in the classical authors. The evolution of the kind of prose written by Procopius was arrived at by arduous study and years of working over exactly those classical texts. Thus it was both intentional and inevitable in itself that his work should at times recall the memory of specific passages in his models. To regard this as plagiarism, damaging to his integrity as a writer, is to misunderstand the process completely.[37]

Nor was it simply at the linguistic level that the influence of Thucydides was felt. Procopius patterned his whole conception of the *Wars* on the model of secular military history based on autopsy. It was a mode of history that must explain human behaviour without setting it within an overriding religious interpretation. It set a premium on diplomatic exchanges and expressed the author's ideas through dramatic speeches. Since its horizon was human, personality and the depiction of individuals played a large part too. Procopius was remarkable for the persistence with which he struck to these aims, when contemporaries were apparently writing so differently, and the superficial imitation of

[33] Suggested by the constant use by different authors of the same standard passages. The total effect could only have been achieved by extreme and deliberate effort.

[34] See Haury 1896, 5f. and Soyter 1951 (arguing against). Though understandable, such accusations start from the false position that *mimêsis* entails copying, i.e. that it is a form of cheating. Recently on Priscus' imitation of Thucydides' account of the siege of Plataea: Baldwin 1980, 53f.

[35] Hunger 1969-70, 26-7, and the many examples cited in Lucian's *How to write history*.

[36] Hunger, ibid.

[37] Ibid.

Thucydidean language and phraseology is only the outward sign of a much deeper dependence.

But of course, we sometimes want to know whether something described by Procopius in Thucydidean or Herodotean language did actually happen as he says it did. Take for instance the episode when Procopius describes the Berber tactic of arranging their camels in a circle round their troops, baggage, women and all, so that their attackers could only get through by hacking their way through the camels.[38] Clearly this was a genuine contemporary practice, as it is described also by Corippus,[39] but Procopius gave his description a classical tinge by recalling Herodotus on Cyrus.[40] It is usually too simple, then, to suppose that the classicising and the 'genuinely contemporary' elements are clearly separable; much more often they are mingled together, and in differing degrees, from the simple use of classical vocabulary to the conscious evocation of a particular passage.

Some parts of the work lent themselves more readily than others – too readily, perhaps – to classical imitation. The Lucianic pamphlet on the writing of history points to prefaces and battles, especially sieges, as obvious candidates.[41] But plague, too, was such an obvious point of imitation that it could not be missed. Yet here, though the imitation of Thucydides in Procopius' set-piece on the plague in Constantinople in AD 542 is apparent throughout, there are striking differences,[42] such that while there is much superficial resemblance there is a deep underlying divide. Like Thucydides, Procopius here discusses possible causes, using the Thucydidean *aitia* and *prophasis*;[43] but he can find no human explanation. The Thucydidean causation will not do for Procopius; indeed, he is here more than usually suspicious of scientific analysis, which he declares to be 'deceit', 'fashioned by the clever' by deceivers who know that such things as the plague are beyond human comprehension.[44] The plague, then, like the sack of Antioch by Chosroes, is to be explained only in terms of the will of God, however obscure that may seem to men. So Procopius actually comes very close to his successor, Agathias, a more obviously Christian writer in general, and one who also professes Christian resignation in the face of disaster.[45] The

[38] *Vandal Wars* I.8.25f., II.11.17f.

[39] *Ioh.* IV.595-99; VIII.39-40. On this tactic (see Ibn Khaldun, XX.20) see Bulliet 1975, 137; Gautier 1927, 170ff.

[40] Herod, I.80.

[41] *Hist. Conscr.* 45.

[42] See Soyter 1951; on the plague in general, Allen 1979, Teall 1965, 306f., McNeill 1977, 123f., Patlagean 1977, 85ff., Biraben and Le Goff 1969. I am glad to have seen an article on the comparison of Thucycides and Procopius by Dr S. Draghici. It was a disaster of the highest order, comparable with the Black Death; to do justice to it, Procopius' treatment should far transcend mere literary imitation.

[43] *Persian Wars* II.22.1-5, a key passage.

[44] II.22.1.

[45] *Hist.* II.15.5f. (compare his language with Procopius' on those who claimed to be 'clever'); see Averil Cameron 1970, 103f., 113.

course of the plague Procopius considers a proper subject, and the influence of Thucydides is apparent throughout his account; but explanation he will leave to others.[46] His scorn for the 'sophists' and 'high thinkers' who do rush into such explanations comes not from Thucydides but from the language of Christian polemic against scientific or pseudo-scientific thinking.[47] This divergence is all the more striking for coming in a passage where he would certainly be expected to be at his most classical. Instead, or as well, he chooses to distance himself from the approach of Thucydides, and we should take due note of that.

There are other ways in which he has diverged from his model, too. Admittedly, he describes the course of the disease with the clinical detachment which he had learnt from Thucydides, and without the evident pain with which Evagrius wrote about the deaths of his own loved ones from plague in Antioch.[48] Yet there are touches which Procopius – who was living in the city for at least part of the outbreak[49] – has added from his own experience. He lays stress, for instance, on the awful experiences of those who had to nurse the sick, especially because of the manic behaviour of the stricken,[50] He describes in detail the hallucinations which are a noted feature of the disease,[51] and emphasises the reactions of the doctors and the impossibility of accurate prognostication, in a manner which suggests close experience.[52] Like Thucydides, Procopius too (inevitably) writes of the difficulties in dealing with the bodies,[53] but his account here is entirely circumstantial, focussing on the emperor's attempts to deal with the situation and the consequences when the number of deaths rose beyond bounds and bodies were simply thrown into the towers of the city walls. All normal procedures were forgotten; there were no funeral processions or chants and in the crisis even the Blues and Greens forgot their differences and helped to bury the dead.[54] Thus Procopius places his emphasis on the unity and solidarity which the disaster called forth from the citizens, though he recognises that the strong effect it exerted on the minds of the wicked was only short-lived.[55] This is not just any city in the grip of plague; it is clearly Constantinople in the sixth-century, where the price of bread rose so high that some starved, and where no one wore the

---

[46] *Persian Wars* II.22.5.
[47] Above, n. 45. Cf. Philoponus, *De Op. Mundi*, p. 204 Reichardt (against astrology), and Theophylact, *Hist.* VII.6.8 (on a comet).
[48] *HE* IV.29, on which see Allen 1981, 190ff.
[49] See *Persian Wars* II.22.9.
[50] II.22.22f.
[51] II.22.21f.
[52] II.22.29f.
[53] II.23.3f.; similarly Malalas, p. 482 Bonn.
[54] II.23.12f. Procopius sees this in terms of the reversal of the expected order (see especially Chapter 13 below), as with his remarks on dress (n. 56). The plague turned things upside down (II.23.14).
[55] II.23.14-16.

chlamys any more but stayed at home and wore ordinary clothes, especially when they heard the news that the emperor himself was stricken.[56]

The general shape, then, of Procopius' description is conditioned very much by the famous account by Thucydides of the Athenian plague in 430, whatever the difference in the actual diseases described by the two writers.[57] Procopius' too is a relatively detached, clinical description, and after it he returns to the main theme with a certain artful self-consciousness.[58] But still, there is also much here that comes from his own personal observation, and the expected *mimêsis* is only one of the influences shaping his description. In the *Secret History* the plague reappears – as a sign of Justinian's demonic nature,[59] one of the catastrophes which 'some' attributed to the rule of Justinian, and 'others' to the work of avenging demons to whom God in His hostility to Justinian had given up the empire. Here Procopius claims that half the surviving population perished in the plague. It is also interesting that in the *Wars* his comments suggest that he believes in a religious explanation for the plague, though he does not here ascribe it directly to the wrath of God, as did so many of his contemporaries,[60] nor does he build up the theme of the financial crisis which it produced (and which he had certainly noticed).[61] But this may be an effect of his consciousness of the Thucydidean model. Procopius' plague description in the *Wars* is very clearly a set-piece, a *tour de force*. It may have personal and contemporary touches, but still he will not go so far as to launch into the kind of confident Christian explanation we find in the chroniclers. Nor, here, could he consider the wider implications of the disaster for the city and the empire, which he does, in however a distorted form, in the *Secret History*. He has, in the *Wars*, limited himself and reduced the sense of the real magnitude of the disaster by confining his description to a classicising digression. Procopius did realise the extent of the plague's effects, for in the *Secret History* he writes that they spread over 'half the human race'.[62] But he did not choose to emphasise this aspect in his

---

[56] II.23.17-21. This concern for the proprieties of society is typical of Procopius, critic of 'innovation' and spokesman for 'law and order' (below, p. 240).

[57] For the Thucydidean plague see Littman and Littmann 1973; the sixth-century plague was certainly bubonic, with all that that implies for the demographic consequences.

[58] II.24.1 – a sharp break, signalling the end of a set-piece.

[59] *SH* 18.44.

[60] Malalas, p. 482; Evagrius, *HE* IV.29 and see Allen 1981, 194. Justinian took the same view – *Edict* 7, pref.

[61] II.23.19. Justinian legislated to help bankers who complained that they were being cheated by heirs defaulting on the debts of the deceased (*Edicts* 7 and 9). For similar financial crises causes in the Italian cities by the Black Death, see Ziegler 1969, 44f.

[62] *SH* 18.44. Effects on the Persian army: *Persian Wars* II.24.12. The worst effects were admittedly the long-term ones, caused by successive recurrences of the disease, while Procopius was writing, even in the *Secret History*, within only a few years from the first onslaught.

major account in the *Wars*. In fact, therefore, the influence of classical imitation was very complex. It worked at many levels, and, as this section seems to show, even while Procopius could blend the classicising with the contemporary, the influence of tradition and the expectation of his audience could exert subtle pressures on him which affected the way in which he presented major events and major historical factors at the deepest level. In these circumstances, then, it is hardly possible to separate the form from the content, or to say which (of the *Wars* and the *Secret History*) is Procopius' real statement. It is striking, finally, that the illness of Justinian is given such low prominence in the *Wars* when the plague is so intimately connected in the *Secret History* with the personality of the emperor himself.[63] But it is hard to know whether to attribute this, like the relative failure to place the disaster in a political context, to the influence of the rhetorical model or to the real political difficulty of expressing oneself openly in a public history. Either would have damaged the value of this part of the *Wars* as Procopius' 'real' views; probably in practice both pressures were operative together.

There are similar ambiguities at the linguistic level. On the whole Procopius tried to maintain an acceptably classicising Greek, using archaising features like the optative mood and the dual, and for his time he was remarkably successful.[64] He certainly used Attic and archaic vocabulary, and parts of the *Buildings* and even the *Secret History* adopt a more florid style suited to the rhetorical forms of panegyric, *ekphrasis* and invective.[65] We have seen already with what care he achieved his rhythmical prose effects.[66] But Procopius' style overall is far more straightforward than that of many of his contemporaries; the Gaza school, for instance, practised an elaborately rhetorical literary style, shared by historians who followed Procopius, especially Theophylact Simocatta.[67] By comparison with writers such as these, Procopius seemed a model of clarity, and it was easy to assume that this refreshingly straightforward writer was also a model of rationality and logic in a sadly superstitious age. Such a rash conclusion lies behind the embarrassment with which J.B. Bury, for instance, greeted the fact that

[63] Again, *SH* 4.1 takes a different line, revealing that Justinian was actually believed to be dead of the plague, and thought was being taken for the succession, whereas in the *Wars* Procopius limits himself to the mere statement of the emperor's illness. It was inevitably a far more serious matter than his bland words suggest; for a later incident of a similar kind, see Theophanes, p. 235 de Boor.

[64] See Rubin 1954, 37f., the best available guide in the absence of any full study of Procopius's language. We still have to fall back on the demonstration of Procopian authorship of the *Secret History* by Dahn 1865, 416ff. for anything like a solidly based discussion.

[65] Below, pp. 93f., 58f.

[66] Also Rubin 1954, 39.

[67] Again a full discussion of literary style in this period is lacking: but see Kustas 1973, 59ff.

Procopius also wrote the *Buildings* and the *Secret History*.[68] But of course, though his style may be more straightforward than the rhetorical effusions of some others, it remains an artful construction. Neither here nor anywhere else must Procopius be taken at face value. Better to discard both the prejudiced distaste for late Greek rhetoric and the assumption that Procopius wrote as he felt, without art.[69] We shall see then (though not properly so long as there is no full linguistic study) that his language and style are indeed complex. That though he carefully observed his own rules of accentual prose, and sought to imitate Herodotus, Thucydides and other classical or near-classical authors, his sentence structure is anything but Thucydidean; instead of elaborate subordination and antithesis, we find participles serving almost as main verbs and stringing sentences together in what Browning calls the 'Hellenistic sentence pattern'.[70] This, perhaps above all, is what gives Procopius his air of simplicity and modernity. But it is an indicator of the complexity of the tradition of Greek historical prose as it came to him, after a thousand years of practice. He had read not only Thucydides, but also, more realistically, more recent authors such as Priscus.[71] Not surprisingly, he also admits many post-classical usages of a sort standard in Byzantine authors – confusion of prepositions, pronouns used for demonstratives and so on.[72] But these too, like the Hellenistic or late Greek sentence structure, are part and parcel even of high-style prose as Procopius knew it. They indicate the long and complex tradition of Greek historiography, and the many different sources of Procopius' Greek style. Certainly this 'simple' narrative style is not to be confused with artlessness.

But if the language of history was only achieved with difficulty, and if there are so many layers of selfconsciousness in Procopius' writing, how are we to assess what he actually says? The plague description has provided one example of this problem, but its most acute presentation lies in what he says on religious matters, where artificiality often very obviously stands in the way of clear understanding.[73] But there are also deficiencies in Procopius' own expression. In particular, he tends to fall into his own clichés of praise and blame, especially in his judgments on character.[74] A complete study of his style would in fact reveal that his

[68] At least in his early days – Bury 1889, I, 359ff.

[69] Unfortunately, Kennedy 1983 has left out the sixth century altogether. Only an understanding of the rhetoric of high level authors such as Procopius in a social and intellectual context will prevent the naive misunderstandings that have been standard up to now.

[70] Browning 1978, 109, an excellent brief characterisation.

[71] Or so it seems, though it is hard to demonstrate directly; see below, pp. 208f. and Rubin 1954, 50.

[72] Rubin, 1954, 38.

[73] Below, chapter 7. This is probably the most misunderstood aspect of Procopius, and largely so for linguistic reasons.

[74] Below, p. 240.

writing is both repetitive and self-referential. He likes periphrases and intensifications – 'good at warfare', 'very friendly', 'extremely keen' and so on – and often turns to a limited and colourless vocabulary that has actually hampered exact description. This is as true of the speeches, often empty of real content, as of the main body of the narrative.[75] In fact the 'real' Procopius is far from being the penetrating and critical thinker that he is usually supposed to be. Certainly that is suggested when we consider the recurring attitudes expressed in his work as well as the recurring phraseology and vocabulary.[76]

I have used (and will continue to use) the term 'Thucydidean history' in relation to Procopius *Wars*, because it does usefully denote a whole set of external characteristics to which Procopius largely conforms. Later chapters will explore the extent of this conformity and the tension in his work between classicising expectations and contemporary attitudes and assumptions. It is clear that in his works taken as a whole he also shares many of the supposedly 'popular' features of contemporary literature. His classicism is an amalgam, like his literary style, and in both he was often nearer the 'literary Koinê' of writers like John the Lydian than to genuine high style.[77] As a result, the proper assessment of the effects of literary self-consciousness on Procopius' writing is the hardest but the most necessary task that we have to face; above all, facile assumptions will not do.

It was not surprising that Procopius' achievement was inconsistent or even apparently self-contradictory. His ability places him in a class above the rest of the early Byzantine classicising historians, and his subject matter and reporting gave him a unique advantage. All the same, he was as much exposed to the influences of the age in which he lived as anyone else, and it was an age in which there was, as we have seen, wide artistic variation, even within the élite sphere. It was also an age of rapid change, one in which Justinian's own policies did more than anything else to destroy the cultural patterns that had prevailed for centuries in the Greek east. No one wrote quite like Procopius after Procopius, and within hardly more than two generations the whole tradition of secular history, changed though it already was, was abruptly broken off. In the

[75] Rubin 1954, 84. Below, pp. 148f. It is well known that Procopius sometimes uses speeches to express his own (thus indirect) criticism of the régime, and the same applies to letters, which fall into the same rhetorical category; below, p. 149. Thus the speeches do at times relate thematically to the main narrative, as has been shown for Thucydides by de Romilly 1956 and Hunter 1973, but as often they are mere exercises.

[76] See especially Chapter 13. The approach of Hunter 1973 to Thucydides (asking 'how' rather than 'what' or 'when') is very instructive for Procopius, who suffers similarly from being thought an 'objective' writer. The analyses of the individual works which follow in subsequent chapters aim at providing the skeleton for a more promising approach.

[77] Browning 1978, 109: on the whole, he 'handles the traditional *Hochsprache* easily and flexibly'. Nevertheless, while there is a world of difference between Procopius and a popular saint's life (see Ševčenko 1981), nobody would actually think in reading Procopius that he was reading a classical author.

main, Procopius' views were traditional and conservative, and his aim in his major work, the *Wars*, was to emulate the histories written in the past. Even that aim, however, was not to be easily achieved for someone writing as late as the sixth century, and the *Wars* itself, as we shall go on to see, exhibits a subtle mix of the personal and the imitative, the traditional and the contemporary. Since, however, nearly all previous interpreters of Procopius have privileged the classicising and 'rational' historian, and usually without even considering their justification, I shall here begin with the other Procopius of the *Secret History* and the *Buildings*, only then looking at the historian of the *Wars*. That will help us to see what to look for in the *Wars*, and lead to general conclusions based on all three works.

PART II

CHAPTER FOUR

Procopius and the *Secret History*

It was of the *Secret History*, or rather the *Anecdota* (literally 'the unpublished work'), that Gibbon wrote that it must 'sully the reputation and detract from the credit of Procopius', and of which he decreed that certain passages must, in his inimitable phrase, be left 'in the obscurity of a learned language'. At the same time he took the trouble to inform the reader with relish of Alemanni's bowdlerisation of the notorious chapter nine on the sexual habits of Theodora, and to note with mock solemnity that 'a learned prelate, now deceased, was fond of quoting this passage in conversation'.[1] Thereby he set the tone of all subsequent reactions. Whereas however Gibbon (unlike the seventeenth-century lawyers),[2] had felt no doubts about the authenticity of the *Secret History*, J.B. Bury argued in 1889 that it could not be by Procopius; he had changed his mind by 1923, but still supposed that Procopius must have suffered a 'brainstorm' before writing it.[3] More recently, A.J.M. Jones, while criticising the *Wars* for the 'childish credulity' displayed there towards everything of which he had no personal knowledge, described the *Secret History* as 'a venomous pamphlet' which 'does not deserve the respect which is often accorded to it'.[4] B. Rubin reversed the trend by elevating the work to a primary place in Procopius' oeuvre, while for Z.V. Udal'cova it represented a unique document for perceiving the situation of the discontented masses under Justinian.[5] The Penguin translator was uncertain what to make of it, but gallantly defended Procopius: 'Procopius was unquestionably on the side of right, and the things which are disgusting to us were equally disgusting to him.'[6]

As we see from this small conspectus of views, the *Secret History* has left modern scholars bewildered. The question of authorship first assumed importance, and after that the problem of finding a psychological or developmental view of Procopius' writing that would

---

[1] *Decline and Fall*, ed. Bury, IV, 211, 213 with nn. 23 and 24.
[2] Above, p. 4.
[3] Bury 1889, I, 355, 359ff.; 1923, II, 417. Evans 1968, 136 supposes schizophrenia.
[4] Jones 1964, I, 266.
[5] Rubin 1951, 1953, 1960; Udal'cova 1974, 171ff.
[6] Williamson 1966, 31; another defence: Holmes 1912, I, 340 n. 2.

accommodate the work.[7] Both attitudes stem from the asumption that the work is something of a freak. But in fact there are many links both between this and Procopius' other works and between the *Secret History* and other contemporary writing. We must make these links our starting point.

The very preface ties the work intimately to the *Wars*. Like the *Wars*, the *Secret History* will be concerned with 'reasons' (*aitiai*); that is, Procopius claims the Thucydidean and Polybian affiliation here too. The subject matter will also be that of the *Wars*, except that now Procopius will give the true reasons for events. Clearly the work was meant for publication after the deaths of Justinian and Theodora; certainly it was not something written for private purposes, as its elaborate preface, modelled on Diodorus and Polybius, and its linguistic homogeneity with the other two works demonstrates.[8] As for the title *Anecdota*, given in the *Suda*, we are reminded of the *anecdota* which Cicero said he could write in the manner of Theopompus, *aut etiam asperiore*;[9] but the title may not be Procopius' own, and indeed the *Suda* entry looks like the deduction of a later author. The only other Byzantine to cite the work explicitly – Nicephorus Callistus – calls it an *antirrhêsis*, a kind of palinode.[10] Probably no Byzantine author knew of it until the tenth century,[11] and this may support the conjecture that Procopius died before Justinian, leaving this and the *Buildings* without their final touches. There are constant cross-references in it to the *Wars*,[12] especially in the first section and as far as the end of chapter 5. From that point Procopius launches into a description of the characters of Justinian and Theodora,[13] prefaced by an account of Justinian's accession. A final, and again rather different section begins with chapter 13, from which point Procopius dwells on a generalised critique of imperial policies with certain recurring themes: Justinian's depradations on the property of the rich, his blood-lust, his demonic nature, Theodora's spite, Justinian's greed. Only the first part, therefore, actually fulfils the promise of the preface to give specific reasons for the incidents narrated in the *Wars*, while the rest of the work broadens out in scope. There are many signs of loose construction in it, and plural authorship has even been suggested;[14] lack of final revision is the more likely explanation.

[7] For the dating of the works see above, Chapter 1. The *Secret History* belongs in 550, though some, e.g. Evans, still put it in 559/60; see also Hunger 1978, I, 293.

[8] Rubin 1954, 258-9; above p. 16.

[9] *Ad Att.* II.5, XIV.17.

[10] *HE* XVII.10.

[11] See Rubin 1953 for discussion and p. 16 above.

[12] Haury 1980/81, 21f. E.g. *SH* 1.13, 28; 2.15, 26; 4.1; 5.1, 17; 6.22; 16.1; 17.38; 18.44. The openings of *SH* and *Wars* VIII correspond closely. Chapters 1-5 are closely based on the *Wars* narrative (see below). Compare Chapter 3 n. 7 above for cross-references to the *Wars* in the *Buildings*. Forward references in the *Secret History*: 1.10; 11.33; 18.38; 26.18.

[13] For Theodora see below, Chapter 5.

[14] See Rubin 1954, 257.

Procopius does not begin with Justinian but with Belisarius, with the latter's relations with his wife Antonina at the point where she brought about the fall of the hated John the Cappadocian (AD 541). Theodora was herself a bitter enemy of John, and Antonina, her close friend, assisted her to bring him down by inducing him to compromise himself through his daughter, who was easily influenced. Though Justinian got wind of the plot and sent word to warn him, John foolishly disregarded the warning and extricated himself from a dangerous situation only by seeking asylum in a church. This however is not the account of the *Secret History*; it comes from the *Wars*.[15] Even there Procopius is surprisingly critical of Theodora and Antonina. He merely adds in the *Secret History* that Antonina's plots were the more wicked because she swore to John and his daughter simultaneously that she would do him no harm, using 'the oaths which the Christians hold to be the most terrible of all',[16] a detail which Procopius says he was afraid to include in his earlier work. After this she joined her husband in the east, where he was engaged in the second Persian expedition. Belisarius had just taken the fortress of Sisauranon (AD 541), but when he heard of Antonina's arrival he abandoned the campaign and retreated. In the *Wars*, the reason is given as sickness in the army, at which the soldiers grew restive and demanded to retire.[17] In the *Secret History* Belisarius retreats because he is so preoccupied with his wife's infidelities.[18] At this point Procopius explains:

> As I explained earlier, some events had also happened in the army which caused his retreat. This, however, led him more quickly to the decision. But as I said at the beginning of this account, it seemed to me to be dangerous to explain all the reasons for what had happened. As a result all the Romans blamed Belisarius for thinking more of his own family than of the vital affairs of the state.

But then Procopius goes on to add a more serious criticism: had Belisarius only crossed the Tigris with his whole army at the start of this expedition he could have plundered all Assyria and reached Ctesiphon itself.[19] Wild words, no doubt, but symptomatic of the sharp criticism of Belisarius which is to follow. For Procopius now accuses him of thus allowing Chosroes to move his army back into Persia unimpeded. After Chosroes had taken Petra, he says, the Persian army was weakened by fighting, disease and hunger. Moreover their Hun allies had been defeated and this caused disaffection within Chosroes' camp. The way

[15] *Persian Wars* I.25.
[16] *SH* 2.16.
[17] 2.19.
[18] 2.18f.
[19] 2.25.

was wide open for an attack by Belisarius which never came, for the general was too interested in his marital problems to care.[20]

The next chapter contains still more direct criticism. Procopius presents Belisarius as entirely helpless at managing his own affairs, a tool of the empress, who can even settle the quarrel between him and his wife and marry off her grandson to Belisarius' daughter.[21] In case we should assume that as a desirable connection by marriage his position cannot have been so abject as Procopius would have us believe, we are told that Theodora's motive was to get her hands on Belisarius' wealth.[22] The triviality of this accusation is shown up when we hear immediately afterwards that Belisarius was put in charge of the Italian expedition – presumably he had never actually been so much in disgrace as Procopius implies. Even in mentioning this military command Procopius slips in an innuendo – Justinian refused to grant Belisarius adequate supplies, and the general paid them out of his own pocket because he was so keen to get away from his wife.[23] Everyone expected him to behave like a man, says Procopius, but he simply swallowed the insults, so much was he in the sway of Antonina.[24] Yet mixed in with this low-level taunting comes serious criticism: the second Italian expedition was a total disaster, for in five years (AD 544-9) Belisarius never set foot on land, save at Roman fortresses, while Rome itself and virtually everything else was lost. Moreover Belisarius was only interested in getting money.[25] In the end two of his leading officers quarrelled, and in total ignominy he was forced to ask Justinian to be recalled. Again Procopius specifically refers back here to the *Wars*, and a comparison of this passage in the *Secret History* with *Wars* VII.35 strikingly underlines their interdependence. For there too Procopius paints essentially the same picture of the second Italian expedition, though of course less overtly critical than in the *Secret History*. He even uses the same terminology in both places. In the *Wars* we read: 'as a result the enemy were enabled to enslave Rome with greater impunity, and virtually everywhere else'; while in the *Secret History*[26] he says 'not only did Belisarius fail to recover any of the losses which the Byzantines had sustained, but also lost Rome and virtually everywhere else'.

All this section is devoted to Belisarius. It is very probable that it was written shortly after, or rather, simultaneously with, the later parts of the *Wars*, when Procopius' grievances against Belisarius were still fresh. This was perhaps the first impulse for the work, and it may be what he means

[30] 2.37.
[21] 3.12; 5.18f. (see Alan Cameron 1978, 270f.).
[22] 4.37.
[23] 4.41.
[24] 4.40.
[25] 5.1.
[26] 5.3.

when he says that he intends in the *Secret History* to fill in the enforced gaps in the *Wars*. It would be hard to see him doing this in 559 or 560, when Belisarius was the aged hero who had just saved Constantinople from the Huns. Furthermore it is hard to believe that the section on Theodora was not written while she was still alive.[27] Had she been dead already when Procopius wrote, he would hardly have refrained from saying so, or rather from exulting over her death. The dating references which seem to point to AD 550[28] do not after all imply that the whole work was written then, and it would be natural to suppose that as Procopius' attitude changed in the writing of the final parts of the *Wars*, especially *Wars* VII,[29] so he was writing down his unpublishable thoughts at the same time. But even if the Theodora section was written in 550 too it would have been composed while the memory of the empress was still very strong, and perhaps to counter the eulogies which must have been pouring out. Impossible to think that Procopius or others would still be interested in this sort of thing as late as 560.

From here the *Secret History* moves to a general attack on Justinian and Theodora. It ends abruptly, with no proper conclusion: merely one sentence in which Procopius says that when Justinian is dead, people will know the truth.[30] Justinian at least was therefore still alive when this was written.[21] Yet in the preface Procopius refers to the reign as if it was already over: 'while the agents were still alive (presumably he means Belisarius and Antonina too) I could not record these things ...' Even more explicitly, he goes on to say that his work will be of use to future generations, who will see that evil is likely to be punished, *as it was* in the case of Justinian and Theodora.[32] But Procopius must have written this bombastic preface with a view to later publication after both Justinian and Theodora were dead, or we would have to deduce that the work was not written until after 565. For some reason, the end of the pamphlet as we have it was never brought to cohere with the preface; nor does Procopius make any of the obvious moral points about the death of Theodora. For all these reasons, and in view of the sudden change of subject at Chapter 17, it seems most likely that the work was left unfinished or unrevised, but that it took shape substantially in the late 540s when Procopius' disillusionment both with Belisarius and with imperial policy was rapidly growing. This impression is confirmed by the

[27] 5.23, 27; 30.34 certainly refer to her death, but there are no such allusions in *SH* 9 f.

[28] 18.33; 23.1; 24.29, 33, all from the section beginning at Chapter 18. Veh 1951/52, 32, dates 1-17 to the years 548-49, supposing them begun immediately after Theodora's death; but this is to overlook the importance of Belisarius and Antonina in 1-5.

[29] Chapter 11 below.

[30] 30.34.

[31] And see 18.33, 23.1, 24.29.

[32] 1.12. Note that at 1.6f. Procopius indicates that he had been considering writing the *Secret History* 'for a long time'.

preface to the last book of the *Wars*, added in 554, for there Procopius
announces a procedure identical to that set out in the preface to the
Secret History: whereas previously he had grouped events geographically, he now proposes to bring the story up to date on all fronts with
what had taken place in the intervening period.[33]

Many modern views hardly take into account this intimate connection
between the *Secret History* and the *Wars*. For instance, Downey writes:
'The Emperor did not realise that ... this distinguished author was
writing a scandalous *Secret History* not to be published until after his
death, in which he cruelly libelled the Emperor and Empress, who, he
believed, had failed to do justice to his hero Belisarius.'[34] Yet criticism of
Belisarius is as prominent as criticism of Justinian; when the *Secret
History* was written Belisarius was far from still being Procopius' hero.

We must link the *Secret History* just as closely with *Wars* VIII.
Theodora died in 548, and immediately afterwards Belisarius was
recalled to Constantinople from his unsuccessful second Italian
expedition, after which he never returned to the west.[35] The year 550 saw
Justinian's cousin, Germanus, appointed in Belisarius' place.[36]
According to Procopius, no one knew exactly what was happening:
Justinian first changed his mind about Germanus and then changed it
back again.[37] When a crisis arose in Italy, it was Liberius who was sent
out, only to have Germanus appointed general-in-chief over him. The
expedition was celebrated by the famous marriage of Germanus and the
Gothic princess Matasuntha, grand-daughter of Theodoric, with which
Jordanes's *Getica* closes.[38] Hopes ran high, but on his way to Italy
Germanus fell ill and died.[39] For Germanus Procopius has nothing but
praise; but he was succeeded first by Belisarius' old rival, John the
nephew of Vitalian, and then by the eunuch Narses, Theodora's protégé
and Belisarius' opponent, and it was Narses who won the final victories,
though Procopius broke off his history before he had to record them.

There is an unmistakable difference between the first seven books of
the *Wars* and the last. For the first time the Goths take on a heroic
stature; but Procopius turns again to Belisarius with a striking defence.
He claims that the emperor kept him in Constantinople even after the
death of Germanus (and did not give him the command in Italy) because
he wanted his presence there:[40] even after he had been appointed

---

[33] *Wars* VIII.1.1; cf. *SH* 1.1.
[34] Downey 1960, 158.
[35] *Gothic Wars* III.35.1. Death of Theodora: Fitton 1976.
[36] Ibid., 38.24, below, pp. 139, 195.
[37] Ibid., 38.27f.
[38] Jord., *Get.* 314; see Momigliano 1955, 1964; O'Donnell 1979, 271f. with *JRS* 71 (1981),
183-6; below, pp. 195f.
[39] *Gothic Wars* III.40.9.
[40] *Gothic Wars* IV. 21.1f.

commander in the east, he was kept in the capital to head the imperial bodyguard, and yet according to Procopius his prestige was greater than that of the highest aristocrat.[41] This is an amazing reversal of the *Secret History*, and is obviously quite deliberately placed, just as in *Wars* VII the eulogy of Belisarius is put immediately after his refusal of the offer of kingship from the Goths.[42] Something has caused Procopius to turn back to Belisarius, if only in protest about Justinian's handling of affairs, and this series of excuses is part of that change of view.

The *Secret History*, therefore, belongs precisely to the period of Belisarius' return from the second Italian expedition, when Procopius was most hostile to him. Not only would he not take steps against Justinian; he was not even capable of managing the war. In the *Secret History* the chapters about Belisarius are relatively short in proportion to the work as a whole; yet they are placed first, and they alone fulfil Procopius' aims as stated in the preface. By 554 they perhaps seemed untimely. Would Procopius have toned them down had he revised the *Secret History*? It is at least possible; for these sections, so intimately connected with the chapters about Belisarius' return from Italy in *Wars* VII, seem to belong to a very specific moment in a rapidly moving situation. We have no idea whether the connection between Procopius and Belisarius was now close enough for the latter to have seen the work; presumably he did not. Procopius' criticism is all backward-looking, and mostly very personal. It was not such as would have brought about a change of policy or suggested different options for the future. Yet soon afterwards Procopius was looking to Belisarius again. The work as a whole, then, took its stimulus from personal rather than political factors. Procopius was dredging up the events of twenty years ago. The incentive for the work came from two sources – the profound disappointment Procopius felt with Belisarius on his return from Italy and the difficulty of treating this adequately in the *Wars*.[43] He may have begun writing the *Secret History* a little before Belisarius' actual return, and while Theodora was still alive. But her death will have made her old activities suddenly news again, like her relationship with Antonina which is a prominent theme in the work. The scope of the work noticeably alters as it progresses, and as Procopius moves from Belisarius to a far more generalised critique of the reign. The bridge passage is the description of the origins and unsavoury background of the empress, and it was she, not Justinian (about whose origins little is said), who provided the stimulus. Her death, occurring perhaps after this section was written, gave the work a new point but did not cause Procopius to undertake a major revision. Even before that it had broadened out into a general diatribe.

[41] Ibid. 21.2.
[42] *Gothic Wars* III. 1.1-22; cf. II.30.25-30.
[43] Below, pp. 137ff.

The most difficult sections by far for a modern reader to accept are these bridging passages between the political/personal opening and the long diatribe at the end – the demonological and pornographic sections about Justinian and especially Theodora.[44] These have done most to 'sully Procopius' reputation'. Yet both are explicable, though in different ways.

Let us begin with the demonological element. In chapter 12, Procopius calls Justinian and Theodora demons (*daimones*) in human form, while Justinian is later called the 'prince of demons' (*archôn tôn daimonôn*).[45] His courtiers saw a demonic apparition sitting on the imperial throne; one saw his body walking around without a head; another saw his features melt and dissolve and then reshape themselves. A monk said that he saw the 'prince of demons' sitting on the throne, while Justinian himself is said to have believed himself capable of levitation.[46] Similar tales circulated about his mother and his wife; both were said to have been visited by demons. Finally, Procopius says very firmly that only the hypothesis of Justinian's demonic nature could be sufficient to explain the slaughter which his policies brought about in the empire.[47]

These stories and their acceptance by Procopius naturally caused most difficulty to those scholars who clung to the identification of the *Wars* with the spirit of rationalism. The most popular solution has been to doubt Procopius' seriousness.[48] But there is no reason to doubt that he meant these sections to be taken seriously. Procopius lived in an age when at any moment it was felt that men could be taken over by demons. Demons offered a ready explanation for misfortune or evil – the natural reverse of the resort to the miraculous which was integral to Procopius' historical explanation. Extraordinary events on earth must be explained by references to supernatural forces, either to the incomprehensible providence of God, as with the plague or the sack of Antioch, or to the workings of the Devil. One of the main themes of the *Secret History* is Justinian's 'lust for slaughter'. How else to explain this except by reference to demons; and if one man is responsible, would he not appear as the very prince of the demons himself – Satan or Antichrist (though Procopius does not use that word)? Just as good emperors assumed supra-human characteristics, so Justinian assumed diabolical ones.[49]

[44] Chapters 9 and 12 in particular.

[45] *SH* 12.26; cf. 32; 30.34. Compare 18.1 with 30.34.

[46] 12.18, 28. On the motif of the 'headless demon' see Gantar 1961, suggesting antecedents in the apocryphal *Testament of Solomon*. Apparitions of demons seen by plague victims: *Persian Wars* II.22.10.

[47] 12.14-17; 18f.

[48] P. 49 above. Terminology referring to 'humour' or 'satire' in the *Secret History* alike denies that these demonological passages can be interpreted at face value.

[49] As Justinian was larger than life, so must the explanation be. Procopius' was a very natural reaction – see Hanson 1979; the underside of Byzantine reverence for the emperor as close to God was always a sharp imperial critique and a readiness to conspire against the throne. See Tinnefeld 1971; Evagrius on Justinian and Justin II provides a good example. It

The mode of thought was well established in contemporary works,[50] and even though Procopius does not use eschatological language,[51] he surely did mean to imply that Justinian was the Devil incarnate, as earlier 'bad' emperors had seemed to be.[52] His disingenuous comparison of Justinian with Domitian shows us his intentions even though he has dressed it up in literary form.[53] Like other 'bad' emperors. Domitian had derived his reputation as Antichrist chiefly from his identification as a persecutor, and while Justinian is not here presented in those terms, his persecution of heretics is a major theme in the work, and Procopius' hatred of him rests fundamentally on the claim that because of Justinian many thousands have died either through his military policies or for their faith.[54] If Christian political theory since Eusebius saw the emperor in a special and supra-human way, it could be envisaged that if ever there was a truly 'bad' emperor, he too must be explained in supernatural terms. We shall see that the *Buildings* set forth the other side of this duality. Between them they recognise that an emperor, and above all an active and innovating emperor (a feature which as we shall see is not necessarily a good recommendation in Procopius' eyes),[55] is to be seen as having a special relation to the supernatural powers. To dismiss the demonology of the *Secret History* as some kind of bad joke, and the Christian political theory of the *Buildings* as insincere flattery, is to miss the coherence and seriousness of Procopius' vision.

However it was originally intended, the *Secret History* emerged as the

---

was easier for Theophylact dealing with Phocas, for he could dismiss him as a usurper (not a proper emperor): cf. *Hist.* VIII.7.7, 10.4 etc. Maurice's death was thus explained, and the religious element already present in Theophylact's account (VIII.11) was further developed in later hagiographical accounts interpreting the Avar and Persian invasions under Heraclius as divine retribution for Maurice's murder. Further, Whitby 1983, 318, 336-7, 340; Wortley 1980.

[50] E.g. in the *Oracle of Baalbek*, ed. Alexander 1967, 97f. The eighth-century *Parastaseis* hints at an equally hostile attitude to certain emperors (Cameron and Herrin 1984, 227).

[51] See further Rubin 1951.

[52] Nero, Domitian, Decius, Constantius, Julian, for example – Rubin 1951, 478-9. For Julian the sons of Constantine also represented *daimones palamnaioi* (X, 335b, cf. *SH* 12.14; Athanassiadi-Fowden 1981, 172f., 180). But for Procopius classicising language did not rule out a Christian intention. Clement of Alexandria similarly uses the Homeric language of Ares (*SH* 12.14) for the Devil – Rubin 1951, 471. Cf. too the *princeps daemonum* in the eschatology of Lactantius:*Epit.* 67.2, *Inst.* VII.24.5. In general: Rubin 1960, I, 441f., 445ff.

[53] *SH* 8.12f.; see below, and Rubin 1951, 480. Ammianus had used the same comparison of Constantius II (XV.5.35) and it was a standard technique to compare emperors with earlier 'good' or 'bad' rulers, but no other example can match the art which Procopius shows here. The converse is represented by his comparison of Justinian to Cyrus in the *Buildings* (I.1.12f.; Persian Wars II.2.14; for the ideal monarch see too on Theodoric, *Gothic Wars* I.1.27f. and on Trajan, *Buildings* IV.6.11; see Sauciuc-Săveanu 1964).

[55] Below, pp. 59, 228. Again the restlessness of which Procopius complains in Justinian is a standard form of critique of 'bad' emperors (cf. *SHA, V. Hadriani* 14.11). For the special relation of the emperor to the supernatural see too Cracco Ruggini 1979, 601f.

opposite of the panegyric represented by the *Buildings* – in fact as an
invective.[56] Its principal characters, then, must inevitably be represented
as larger than life, and this must be even more the case with panegyric or
invective directed at an emperor. It had been taken for granted, after all,
since Eusebius, that a panegyric of a Christian emperor would link him
with God's providence for the world. The lesson for an invective against
an emperor was quite obvious. Yet the demonology of the *Secret History*
is only a part of the whole: it does not pervade the entire work, and this
very fact has made it easy for modern scholars to find a way of dismissing
it.

Another feature of these sections leading to confusion in interpretation
is Procopius' obviously classicising presentation, which leads to some
odd effects. For instance, he calls Justinian and Theodora 'a pair of
blood-thirsty demons, and what the poets call "plaguers of mortal
men" ',[57] deliberating evoking Homer.[58] Having set forth his claim,
which, he says, is a belief shared by 'most people', he then explains what
he means, as if such terminology is unsuitable in a classicising history,
and declares that Fortune (Tychê) cooperated with Justinian and
Theodora to destroy mankind. The laboured explanation of the meaning
of *to daimonion* and the introduction of Fortune thus seem to us to
undercut the force of Procopius' statements. But that is a mistaken
reaction. We must simply accept that Procopius is dressing up in literary
guise a basically very serious interpretation.[59] The comparison with
Domitian is an even more striking example, not for its classicising
vocabulary but for its disingenuous presentation of Justinian in a totally
antique and historical comparison, with an underlying meaning of quite
a different sort. Procopius sets up a comparison and includes a piece of
personal verification – he had seen the statue of Domitian himself in
Rome, where his wife set it up 'on the road leading up to the Capitol, on
the right coming from the Forum, where it displays the appearance and
fate of Domitian until today'.[60] 'One might guess that the figure of
Justinian and his very countenance and all his features are clearly there
on this statue.'[61] Yet of course – a casual after-thought, as it seems –

[56] Cf. *Suda* s.v. Procopius, calling it a *psogos* and a *kômôdia*. The *Secret History* as
invective: Tinnefeld 1971, 29f.

[57] *SH* 12.14 (see n. 52).

[58] As he elsewhere evokes the language of tragedy (Averil Cameron 1966 (= 1981, I), 477).
Here he draws attention to the allusion ('as the poets say').

[59] For Procopius this was evidently one of the key passages in the work, and he takes care
that its effect is not lost. What may seem an odd combination of ideas to us is a sign of
Procopius's extra effort. It is followed by 'signs' of the demonic nature of Justinian and
Theodora.

[60] *SH* 8.20.

[61] 8.21. The whole story: 8.12-21. Destruction of Domitian's statues: Pliny, *Paneg.* 52.
After this, the description of Justinian's statue in the guise of Achilles in the *Buildings*
(I.2.10) might well seem deliberately ironic (below, p. 87), but that too has to be read in its
context. Physical descriptions of emperors were important in Byzantine historiography

Domitian had been the most hated of Roman emperors, and the statue in question was made only after Domitian's wife had collected up his dismembered corpse and had it all stitched together. Procopius does not refer to Domitian's reputation as a persecutor, but in recalling a classic 'bad emperor' his intentions are unmistakeable.

Classical invective has shaped the whole section on the appearance, origins and character of Justinian and Theodora; the narrative announced in the preface is totally forgotten. And in literary terms this is one of the most polished sections in the work. Immediately after the comparison with Domitian, Procopius sums up the character of Justinian: 'both foolish and vicious.'[62] He explains his nature as compounded of a mixture of folly and wickedness, according to Peripatetic definition.[63] He spells out what he means: 'This emperor was dissembling, treacherous, false, secret in his anger, two-faced; a clever man, well able to feign his opinions, one who wept not from joy or from sorrow but deliberately, at the right moment when needed ... he was an unreliable friend, an enemy who would not observe a truce, a passionate lover of murder and of money. He was constantly stirring up trouble and change;[64] he was easily led to evil, but never for any reason did he turn to good ...'[65] Procopius was well able, therefore, to turn to classical models for this aspect of the *Secret History*, and in the rhetorical genre of invective it was well-established practice to present one's target as a 'demon'.[66] There is also a certain degree of literary affectation in the *Secret History* – an explanation of 'heresy', for instance, or a reference to 'those who were pure in heart', apparently clergy.[67] It is a selfconscious work, as artificial in its way as the *Wars*, if less finished. But that does not detract from its seriousness.

In the pornographic section, however, literary tradition probably did have more real influence. Those who have found this section so offensive have failed to realise that its literal truth or otherwise is hardly relevant, for its extreme sexual abuse is demanded by the rules of invective.[68] Procopius clearly enjoyed developing the theme, and that, writing twenty-five years after Theodora's repentance and marriage,[69] is exactly what he did. We only need to look to Claudian to see the unpleasant

---

(Head 1980; Baldwin 1981), following Roman tradition (Evans 1935), and physical description is prominent in Malalas; Procopius knew exactly what he was doing in making this comparison with Domitian. See further Comparetti 1925.

[62] *SH* 8.22.

[63] 8.23.

[64] Cf. *SH* 20.15; 30.21f. (innovation).

[65] 8.24-6.

[66] As Claudian did with Rufinus in the *In Rufinum* (see Alan Cameron 1970, 68f.).

[67] *SH* 11.14; 12.20.

[68] See Nisbet 1961, 194f.

[69] For which see Daube 1967.

things that could be included in an invective.[70] Claudian's Eutropius was made the target of sexual abuse and allegations more disgusting than anything in the *Secret History*, but no one was expected to take them literally.[71] In this case, with Theodora, there is only one place where Procopius is even very explicit,[72] and modern reaction stems from the fact that we cannot forget that this is the empress of whom Procopius is writing. There has been a strong tendency, even in recent times, to romanticise and 'explain' Theodora in the face of Procopius' allegations.[73] More seriously, though, we also tend to modernising reactions in that we are not accustomed, as Procopius' generation was, to the overwhelming influence which panegyric exerted on the modes of thought of late antiquity. In any culture in which political expression finds a primary form in panegyric, we must expect traces of its opposite, invective. There is no room for an unbiassed mean when literary expression is forced habitually into extremes. It is simply therefore that the *Secret History* offers the understandable counterbalance to the excesses of panegyric. Its content – which includes these sexual passages – is conditioned by these factors as much as its form.

We must still ask in what sense it may be right to call the work a satire, as many have done from Gibbon on. Indeed, the *Suda* calls it a *kômôdia* (satire), though it links that term closely with *psogos* (invective). Before now the *Secret History* has been compared with the *Apocolocyntosis* of Seneca, whose history, subject matter and problems of authorship bear some similarity to it. But any direct connection is totally improbable.[74] There are certainly formal elements in the *Secret History* which link it with satire, and traces of the kind of exaggeration and distortion typical of that genre. There was also something of a tradition of a literary or even poetic opposition to imperial policies.[75] But to explain the *Secret History* in such simple terms is to do less than justice to its complexity and its earnestness, and should not be allowed to obscure the substantial proportion of the work that is devoted to detailed political accusation.

We find most of this in the last part of the work,[76] which contains a detailed and passionate, if one-sided, attack on Justinian's policies. There are certain recurring themes and motifs. Thus Justinian was a

---

[70] See Alan Cameron 1970, 68f., 83f., 255f.

[71] E.g. *In Eutrop.* I.66-8, 101-2, 280, 360-70.

[72] Namely *SH* 9.18. In comparison with modern pornography this section seems mild, or even absurd.

[73] See further below, Chapter 5.

[74] Bagnani 1954, 38 'the comparison with Procopius and the *Secret History* is good journalism but can hardly be taken seriously', with earlier references.

[75] Besides the long tradition of scatological imperial biography, there were examples closer to hand of political lampoon; Timotheus of Gaza, for instance, is said to have composed a *tragoedia* on the *chrysargyron* tax (*RE* s.v. Timotheus 18).

[76] *SH* 13-30.

treacherous friend;[77] no respecter of any law,[78] ready to do anything for gain.[79] The fasting and sleeplessness which in the *Buildings* are proof of piety[80] are here used to signify the paranormal strength of someone essentially demonic.[81] What hagiographic works present as obvious signs of sanctity here signifies the capacity for destruction.[82] Indeed Procopius seems himself to be thinking of the usual hagiographic interpretation of such physical endurance and asceticism when he criticises Justinian for failing to use it for its proper ends, but only to bring about still greater disasters for his people which he can then boast about himself.[83] At another time he will explain Justinian's famous lack of sleep as a way of checking up on his subjects.[84] Much of Justinian's activity resembles a farce ('like something on the stage')[85] or a children's game.[86] He wears the wrong clothes and neglects established customs by doing things himself.[87] Above all, he loves destruction and gain:[88] both Italy and Africa were emptied of their populations to satisfy his greed. If he seems to show gentleness (*prâotês*), the required quality of a Byzantine ruler,[89] it is only to deceive.[90] Like that of Leo I according to the Oracle of Baalbek, Justinian's reign was marked by natural disasters – floods, plague, urban riots – and here Procopius makes the connection explicit: some, he says, attributed them to the presence in this world of this demon, while others thought that God had abandoned the Roman empire because of Justinian's evil deeds.[91]

[77] *SH* 13.1-3, 16; cf. 8.26.

[78] 13.21, 23; 14.1, 20; 28.16 etc. Procopius praises the quaestor Proclus for precisely the opposite: *Persian Wars* I.11.12.

[79] See especially 19.1f.

[80] *Buildings* I.7.7.

[81] *SH* 13.28f.

[82] 13.32. In each case Procopius picks out Justinian's Lenten practices for special comment – for good or ill. Abstinence and extreme asceticism, standard signs of holiness, are also taken for its opposite. The logic of Procopius's position would dictate that he accuse Justinian of sexual excess, as he does with Theodora: that he does not is striking, and must mean that Justinian's character on this point was unassailable.

[83] When Tribonian said that he had seen Justinian levitating, the emperor took it entirely seriously (13.12). His nocturnal wanderings round the Palace, coupled with his extreme asceticism, are proof enough for Procopius of his demonic nature (12.17). Yet the same asceticism was the mark of a holy man (*Persian Wars* I.7.7; *Buildings* V.8.4. Cf. e.g. Athanasius, *Life of Antony* 7, 14; Cyril of Scythopolis, *V. Sabae*, 4). For this aspect of the *Secret History* see Patlagean 1968, 115f. (as inverse hagiography).

[84] *SH* 13.32-33; cf. 15.11.

[85] 15.24f.

[86] 14.15 'the commonwealth was like children playing "King of the Castle" '.

[87] 14.5.

[88] 18.10f., 19.

[89] Cf. *Buildings* I.1.15; Corippus, *Iust*. III.308 with note at Averil Cameron 1976, 192; Agapetus, *Ekthesis* 58. Constant change was also the opposite of what was expected – Agapetus, 13.

[90] 13.1.

[91] 18.45; cf. 31f. and especially 18.37. Cf. *Oracle of Baalbek*, 135f., on which see Alexander 1967, 111.

By this point (chapter 19) Procopius has set out the main grounds for
his attack. It remains for him to give specific examples, and it is here that
Procopius' evidence has been thought most suspect, especially where he
deals with detailed actions not attested elsewhere.[92] He has now departed
a long way from his announced purpose of commenting on the *Wars*;
many of the items singled out for criticism in this section are not political
or military events, but economic or administrative policies on which
Procopius lets loose a flood of accusations designed to show exactly how
Justinian's rule brought financial ruin to the state.[93] Many of the
criticisms of neglect of public services, for example the water supply,[94]
are naturally explicitly or implicitly contradicted in the *Buildings*.
Without other evidence it is not easy to decide which to believe. While for
instance many of the points made in this section are blatantly prejudiced
or at odds with what Procopius himself says elsewhere, there is sufficient
mingling of truth to make it dangerous to condemn the *Secret History*'s
accusations *en bloc*. To illustrate Justinian's 'lust for blood', Procopius
cites the case of Africa, so depopulated from the Byzantine occupation
that no matter how far you travelled you would hardly meet a human
being.[95] To drive home the point he appeals to his own personal
experience of the large numbers of Vandals, Romans and Moors who were
living there when the Byzantines arrived. There is probably some truth
in this accusation, if we consider the complaints of Corippus about the
woes of Africa only a few years after the occupation, and which were not
much improved when he wrote the panegyric to Justin II nearly twenty
years later,[96] though obviously Procopius's figure of five million dead is
pure rhetoric. But true to form Procopius produces a personal reason for
all this – he blames it on the recall of Belisarius, who would have acted as
a brake on Justinian's blood-lust.[97] Still, he can point with perfect justice
to the problems that did follow the victory, especially the very serious
mutiny in the Byzantine army.[98] So there is a mingling of the
circumstantial and the generalising, and the effect of these verifiable
details is spoilt by the blanket way in which the theme of the destruction
caused by Justinian's supposed victories is applied indiscriminately to
all battle-fronts – Italy, Persia, the incursions of the Huns and so on.[99]

[92] On this section see Gordon 1959.

[93] 19.1f.

[94] 26.23f.

[95] 18.4. The opposite point – how glad the local people were at the arrival of the
Byzantines – is made at *Buildings* VI.6.3-6. At *Vandal Wars* I.16.2f., 9f., however,
Procopius implies that the Byzantines may have been less than welcome in Africa: see
Averil Cameron 1982, 33. He makes Belisarius remind his soldiers that in fact the 'Africans'
were originally Roman: *Vandal Wars* I.20. 19f.

[96] See Averil Cameron 1982, 32f. and see below, Chapter 10.

[97] *SH* 18.9.

[98] 18.10-12.

[99] 18.5-30.

When he turns to internal affairs, we can see that Procopius is simply working out the idea that the reign of Justinian, this Devil in human form,[100] was inevitably accompanied by every kind of natural disaster – flood, plague, riot and so on.[101] This is indeed less history or criticism than apocalyptic: the tone suggested but not explicitly expressed in the demonological section thus returns in the more 'historical' sections.

Even making large allowances for exaggeration, this part of the *Secret History* must show how limited was Procopius' sympathy with the general aspirations of the régime on the domestic front. The duties of the quaestor, for example, are dismissed as consisting of rounding up pederasts and fallen women, with plenty of opportunity for lining one's own pocket.[102] So easily does Procopius dismiss the great body of Justinian's legislation, the framing of which was the main duty of the quaestor. For him, what matters is the personality of individual quaestors, first Tribonian, the agent of Justinian's codification, who gets nothing but contempt from Procopius, and then Junillus, against whom his complaint is that he spoke Greek with a broken accent[103] (it does not strike Procopius that as an African Junillus was under something of a handicap). In his view all Justinian's officials were corrupt – indeed, they were chosen for that very reason.[104] There is probably truth in the accusations against Peter Barsymes and his management of the grain supply,[105] but Procopius is ready to attribute his success to magic.[106] There is truth too in some of the bad effects of the sale of offices,[107] but Procopius neither understands the function of the policy nor the reasons for it. The rest of his tirade is very similar and equally biassed. Thus the neglectful handling of the army, the pressures of taxation, the economic chaos that followed the first outbreak of plague in 541-2, when the government was as desperate for the lost tax revenue of the dead as the survivors were unwilling to take it up,[108] all offered justifiable grounds for complaint, but naturally there is not the slightest hint in the *Secret History* that there might be another side to the question, or that the

---

[100] 18.1, 36.

[101] Cf. *Oracle of Baalbek* (n. 91). This is the complement to the theme familiar in sermons of the sympathy of the elements with the death of Christ (Alexiou 1974, 70f.; cf. George of Nicomedia, *PG* 100. 1485) or the Resurrection (ibid., 1501). Similarly the world reflects the presence of the demonic. The baroque dream reported at 19.1-3 is another example of the effect of Justinian on nature.

[102] 20.9f. For the office of quaestor, see Honoré 1978.

[103] *SH* 20.16-23; *Persian Wars* I.24.16. See below, p. 231.

[104] 21.9; 22.3 (Peter Barsymes).

[105] 22.14-21.

[106] 22.25. Procopius here shows the religious prejudice that he condemns elsewhere (e.g. 11.14f.), for he adds as an extra taunt that Peter was suspected of being a Manichaean.

[107] 21.16f., 20f. Sale of offices: Guilland 1953; Veyne 1981.

[108] See *SH* chs. 22-3. On this financial crisis (not emphasised in Procopius' account of the plague – see above, p. 42) see Averil Cameron 1976, 176f. on Corippus, *Iust*. II.361ff.

government was faced by genuine problems. Yet these and other
difficulties of Justinian were the direct consequences of the policy of
reconquest which Procopius favoured. The critique of the *Secret History*
is a critique of the 'how'. It focusses on personalities and complains about
the results without questioning the fundamentals. 'Those who owned the
land' in the provinces[109] and the professional classes in the capital and
other cities[110] – that is, Procopius' own class – were in his opinion the
main sufferers from Justinian's régime. How he expected massive
reconquest to be achievable without increased taxation and without
cooperation is not explained. In the *Secret History* Procopius is satisfied
with a very simple level of explanation – reasonably enough, one might
think, in a work of this kind, were it not that the *Wars* is not much better.
Here when he does not appeal to supernatural factors he is content to
invoke 'greed' or 'blood-lust', while a high proportion of his resentment is
simply directed at specific individuals whom he personally dislikes. In so
far as he has a general political stance, it is one of blind resistance to any
kind of innovation.[111] Thus the political criticism in the work is in a
tradition of senatorial opposition to autocratic government; but its level
of analysis is not much higher than that of abuse. It is typical that
though here the Nika revolt is given a crucial role as marking the turning
point in Justinian's attacks on the senatorial class,[112] Procopius has
essentially nothing to add to the very inadequate account given in the
Wars;[113] above all, he does not explain why, as he alleges, the revolt
caused Justinian to take reprisals from senators. In the main account,
the blame is given to the Blues and Greens; yet Procopius is so little able
to explain their role that he has to fall back on saying that he can 'only
describe it as a psychological disease' (*psychês nosêma*).[114] As for the
senators, the only specific reference to them places them on the side of
the emperor.[115] Neither of these two versions is satisfactory, therefore,
and if Procopius is right in attributing Justinian's reaction after the Nika
revolt to the belief that it represented a senatorial conspiracy, not merely
factional violence, he is not prepared to say so openly. While in the *Wars*
he does not wish to stress the role of the senate in an unsuccessful coup in
which Belisarius had the job of putting down the revolt on imperial
instructions, in the *Secret History* an admission of real senatorial
involvement would spoil the effect of his claim that Justinian's attacks
on the class were unprovoked. In each case the logic of the work itself has
conditioned the treatment of the subject matter, and we shall see that

[109] 22.39.
[110] 26.1f.
[111] Especially evident in chaps. 29-30. See Chapter 13 below.
[112] Especially chapter 12; 14.7.
[113] 12.12f.; cf. *Persian Wars* I.24, and see below, pp. 144ff.
[114] *Persian Wars* I.24.6.
[115] Ibid.

this is also true of the *Buildings*.[116] Ironically enough, the version of the *Wars*, which played down the grievances of both senators and factions,[117] was the version preferred by the emperor, who did not choose to acknowledge that there might be good reasons behind the uprising, or that (as is clear from the account in Malalas) it had been mishandled by the authorities from the start.[118]

Procopius' criticism in the *Secret History* therefore is not based on theoretical opposition to autocracy. He does not question the basis of Byzantine kingship, like a contemporary political theorist;[119] on the contrary, he would be satisfied if only Justinian were better able to control wayward elements, more successful in his wars and less inclined to tax the rich. He does not long for a philosopher-king, like Synesius, though he shares with him dislike of appeasement, hostility to barbarians and opposition to high taxation.[120] It does not seem to have occurred to him that his expectations were unrealistic. Nor was he alone in his views. Agathias, for instance, criticises Justinian rather sharply for being neglectful of military affairs,[121] and Corippus' poem on the accession of Justinian's successor seems to show that there was a reaction against him.[122] Near the end of the century Evagrius, using Procopius but probably not the *Secret History*, expressed himself with great force against Justinian, inveighing against his greed, his hostility to the Greens and finally his lapse into heresy.[123] The violent tone of Evagrius' remarks on Justin II (565-78), again making greed a central accusation, is a very good illustration of the lengths to which criticism could go,[124] and we have the *Church History* of John of Ephesus for the same reign, though here it is interesting to see the deranged Justin presented as pathetic rather than vicious.[125] There seems, therefore, to have been a surprising amount of opposition literature in the sixth century, but it was probably less possible under Justinian than later, though Agathias

[116] Cf. *Buildings* I.1.20f.

[117] *Persian Wars* I.24.10.

[118] It is suggested by Malalas that the uprising was caused 'by some avenging demons' (p. 473) and that the Blues and Greens were urged on by the Devil (p. 474.9). Mismanagement of the initial stages of the affair: pp. 473-4. While John represents the revolt as a 'rising of the multitude' with justifiable grievances against Justinian's ministers (III.70.2), the emperor publicised its ending as a victory over 'tyrants' (Malalas, p. 476.23f.).

[119] See Chapter 14 below.

[120] Synesius, *De Regno*, 5ff. (philosophy); 13ff. (military duties); 20f. ('Scyths'); 25 (taxes).

[121] *Hist.* V.14.

[122] Cor., *Iust.* I.170, 250f.; II.249ff., with comments in Averil Cameron 1976.

[123] *HE* IV. 30f., with comments in Allen 1981, 194ff. Evagrius does not seem to have used the *Secret History*, which makes the violence of his criticism and its similarities with Procopius all the more striking.

[124] *HE* V.1; see Tinnefeld 1971, 45f.; Averil Cameron 1977 (= 1981, IX), 9f.

[125] *HE* II.25, 29; see my art. (n. 124), 11.

mentions that criticism did exist.[126] Neither in these authors nor in the *Secret History*, however, is there fundamental criticism of the institutions of the empire.[127]

The *Secret History*, then, is far from being a polished work, and it contains only some of Procopius' thinking about the régime. The next chapter will consider its presentation of Theodora, which is even less to Procopius' credit than his view of Justinian. In general, however, the *Secret History* is a mixture of material of differing literary levels. Nor does it rate highly as an example of political thought. Interestingly, Procopius's characterisation of Justinian's main enemy, Chosroes I of Iran, is where he most effectively summarises the view he held of Justinian himself – vicious, treacherous, money-loving, preoccupied with theology, bloodthirsty and war-mongering, mean-spirited.[128] But this is far from reassuring as an indicator of Procopius' insight; rather, it suggests that he was applying a standardised vocabulary of abuse to both rulers. One feature alone, to which we shall return, sets the *Secret History* above the common level for the quality of its thought, and that is Procopius' unusual distaste for religious persecution, which he attributes to Justinian's greed for confiscation and desire to see as many of his citizens killed as possible[129] Consider, however, the words of Procopius himself:

> The citizens of my own town, Caesarea, and the other cities regarded it as stupid to undergo suffering for the sake of a foolish dogma, and were able to shake off the danger from this law by adopting the name of Christians instead of that which they then bore. Those of them who were sensible and reasonable were quite willing to practise this faith.[130]

The rest of these Samaritans chafed at the bit and went over to paganism and Manichaeism and even into open revolt against Justinian. Procopius' view is quite clear: he thinks that such behaviour was short-sighted and brought unnecessary death and extra costs to their Christian neighbours who had been more amenable. Not a comment based on principle, therefore, but on pragmatism. The *Secret History* is not a document in the history of freedom of thought,[131] but something less – an angry pamphlet, finished in parts, but without much that was new to contribute to opposition literature over and above its scandal value. It will be as well to bear this in mind when the time comes to approach the *Wars*.

[126] *Hist*. V.20, 24.

[127] See Chapter 14 below on the anon. *Peri politikês epistêmês*.

[128] *SH* 18.28f. See Chapter 13 below on the characterisation of Justinian, and the extent to which it is cliché-bound in all Procopius' works.

[129] 11.14f.; 13.4f.

[130] 11.25-6. On the Samaritan revolts see Avi-Yonah 1976, 241ff.

[131] Bury 1923, II, 428 of the projected ecclesiastical history: a book which 'would have been of some significance in the literature of toleration'.

CHAPTER FIVE

Procopius and Theodora

The treatment of the Empress Theodora has been one of the most intractable features of the *Secret History* in modern scholarship. To understand Theodora it is essential to begin with these chapters, and yet impossible to get beyond them. Since Gibbon, a stream of 'biographies', novels and plays with titles such as 'Empress of the Dusk' or 'Theodora and the Emperor' typify the fascination and the dilemma.[1] All their authors must use Procopius even while sneering at him, just as a recent book, drawing almost exclusively on his material, calls him 'sick and unbalanced'.[2] Surprisingly enough even now Theodora suffers from approaches limited by prejudice or romanticism, quite apart from the methodological problem posed by Procopius' evidence, and the great Diehl's romantic vignettes[3] have yet to find a satisfactory replacement. That this should be so, even after the belated entry of women's studies to the field of Byzantine history,[4] is one of the major deficiencies in Procopian scholarship.

It is easy to understand the romantic appeal of Theodora, even without the *Secret History*, for the famous Ravenna mosaic showing her in procession with her attendants has probably done as much to form modern impressions. There she looks pale and interesting, far more intriguing than her somewhat podgy husband, and her appearance coincides so well with Procopius' description of her pale skin, small stature and careful attention to her beauty regime.[5] As it happens, no other certain portrait survives, though she must have been depicted hundreds of times, as we know she was on the ceiling mosaic of the Chalke entrance to the imperial palace, receiving with Justinian the

---

[1] For instance Stadelmann 1926; Grimbert 1928; Underhill 1932; Vandercook 1940 (dedicated to the author's mother); Masefield 1940; Lamb 1952; Welland 1966; de Lancker 1968, Olek 1971. Robert Graves's *Count Belisarius* is in a different class from most of these.

[2] Bridge 1978, 19.

[3] Diehl 1904, 1909. On the treatment of Theodora in modern works see also Holmes 1912, I, 338ff., himself comparing her with Messalina and Lola Montez.

[4] That is, women's studies as opposed to romantic biographies of Byzantine empresses.

[5] *SH* 10.11f., 15.6f. For the mosaic of Justinian and Theodora in S. Vitale, Ravenna, see Volbach 1962, no. 165; Grabar 1936, 106.

spoils of victory from Belisarius.[6] But the Ravenna mosaic is so often
reproduced that it has set Theodora for ever in one likeness, that of the
mysterious and haunted beauty of the *Secret History*, so different from
the squat figure of a sixth-century Byzantine empress shown on the
Vienna and Florence ivory diptychs.[7] Over the pale slight figure hangs
the glamour of early death and a sorrowing imperial husband. The
combination was irresistible.

However, entirely the wrong conclusions have been drawn. 'Le
féminisme de Theodora', 'feminine and feminist to her fingertips'[8] –
these are the admiring phrases of male writers, drawing on the anecdotes
in the *Secret History* and certainly not referring to feminism in any
modern sense of the term. Procopius tells us that Theodora would
intervene to help marriageable girls at court and women in distress;[9] she
founded a famous Convent of Repentance for reformed prostitutes.[10] But
these were the traditional actions of a great lady, hardly attempts to
improve the status of women, as some books come near to suggesting. In
fact it is the 'feminine' rather than the feminist aspect of Theodora that
predominates in these male accounts, as it does with Procopius, and then
not to the credit of women. For him, 'feminine' means 'intriguing',
'interfering' and the like.[11] Nearly all the 'true reasons' offered in the
Secret History for the events narrated in the *Wars* have to do with
women, Antonina as much as Theodora. Whereas modern 'biographers'
of Theodora view her sympathetically or sentimentally in the guise of the
reformed Magdalene, Procopius is unreservedly hostile, and his
description of her early life totally devoid of romanticism. One looks in
vain for humour, understanding or sympathy. By contrast, Diehl
persuaded himself that she must have truly repented of her past life, or
(even better) that she was never willingly a prostitute in the first place
and naturally never derived pleasure from it. But this is to give to the
scabrous sections of the *Secret History* an importance which, as I have
suggested, they probably did not have for Procopius or his contemporary
audience, for whom they are partly a literary convention, partly a vivid
way of showing the truly exceptional evil of Theodora's nature, whose
real sin lay in the harm she had done to the state together with Justinian.
Lacking Procopius' political perspective, modern scholars have in fact
trivialised Theodora by reducing her to a romantic stereotype. The

[6] *Buildings* I.10.17.

[7] See Delbrueck 1929, no. 51. For the marble head sometimes thought to be of Theodora,
see J.D. Breckenridge in Weitzmann 1979, 33, accepting the identification on grounds of
similarity with the Ravenna mosaic portrait and the description at *Secret History* 10.11.

[8] Diehl 1904, 217f.; Bridge 1978, 94. Thus modern admirers of Theodora present her
through a rhetoric of sentimentality which is the inverse of Procopius' misogyny.

[9] *SH* 17.7ff. and see below.

[10] *SH* 17.5-6; below, pp. 92f., 102.

[11] Fisher 1978, 294f. (views of women in the *Wars*). Typically, Procopius makes the
Gothic women at Belisarius' entry to Ravenna interested in the comparative physique of
the Byzantines and their own husbands (*Gothic Wars* II.29.34).

details of her toilette which for Procopius are simply there to illustrate her vanity and pride[12] are given magnified importance and stitched together into a women's magazine character piece. Procopius' presentation of her may be partial and one-sided, but at least it is neither trivial nor sentimental.

Besides the *Secret History* a famous passage from the *Wars* has also contributed to these modern misunderstandings. That is the episode from *Wars* I during the Nika revolt when she is made to deliver a memorable speech dissuading Justinian from flight.[13] 'The empire is a fair winding sheet', she is supposed to have said.[14] So we read that 'the throne of Justinian was saved through the moral energy of Theodora and the loyal efforts of Belisarius'.[15] Bury assumes (but I choose him only as an example) that Procopius heard about the speech from Belisarius, and his whole account of the revolt is a virtual paraphrase of the narrative of Procopius, and totally premised on his reliability. As a result of this famous scene, Theodora has gone down in history as the brave queen putting backbone into her wavering husband. Yet we have only Procopius to thank for the story. On closer inspection, the speech itself is part of a rhetorical set-piece, as its introduction betrays: 'many speeches were made putting opposite points of view.'[16] Procopius only gives us this one, ascribing it to Theodora, possibly purely for dramatic and rhetorical effect. At least, he makes the speech begin from the obvious theme of Theodora's sex: the present crisis is too serious to worry about the conventional role of women. Then she goes on – not to discuss the situation in general, or even the best course for Justinian, but her own resolve to die in the purple. In other words, the speech is an illustration of the theme of the resolute female, not a discussion of the situation in hand. Procopius was very well aware of the irony and the rhetorical possibilities of women acting seemingly out of character.[17] It is hardly possible to believe that this speech was delivered as Procopius gives it. Amazingly, it has nearly always been taken at face value.

Most of the modern novels and 'biographies' have only two substantial episodes apart from their versions of Theodora's early life as a courtesan – the Nika revolt scene and the account of the second fall of John the Cappadocian,[18] which is Procopius' other main (equally questionable) presentation of Theodora in action. John's administration as Praetorian

---

[12] *SH* 15.9 ('self-indulgence').

[13] *Persian Wars* I.24.33f.

[14] I.24.37. On this passage see Baldwin 1982. The saying derives from Isocrates (*Archidamos* 45), but may have been transmitted via Diodorus 14.8 (Baldwin, following Rubin 1954, 35). Baldwin supposes that this was a real speech by Theodora.

[15] Bury 1923, II, 48.

[16] I.24.32.

[17] Below, chapter 13. For one so keen on the maintenance of order as Procopius (ibid.) the prospect of women getting out of hand was intolerable; see below, p. 241.

[18] *Persian Wars* I.25; see Bury 1923, II, 55ff.

Prefect had been a major factor in the Nika revolt and he had been dismissed then by Justinian to placate the rioters; but within a year he was restored. Hated by Theodora, he was also the enemy of Belisarius, and the latter's wife Antonina was instrumental, if we believe Procopius, who is typically the only source, in bringing to fruition an elaborate plot for his destruction.[19] She is supposed to have deluded John's daughter Euphemia into believing in a fabricated plot against Justinian on the part of Belisarius, and of persuading her father to go along with it, so that Antonina was able to supply 'evidence' of John's treachery. The result was that he was duly exiled to Cyzicus. After this worse was to follow for him, for there he fell under suspicion for having connived at the murder of the local bishop, as a result of which he was roughly treated, scourged and shipped to Egypt.[20] Still more was to come: Theodora, according to the *Secret History*, remained unsatisfied, for John's guilt had never been proved, and she now went to extreme lengths to get her proof. Two young men were tortured to extract a confession implicating John, and when this attempt was unsuccessful the hands of both were cut off.[21] Only after Theodora's death did John attain any respite, when Justinian allowed him to return from Egypt to Constantinople and live there in orders.[22]

According to this famous and circumstantial story, which figures large in modern books, the empress appears as a vindictive monster. But caution is needed. Procopius certainly intended to convey that impression, and several other stories in the *Secret History* converge in the same direction.[23] But though the manipulation of the unfortunate Euphemia is told in the *Wars*,[24] in a passage written only three years after the event and indeed with much inside knowledge, the more lurid account of Theodora's continued pursuit of John comes only in the *Secret History*, where it is connected with Procopius' other main theme in connection with Theodora, her fanatical support of the Blues. It is also intimately bound up with the presentation of Antonina. Belisarius' wife features as the aide and confidante of Theodora in both the *Wars* and the *Secret History*, and it is not dificult to show that here too the facts are touched up in the light of Procopius' own prejudices.[25] Antonina, whom he did know well,[26] is here both the foil and the touchstone for Theodora.

---

[19] For Antonina, below, pp. 71f. and Evert-Kappesowa 1964. For an intelligent discussion, prefiguring the approach taken here, see Fisher 1978.

[20] *SH* 17.38f.

[21] 17.44.

[22] *Persian Wars* II.30.49.

[23] *SH* 15.24f.; 16.6f. etc.

[24] *Persian Wars* I.25.13f.

[25] See Evert-Kappesowa 1964 and (better) Fisher 1978.

[26] *Vandal Wars* I.12.2-3; 13.24; 19.11; 20.1 (left with the army by Belisarius); *Gothic Wars* II. 4.14 (undertakes duties in Campania during first siege of Rome and joins up with Procopius, 4.20); clearly, during the good days, she had acted as an aide to Belisarius in much the same way as Procopius himself and often enough together with him.

The two couples, Justinian and Theodora, Belisarius and Antonina, set
each other off. With the utmost irony, Procopius' hero Belisarius is seen
in the same light as Justinian – weak, uxorious, dominated by a
masterful wife. The techniques which Antonina and Theodora use are
the techniques of women – intrigue, sex, manipulation. But of the two, it
is Antonina who is actually the most active according to Procopius. Her
life allowed her even to go on campaign with her husband, and there
exercise male functions, even to the control of troops,[27] while Theodora
was confined to the restricted ceremonial life of the palace. Even this
Procopius turns to her discredit, complaining of her haughty behaviour
to elderly senators, and her insistence on extreme deference.[28] There was
not much that Theodora could actually do directly, and even her most
active interventions, such as that in the fall of John, are achieved by
indirect means. It is probable that the general outlines of the plot against
John are true enough, and that Procopius had genuine inside knowledge.
But in the *Secret History* he could develop the theme more fully, bring
out its sensational side, and use the character of Antonina to give it extra
weight. A too hasty reading of the episodes in the *Wars* and the *Secret
History* would miss these differences.

It is worth staying with Antonina. For all his faults, Procopius did
know Belisarius and Antonina well, and when he refers to the latter in
the *Wars* as taking the initiative, or undertaking the same kind of
mission as he himself was engaged in, we must believe him. At the same
time she has undoubtedly been developed in his works as a female
character parallel to Theodora on the non-imperial plane. Antonina is
introduced in the first chapter of the *Secret History*.[29] Just as with
Theodora, Procopius begins with her origins as a mime. The balance
between the two conjugal pairs is very striking; it is a balance achieved
through the women. They are the recipients of moral and sexual
criticism, while their husbands, in both cases, are relatively spared. The
women, then, whether imperial or not, are dealt with under different
categories from the men: one of the chief charges levelled against both
Belisarius and Justinian is precisely their subjection to their wives.[30]
There is a good reason for this imbalance, which has contributed to the
distorted prominence given in the modern books which follow Procopius
to the sexual aspects of Theodora's life. For if a writer like Procopius
wanted to make a woman the object of attack, the obvious sphere in
which to locate his accusations was the sexual. Thus Antonina is first
charged with generalised immorality and sexual offences in her early
days, and then with love affairs carried on after her marriage, and with

---

[27] *Gothic Wars* II.4.20. See *PLRE* III s.v.
[28] *SH* 15.13f.
[29] *SH* 1.11.
[30] Cf. *SH* 1.18 (Belisarius; cf. especially 2.12, 21, 3.1); Procopius accuses Antonina of
bewitching her husband (2.2, 3.2); 9.29 (Justinian).

magic and vindictive measures against anyone who crossed her, especially in her sexual desires.[31] It was particularly unpleasant in Procopius' view that Antonina and Theodora should have conducted love affairs with young men,[32] and that Belisarius should still have cared for Antonina when she was already a woman of sixty.[33] Both women are said to have given birth to children in their dissolute days – an accusation of promiscuity rather than a statement of fact.[34] Abortion, infanticide and lack of maternal feeling are all brought into play as charges against Theodora.[35] Again, we are more in the realm of ideology than of fact. Elsewhere Procopius admits that Theodora had a grown daughter with a son of marriageable age, to whom Antonina betrothed her own daughter Joannina.[36]

Some of these accusations, for instance those about the son called John, born in Egypt, whom Theodora is said to have disposed of when he came to Constantinople, fall the more easily into place when set in the broader context of Procopius' views on women, for whom (he alleges) Theodora set the prime example:

> At that period almost all women had become morally depraved. For they could play false to their husbands with complete impunity, since such behaviour involved them in no danger or harm. Wives proved guilty of adultery were exempt from the penalty, as they only had to go straight to the Empress and turn the tables by bringing a countersuit against their husbands, who had not been charged with any offence, and dragging them into court. All that was left to the husbands, against whom nothing had been proved, was to pay twice the amount of the dowry they had received, and as a rule to be scourged and led away to prison – and then once more to watch their faithless partners showing off and inviting the attentions of their paramours more brazenly than before. Many of the paramours actually gained promotion by rendering this service. Small wonder that from then on most husbands, however shocking their wives' behaviour might be, were only too glad to keep their mouths shut and avoid being scourged, conceding every licence to their wives by letting them believe that they had not been found out.[37]

[31] 1.11f. See Fisher 1978, 308f. Theodora and Antonina in the *Wars*: ibid., 300f.

[32] 1.15f. (Antonina); 16.11f. (Theodora). In general, Procopius cannot seriously accuse Theodora of sexual excess after her marriage, any more than he can Justinian (thus Justinian's chief offence is to have fallen in love with Theodora). Consequently he piles up virtually all his sexual accusations against her into the section about her life in the Hippodrome (chapter 9), whereas with Antonina he can be more expansive.

[33] 4.41 'completely oblivious and indifferent to the oaths he had sworn to Photius and all his most intimate friends, he went where his wife directed him; for he was hopelessly in love with her, though she was already a woman of sixty'. Procopius links this criticism with the claim that God was against Belisarius (4.42).

[34] 1.12 (Antonina); 9.19 (Theodora).

[35] 9.19, 10.3, 17.16f., implying that she did away with a son who had survived to adolescence and appeared in Constantinople to embarrass her.

[36] 4.37, 5.18f.; see Alan Cameron 1978, 270ff.

[37] 17.24f (Penguin trans.).

It is likely, then, given such an attitude to women in general as appears from this passage, that Procopius' presentation of Theodora is itself shaped according to it, rather than that it should be understood as a literally true description. In any case, it is significant that the areas of attack are private, not public. Most of what Procopius actually has to say about Theodora lies in the private sphere or in the indirect realm of women's activity. Antonina has been built up as her foil and parallel. Similarly, the alliance between the two women, structurally so important to Procopius, has probably been exaggerated.[38] Its peak was the fall of John the Cappadocian, a petty enough aim, and it is hard to follow Procopius when he tries to lay on Antonina the blame for Belisarius' military failures. After Sisauranon, when Procopius claims that Belisarius retreated because of the arrival of Antonina, even he admits that there were other good reasons.[39] His remarks about the dispatch of Belisarius to Italy for the second time are simply absurd:

> It was universally surmised that Belisarius settled the problem of his wife in this way ... simply with the object of getting away from life in Byzantium.[40]

When women intervene in public affairs it is obvious, so far as Procopius is concerned, that they must do it for private reasons. The description of Belisarius' abject state before his reinstatement is even more fanciful. He had been accused of plotting for the succession while Justinian lay ill of the plague; but the emperor recovered and Belisarius and Buzes fell under suspicion. Buzes, we are told, was cast into the most appalling imprisonment in an underground cell, while Belisarius, whom Theodora dared not attack openly like this, nevertheless met with so cold a reception when he dared to venture to the palace that he was in terror of his life:

> In the grip of this terror he went upstairs to his bedroom and sat down on his bed alone. There was no honourable thought in his head; he was not conscious that he had once been a man. The sweat ran down his face unceasingly; his head swam; his whole body trembled in an agony of despair, tormented as he was by slavish fears and anxieties utterly unworthy of a man.[41]

All this is said to be the doing of Antonina and Theodora, who also have the power to restore him. While he is in this state, a letter arrives from

---

[38] At 22.1 it is 'the emperor and Theodora' who bring about John's fall; contrast 4.18. But Theodora is said to be highly suspicious of Antonina (5.20f.) – rightly (5.23f.).

[39] 2.18f.

[40] 4.40; cf. 2.21; 3.30f. (Belisarius loses the favour of God because of his blind infatuation with Antonina and its effects; he therefore exposes himself to charges of cowardice on his next eastern campaign). All Procopius' disappointment with Belisarius finds a focus in these accusations of enslavement to a woman: 4.32 'such was the fate of the general Belisarius, to whom not long before Fortune had given Gelimer and Vitigis as captives'.

[41] 4.22f (Penguin trans.).

the empress. Dreading that it is the order for his death, Belisarius finds
that he is forgiven. But it is Antonina who gets the credit:

> He sprang up at once, threw himself at his wife's feet and flung his arms round
> both her knees. Then, raining kisses on each ankle in turn, he declared that he
> owed his life entirely to her, and swore that henceforth he would be her faithful
> slave, not her husband.[42]

But Procopius lets slip that Justinian as well as Theodora had been
jealous of Belisarius for some time; both of them had spurned him when
he came to the palace.[43] So all this elaborate scenario of feminine intrigue
is merely a device; the real reason for Belisarius' eclipse should be
ascribed to Justinian and seen in political terms. As for Antonina's great
friendship with Theodora, she was quick enough to break off the betrothal
of her daughter to Theodora's grandson on the empress's death, knowing
that Theodora dead was no use to her.[44] No doubt they were allies when it
suited them both; Procopius however has implausibly built up this
friendship for structural reasons into something which could even affect
affairs of state.

Obviously highly-placed women could, in this 'Byzantine' court, in
some cases exert political influence. In the tensions of Justinian's
reconquest policy the wives of generals might be well placed for such
intrigue. At the same time, the increasing court ceremonial gave the
empress more of a ritual role, in which some of the other women
inevitably shared – Procopius of course represents Theodora's concern for
court etiquette as merely indicating her haughtiness and vanity.[45] Yet
Theodora did not achieve the official role of her niece, Sophia the wife of
Justin II, who appeared on coins with her husband and ruled after his
derangement, even if through a male Caesar.[46] We are commonly
assured, on the basis mainly of Procopius, that Theodora was effectively
co-regent with Justinian, and it is true that Byzantium was receptive to
powerful empresses.[47] But Theodora was not one of these. She did not
reign alone, and influential though she may have been, she largely
worked behind the scenes and through processes of intrigue.[48] In fact she

[42] 4.34f (Penguin trans.).
[43] 4.20f., following the suspicion that he had been involved in plotting for the succession
during Justinian's illness of the plague (4.1f.); cf. also 4.33 (envy of his wealth) and 4.39
(second Italian expedition to be at his own expense).
[44] 5.27.
[45] 15.13f.; 30.21f.
[46] Averil Cameron 1975 (= 1981, XI).
[47] Maslev 1966; Holum 1983.
[48] See on this Lefkowitz 1983; Theodora was very unlike the energetic and powerful
empresses studied by Holum (Holum 1983). The oaths taken in the names of both Justinian
and Theodora (see Bury 1923), II, 30 on *Nov.* 8, AD 535) do not outweigh this general
impression; despite Bury's statement that 'she did not scruple to act independently' (ibid.,
31), most of the examples he goes on to cite (from *SH*) are of traditionally indirect action.

led an extremely private life, the life of a queen in a traditional court. Most of Procopius' criticisms are in line with such a view of her, above all the striking difference of emphasis in the type of critique directed at her compared with that directed at Justinian. If one wanted to attack a woman, even an empress, the way to do it was through her private life. But such criticism – which allowed a misogynist like Procopius to vent all his dislike and distrust of women on to this useful scapegoat – is neither serious criticism nor serious description.

A more substantial theme, however, in relation to Theodora, is that of her religious and factional predilections, in which she is said to have exercised a real and important influence on policy. There are some difficulties in Procopius' treatment of both of these. Again we can see that he has used the character of Theodora to work out certain thematic points for himself.

We are told repeatedly by Procopius, then, that Theodora was a rabid supporter of the Blues.[49] When her step-father, Bearkeeper of the Greens, had lost his job and moved over to the other faction, she had evidently transferred her allegiance too, and no doubt (though Procopius does not say so) started her career as a performer with the Blues.[51] It was awkward for Procopius, however, that both the emperor and empress should have favoured the Blues. How much easier if they had taken opposite sides, as they did in doctrinal matters. He has to resort to a very forced explanation:

> They began by creating a division between the Christians; and by pretending to take opposite sides in religious disputes they split the whole body in two, as will shortly be made clear. Then they kept the factions at loggerheads. The Empress made out that she was throwing her full weight behind the Blues, and by extending to them full authority to assail the opposite faction she made it possible for them to disregard all restrictions and perform outrageous deeds of criminal violence.[51]

But Justinian also favoured the Blues, as Procopius often tells us,[52] so that the passage does not develop in the way its opening suggests. So widely known was Justinian's preference that when Chosroes conquered Apamea and held chariot races in the Hippodrome there in imitation of Constantinople he naturally took the Green side.[53] The most that Procopius can now do is to say weakly that Justinian 'was determined to punish the Blues as criminal offenders',[54] though they were actually the most law-abiding. This is not only feeble but illogical. Elsewhere

---

[49] *SH* 9.33; 10.16.
[50] 9.2-7.
[51] 10.15f. (Penguin trans.).
[52] 7.1f.; 9.33.
[53] *Persian Wars* II.11.32f.
[54] *SH* 10.18.

Procopius is quick to condemn them.[55] He can only be so ready to defend them here because he is using the factions as a tool of criticism against Justinian and Theodora, while also somehow having to sustain the opposition he has set up between the imperial couple and their individual policies. For in general, for Procopius, factions stood for trouble.[56] If he could associate the imperial couple with them, he would be suggesting that they were responsible, however indirectly, for the faction rioting. As in other things, however, Theodora bears the brunt of accusation while Justinian gets off relatively lightly. In fact Procopius cannot produce much hard evidence, and Theodora's alleged crimes against the Greens amount to no more than personal attacks of dubious credibility.[57] So our understanding of the social role of the factions, difficult enough already, is made harder by the recognition that Procopius is using them simply to play a functional role in his work. There is a blatant contradiction, for instance, between the present passage, where Procopius attempts to set up the theme of 'opposition' between Justinian and Theodora, and the famous one a little earlier where he describes the dress of the factions,[58] for there Justinian is actually said to have spurred on the extremists among the Blues against opposition from their quieter members – quite at odds with the claim that he wanted to bring them to trial. But it was inevitable that Procopius would use the factions as a stick to beat Justinian and Theodora if he possibly could, for he associated their violence himself with a general decline in morals and with the plight of the state for which he held Justinian and Theodora responsible.[59] It is noticeable yet again, however, that while Justinian can be charged outright Theodora is made the object rather of innuendo, and accused of working behind the scenes.

On Theodora's religious preferences Procopius is more plausible, and we have plentiful evidence from elsewhere. Her support of Monophysitism is amply confirmed in other sources, above all by John of Ephesus in his *Ecclesiastical History* and especially his *Lives of the Eastern Saints*.[60] She was an intimate of the great Severus of Antioch; she sheltered Monophysite monks and clergy in large numbers in the palace at Constantinople for years on end; she sent Monophysite missionaries to Nubia and she did her best to end Monophysite persecution and promote Monophysite ecclesiastical policies.[61] Especi-

---

[54] *Persian Wars* I.24.1f. (both colours condemned); at *SH* 7.1f. however, Procopius does again defend the majority of Blue supporters.

[56] See his set-piece on the subject at *SH* 7.1-42, ending with complaints that Justinian favoured and supported them. Similarly *Persian Wars* I.24.1-6 (the Nika revolt: factions have no regard for God or the law).

[57] *SH* 16.18f.

[58] 7.1-42.

[59] See below, Chapter 13.

[60] *PO* 17-19.

[61] *PO* 17.27, 35, 157, 195; 18.529f., 676ff. After her death John claims that Justinian

ally, she supported James Bar'adai, who effectively created the Monophysite institutional structure in the eastern provinces which carried the church in those parts through to the Arab invasions and beyond the break from Byzantium.[62] John makes it clear that she was indeed regarded by the Monophysites themselves as their champion and protectress, with a veneration that has survived to this day, as evinced in the play 'Theodora' composed in Arabic in 1956 by Mar Faulos Behram, Metropolitan of Baghdad, and translated into Syriac in 1977 by the Metropolitan of Mardin.[63] The Monophysites were naturally embarrassed by Theodora's origins, and a more comfortable version evolved, according to which she was the chaste daughter of a Monophysite priest from the eastern provinces whose parents opposed her marriage to the Chalcedonian Justinian.[64] But John of Ephesus made no attempt to deny her real background, referring to her as 'from the brothel'.[65] Unlike modern scholars, who have found Theodora's past history a major stumbling block, the eastern church found the idea of the repentant sinner attractive, and Theodora herself underlined it with her foundation for reformed prostitutes.[66] There may be another slight confirmation of Procopius' version also in the eighth-century patriographic work known as the *Parastaseis Syntomoi Chronikai*, which refers to an empress, surely in the context Theodora, as 'formerly shameless but later chaste'.[67] It is surprising to us that there is no emphasis on Theodora's background in other contemporary writers besides Procopius, but it was a feature of Byzantium that outsiders could be readily accepted into the imperial purple, especially as empresses.[68] If we discount some of the 'circumstantial' details from the *Secret History*, Theodora was debarred from marriage to Justinian because she was a performer, not for the alleged immorality itself, and the opposition to the marriage came not from popular opinion but from the old empress, herself of humble background.[69] Once she had become empress herself her past seems to

---

carried out her wishes by continuing to protect the monks and clergy in the Palace of Hormisdas.

[62] *PO* 18.690ff.; 19.153ff., 228ff. See on this Honigmann 1951; Frend 1973 (= 1976, XIX) and on Theodora's Monophysitism, Frend 1972a (= 1976, XVIII), 20f.; Frend 1972b, 80ff.

[63] *Theodora suryoyto* (Southfield, Michigan, 1977), trans. P.Y. Dolapönü. I owe this information to Susan Ashbrook Harvey.

[64] Michael the Syrian, *Chronicle* IX.20; *Chron. ad 1234*, LV.

[65] *PO* 17, 189. Not unnaturally, this has been taken to be suspect (Holmes, 1912, I, 345, n. 2, citing Diehl; but Diehl 1904, 68 admits that before her marriage Theodora was a courtesan, 'obscure ou célèbre, peu importe', though he has a chapter entitled 'La vertu de Theodora' about her life subsequently; Bury 1923, II, 28, n. 5, also citing Diehl and supposing the words to be an interpolation). There is no reason however to doubt the text.

[66] *SH* 17.5; *Buildings* I.9.5f. See p. 102.

[67] *Parast.* 80. See Averil Cameron and Judith Herrin 1984, p. 271.

[68] Thus empresses could be actively sought for their beauty rather than their high birth; cf. the intriguing case of Eudocia, Holum 1983, pp. 112f.

[69] For the marriage and the objections to it, see Daube 1967.

have been irrelevant. For John of Ephesus and others like him what mattered was her piety and her support for their cause, and his glowing picture of her in the *Lives* in fact confirms, from a very different point of view, Procopius' own presentation of her interventions.

Nevertheless, Procopius, in his usual way, distorts Theodora's actual religious role by forcing it into a stereotyped model of opposition to Justinian. 'They began by creating a division between the Christians, and by pretending to take opposite sides in religious disputes they split the whole body in two ...';[70] Theodora 'kept up a pretence of going against the Emperor in doctrinal matters'.[71] For Procopius, everything is to be explained in terms of dissembling – neither Justinian nor Theodora can be assumed to be sincere. Since he so strongly disapproves of doctrinal dispute himself,[72] he must assume that Theodora's undoubted support of Monophysites is dictated by malice, or else that it is a cunning political ploy. Not seeing the illogicality of holding both these views, and believing himself that persecution is folly, religious differences not to be thought of as a matter of principle,[73] he reduces Theodora's actions to the level of commonplace intrigue, and explains that as motivated by personal spite or wilful interference.

In fact Theodora was acting in this sphere within a totally traditional role. Despite Justinian's fulsome allusions to her and Prcopius' emphasis on her power and influence, she could only hope to work through personal intrigue or persuasion. The real limitations on her as an empress within a traditional society have, paradoxically, given Procopius the material for his presentation of her in terms of 'feminine' guile. Thus she could protect individual Monophysites, supposedly for years on end and completely without the knowledge of Justinian,[74] but she could not pass laws to better their situation as a group. We know from Zachariah of Mytilene as well as Procopius and John of Ephesus that she did indeed protect and show respect to Monophysite leaders – Severus of Antioch, Theodosius of Alexandria and Anthimus of Constantinople, all condemned by the orthodox state.[75] That she tried to make a deal to establish the complaisant Vigilius as Pope after Agapetus we know from the western sources,[76] and that she removed the wretched Silverius who had just been elected is confirmed by the *Liber Pontificalis*, though only

[70] 10.15.

[71] 27.13.

[72] See below, Chapter 7.

[73] As he makes clear in his comments on the Samaritans: 11.24f. The 'sensible course' is in his view to convert to Christianity and stick to it; it is the Samaritans who refused to make a permanent change who are condemned. Cf. too 27.26f.

[74] John of Ephesus, *PO* 18.686f. (Patriarch Anthimus of Constantinople); but at 676ff. he implies that there were more than five hundred Monophysites berthed in the Palace of Hormisdas and visited for regular blessing by Justinian as well as Theodora (p. 680).

[75] See Bury 1923, II, 377.

[76] Liberatus, *Brev.*, 22 (*PL* 68); *Lib. Pont.*, 292, 297; Victor Tonn., *Chron.*, s.a. 542.

hinted at by Procopius.[77] Naturally she supported Justinian's condemnation of the Three Chapters, which was seen by the west as a dangerous concession towards Monophysitism; but she died while the disputes between Justinian and the Pope were still at their height and before the Fifth Ecumenical Council. Procopius' picture of her as intriguing behind the scenes must be understood in relation to these fraught years in the 540s, when ecclesiastical disputes were raging. If Theodora was in any way as influential as Procopius suggests, she was bound to become involved. But Procopius manages to give the impression that her involvement consisted of gratuitous meddling and interference – part of his generally trivialising technique.

This is especially the case since he does not choose here to go into any detail, promising a full treatment elsewhere.[78] Nevertheless, however natural it was that Theodora should become involved, and that her sympathies should be enlisted, it remains true that her main way of supporting the Monophysites was through her personal protection. Typically, she bypassed official channels. Thus one of the most important developments during her ascendancy was the dispatch of James Bar'adai to Syria as nominal bishop of Edessa, and his subsequent large-scale ordinations of Monophysite clergy, mostly conducted in clandestine journeying throughout the eastern province.[79] So an alternative church was created in the east, and it was this church that was to last. It would be difficult to overestimate its importance. But James himself was ordained by the Monophysites – later called Jacobites after him – under Theodora's protection in the palace. Whatever her personal involvement, this development certainly took place in direct violation of official policy. Another way in which the empress's influence was diffused with lasting effects was through missionary work, especially in Nubia if we are to believe John of Ephesus, where, extraordinarily enough, the imperial couple do seem genuinely to have sent separate Chalcedonian and Monophysite missions.[81] In the end the Monophysites prevailed, but less due to the ingenuity of Theodora (exaggerated by John as much as her crimes are by Procopius) than to that of existing contacts with Monophysites, and to the course of events after her death.[82]

But it is hard to understand what these 'rival' actions really mean. For Justinian himself would sometimes visit the Monophysite monks and clergy lodged in the Palace of Hormisdas, and he was willing to send out the very John, later Bishop of Ephesus, who is our main source for

[77] *Lib. Pont.*, 292f.; cf. *Gothic Wars* I.25.13.
[78] *SH* 1.14.
[79] N. 62, with John of Ephesus, *PO* 18.690ff.; 19.2, 157ff.
[80] *PO* 18.692.
[81] See on this Frend 1975a (= 1980, XXII), 10f.; 1975b (= 1980, XXIV), 20.
[82] Frend, 1975a, 11.

Theodora as the protectress of Monophysites, on a grand proselytising tour of Asia Minor where some 80,000 souls were claimed, presumably for the Monophysite faith.[83] We are again up against Procopius' tendency to the stereotype. It is easy, after all, to present Justinian and Theodora as pursuing diametrically opposing policies, if only for political advantage; as in the case of the Blues and Greens, though less happily there, it makes for more lively reading. But in reality the boundaries were not so firmly drawn. Justinian was sincere in his efforts to reconcile the warring factions, and he was not prevented from feeling respect for the Monophysite leaders even if he was forced as ruler to exile them. The concessions which he made to Monophysitism in the interests of church unity indeed seemed intolerably large to the westerners. Conversely, Theodora did not refuse to associate herself with Justinian's church dedications – SS. Sergius and Bacchus in Constantinople, or the monastery on Sinai,[84] even though they were officially orthodox. Procopius' over-simplified picture, together with the naturally one-sided version in John of Ephesus, have probably given us a distorted view of Theodora's religion when the truth is far more complex. She did favour Monophysites, and is still remembered in the eastern church for her help, but she did so only in limited ways, and as part of the far more complicated and subtle whole of Justinian's ecclesiastical policies. And because she died in 548, at the very height of the Three Chapters affair, these urgent concerns in her last years gave an impression that her influence overall on religious matters was greater than it probably had been, and led Procopius to his exaggerated and inadequate picture of her religious activity.

There was a further side to her influence to which Procopius failed to do justice – the skilful way in which she manoeuvred her family into the highest place in Byzantine society. Again Procopius reduces this, where he mentions it, to gossipy and spiteful anecdotes about individuals. Despite his claims that she often resorted to abortion in her early days, she had a daughter who grew to adulthood to see her mother as empress, and produced at least three sons, of whom one, Anastasius, married Joannina, the daughter of Belisarius and Antonina.[85] The others are named by John of Ephesus as John and Athanasius; another 'kinsman' is named as George.[86] Both John and Athanasius were clearly Monophysites, and it is fair to conjecture that their father, the son-in-law of Theodora, belonged to the family of the Emperor Anastasius, perhaps his brother Paul.[87] The grandson John married into another ardent and wealthy Monophysite family, for his wife and mother-in-law Georgia and

[83] John of Ephesus, *PO* 18. 681; see Stein 1949, 371ff.
[84] For SS. Sergius and Bacchus, Mango 1972; for Sinai, Ševčenko 1966.
[85] See Alan Cameron 1978, 269f.; *SH* 4.37, 5.18f.
[86] John of Ephesus, *HE* II.11 (*CSCO* 106, *Script. Syri* 55); V.1.
[87] Cameron, 272.

Antipatra are described by John as high-born and wealthy, of consular rank and patrician respectively.[88] These clear connections between the descendants of Theodora and the lineage of Anastasius show how far she had been able to place her relatives in the highest circles; her illegitimate daughter could evidently live in honour in Constantinople and then make an illustrious match. Even Procopius mentions her descendants without a sneer at their birth.[89] But besides the direct line there were Theodora's sisters, of whom Comito married the general Sittas, one of Justinian's most trusted military men.[90] Indeed the marriage of Justinian and Theodora in *c.* 524 brought in its wake that of Comito and Sittas and also that of Belisarius and Antonina, each uniting a self-made general with an actress. The future empress Sophia, wife of Justin II, was Theodora's niece,[91] and her husband Justin himself the son of Justinian's sister Vigilantia. These are complex connections. The marriage alliances of Theodora's descendants conveyed wealth, position and lineage; they also carried influence and availability for office (her grandson John acted as ambassador and was a consul and patrician, while Athanasius went into the church).[92] Besides that, the Monophysitism of some, though not all, made of them a distinctive group in the élite of the capital. And they are a testimony to the surprising degree of upward mobility at the top of Byzantine society epitomised by Theodora herself.

*

Deeply suspicious of women, especially if they have acquired power, Procopius was hostile to Theodora from the beginning. One of her worst crimes, according to him, was that through her 'almost all women had become morally depraved' – that is, they achieved some degree of protection under the law.[93] He attributes all her actions to the lowest 'feminine' motives. Thus the murder of the Gothic queen Amalasuntha was Theodora's doing, out of jealousy and the fear that she might attract Justinian; [94] tellingly, Procopius says that Theodora feared Amalasuntha because of her 'splendid and extraordinarily masculine bearing'. Procopius' Theodora is not presented as a masculine woman, or as

---

[88] *HE* II.12.

[89] *SH* 5.18f.

[90] Malal., p. 430 Bonn; Theophanes, p. 175 de Boor.

[91] John of Ephesus, *HE* II.10; cf. Vict. Tonn., s.a. 567 (*neptis*).

[92] Cameron 1978.

[93] *SH* 17.24. Cf. Procopius' remarks on the factions at *Persian Wars* I.24.6: he is outraged that women also participated, sometimes even opposing their husbands, though in his opinion they had no motive, for they did not even go to the theatre. This is why he can only call faction rivalry a 'disease'. For a similar view taken of women supposedly participating in tournaments in the fourteenth century by Knighton see Ziegler 1969, 36. In this case the chronicler sees the Black Death as a punishment sent on them.

[94] 16.1f.

transgressing or exceeding her sex, like Clytemnestra; rather she is the epitome of the 'feminine', with all the limitations that that implies to Procopius. By comparison with the range of modern attitudes, Procopius' are limited. He dislikes women in power; he dislikes low-born people who give themselves airs; he came to dislike anyone too closely associated with Justinian. His unpleasant detailing of Theodora's activities in the Hippodrome is not softened by any tinge of romanticism – it is unmitigated venom. There is certainly none of the idealisation of Theodora as the champion of womanhood that we find in some modern books.[95] To him, emancipation of women, in whatever form, would be an unmitigated evil. He does produce some examples of Theodora helping individual women.[97] But here Procopius correctly sees that her actions were on the personal scale; she can hardly have considered the lot of women in general, and indeed she was a fierce supporter of marital fidelity and the status quo.[98] Her power and influence derived as always from personal proximity to Justinian and from his generosity to her.[99]

Even in his physical description of Theodora, Procopius is hostile. The 'eternal feminine', an idealised concept which Theodora has seemed to typify for many moderns,[100] was not at all an object of admiration to Procopius. He describes her coldly and dispassionately:

> She had an attractive face and a good figure, but was short and pallid, though not in an extreme degree, for there was just a trace of colour. Her glance was invariably fierce and intensely hard ... to her bodily needs she devoted quite unnecessary attention, though never enough to satisfy herself. She was in a great hurry to get into her bath and very unwilling to get out again ... again and again she would sleep for hours on end, by day until nightfall and by night until sunrise. And though she had strayed thus into every path of self-indulgence for so great a part of the day, she thought fit to run the whole of the Roman empire.[101]

With this physical description Procopius shows the characteristics and the limitations of his treatment of Theodora, which is not so untypical of his treatment of other main characters in his works. Prejudiced, one-sided and biassed as his presentation is, it is ironic that it should have been for so many the starting point for so different an impression. Yet the aspects which they have chosen to emphasise are more indicative of their own background than of the reality of either Procopius or Theodora. Because of the modern preoccupation with sex, the

[95] E.g. Lamb 1952, 1977, 87; Bridge 1978, 94 'she was a feminist. She fought tirelessly and at times ruthlessly to improve the lot of women.'

[96] *SH* 17.24f.

[97] Malalas, p. 440f.; *Nov.* 14 (AD 535); cf. Bury 1923, II, 32.

[98] 17.7f., 28f.

[99] See Bury 1923, II, 31.

[100] Vandercook 1940, 141; Diehl 1904, 122 'séduisante toujours infiniment'.

[101] *SH* 10.11ff. (Penguin trans.).

romanticising and the idealising views alike dwell on the sexual details which for Procopius were probably never to be taken absolutely at face value. The demonological section on the other hand is usually simply ignored. It is not in tune with modern times; nor can devils be made sympathetic. But it sums up all that Theodora meant for Procopius.

CHAPTER SIX

Procopius and the *Buildings*

If anything, the *Buildings* has caused more problems for interpreters of Procopius than the *Secret History*. It has certainly been taken less seriously, and too often simply dismissed with expressions of distaste, to be left as a source book for archeologists.[1] This view, which emphasises Procopius' supposed 'insincerity', as against his 'real feelings' expressed in the *Secret History*, totally fails to appreciate the importance of panegyric in late antique literature as a whole and the code in which it was written. If the *Secret History* is not the unrestrained outpouring of Procopius' real feelings that it has so often be taken to be, neither is the *Buildings* to be so easily dismissed with the epithet 'insincere'. More than the *Secret History*, the *Buildings* needs to be rehabilitated into a central position in Procopius' writing, especially now, when a growing interest in the archeology of this period is focussing increased attention on the quality of the work as evidence for Justinianic building.[2] But before its evidential value can be properly appreciated, the work itself must be understood as a whole and in relation to Procopius' writing in general. We shall find that there is certainly distortion in it, which could be used to fuel the 'insincerity' interpretation, but that this work too expresses Procopius' attitudes and reveals his strengths and limitations in much the same way as the *Secret History* and the *Wars*.

It seems very likely that the *Buildings* as we have it is unfinished[3] or at least unrevised, as I have suggested may also be the case with the *Secret History*. Not only is Italy entirely omitted: the scale of the work changes dramatically after Book III, so that parts of Books IV and V consist merely of lists, whereas in Book VI (Africa) Procopius returns to a treatment as polished as that of the early books. The lists in Books IV

---

[1] E.g. Dahn 1865, 361f., Downey 1947, 191. From this attitude stems the assumption that the work must be pervaded with sarcasm or at least irony.

[2] See Croke and Crow 1983. The commentary by W. Pülhorn (1977) is indicative of this newer approach, but could now be much extended; see now also R. Hodges and D. Whitehouse, *Mohammed, Charlemagne and the Origins of Europe* (London, 1983).

[3] As suggested in Downey 1947. Downey 1953 points out the formal and hierarchical arrangement of the subject matter in Book I, and suggests that this book was written separately for public performance.

and V are hard to evaluate, since they are repetitive and inaccurate;[4] nevertheless, the polish of the other parts of the work suggests that Procopius intended to work them into a more literary form.[5] It would also seem an obvious conjecture that he meant to include Italy;[6] if the work dates from 554,[7] Procopius may have left Italy out so far as not being finally under Byzantine control, as in the *Wars* he does not carry the narrative up as far as the final victories of Narses, but it is harder to account for its absence if he was writing in 559/60. Rubin's suggestion that Italy was omitted because it shed little glory on Belisarius[8] misunderstands the nature of the *Buildings*, which is addressed directly to the matter of imperial achievement, not the fame of Belisarius,[9] who is largely irrelevant to it.[10] The one place where he does feature prominently, however, in the description of the mosaic on the ceiling of the Chalke,[11] links Italy and Africa as representative of Justinian's victories through the agency of Belisarius, thinking of his early and splendid achievement in Italy before the ignominy of the second Italian expedition.[12] So it is surely likely that Procopius would indeed have included Italy in his general survey. But even if we could accept that Italy was not to be included, the raggedness of the work as it stands still makes it likely that it is unrevised, if not actually unfinished. It was clearly meant as a work of high style, as its preface suggests,[13] but the high style is not sustained throughout. If it was indeed composed *c.* 554, the simplest explanation of this raggedness is to suppose that Procopius

---

[4] IV.4, 11; V.9. See Downey 1947, 173f. and below, Chapter 12. They are too often assumed to be official lists without asking what 'official' might mean, or even whether these are actually lists of finished building projects. See also Perrin-Henry 1980.

[5] See Downey 1947, also for the argument that there were two recensions of the work (criticised by L.M. Whitby in a forthcoming article). Menander Protector, fr. 12, apologises for leaving in the original words of a treaty and not improving on their style. It is not always remembered that Procopius was a considerable stylist too, and that *Buildings* I, for instance, represents his art at its most deliberate. It is surprising then that he should leave in these lists, especially as Book VI returns to the previously high literary level (though see n. 6).

[6] So Downey 1947, 172f. Book VI as it now stands, though highly finished, is rather short, and might originally have been part of Book V.

[7] See Chapter 1 above.

[8] Rubin 1954, 299-300.

[9] See I.1.6f., 17.

[10] Had Procopius wanted to underline the connection between Justinian's achievements and Belisarius's (Rubin 1954, 299), he was quite capable of doing so explicitly; as it is, Belisarius is remarkably absent from the work. Furthermore, although he busied himself with building when militarily necessary (as at Carthage and Rome), it was not on the whole Belisarius who was concerned with the churches and forts detailed in the *Buildings*, which belonged to a much slower and longer-term process. In any case, by 554 (and still more by 559/60) Belisarius was off the scene so far as Procopius was concerned.

[11] I.10.16, where his presence is of course demanded by the subject, on which see Mango 1959, 32f.

[12] So too Jordanes, *Get.* 313-14; Corippus, *Iust.* I.276ff.; III.121ff.

[13] Below, p. 86.

himself died soon after, for if we discount the prefect of the city of 562, we
do not hear of him again.[14]

As a finished panegyric, then, the *Buildings* is problematic. It could be
said to have three main themes – church building (especially as
instrumental in advancing the process of conversion to Christianity),
fortifications and the water-supply. But it is less clear whether Procopius
had made a conscious decision to concentrate on these topics, or how in
practice he meant to arrange his material. Not only are there notable
omissions (for the work is by no means an exhaustive record of
Justinian's building work), but the material that is included often seems
to be strung together in an arbitrary kind of way. Procopius does not
often relate the building works mentioned to their geographical location
or explain any overall strategy of building in an individual province, not
even for the fortifications where it would have been most welcome. While
it seems likely enough, even without the lists in Books IV and V, that he
had access to official records,[15] it is not at all easy to trace their use in the
work as a whole, much of which is anecdotal in character. It is certainly
unsafe therefore to make assumptions about dating on the basis of
omission of a known work in the *Buildings*; equally, we are not in a
position to understand Procopius' principles of inclusion. Certain
sections stand out as having unusual detail and emphasis, notably Dara
and Antioch; unfortunately, though, both of these, and other set pieces
so far as they have been analysed, reveal the deficiencies of Procopius as
a reporter even for places which he knew well through his own
experience.[16] So, like the *Secret History*, and like the *Wars* too, as we
shall see, the *Buildings* turns out to consist of an uneven mixture of the
reliable and the unreliable, the finished and the sketchy. As with the
Secret History, again, it shows a preoccupation with the Empress
Theodora[17] which surely must put its date nearer to her lifetime than
560. Just as 550 seems most likely for the *Secret History*, so 554 or
thereabouts seems most probable for publication of the *Buildings*.

The element of panegyric in the work is apparent throughout, though
Procopius masks it in the opening sentences by moralising about the
benefits accruing from writing the history of cities.[18] The main theme is
however soon announced: the advantages brought to the empire by
Justinian's building policies.[19] We therefore find Justinian treated in the
first chapter in panegyrical terms: he is a restorer of the state through

---

[14] See above, Chapter 1 and cf. the useful discussion by Veh 1952/53, 12ff., arguing that
Book V was added later than the rest, which took its shape in close connection with the
Wars.

[15] Though he only cites explicitly from oral sources, besides alluding to what he had seen
himself, e.g. VI.7.18.

[16] II.1-2 (Dara, see Croke and Crow 1983); 10 Antioch, see Downey 1953.

[17] See I.11.9, 27, with I.9.5.

[18] I.1.1-5. The preface is based to a large extent on Diodorus (Lieberich 1900, 4f.).

[19] I.1.12.

victory; a builder of cities, supporter of the true faith, codifier of the laws, bringer of internal harmony and external peace, strengthener of frontiers.[20] He is gentle like a father, more kingly than Cyrus of Persia,[21] merciful to those who have plotted against him.[22] Already Procopius has invoked Diodorus, Themistocles, Homer, Xenophon and Pindar.[23] And the themes enunciated here recur throughout the work, in varying degrees: thus the piety of Justinian and Theodora,[24] Justinian's initiative, often divinely inspired.[25] The emperor is called 'builder of the world'.[26] and the main claim to fame of Justiniana Prima in Illyria is said to be that it was his birthplace.[27] All that Procopius describes he attributes to Justinian alone, as though he had personally initiated it and carried it through; sometimes Procopius underlines this common panegyrical device by insisting that this really was the case.[28] He hammers home the lesson by constantly bringing to the reader's attention the name of 'Justinian our emperor'.[29] And as in the *Secret History* Justinian's imperial activity is reckoned by Procopius from the beginning of his uncle's reign, as if to extend his influence.[30]

One of the most prominent of the panegyrical themes in the work is that of the emperor's closeness to God, the reverse of the demonology of the *Secret History*. Procopius is following the firmest assumption in sixth-century imperial literature – that the emperor was in some sense God's special representative on earth, occupying a place nearer to the supernatural than ordinary men.[31] It was an idea built into Byzantine political thought since Eusebius.[32] Thus while Procopius sets the *Buildings* in the tradition of kingly biography, he also draws on the contemporary view of the Christian monarch. While the *Secret History* sees Justinian as demonic, the *Buildings* presents him almost as reaching

[20] I.1.6-11.

[21] I.1.12-15. Justinian's rule makes that of Cyrus seem like a game (I.1.15); cf. *SH* 14.14, and cf. 14.1; again at *Persian Wars* II.2.14. The *Buildings* passage might indeed seem like deliberate irony, but could as well derive from the extreme limitation of Procopius' vocabulary and range of critical concepts, for which see Chapter 13 below. Gantar 1962 sees the entire preface as ironic.

[22] I.1.16. Cf. *Gothic Wars* III.39.8 (Artabanes).

[23] I.1.19; cf. Pindar, *Ol.* 6.4.

[24] I.8.5.

[25] I.1.67, 4.7, 10.10; II.1.11, 2.8, 3.8, 13f.; V.1.13, 3.14, 5.2, 19, 6.16, 7.15; VI.2.2.

[26] IV.1.17.

[27] IV.1.19-27. On Justiniana Prima (Caričin Grad), see Grabar 1948; Claude 1969, plan I; Hoddinott 1964, 188ff.

[28] VI.5.6.

[29] VI.7.17-18; cf. e.g. V.2.3, 5.7.

[30] I.3.3; cf. 4.29. It also made it easier for Procopius to claim that work mainly done earlier, especially under Anastasius, was actually the work of Justinian; see below, pp. 107ff.

[31] See Corippus, *Iust.* II.425f. with note in Averil Cameron 1976, 178 and below, Chapter 14. Procopius' ideas about emperors, ideal and less than ideal: Veh 1951/52, 3-10.

[32] See Baynes 1955, 168ff., and, for the sixth century, Henry 1967, 298ff.; Dvornik 1966, II, 611ff.

sainthood. The asceticism and the extreme Lenten observance which are there interpreted as signs of his evil nature are here taken as proof of his holiness and piety, a signal for favours from God.[33] He tells the story of the miracle that occurred when Justinian's rheumatism (the result of excessive mortification of the flesh) was cured by the relics of the forty Martyrs held in the church of S. Irene, and which had miraculously revealed themselves when the foundations of the church were dug.[34] When Justinian went there he immediately received the reward of his faith and orthodoxy: oil flowed from the holy relics and soaked his feet and purple robe.[35] Procopius adds that this robe was preserved, still soaked in oil, in the church, to cure others suffering from incurable disease. Another time, he tells us, when Justinian was critically ill and the doctors had given up hope, the saints Cosmas and Damian came to him in a dream and cured him, whereupon he rebuilt their church across the Bosphorus.[36] In much the same way as the relics of the Forty Martyrs, the remains of the apostles Andrew, Luke and Timothy were revealed to Justinian when he was building the church of the Holy Apostles.[37] Again Procopius goes further and adds an extra comment: these apostles, he says, have since repaid the piety of the emperor in giving them splendid reburial, for 'when an emperor shows piety, the divine and the human are not divided, and God remains at hand in human affairs' (my paraphrase). When Justinian's architects were planning the rebuilding of Dara, Justinian himself, with God's aid, came up with the right solution, so that everyone was amazed at how God advised Justinian as to what was best for the state, and Justinian's idea prevailed when the cleverness and skill of the builders had been of no avail.[38] Of the Sangarios bridge, Procopius gives it as his own opinion that it will be finished, since God takes a part in everything that the emperor does.[39]

It is not particularly helpful to categorise all these statements as 'insincere', on the basis of the *Secret History*. The *Buildings* is characterised by a sustained Christian interpretation of the reign, to which Procopius often contributes his own comments, as we have seen, and in which the conception of the emperor's special role is central. It is precisely that conception of the unique nature of the position of the emperor that could lead Procopius, in a darker moment, to conclude that Justinian's power was demonic. The two views are complementary. We

[33] I.7.6; cf. *SH* 13.28f.; above p. 61.
[34] I.7.
[35] Ibid., 13, 15
[36] I.6.5.
[37] I.4.20-2.
[38] II.3.13-14.
[39] V.3.10. For the date of this bridge (which still stands), see below, Chapter 1, and for pictures and discussion, see Mango 1976, 126, 129.

do not know exactly what Procopius' political views were when he wrote the *Buildings*, but we are not thereby entitled to conclude that it is not representative of his own thinking, just because it seems to differ from an earlier work. There is no reason to believe that he could not have accepted the standard view of God and emperor which he here enunciates, even if, in the case of Justinian, it represented an ideal more often than an actuality.

The work is imbued with the assumption that conversion of pagans was a prime aim of Justinian's building policy. The church of the Virgin at Augila is a good example: Procopius explains in some detail that the inhabitants of those parts suffered the 'disease' of paganism even in his own day, and that this was the site of the shrine of Ammon visited by Alexander the Great.[40] 'And now this emperor not only offered physical security to his subjects but was also concerned to save their souls.' Similarly, the newly converted Tzani who bordered on Armenia and practised animism were given a fine church so that they might cease living like beasts and learn from participation in prayers and the liturgy that they were human beings.[41] When he writes of the Lazi, Procopius brings out especially clearly the process of cementing ties of loyalty, in which church building was an important element – but in this case it was a matter of restoring an ancient church which had fallen into disrepair.[42]

At the same time, the *Buildings* is unlike other contemporary panegyrics in form. It is not a sustained *ekphrasis* like Paul the Silentiary's poem on the restored S. Sophia, unless Procopius intended in the finished version to write up more sections on the scale of his own description of S. Sophia in Book I.[43] Nor is it wholly on imperial themes, like Corippus' panegyric on Justin II, or the preface to Agathias's *Cycle*.[44] It does not, except in the first chapter, attempt direct description of Justinian according to the standard divisions of rhetoric (contrast parts of the *Secret History*).[45] Nevertheless, the objective of the work is obviously to shed glory on the emperor through the catalogue of his achievements as a builder, a theme closely tied in to imperial ideology from the beginning and reinforced for the Christian empire by Eusebius'

---

[40] VI.2.14-20. There is a good deal on the shrine of Ammon in Corippus' *Iohannis* (III.81ff.; VI.145ff.; see Averil Cameron 1974, 40 and 1983, 173f.). Since there is no good evidence for the actual working of the shrine in the late imperial period, Justinian's action was more for show than Procopius admits; similarly, Corippus' elaborate emphasis on the supposed devotion of the Berbers to the shrine is almost totally literary.

[41] III.6.1f., especially 12.

[42] III.7.5-6.

[43] I.1.20ff. Downey 1953b, 722, suggests that book I was written and delivered separately (cf. I.8.15; 11.8-9) and the rest added later. For Paul the Silentiary see Friedländer 1912 and p. 20.

[44] For the form of Corippus' panegyric, see Averil Cameron 1975, 1976; the preface to the *Cycle: AP* IV.3.

[45] Above, p. 59.

Life of Constantine.[46] If there is no exact surviving parallel for Procopius' *Buildings*, it is not because Procopius' work was in itself innovatory, for the subject was an obvious one in relation to imperial ideology, and Justinian's extensive programme (even allowing for exaggeration) demanded commemoration. Procopius' originality, if it be that, lies rather in his treatment of the material. He shows little interest for the most part either in the aesthetic qualities or even simply in the appearance of the works that he describes, nor in the overall logistics of Justinian's building, whether ecclesiastical or defensive. In most of the work, after the first book, which is on an altogether larger scale, he is more concerned to list and catalogue, while at the same time constantly turning his material to panegyrical purpose. He may therefore be reflecting a growing contemporary taste for the cataloguing of buildings, which we can see reflected in sixth-century chronicles and in the growth of a patriographic literature about the physical history of cities.[47] As it stands, the *Buildings* oscillates between lengthy ekphrastic description and mere cataloguing. At the same time its reliability varies; the most finished and developed sections are far from being the most reliable. Like the *Secret History* and, as we shall see, the *Wars*, it has a texture that is complex; this lack of homogeneity is basic to Procopius' work, and means that it can be used only after careful and detailed assessment of individual passages.

One feature of the *Buildings*, however, is quite consistent – its Christian framework. This is a work written with a certain purpose – to appeal to the imperial court – and it would be extraordinary if it did not make use of imperial Christian ideology. Nevertheless, it would be premature to conclude that this feature is purely literary on the grounds of the sceptical tone adopted in parts of the *Wars*. We should rather ask first how the Christian framework of the *Buildings* is constructed, and then (but this will be possible only in a later chapter) whether it really does conflict with the *Wars*.

In Book I, then, Procopius says: 'We must begin with the churches of the Virgin Mary. For we know that this is what the emperor wishes, and the reason is clearly given by the true saying that one should proceed from God to His Mother.'[48] He declares that it was the will of God that the old S. Sophia should be destroyed, so that Justinian could build a

---

[46] See *Life of Constantine* III.25ff., with the remarks of MacCormack 1974, 168ff. (imperial church building as a theme in Christian panegyrics). Further in Geanokoplos 1966, 1976, 118ff.; Armstrong 1969; Irmscher 1977. The tendency to exaggeration of Justinian's achievements (discussed below) was a feature built in to the genre (see on Augustus's *Res Gestae* Gros 1976, 15.

[47] Especially in Marcellinus and Malalas (on whom see Downey 1938); the patriographic literature as such begins for us with Hesychius of Miletus (sixth century). Besides these works, there were many contemporary epigrams celebrating buildings, and building is a prominent theme in the *History* of John of Ephesus.

[48] I.3.1.

new one;[49] God supplied the best craftsmen as well as the best inspiration.[50] The description of the reaction of someone entering the church is famous: 'Whenever anyone enters it to pray, he understands at once that this edifice has not been built by human capability or skill but by the inspiration of God; his mind is lifted up and flies up to[51] God, whom he thinks must be near at hand, wishing to associate with those He has chosen.'[52] In fact the treatment in his passage of the Nika revolt, the cause of the destruction of the original church,[53] is of some interest, since whereas in the *Wars* and the *Secret History* he gives a secularised version of its causes here he comes much closer to the 'official' version that we find in Malalas. It is part of God's plan, therefore; but the agents of the destruction are the 'rabble'[54] who 'took up arms against God.' Neither the Blues and Greens (made responsible for the riot in the *Wars*) nor the senatorial class (which the *Secret History* implies was blamed by Justinian) appear in the other works in this religious light. But the allusion to 'taking up arms against God' is in conformity with the general logic of the *Buildings*, while the elements singled out in the other works correspond equally well to the demands of those contexts. Another striking passage here where imperial experience coincides with what are presented as general attitudes is the description of the church of SS. Cosmas and Damian,[55] rebuilt and extended by Justinian after his cure. Procopius memorably describes how now when people are sick and in despair they get into their boats and sail across to 'their only hope', and that when they embark they see the great church 'like an acropolis', reminding them of the emperor's generosity. With the famous Convent of Repentance founded by Theodora there are again differences between the emphasis here and that in the *Secret History*.[56] The prostitutes there 'forced' to repent are here said to have been 'forced against their will' into the profession in the first place. It might seem as though Procopius is playing with ideas. Here Theodora is inspired by pure piety,[57] whereas there her piety forces others to do what they don't want to do.[58] But the foundation itself could be seen in different ways, after all, though there is certainly in both works a degree of forcing the facts: here, where we are

---

[49] I.1.21.

[50] I.1.24, 69.

[51] For the language, see p. 35 n. 8.

[52] I.1.61.

[53] See n. 49. Procopius' other treatments of the Nika revolt: *Persian Wars* I.24; *SH* 12.13f. See pp. 144f., 166f.

[54] I.1. 20-21; cf. Malalas, pp. 473f.; below, pp. 166f. In the *Persian Wars* it is largely the factions who are blamed, while in the *Secret History* it is implied that senators are seriously involved.

[55] I.6.5-8.

[56] I.9.1f. Above, p. 68.

[57] I.9.5.

[58] *SH* 17.7f.

told that the girls were unwilling prostitutes, they nevertheless have to be enticed into the convent with fine living quarters,[59] while in the *Secret History*, where the same argument would have done so well, Procopius claims that most of them were previously only just getting a living.[60]

In general, however, the Christian interpretation in the *Buildings* is both central and consistent. During the rebuilding of Dara, Procopius says, God miraculously revealed to Justinian exactly the plan which later arrived from the architect Chryses of Alexandria and was then adopted;[61] that is, Procopies implies, the technical skill of Anthemius and Isidore was inferior to true piety. The same point is made in the description of the great Nea church of the Virgin in Jerusalem, whose recent discovery strikingly confirms the accurate description of which Procopius was sometimes capable.[62] On this occasion the problem was how to support the weight of the columns. God revealed to Justinian a special kind of stone in the neighbourhood which would remove the difficulty.[63] Procopius comments that this is entirely credible since we humans, judging by human standards, often think something is impossible, whereas God can do anything. When he mentions Mt. Gazirim, he retails the account of the Samaritan incident under Zeno after which the mountain was handed over to the Christians and put under guard; then he goes on to the insurrection under Anastasius, put down firmly by Procopius of Edessa the governor of Palestine,[64] and describes how although the Samaritans had now mostly adopted Christianity Justinian rebuilt and increased the fortifications on the mountain, restoring five churches burnt down by the Samaritans. It seems impossible to suppose that Procopius is so deliberately disingenuous here as to have knowingly omitted the second Samaritan revolt of 555 in which the governor was killed.[65] The whole sequence is told from a straightforwardly Christian point of view, quoting from John's Gospel[66] and using the simple phrase 'when Jesus the Son of God was in the flesh'.[67] Even this could perhaps be adopted simply for panegyrical ends. But Procopius gives it as his view

---

[59] I.9.10.

[60] SH 17.5-6. It is not then entirely logical when he continues with the claim that some of them threw themselves over the walls rather than stay in the convent.

[61] II.3.8-15.

[62] V.6.1; see below, p. 95.

[63] V.6.19.

[64] V.7. For the unlikely suggestion that this was the historian's father see Haury 1891 (retracted, Haury 1898, 17).

[65] For the implications of this passage for the dating of the *Buildings* see Chapter 1.

[66] V.7.3 (*Jo.* 4.7). For this extremely unusual Scriptural citation (in the context of Procopius' work) see Rubin 1954, 45, 68f.

[67] Cf. *Persian Wars* II.12.22; on Procopius's formula, Rubin 1954, 68. The fact that he does (exceptionally) use similar language in the *Wars* shows that it is not merely assumed in the *Buildings* because this is an official and necessarily Christian work.

that the words of he who is God must be true;[68] and the Samaritans are presented as wicked desecrators of the holy altar and the ineffable liturgy,[69] profaners of the mysteries, which 'Samaritans might do, but about which we should be silent'. Elsewhere he expresses himself rather differently, in suggesting that sensible Samaritans would convert to Christianity rather than rebel;[70] but the two positions are not opposed, except in emphasis. When Procopius goes on to write of the monks on Mt. Sinai[71] and says that their asceticism places them above all human wants,[72] he is expressing the same ascetic idealism which leads him to approve Justinian's mortification in this work and see the same feature as a sign of evil in the *Secret History*.[73]

This pervasive Christianising interpretation did not prevent Procopius from sometimes adopting the affected ignorance of the technical terms of Christianity that is common in the *Wars*. He writes in an apparently artless way of John the Baptist that 'this apostle is called Theologos, because he explained about God in a more than human way',[74] or says of S. Anne that 'some think' that she was the mother of the Virgin,[75] or that the most holy place in a church 'is called' the sanctuary.[76] In the case of the reference to S. Anne Procopius might be alluding to the fact that we know of her only from the Apocrypha;[77] but usually the motivation for such 'explanations' is purely stylistic. They are not different from his explanation of the name S. Sophia ('the Byzantines call the church Wisdom, having given it the name most suitable to God'),[78] or of the architectural term 'hemisphere' or the technical use of 'metropolis'.[79] In neither case do they mean that Procopius himself was ignorant of these terms, and they do not affect the fact that the *Buildings* is a Christian panegyric, and usually an explicitly Christian one; instead, they merely underline that it is also an ambitious piece of high-style literature. It is no doubt the case rather that Procopius has actually enhanced the Christian element in his explanations, as we have seen in the examples of the Nika revolt and the Convent of Repentance. But discarding both the 'unfamiliar' look of the periphrases and the element of exaggeration which panegyric is bound to bring out, it remains the

[68] *Buildings* V.7.4.
[69] V.7.5.
[70] *SH* 11.25f.; see above, p. 66.
[71] V.8.5.
[72] On this passage see below.
[73] Above, p. 61.
[74] V.1.5.
[75] I.3.11-12.
[76] I.1.65; cf. V.7.5 (Pentecost).
[77] Notably the *Protevangelium Jacobi*, whence she became an important figure in Byzantine homiletic touching on the birth and upbringing of the Virgin (see e.g. *PG* 96.708 (S. John Damascene); 100. 1408f. (George of Nicomedia)).
[78] I.1.21.
[79] I.1.32; V.4.18. Further below, Chapter 7.

case, as I shall go on to argue further, that in all three of his works
Procopius is operating within the same overall set of assumptions, and
that they are the Christian assumptions shared by his society at large.
From this point of view – to which the next chapter will return – it is less
useful to concentrate on the differences between the works than on their
fundamental similarities.

Because of the literary elusiveness of the *Buildings* – and for other
reasons – it is far from easy to establish its specific contribution to our
understanding of the places and buildings which it describes. Even
within the work itself, there are great variations. Some parts are full and
detailed, others cursory and vague, while whatever the documentary
sources to which Procopius had access, it is obvious that there is a great
difference between the parts where he discusses places he knew well and
those where he deals with parts of the empire to which he had never been.
Book IV, where he deals with the Balkans, is a case in point. Twice the
narrative peters out into lists, and whatever their credentials it is hard to
avoid the conclusion that Procopius himself was at a loss for more
congenial material. Even his description of Justiniana Prima, birthplace
of Justinian and showpiece of the regime, is surprisingly vague and
lacking in detail;[80] he simply lists the stock attributes of a late antique
city – churches, official buildings, stoai, fora, fountains, streets, baths
and market-places.[81] By contrast, when he describes Carthage, which he
knew well himself, and mentions many of the same features, he gives
them individual names and locations.[82] Book IV bears all the signs of
something written quickly, perhaps to order, and often without access to
solid material (the lack has to be made up with panegyrical in-fill).[83] By
contrast, Book VI is shorter, but much denser and with less padding.[84]
The briefest look at the varying scales and methods used in the *Buildings*
makes it clear that every section must be reviewed individually before its
value as a source can be assumed. I shall take a few examples to show the
strengths and the limitations of the work.

In Book V Procopius announces that he will cover all those parts of
Asia not already discussed, and Africa too.[85] After a geographical ramble
from Ephesus to Cilicia, he reaches the Holy Land, Mount Garizim and
Mount Sinai.[86] The second of these is the occasion for a rather lengthy

[80] N. 27. Book IV is discussed below, pp. 219f.
[81] See in general Claude 1969, 69ff. It is similar with Caput Vada in N. Africa (VI.6.8-16);
see p. 182.
[82] VI.5.8-11, on which see Averil Cameron 1982, 33f. and pp. 181f. below.
[83] E.g. IV.4.1.
[84] For Book VI see Chapter 10 below.
[85] V.1.1.
[86] V.6-8. V.9 consists of a list of monasteries, wells and other buildings in Jerusalem
restored by Justinian, without further explanation or comment from Procopius. His whole
account of the Holy Land is bare by comparison say with that of the pilgrim Antony of
Piacenza (Geyer 1965), and with much less sense of the holy places; Procopius is more
interested in architectural marvels like the Nea and the Sinai monastery.

account of Samaritan/Christian relations,[87] but very little is actually said abut the place itself, and nothing whatever about the nature of the alterations to Zeno's church. This is not, then, in any sense a complete or comprehensive account of Justinianic building in the Holy Land, nor does Procopius even attempt to justify his principles of inclusion. To get a better sense of the scope of Justinian's activity here we have to turn to other sources – the *Life* of S. Sabas by Cyril of Scythopolis, the *Annales* of the tenth-century patriarch Eutychius, pilgrim itineraries. In particular, Procopius says nothing about the Church of the Nativity at Bethlehem noted at some length by Eutychius.[88] Yet both the description of the Nea church and the section on Sinai are of considerable interest. Procopius' lengthy and detailed account of the Nea church of the Virgin in Jerusalem seems indeed to have been startlingly vindicated by the discovery of a well-preserved imperial inscription in 1977 inside a subterranean structure in the Old City which had been in use as a cistern as late as the nineteenth century.[89] It is clear that this inscription, dated by indiction to 534/5 or 549/50, belonged to the massive complex found not long before and identified already as the Nea church, which is situated in exactly this position in the sixth-century Madaba map of Jerusalem,[90] for it names not only Justinian but also the hegumen Constantine, whom John Moschus also names as abbot of the Nea.[91] The earlier of the two dates is the probable, since Cyril of Scythopolis was granted funds for the church in 531.[92] It is noticeable that Procopius gives relatively few details about the complex centring on the church,[93] and concentrates almost exclusively on the technical problem of building out the foundations on the side of the hill. He had good information about the construction of this church, clearly from local sources, but he made no attempt to link it with a wider view of Jerusalem under Justinian, or to describe the appearance of the church itself; nor does he see fit to mention Cyril's visit to Constantinople. He describes the church as a 'wonder', an illustration of the miraculous benefits which came to Justinian from God. The whole account, in fact, is a good indication of the objectives of the *Buildings*, and a warning that we must not expect too much from the work in terms of general completeness or aesthetic analysis. Perhaps, like Thucydides, Procopius would have worked his lists into the main narrative in a finished work, but even so the final

[87] See p. 93, cf. p. 66. Procopius' account of the Samaritan revolt is cast more in terms of the triumph of orthodoxy than of precise detail, and the need for rebuilding churches burnt during the revolt, which is described in detail by Eutychius (see Vincent and Abel 1914, 118ff.), gets only a cursory mention here (V.7.17).

[88] Thus dated after *c.* 560 (sic) on grounds of Procopius's silence: Harvey 1910; Bagatti 1952, perhaps rightly, though this section of the *Buildings* is too selective to be sure.

[89] See Ben-Dov 1977; Avigad 1977.

[90] See Avi-Yonah 1954, 57.

[91] *PG* 87.2857; see Milik 1960-61, 145f.

[92] *V. Sabae* 73 (Schwartz 1939, 176-78).

[93] See Avigad 1977, 148; Vincent and Abel 1926, 913ff. I am grateful to Dr Tsafrir for information about the Nea church.

version would have been far from homogeneous, to judge by the more polished sections that we do have.

When we come to Procopius' account of the Justinianic monastery and fortress on Sinai, we shall see again that his description is incomplete, and influenced by the logic of the *Buildings* as a whole. On the other hand, the problems raised by this passage are not a simple matter of a contradiction between Procopius and the *Annales* of Eutychius, to the detriment of the reputation of Procopius.[94] If we actually look at Procopius' account, we can see at once that it is by no means a straightforward description of Justinian's fortified monastery, and that Procopius makes no attempt to analyse its function or even describe its appearance in detail. As with the Nea church, he is interested in the sensational and the dramatic. He starts with a highly literary reference to Mount Sinai, which leads him into a rather long recapitulation of his account in the *Wars* of Justinian's relation with the Arabs and others in that area.[95] After this self-reference, he says that he will say no more for fear of being accused of vulgarity. So far there has been no description of Sinai itself whatever. Nor does he go on to the monastery even now. He remarks next that there are monks living on Sinai (no affectation here over the term 'monk', though it usually calls forth elaborate explanation).[96] In the logic of this account, the monastery itself is secondary to the prominence accorded the monks; the fortifications, surprisingly enough, come after both. The monks are interestingly described: Procopius says that their way of life is a living death.[97] It is hardly appropriate to attack the credibility of his evidence on the grounds that the Sinai monks did not practise this supposed special form of eremiticism.[98] Procopius was not setting out to give a detailed and impartial account of their exact practices. On the other hand, it is not so certain that he was wrong: however much the comment that the Sinai monks sought to 'practise death' looks like a typical remark by Procopius himself, it was in fact a cliché of Syriac asceticism. In the works of Ephraem Syrus the metaphor 'like dead' is used as one of the highest terms of praise for monks, while 'death' itself can be used as a metaphor for the ascetic life: 'everyone that bends his neck (i.e. to the monastic life) and serves in this institution is regarded as dead.'[99] The idea might well have been familiar to Procopius too. In any case, to pick up this

[94] So Mayerson 1978. For Eutychius see Griffith 1982.

[95] *Persian Wars* I.19.17ff.

[96] *Buildings* V.8.4; contrast Persian Wars I.7.22; *Vandal Wars* II. 26.17. Cf. Averil and Alan Cameron 1964, 317f.

[97] V.8.4. Procopius' presentation of the Sinai monks is highly intellectualised; it lacks the personal detail of Antony's remarks (*Itin.*, 37f.), nor does he know them by name (see further Devreesse 1940).

[98] Mayerson 1978, 35.

[99] See Vööbus 1958, 102f. and see too Evagrius Ponticus, *PG* 40.1229.

detail and use it to beat Procopius with is to miss the articulation of the passage as a whole. Only after he has written of the monks and the strength of their asceticism does he introduce the church – which he ascribes to the Virgin, in common with all the early accounts.[100] Here again his credibility has been impugned, and it is true that he seems to have only a rather vague idea of the physical arrangement of the buildings; he writes as though church and fortress are separate, and fails to give the real reason for the location of the monastery, which was to include the site of the Burning Bush,[101] instead adding apparently lamely that 'they say' that it was on Sinai that Moses received the tablets of the Commandments. But the defensive purpose of the fortress as expressed by Procopius is more credible than has been allowed. Thus his statement that it was meant to prevent the Saracens from entering Palestine[102] has seemed no more believable than the siting of the monastery itself, at the base of a slope where it was open to attack from above.[103] Yet in a general sense – which is what Procopius intended – he was correct, for the great monastery and fortress was a prime instrument of Byzantine diplomacy and would have had the effect of deterring the razzias that were the predominating method of attack in that region by its strong statement of Byzantine authority. It could not 'bar the way into Palestine', but it had a major role to play in the complex mechanics of Byzantine control in Palestina Tertia, even though in its early period it seems to have functioned rather as a refuge and stopping place for pilgrims and as the home of ascetics, many living outside the walls, than a functioning military unit. Procopius had not himself been to Sinai. His account is (unsurprisingly) strictly inaccurate in detail, as when he says that Sinai was near the Red Sea and that Palestina Tertia was barren, when in fact the slopes have always supported sheep and goats and a modest degree of

[100] On the monastery, see Ševčenko 1966; Forsyth 1968; Forsyth and Weitzmann I, 1973. Procopius writes vaguely about a site and a project only recently under way, and of which he could have had no personal experience. Since his is the earliest account, it is natural to think it should be the most authoritative, and to cast aspersions on Procopius' credibility if it is seen to be deficient; we must however interpret it in the context of Procopius overall methodology in the *Buildings*, instead of in isolation.

[101] For the site, see Forsyth 1966; Tsafrir 1971 (a popular but helpful account), 1978.

[102] V.8.9. For Palestina Tertia see Gutwein 1981, especially 23f. (Sinai), 309ff. (defences). Procopius does not attempt to relate Sinai or the monastery to the situation of the province in general, nor does he give any hint that monks were scattered over the mountain area outside the monastery, and thus highly vulnerable to nomad attack; his account has one purpose – to cast maximum glory on the monastery as a prestige project of Justinian – and it is simplified to that end. Procopius is not interested in surveying whole provinces, only in selected imperial sites within them. For a more general view of the defences of this area see Devreesse 1940, and see Chapter 7 below on the Arabian phylarchates. Naturally Procopius prefers to emphasise this showpiece of Byzantine strength rather than the less glamorous reality of subsidies and shifting alliances (Sartre 1981, 194ff.; Liebeschuetz 1977, 494f. – and in general on the practicalities of the eastern frontier).

[103] Mayerson 1978, 34f.; Forsyth and Weitzmann I, 6. Procopius evidently thought the same (V.8.6-9). There is however no water on the top of the mountain.

cultivation. In the light of the long history of the monastery up to the present day, Procopius' emphasis on its military aspect may seem misplaced. But every peculiarity in Procopius' account is the product of an intensely literary treatment in a context in which, after all, the main subject matter is provided by fortifications and churches. He was not writing a dispassionate description for our convenience. By contrast, our other main source, the tenth-century *Annales* of the patriarch Eutychius of Alexandria, is written from the opposite point of view, that of monasticism, and reflects a situation five hundred years after the foundation of the monstery, during which time its severe deficiencies as a fortified site had been forcibly revealed.[104] For that reason Eutychius' comments have more appeal to modern scholars who have noted the same faults for themselves. But Procopius' version was dictated by the general logic and emphasis of the *Buildings*, in which a main theme was to emphasise the grandeur of imperial achievement. Had Procopius been conscious, then, of the military weakness of the site, he would hardly have spelt it out in this work. More likely, though, the monastery appeared to him as to others at the time, and credibly enough, a magnificent demonstration of Byzantine arms and religion.

The same need to interpret individual accounts in relation to their general aim is well illustrated by the treatment in Book I of the buildings in Constantinople itself. In no sense does Procopius provide a guidebook, or even a comprehensive idea of what the city looked like in the sixth century. Yet the concentration of Justinianic building in the capital naturally made this part of the work fuller than most other sections, and enabled Procopius both to collect material more easily and to draw on his own observation; it also dictated the emphasis on churches, whether or not this was suggested to Procopius as part of an imperial commission. Even here, however, there are certain signs of strain in the organisation. Chapter 1 to 9 are taken up with a catalogue of Justinian's church building and restoration in Constantinople, warranted partly topographically and partly by subject.[105] But Procopius has not found it easy to deal with this mass of detail. He resorts to the rhetorical question,[106] the

---

[104] See Mayerson 1978, 37 and in general. Mayerson attacks the credibility of Procopius' account (also Mayerson 1963) but does not ask why Procopius wrote it as he did. One of his arguments against Procopius is that the physical remains of the early monastery do not support the assertion (V.8.9) that Justinian established a garrison there. But the contemporary Jebaliyeh, hereditary servants of the monastery, persistently trace their origins back to the foundation, and claim to have been originally Christian; whatever their actual origin, these are perhaps the 'soldiers' mentioned by Procopius (see Nandris 1980, 1981, forthcoming). I am grateful to both Dr Mayerson and Dr Nandris for discussion on this passage.

[105] The account begins with S. Sophia, then moves to the Augusteum, then to S. Irene. Next Procopius aims to treat churches of the Virgin and S. Anne, then of other saints, and finally returns to a topographical arrangement. For discussion see Downey 1953b.

[106] I.4.25 'why omit the church of S. Acacius?' (so too I.8.13).

favourite device of panegyric, and parts of this section read more like a
list than a literary work. When he passes to secular works the scale
changes to become less full, but here too he describes a series of
individual works without giving a sense of the overall impact of Justinian
on the appearance of the capital. Ironically, the *Buildings* was quite
unknown to the compilers of the *Patria* of Constantinople, and by the
eighth century Procopius' description of the churches and other buildings
in Constantinople had been forgotten; despite his efforts as a panegyrist,
Justinian was no longer remembered as one of the major imperial
builders.[107] Among the reasons for this is the nature of the *Buildings* as a
high literary text, and its share, therefore, in the fate of other such texts
in the Byzantine Dark Ages.[108] Contemporaries and near contemporaries
did not assume, as moderns have tended to do, that it was a
straightforward source of information.

Indeed, the work's literary aims have done much to shape Book I,
particularly of course in the description of S. Sophia.[109] Certainly,
Procopius gives us a good deal of information not found elsewhere about
the technical problems of construction and the progress of the building,
but he has also written here a rhetorical *ekphrasis* in the manner of those
by Choricius of Gaza on the Gaza churches.[110] The technique of
description is similar, emphasising the effect of the church on the
beholder, its colours, the variety of materials, and expressing all this in
elaborate language with plentiful use of simile and metaphor.[111] It is a
description, clearly, of the first church put up by Justinian after the Nika
revolt of AD 532: there is so much emphasis here on the paradoxical
safety of the church even when it seems so precarious that we cannot
believe that Procopius was simply failing to mention the disastrous
collapse of the dome in December, 557.[112] He concentrates on the
architecture, the light pervading the interior, and the colours of the
marble. Justinian's S. Sophia was probably aniconic in decoration,[113]
though it would be rash to infer this from Procopius alone, for he never

[107] See Averil Cameron and Judith Herrin 1984, 38.

[108] Ibid., 40f.; for the lack of availability of books in the early eighth century see Mango
1980, 137; cf. also 79f. on the situation in Constantinople; Wilson 1983, 61ff.

[109] I.1.20-77.

[110] For *ekphrasis* in general, see Downey 1959a; for a translation with notes of this
description, see Mango 1972, 72ff., with other comparable material (Choricius' *ekphraseis*
of the churches of S. Sergius and S. Stephen at Gaza, ibid., 60ff.). Procopius description is a
piece of high-style writing; it does not convey the living connection of church and liturgy or
its mystical significance.

[111] It is therefore dangerous to treat Procopius' as necessarily either a straightforward or a
complete description.

[112] See especially I.1.34f., 50f. Those who favour the later date for the *Buildings* (*c.* 560,
see Chapter 1 above) have to assume that Procopius was ignoring the collapse for
panegyrical purposes.

[113] See Mundell 1977, 70. Contrast Choricius on the pictorial decoration of S. Sergius at
Gaza (Mango 1972, 62f., 64ff.).

mentions pictorial decoration in Justinian's churches. And while the whole section on S. Sophia is written within a typology of divine inspiration and intervention, it lacks the explicit connection of parts of the church with theological meanings found in other sixth-century texts.[114] Even in its emphasis on the miraculous in the building of the church it is a long way from the eighth or ninth-century *Narratio de S. Sophia*, according to which an angel revealed the new church to Justinian and another appeared to 'Ignatius' the master-builder picturesquely dressed in imperial vestments and red buskins.[115] Another difference from this later text lies in Procopius' complete failure to detail the furnishings of the church, which he neglects totally in favour of its architectural features. Like many of his other set-pieces, this one is one-sided, shaped by certain literary aims and personal emphasis; certainly not a complete or objective description.

It is the same with the other church descriptions. Rather than give the detail we might like, Procopius tends to lapse into vaguely rhetorical vocabulary. The great Blachernae church, blatantly ascribed to Justinian,[116] is 'by the sea', 'very holy', 'high' – but Procopius quite fails to mention that it was the home of some of the city's most precious relics and a major site of ceremonial.[117] The church of the Virgin at Pege is 'not easy to capture in the right words or sketch with the imagination'; here Procopius is content with the banal observation that it is the most beautiful and large of the churches.[118] The church of S. Anne gets no description at all, and that of S. Michael in Constantinople only an architectural comment.[119] Nearly the whole of the treatment of Justinian's great church of the Holy Apostles is taken up with the story of the miraculous discovery of the relics of SS. Andrew, Luke and Timothy.[120] Again and again Procopius merely mentions a church or is content with trite indications of its 'splendour' or its size; probably the most explicit description is of the twin churches of SS. Peter and Paul and SS. Sergius and Bacchus, where he is unusually specific about their physical

[114] Corippus, *Iust*. IV.288ff., a passage wrongly taken in the past as a literal description of the church. See also Mango 1972, 55ff. on the Syriac description of the cathedral at Edessa, rebuilt in the mid-sixth century; McVey 1983. These ideas were most highly developed by Maximus Confessor (d. 662), following ps.-Dionysius the Areopagite.

[115] For a convenient translation, see Mango 1972, 96ff.

[116] I.3.3. On the Blachernae church see Janin 1969, 161ff. In the first place, Procopius attributes to Justinian what he knows to have been the work of Justin I, justifying that as part of his general and proper procedure; but even that was a restoration or extension, not an actual foundation, for many sources attest the church's foundation in the fifth century, soon after which it became the repository of the Virgin's robe (Janin, loc. cit.; Baynes 1955 (1949), 240ff.). This very clear example should make us suspicious of other attributions to Justinian.

[117] See Averil Cameron 1979 (= 1981, XVIII), and for these churches, besides Janin 1969, Mathews 1971, 1976.

[118] I.3.7-8.

[119] I.3.11-18.

[120] I.4.9f. For this church, see Downey 1957, 1959b; Grierson 1962.

arrangement – uncommon enough indeed for his notice.[121] But he is interested neither in their early date in Justinian's reign nor in the great inscription which still runs round SS. Sergius and Bacchus. The touchstones for him are beauty, size and cost,[122] and those churches that receive more detailed descriptions are in the minority.[123]

Of course this section is full of useful information which we might not otherwise have. But Procopius is not at his best here. He felt bound to begin with Justinian's churches,[124] and S. Sophia offered a subject to which his rhetorical skill had to rise, if to nothing else. But he often seems perfunctory, or even bored. He shows little concern for the aesthetic qualities of the buildings he mentions, except to draw on the conventional repertoire of expressions for beholder reactions. He conveys no impression of the chronological development of Justinian's church building or of its overall rationale. This is not because Procopius was out of sympathy with Christianity. It springs in part from the characteristic limitations of descriptive vocabulary and response that are perceptible in the *Wars*,[125] and in part too, from the technical requirements of panegyric. Book I of the *Buildings* may be the most finished in literary terms, but it is very uneven in treatment, and while parts are accomplished technically, it lacks in general the liveliness of some other parts of the work.

One positive quality does however emerge in this book – the physical sense of Constantinople as a city on the water. The visitor to Istanbul and the citizen of Constantinople both had the feeling, wherever they stood, of being on the edge of the water, and this comes over strongly in the *Buildings*. One of the beauties of 'Byzantium' (Procopius always prefers the old name) is the sea;[126] it washes round the city and opens out into the ocean, making the city beautiful and providing safe harbours and sure livelihood. In the middle of his catalogue of churches Procopius suddenly introduces a long eulogistic description of the harbours of the city and the meeting of the Aegean and the Euxine. It acts as an introduction for his description of Justinian's churches along the Golden Horn, SS. Laurence and Priscus and Nicolaus, [127] the last of which had its foundations far out under the water, at the top that of SS. Cosmas and Damian, 'like an acropolis',[128] and on the other side S. Anthimus and finally S. Irene the martyr.[129] Procopius loves the idea of the peaceful churches washed by the waves, which they in turn miraculously calm.[130]

---

[121] I.4.1ff. See Mango 1972b, 1975 (stressing the connection of SS. Sergius and Bacchus with the Monophysite monks protected by Theodora; against: Krautheimer 1974).
[122] I.8.19.
[123] Procopius' vagueness: I.9.14, 16.   [124] I.1.25-6.
[125] See below, Chapter 13.
[126] Cf. I.5.2-13.
[127] I.6.2-4.
[128] Above, p. 88.
[129] I.6.9f., 7.1.
[130] I.9.10 (S. Anthemius).

He turns naturally from the Golden Horn to the Bosporus: the churches
of S. Michael on either side the strait,[131] one so like the church of S. John
the Baptist in the Hebdomon, 'save only that the church of the Baptist is
not beside the sea'.[132] On the same promontory Justinian and Theodora
established their new Convent of Repentance, 'on the right as you sail
into the Euxine'.[133] And still further up the coast, on another
promontory, was the church of S. Panteleimon.[134] Procopius' Constantinople was laid out according to its sea-ways and harbours. They gave it
its beauty and its fresh breezes and they determined the arrangement of
his catalogue of churches. If we do not have much of a sense of the main
squares and streets of the city from reading the *Buildings*, we do share
the vivid experience of it as a city on water. Like the author of the
sixth-century *Life* of Eutychius, who describes the scene of a typical
approach to Constantinople by water,[135] Procopius too writes as an
inhabitant of the city whose hour of struggle was to be decided in the
waters of the Golden Horn.[136]

In comparison with the section on churches, Procopius' discussion of
secular building in the capital bears an oddly truncated look. He turns to
the secular theme with the remark that he need not go into detail about
the rebuilding of the palace after the Nika revolt because he has already
described it in detail in the *Wars* – which is not the case.[137] In fact he now
dismisses the palace with no more than a few words,[138] and spends more
time on the Augusteum, the Senate House and the Chalke. The great
Chalke mosaic showing Belisarius with all his army in a triumphal
composition with Justinian and Theodora[139] is the only pictorial scene
which Procopius describes in the *Buildings*, and the choice may have
something to do with the centrality of Belisarius,[140] though the emphasis
in the description is on the emperor and empress. For once Procopius
comments on the detail in the scene: the faces of the senators are smiling
as they offer to the emperor godlike honours for his glorious
achievements.[141] As for the equestrian statue of Justinian on a pillar in
the Augusteum, Procopius has described it earlier in the work, and at

---

[131] I.8.1-2.
[132] I.8.16.
[133] I.9.7.
[134] I.9.11.
[135] *PG* 86.2. 2360.
[136] Above all in the Avar-Persian siege of 626 when fighting actually took place in the
water, and when Blachernae was under serious threat: see Averil Cameron 1979 (= 1981,
XVIII), 18ff.
[137] I.10.1-2; cf. *Persian Wars* I.24.
[138] I.10.3, 10 the palace is 'impossible to describe, but it will be enough for future
generations to know that it is all the work of this emperor'.
[139] I.10.12-20, on which see Mango 1959, 32f.
[140] So Rubin, but see above, p. 85.
[141] I.10.19.

length.[142] Here again he is interested in the iconography and its imperial signification. The statue is in the dress of Achilles; it looks towards Persia; it carries a globe in its hand signifying empire, and on the globe a cross, 'through which alone was granted rule and victory in war'.[143] 'You would say poetically that it was the famous star of evening.'[144] Obviously the placing of this description, near the beginning of the book and out of sequence, second only to the description of S. Sophia, was absolutely deliberate. Procopius chose to emphasise the expression of the imperial theme through warfare, and included the long account of the Chalke mosaic for the same reason. In Justinian's new lay-out of the city he was much less interested, despite its importance for the development of ceremonial and imposition of a strong imperial stamp on the topography of the city.[145] The Senate House of the Augusteum evokes a rare comment about ceremony, when Procopius says that every year the ceremonies for the new year took place there.[146] Otherwise the remaining secular works that are included are the building on the site of the Arcadianai baths, and the palaces of Hieria and Iucundianai.[147] Both evoke the water scenes that Procopius likes so much: the relation between the walking space and the water lapping against it at the Arcadianai is so harmonious that strollers can have conversations with the people in the boats,[148] while bronze and stone statues surround it, so fine that 'you would think they were by Phidias the Athenian or Lysippus of Sikyon or Praxiteles'. One of them was of the Empress Theodora, a thank-offering from the city; it is beautiful, Procopius says, but not so beautiful as the original. As for the two palaces, he cannot describe them adequately, but they are all the work of Justinian.[149] What he does describe is the safe harbour that Justinian built and which removed the dangers which ships had previously experienced in those waters and made these palaces into suburban pleasure-grounds. The last item in this section is on the still-surviving Basilica cistern, by which Justinian caused a constant supply of water to be available in all seasons; 'in this way the Emperor Justinian brought it about that the people of Byzantium never lacked for drinking water'.[150]

So Book I shows the same idiosyncratic choice of material as the other

---

[142] I.2.1-12. On this famous statue see Downey 1940; Mango 1959, 174f. with note 1; Gantar 1962.

[143] I.2.11-12.

[144] I.2.10. See Gantar 1962, arguing that the evening star is a bad sign (cf. *Il.* X.26-31) and that we are meant to pick up the allusion. If so the sarcasm would be very oblique and Procopius' knowledge of Homer highly sophisticated.

[145] Cf. I.10.3-4; see Averil Cameron 1979 (= 1981, XVIII), 8f.

[146] I.10.7.

[147] I.11.1f., 16f.

[148] I.11.3.

[149] I.11.17; cf. n. 138.

[150] I.11.10-14.

parts of the work. Procopius did not set out to describe the city fully, and certainly does not do so. The churches are included for political reasons and sometimes merit only a cursory description, while the secular buildings seem to have been included on the basis of public and imperial relevance. Naturally major works put up by private individuals are passed over; there is no hint, of course, of the great church of S. Polyeuktos erected by Anicia Juliana when Justinian's power was in its early stages.[151] Nor is Procopius often interested in buildings for their own sake. He likes the curious anecdote, and emphasises anything that illustrates the imperial theme. If there is personal taste to be detected, it is rather for the natural beauties of Constantinople, its position on the shore of the Bosporus, the sight of ships sailing up the Golden Horn, and the romantic idea of great buildings with water lapping round their walls.

After Book I Procopius abruptly changes the subject. He will go on to describe the defences of the empire built by Justinian – not useless ornamental structures like the Egyptian pyramids, but all the fortifications by which the emperor made the empire safe from the barbarians.[152] Three whole chapters deal with the great fortress of Dara, which Procopius had had occasion to know well when Belisarius had been its commander.[153] But then he moves on to the other forts on the Mesopotamian border, some of which, he says, Justinian found 'in a ridiculous condition';[154] we might expect then that he will give some idea not merely of the physical building on the frontier, but also of how Byzantine frontier defences operated in theory and in practice.[155] In fact, since he does not give any indication of the chronological development of Justinian's policy nor in most cases discuss the size of actual garrisons, he has produced an account which is often little more than a list of forts interspersed with general statements to the effect that by building or restoring them Justinian thereby 'made it impossible' for the Persians to overrun Mesopotamia.[156] In practice this was an extremely easy way for them to enter Roman territory. The size of the army stationed there was

[151] Excavated by R.M. Harrison at Sarachane; final publication forthcoming, but see meanwhile Mango and Ševčenko 1961; Harrison and Fıratlı 1965-8; Mango 1976, 98; Harrison, *New Scientist*, 10 Feb., 1983, 388f. The commemorative inscription survives as *AP* I.10, from which it is entirely clear that the foundress, Anicia Juliana, openly vied with the reigning imperial house. We are told by Procopius (*Buildings* I.8.5) that Justinian would allow churches to be built only with public money or at imperial instigation – a clear reaction to Anicia Juliana's pretensions.

[152] II.1.2-3.

[153] II.1.4-3.26; see Croke and Crow 1983 and below, p. 107.

[154] II.4.14.

[155] But see above on Sinai in relation to Palestina Tertia as a whole. Liebeschuetz 1978 and 1981 offers much help towards a view of Syria less heavily weighted towards the major urban centres, and emphasises the serious lack of satisfactory defences. Procopius is as reluctant to give a general assessment when he covers Africa in Book VI: see below, Chapter 10.

[156] II.4.21, 5.1, 6.13. Garrisons: II.6.9 (Circesium), 16; 9. 2, 30; 8.24 (Zenobia); 9.8; 11.4. Much information on these and other sites in the area in Croke and Crow 1983.

by now minimal, and they were able to bypass the forts and penetrate deeply behind the lines with no effective opposition.[157] Perhaps this is why Procopius concentrates on the forts themselves. He does however reveal his awareness of the difference between Arab raids and full-scale Persian invasions, when he says that even a mud and brick fortification would be enough to keep out the former, who had no knowledge of siege warfare,[158] and he was uncomfortably conscious of the contradiction between the message of the *Buildings* and the implication of the Persian successes he had written of himself in the *Wars*.[159] Two ready explanations for Chosroes' early success against Justinian were however to hand – that the Roman fortifications were in a bad state of repair when Justinian found them, and that the Persian successes were due to the deceitful cunning of Chosroes himself, who unfairly surprised the Byzantines.[160] Neither is exactly convincing, but Procopius does his best with them.[161] At least this concentration on a personal explanation fits his own theories of historical causation as shown in his work as a whole,[162] and it is to some extent implied by his model of Byzantine-Persian diplomacy in general as a kind of gentleman's agreement between two equals, in which success for either side will tend to be attributed to the personal factors of the moment.[163] In general in this book, while Procopius gives us quite a lot of data about the Syro-Mesopotamian *limes*, it is given without much attempt at analysis, though in view of the generally vulnerable state of affairs in the region, this may be quite deliberate.[164] Only occasionally is there a sign of the special condition of an individual place – Cirrus, for instance, where Justinian was moved by his special devotion to SS. Cosmas and Damian to build splendid urban buildings in the city near which their remains were preserved.[165] Generally he was not interested in the buildings which sometimes accompanied the strengthening of a fortification: the great church of the Virgin at Antioch merits only the cliché that it would be impossible to describe its beauty and splendour.[166]

[157] See Liebeschuetz (n. 155) for the increasing ruralisation of these eastern border territories, which made them highly susceptible to invasion (see Chapter 9 below). We get a very different impression from the concentration of the *Buildings* on urban sites.

[158] II.9.4.

[159] See Chapter 9 below.

[160] Below, pp. 162f.

[161] The same attitude pervades Corippus' treatment of the Berbers throughout the *Iohannis*: Averil Cameron 1982, 38ff.; 1983. Throwing the weight of explanation on to the 'treachery' of the enemy covered up the defects in one's own side.

[162] See Chapter 13 below.

[163] Here the concentration on the personality of Chosroes, below, p. 163.

[164] We must remember that the Persian war was still going on in the 550s and that the peace of 561, bought at high cost, did not prevent hostilities from breaking out again in the next reign.

[165] II.11.4; cf. I.6.5.

[166] II.10.24.

There are three set pieces in this book – Dara, Edessa and Antioch.[167] Two of them – Dara and Antioch – seem to convict Procopius at least of misrepresentation, if not of deliberate distortion. The best known, since Downey's critique, is the account of Antioch, which describes very fully the rebuilding of the city after its sack by Chosroes in 540.[168] Not only does it omit certain well known features, however: it conflicts with what Procopius himself says in the *Wars*, where he explicitly states that the Persians had left the walls standing.[169] As in the case of Dara and elsewhere, Procopius here enhances the reputation of Justinian by exaggerating the poor condition of the fortifications when he came to the throne; a similar methodology has led him to exaggerate also the danger posed by the large rock which he describes here and in the *Wars* as being the point of entry of the Persians.[170] Panegyrical considerations have therefore certainly dictated the content as well as the form of this account.[171] But there was another problem for Procopius, at a deeper level: he had to come up with some sort of explanation for the fact that Chosroes had been able without difficulty to capture and sack the second city in the empire, without laying blame on Justinian for negligence. In the *Wars* the sack of Antioch calls forth his most agonising speculations about the mysterious and painful workings of God's providence.[172] Here he says as little as possible about the Persian sack itself and minimises Justinian's culpability by emphasising the precarious state of Antioch's defences before 540.[173] Naturally he is not entirely successful. Nevertheless the need to satisfy public opinion on this matter surely accounts for the length of this section in the *Buildings*.[174] As with the Nika revolt, there were certain matters which needed to be dealt with in the *Buildings*, yet which were politically sensitive; we can see Procopius struggling to cope.

The account of the building of a canal at Edessa to divert the river Daisan (Greek Skirtos) should have placed Procopius on less contentious ground, however.[175] He is well informed in general about Edessa,[176] and the *Secret History* refers to a description in another work of the flooding of the river, perhaps this very passage.[177] Thus again we can see how

[167] II.1-3; 7; 10.2-25.
[168] Downey 1939, which provides a translation of II.10.2-25; see too Downey 1953a.
[169] *Persian Wars* II.10.9.
[170] Ibid., 6.11f.
[171] Cf. Downey 1939, 368 n. 1, pointing out the stereotyped description of urban features at *Buildings* II.10.22.
[172] *Persian Wars* II.10.4; below, pp. 145, 232.
[173] See Downey 1939.
[174] Ibid., 374.
[175] II.7.2-10. Cf. Malalas, p. 418. For Edessa see Kirsten 1959, 1963; Segal 1970; Drijvers 1977. But he is wrong again about the dating, attributing Justin's work to Justinian: Wilkinson 1971, 284ff.
[176] Above, Chapter 1, and see p. 116, below.
[177] *SH* 18.38.

closely the three works are linked, and how the *Buildings* slots in to Procopius' writing as a whole. But with Dara there are again serious problems. The great fortress on the Persian border had enormous ideological significance for the Byzantines: 'if anything happens to Dara the evil will not stop there, but the whole empire will be shaken.'[178] It was a show-case of imperial defence, and Procopius needed to do it full justice. Moreover, he could claim to know it personally, since he had been there with Belisarius in his early days, and was present at the battle there in 530.[179] But this did not prevent him from writing highly tendentiously in other instances;[180] further, we do not know that he was back in Dara after this first phase of the Persian war, and since some of what he describes seems to postdate 530, he was not writing throughout from personal experience.[181] Certainly he makes claims for the general decay of Dara's defences at the beginning of Justinian's reign that are in direct contradiction with the other literary sources that for once can be compared with the *Buildings*,[182] and which uniformly emphasise the strength and good repair of these walls. He may even have attributed work to Justinian which was actually carried out by Anastasius; at the least, he exalted minor repairs into full-scale building. Even within his account there are inconsistencies: if the defences were in such a poor state, why does he say that Justinian's builders had only to fill in the apertures and increase the height of the wall?[183] or imply that Dara was in fact fulfilling its defensive function adequately?[184] Again Procopius does his best, within the scheme of the *Buildings*, with awkward material. He makes Justinian the personal agent, 'through God's help', of the entire project,[185] and this device helps him too. Thus it was by the 'inventiveness of the emperor' that the Persian army retreated, for he had been able, with divine aid, to find a way of depriving the besiegers of water.[186] Indeed there is so great a degree of concentration on Justinian

---

[178] *Buildings* II.1.13. See Mundell 1975, 220f.; Mango 1976, 39 and plates 38ff.; Crow 1981; Croke and Crow 1983.

[179] *Persian Wars* I.13.9-14.55. Below, pp. 157f.

[180] Below, e.g. pp. 160f.

[181] See Croke and Crow 1983.

[182] Dara was built on a splendid scale by Anastasius in 507 (Malalas, p. 399; Zachariah of Mytilene, *HE* VII.6; Evagrius, *HE* III.37). When Procopius says that the original walls were built in fear and haste (II.1.7-10), he is in direct contradiction with Zachariah, loc. cit., and Joshua the Stylite, p. 90 Wright; and since he also says that Justinian built on top of these walls (II.1.16), it is clear that they were still standing. Many other places are said in the *Buildings* to have been repaired by Justinian because their walls were in a state of collapse: I.4.9; II.5.1, 6.2, 7.5, 7.17, 8.8-25; III.4.7, 11; 6.14. The claim must be regarded as a panegyrical device on which little credence can be placed even when there is no direct evidence to the contrary, as there sometimes is. For discussion see Croke and Crow 1983, p. 150f. and for the evidence of Marcellinus on the founding of Dara see Croke 1983.

[183] II.1.14f.

[184] *Persian Wars* I.13.9ff.

[185] *Buildings* II.2.9, and cf. the personal language of e.g. II.1.18.

[186] II.2.10-21.

that Belisarius is never mentioned.[187] In fact, however, it seems that this possibility of diverting the water supply in time of siege had been a feature of the fortress since its foundation.[188] It so happens that for Dara, very unusually, there are other good literary sources available which show up Procopius' technique in a rather lurid light. For most of the material in the *Buildings* this is not the case, and Procopius' veracity and credibility has probably been exaggerated as a result. We are still not at an end with Dara, however. He attributes both the great church of Dara and the church of S. Bartholomew to Justinian[189] though the other sources suggest that both were earlier. And if we look more closely at the patterning of the section we can see that the larger part of the three chapters here devoted to Dara is in fact taken up by the thematic demonstration of Justinian's special powers and the ways in which he received divine aid. It is of Dara that Procopius tells the story of the confounding of the clever architects Anthemius and Isidore by the dream received by Chryses of Alexandria, and the miraculous way in which Justinian arrived at the same conclusion before he saw Chryses' diagram.[190] We might attribute this heavy emphasis on the theme of imperial inspiration in an account supposedly of the physical characteristics of a great fortress to Procopius' awareness that he was deliberately having to distort his material to suit the aims of this particular work. He goes as far as he can with manipulation of the physical description, but that can only take him so far; the concentration on God's protection of Justinian is a device which can be exploited at greater length and more easily. But the idiosyncrasies of Procopius show through as well: he is not interested here in the improbable antiquarian detail in Evagrius that the fort was named Dara because it was near the spot where Alexander had defeated Darius,[191] but his attention is caught by the peculiarities of Dara's water supply and their tactical implications. The whole Dara account is given great weight and prominence by Procopius, and as a factual description it is as vulnerable as the Antioch section. But it is also as instructive for Procopius' methods and aims in the *Buildings*, and for the real difficulties he had in dealing with delicate material in a manner appropriate and convincing for a panegyric. It is far from being a simple matter of whether or not Procopius is 'telling the truth'.

In one case, however, the evidence of the *Buildings* does seem preferable to what he says in the other works. In the *Secret History* Procopius states categorically that no public building was restored or

---

[187] Rubin 1954, 304 tries unconvincingly to explain this away.

[188] Cf. the description of Dara in the reign of Anastasius by the pilgrim account of Theodosius, *de situ terrae sanctae* 29 (Geyer 1965, 124).

[189] II.3.26. Cf. Zachariah, *HE* VII.6; Theodore Lector, p. 157 Hansen.

[190] II.3.1f.

[191] *HE* III.37.

anything else done in the whole of Greece, including Athens.[192] But in the *Buildings* he states equally firmly that all the cities south of Thermopylae were made safe and their walls renewed; he mentions specifically Corinth, Athens and Plataea.[193] Not only that: Justinian left nowhere unfortified, building new walls on the Isthmus with forts and towers.[194] Here the building work seems to be confirmed by archeology. In particular, Justinian's Isthmian wall can still be seen in part today. It may have been built after the serious earthquake of 551.[195] When the rebuilding took place material was reused from pagan temples including the theatre and the temple of Poseidon.[196] At Athens, too, signs of repair were seen during excavation of the inner and outer walls.[197] Again, however, and naturally, so, we can detect signs of exaggeration in Procopius' account. He claims that Justinian 'made the whole of the Peloponnese impermeable to the enemy, even if they should succeed in damaging the fortification at Thermopylae',[198] a claim that was to prove quite unfounded when later in the century the Avars and Slavs undoubtedly reached the Peloponnese and further. This enhancement of Justinian's role, the focus on the emperor himself and the tendency to claim repairs as new building is the exact inverse of the technique of the *Secret History*, where he is personally credited with everything that is wrong with the state. Here even the unequivocal statement about the rebuilding of the walls of Thermopylae itself turns out to be questionable, since carbon-14 dating indicates that renovations took place earlier than the sixth century.[199]

In the *Buildings* as a whole, Procopius produces the impression that a sudden and overwhelming change was brought about by Justinian's building policies, as though the empire was restored and revitalised solely through his efforts and within a short space of time. Whether this was how things actually were is another matter. It was standard for rulers from Augustus on to seek to convey exactly this impression.[200] In the case of the *Buildings* archeologists have however been too ready – understandably in view of the lack of better information in so many cases – to believe the claims and to attribute to Justinian any roughly sixth-century fortification. The sections on the Crimea in Book III illustrate both this point and the shortcomings of Procopius'

---

[192] *SH* 26.33.

[193] *Buildings* IV.2.24.

[194] IV.2.27-8.

[195] Hohlfelder 1977, arguing that a previous trans-Isthmian wall held firm against the Persians in 540 (see *Persian Wars* II.4.10f.) and that this partially surviving Justinianic wall belongs to the period after the earthquake of 551 (for which see *Gothic Wars* IV.25.16-23).

[196] Hohlfelder 1977, 178.

[197] Thompson 1959, 65.

[198] IV.2.28.

[199] See Cherf 1982, and now in *AJA* 88 (1984), 594-98.

[200] See n. 46.

geography, for while the area is dotted with late antique fortification, often assumed on the basis of Procopius to be Justinianic, there is no agreement on the identity of the 'long walls' which he mentions here, nor sufficiently precise dating available from archaeological investigation to be certain of identifying sixth-century work; at the same time Procopius' indications as to the position of Dory have given rise to widely differing modern views.[201] It is most unlikely that Procopius knew the Crimea at first hand, and in general it is dangerous, though obviously tempting, to press his statements too hard. Here, typically, he intersperses apparently hard data with hearsay about the Goths in the area, suggesting perhaps that he got his information from Goths he had met on campaign or later. The effects of Justinian's building programme must have varied far more from area to area than Procopius allows us to see. North Africa after the reconquest, for instance, was the scene of much clearer and more deliberate imperial effort.[202] But in many areas it was more a matter of gradual development, following existing patterns of defence building and the works of earlier emperors, in particular Anastasius, or of changing circumstances which permitted the conversion or renovation of classical buildings.[203] Procopius of course was not interested in gradual change, nor was he trying to analyse the broader developments of his own day. The *Buildings* is not a factual record, despite its appearance of documentary authenticity, and it needs extremely sophisticated and cautious interpretation, even in the more 'factual' parts. Its theme is not so much the real physical history of the empire in this period as the innovative and restorative activity of Justinian. In its focus on personality as a main factor in effecting historical change, this was a theme which despite the surface contradictions between this work and the *Secret History*, was curiously close to Procopius' own taste.

There was however a seamy side to the 'official' version of Justinian's building. His constructions, put up in such great numbers and so quickly, were often shoddy.[204] The churches depended for their effect on the splendour of their interiors, and especially the marble that they could still use (it was by now coming to be in short supply and soon virtually stopped being quarried); perhaps this is why so many contemporary

[201] III.7.10-17. Long walls: III.7.17. Dory: III.7.13. Justinianic dating: Yakobson 1964, with Firsov 1979; Dory: opp. citt., with Solomonik and Dombrovsky 1968, Veimarn 1980. There is clear evidence of fifth-century construction in the forts of the S-W Crimea, while work said to be Justinianic by Yakobson is felt by others to be medieval. I am very grateful to Dr John Smedley for this information.

[202] See Averil Cameron 1982. The question is, however, whether reconquest brought benefits or the opposite – and whether it was liberation, as the Byzantines claimed, or rather occupation; also how much of this building was centrally organized and financed, thus 'Justinianic' in Procopius' sense.

[203] A gradual change that was taking place in differing degrees all over the empire: see Averil Cameron 1979 (= 1981, XVIII), 29f. and especially the works of Foss there cited.

[204] There is much interesting discussion of the Justinianic rebuilding in Mango 1976.

ekphraseis, including the section on S. Sophia in the *Buildings*, spend so much of their time praising the coloured marbles.[205] Another side too to the building activity of Justinian is suggested by the circumstances of the rebuilding of S. Sophia: it was made possible by confiscations from the rich, rendered easier by throwing on to the senatorial class the blame for the Nika revolt which made the rebuilding necessary.[206] It was far from inevitable or easy in itself, and the unexpected windfall of the Vandal victory in 534 was another major factor in making it possible. Once started, its prestige value was so great that there is no doubt truth in Procopius' accusation in the *Secret History* that it diverted funds that could have been better used elsewhere.

As a source of information about Justinian's building activity the *Buildings* is both exciting and disappointing. It is the most detailed and varied single source, and presents a wealth of unparalleled information. But its literary purpose, together with Procopius' limitation of interest, means that it presents only a selection of the material, and then with a clear slant.[207] Procopius is not much interested in the sorts of question that modern archeologists and art historians would like to have answered: he does not bother to write about masonry, or style, nor does he concern himself with iconography except when it has an imperial connection. The relation between public and private building, between religious and secular art and architecture, are not matters on which he gives much help. Certain aspects of the Byzantine frontier system and its working emerge from his writing, but he does not often address himself to the question directly, even in Book VI, where the section on the province of Africa is perhaps the most solid and informative part of the *Buildings*.[208] And since he deals with imperial building, he does not often raise the issue of the economics of building – how buildings were financed, who kept them in repair, how they related to the general economy of the area, whether there was significant variation from province to province, and if so, why. He thinks rather in terms of cities, and of the urban stereotypes of the Late Roman period, though the cities themselves were already changing from the classical to the medieval form. All over the empire, archeology shows that a transformation was occuring during the sixth century. The open spaces of the classical city – the baths, fora and public buildings which Procopius records, for instance at Justiniana Prima or Ras Kapoudia in North Africa,[209] were

---

[205] Ibid., 24.

[206] See Downey 1950, 262, and cf. *SH* 12.12f. The rebuilding was announced by Justinian together with the claim of victory over the 'tyrants' – Malalas, pp. 476f.

[207] We would never deduce from Procopius, for example, that there had been population growth and ruralisation in the eastern provinces: see Tchalenko 1953-58 (N. Syria): Liebeschuetz 1981, 19f.; Patlagean 1979; Gichon 1961 (Palestine).

[208] See below, Chapter 10.

[209] Nn. 27, 81.

giving way to the crowded and winding streets of the medieval souks; the houses were soon rather to be found huddling round the fortified citadel enclosing the bishop's palace and the main church.[210] Of this complex and subtle development there is little sign in the *Buildings*, with its bland assumption of Late Roman continuity, any more than there is any awareness of the likely long-term effects of the great plague of 541/2, which Procopius describes in clinical detail,[211] but which was also a major precipitating factor in accelerating these urban changes.[212]

The *Buildings*, more than either of Procopius' other works, is constrained by its political and literary purpose. It ignores so many developments obvious from other sources, such as, for instance, the intimate connection between imperial building and ceremonial in sixth-century Constantinople.[213] It is neither a straightforward description of new building, nor an analytic view of the overall development of fortification or church building. On the other hand, it stands out from the *Wars* by its unforced acceptance of the notion of God-given rule, with its implication of the closeness of the emperor to God, and its assumption of an unhurried progression of Byzantine power, discretely marked off from the surrounding barbarians by a clearly defined system of physical constructions. We are not entitled to dismiss this view as due to the literary conventions and requirements of panegyric, as though Procopius could not 'really' have thought this way. As we have seen, this set of ideas about the world and the place of emperor and state within it in relation to God, is simply the inverse of that in the *Secret History*. Procopius did not question it – only the specific contribution of Justinian himself at a time when all seemed particularly black. It was precisely because Procopius came to feel, during the writing of the *Wars* and at the time of composition of the *Secret History*, that Justinian had deviated catastrophically from the real and necessary role of the emperor that his criticism there was so acute and so passionate. In what may seem a paradoxical sense, the *Buildings*, more than the *Wars* or the *Secret History*, represents Procopius' 'real' views about emperor and empire, while the other two works trace his disappointment that the reality of Justinian diverged so far from the ideal.

[210] See e.g. Foss 1976, 16, 42ff.; Claude 1969, 60ff.; Hodges and Whitehouse 1983 (n. 2), pp. 54ff.

[211] Above, pp. 40f.

[212] Rightly emphasised by Patlagean 1979, 301ff.

[213] For which see Averil Cameron 1979 (= 1981, XVIII), 6ff.

CHAPTER SEVEN

Procopius and Christianity

Procopius did not write a Christian history; yet we have seen more than enough by now to realise that for all its suprastructure of classicising scepticism – manifested, if only superficially, in all three works – the underlying approach of Procopius' writing is thoroughly Christian, and recognisably late antique in type. The older view of Procopius as a 'sceptic', based in general on a misunderstanding of his habit of stylistic affectation, can no longer convince.[1] Nor should we try to save Procopius from himself by attempting to harmonise the apparent inconsistencies in his religious statements. We can admit now that all his works rest on similar basic assumptions about the reality of divine providence, the polarity of good and evil, the special relation of the emperor to the supernatural, the possibility of the miraculous. Further, we can see that for all his élitism and high culture, Procopius' religious position is not so very far from that of his contemporaries. Thus dislodged from the pedestal of his supposed rationalism he seems less impressive, perhaps, but also more interesting. It still remains to look more closely at this aspect of his work and to see whether it is possible to approach it in a less prejudiced manner – to see, in fact, whether we can uncover the basic assumptions which pervade his writing and his thought, the categories within which he operates, and the ways in which he diverges from contemporary religious expression. The three works present a unified system of religious discourse which is crucial to our understanding of Procopius as a historian, since it is within these terms that his historical thinking operates, as much in the *Wars* as in the shorter works.

To begin with the texture of Procopius' writing. It is dominated by statements and expressions which assume familiarity with and acceptance of a Christian world-view. We may cite examples of different kinds as illustrations of this generalisation. Thus, understandably, he will often put Christian sentiments into his speeches;[2] but equally often

---

[1] So Dahn 1865; Teuffel 1871 and more recently Downey 1949; Veh 1952; Evans 1971. Against this approach: Averil Cameron 1966 (= 1981, I); see also Evans 1971, 86f.

[2] *Persian Wars* II.4.17f. (letter of Justinian); 11.30 (Thomas of Apamea); 19.14 (Belisarius); *Vandal Wars* I.9.12, 16 (letters of Justinian); 12.13 (Belisarius); 16.14 (letter of Justinian); 19.6 (Belisarius); 25.18 (letter of Gelimer) etc.

he expresses them himself without equivocation. Narses gives thanks
after his defeat of Totila and never ceases attributing it all to God,
Procopius says, 'as indeed was the case';[3] 'God saved Apamea';[4] only God
knows the explanation for the plague.[5] Assumptions of miraculous
intervention are common: S. Peter protects a broken part of the Roman
walls during the siege by Vitigis;[6] the mosaic of Theodoric at Naples
gradually disintegrates, correctly foretelling Roman victory;[7] Belisarius'
wine jars overflow, indicating victory in Africa.[8] It is clear that all these
are to be interpreted as specifically Christian miracles, even when
Procopius does not actually say so. When, for instance, some Romans try
to open the doors of the temple of Janus and they will not move, he takes
it as a sign that when people try to go back to the 'old belief', i.e. to
paganism, they are bound to fail.[9] Sometimes omens are included as
though simply part of the tradition of classical historiography, like the
woman at Edessa who produced a child with two heads.[10] Procopius is
interested in the Sibylline oracles for their own sake, and disputes the
interpretation placed on them by some Roman patricians during the
siege of Rome not because he thinks they are untrue but because they are
actually confused and rambling, as he knows himself,[11] and he comments
in a worldly-wise manner on the excited recourse to prophecy in 548,
when disasters and portents followed hard on each other's heels.[12] But all
this is in a general context of acceptance. Take the Vandal expedition: no
one, says Procopius, shared the emperor's enthusiasm for the venture
until a bishop ('one of the priests whom they call bishops') relayed to
Justinian a dream in which God had told him that He was on the
emperor's side.[13] Procopius then claims that he too had had such a
dream, which had removed his own doubts.[14] The entry of Belisarius into
Carthage confirmed this belief in divine aid, for then too, Procopius
claims, S. Cyprian advised his people in a dream that vengeance would
come over the Arian Vandals, and, sure enough, the Catholics ('the
Christians who practise the orthodox faith') were able to repossess their
basilica and use the lamps and ornaments put up by the Arians, just as
Belisarius entered the palace and feasted from food prepared for the

[3] *Gothic Wars* IV.33.1. Further, above, pp. 30f.
[4] *Persian Wars* II.11.28.
[5] Ibid., 22.2.
[6] *Gothic Wars* I.23.4-8. But whereas Theophylact Simocatta justifies the inclusion of such stories on religious grounds (*Hist.* VIII.14.1) Procopius includes them without comment.
[7] Ibid., 24.22-7.
[8] *Gothic Wars* III.35.4-8.
[9] I.25.18-25.
[10] IV.14.39-40.
[11] I.24.28-37.
[12] III.29.18.
[13] *Vandal Wars* I.10.1f., especially 18.
[14] I.12.3.

Vandal king.[15] This passage, one of the most colourful and intense in the *Wars*, recording a high peak in imperial achievement through the generalship of Belisarius, is most carefully constructed within a strong framework of Christian providential intervention. A Christian dream marks the achievement of the great expedition as an earlier one, reinforced by Procopius' own, had marked its dispatch.

Even in passages where he pretends unfamiliarity with Christian technical terms, Procopius writes from a Christian point of view. For instance, on the fall of John the Cappadocian, who is forced to live as priest – 'not a bishop, however, but the sort they call presbyter',[16] he remarks: 'God, I am sure, did not want John's punishment to stop here, but was preparing a bigger retribution for him'; and then: 'it seemed as though the judgment of God was exacting from him penalties for the whole world'.[17] The monks who fell asleep after a feast during the defence of Amida and were all killed by the Persians are called 'those who are the most ascetic of Christians, whom they call monks',[18] but are juxtaposed with the story of the holy man James, protected from external harm by his holiness.[19] In the context of the raids of Chosroes on the towns of Syria and Mesopotamia, during which the defences were usually led by the local bishops, Procopius tells quite straightforwardly how Apamea was saved by its relic of the True Cross, paraded through the church to the accompaniment of a miraculous flame over the bishop's head,[20] while the people wept for joy. Even the city's narrow escape and the heavy payment which Chosroes exacted did not dampen Procopius' faith that God had saved it. This story is not entirely satisfactory as Procopius tells

---

[15] I.21.6 (the food prepared for Gelimer); 17-25 (S. Cyprian). For the probable identification of this basilica see Frend 1976, 25, 27f.; Ennabli 1975, 15-6 (the so-called Basilica of Sainte Monique outside the walls, overlooking the sea). Duval 1972, 1075 is more cautious. Very large numbers of funerary inscriptions of the fourth to sixth centuries have been published by Mme. Ennabli from this basilica. For the Arian problem in Byzantine Africa see below, Chapter 10.

[16] *Persian Wars* I.25.31. This kind of affectation is discussed by Averil and Alan Cameron 1964 (= 1981, III). One of the most extreme examples is the passage about Moses at *Vandal Wars* II.10.13f., built into a digression on the Phoenicians. Procopius does not actually use any of his objective formulae here, but to call Moses merely 'a wise man' who led the Hebrews out of Egypt (II.10.13) is extraordinary in a text of the period. Unlike most of his contemporaries, Procopius has almost completely excluded Scriptural allusions from his work; cf. p. 92 n. 66.

[17] *Persian Wars* I.25.36, 41.

[18] *Persian Wars* I.7.23. Contrast Procopius' more admiring remarks on the monks of Sinai in the *Buildings*, V.8.4 (above, p. 96). For the monks of Amida see John Ephesus, *PO* 18. 607ff.

[19] *Persian Wars* I.7.5. Unlike Justinian's asceticism, a sign of his evil nature (or in the *Buildings*, of his virtue: p. 88 above), that of the holy man is his protection. For a convenient selection of examples see Benedicta Ward 1980, 65 (Bees); 80-1 (Amoun; 91 (Helle), all examples of the saint's power over nature and the animals, Procopius actually uses here the technical word *askein*.

[20] *Persian Wars* II.11.14-20; this miracle was witnessed as a boy by the church historian Evagrius (*HE* IV.26).

it. He introduces it with an odd circumlocution – 'a portion of the cross on which it is agreed that Christ once willingly endured His punishment',[21] and he passes from the miracle to the curious tale of Chosroes' circus races, held in the Hippodrome in imitation of Constantinople, and in which the Persian king, supporting the Greens against Justinian's favourite Blues, resorted to cheating when his side was losing and then impaled a Persian whose life he had just agreed to spare (evidence for Procopius of Chosroes' bad character).[22] Still, he has no doubts that the miracle was genuine, or that the relic itself had been brought to Apamea in a romantically secret way, as the locals claimed.[23] Despite its somewhat awkward articulation, then, the whole episode shows Procopius accepting a historical causation in which the key factor is the intervention of God, guaranteed by due deployment of relics.

This is an important realisation. It makes the interpretation of other passages possible. For example, it is highly unlikely that Procopius' failure to mention the Image of Edessa in the context of the miraculous escape of the city from Chosroes in 544 is due to reasons of religious purism or a rationalist distaste for relics.[24] In fact his treatment of Edessa's experiences in 540 (when Chosroes first attacked) is among the most explicitly Christian in the *Wars*.[25] Procopius is sure that it was by the will of God that Edessa was saved,[26] and explains why by telling the famous story of King Abgar's letter to Jesus and Christ's reply, very possibly drawing on Eusebius' *Church History*.[27] It is clear that in Procopius' view the letter and reply really were exchanged in the time of Christ. Of the supposed addition to Christ's letter, he says that even if it did not represent the words of Jesus, nevertheless God deliberately fostered belief in its contents (promising safety for Edessa) so as to protect the city – an equally pious if more sophisticated sentiment.[28] In general, Procopius is completely accepting of the religious explanation of Chosroes' retreat, even if he is critical of the authenticity of the 'addendum' to the letter. If he does not mention the image of Edessa, the icon of Christ not made by human hands reputedly discovered in a niche in the city wall during the siege of 544, it is not because he disapproved of it, but most probably because the story of its 'finding' was not yet known to him, writing as he was only a few years after the event.[29] In his lengthy

---

[21] II.11.14.

[22] Ibid., 31-8. But Belisarius was also capable of impaling offenders – *Vandal Wars* II.1.8.

[23] II.11.14 (brought secretly by a Syrian long ago).

[24] So Runciman 1931, 244. But see Averil Cameron 1980b and 1984a.

[25] *Persian Wars* II.12.6-30.

[26] II.12.30.

[27] Cf. II.12.26, referring to 'those who wrote the history of the time', in contrast to 'the men of Edessa' who are his source for the rider to the letter. See Rubin 1954, 41ff. But we must remember that there were probably many versions of the Abgar legend in circulation, in both Greek and Syriac (see Averil Cameron 1980b, 21, n. 29).

[28] II.12.26, 30.

[29] The author of the Chronicle of Edessa, writing soon after 544, did not know of the

account of the second episode, in 544, which concentrates exclusively on the military side, there is no mention of a miraculous delivery.[30] Procopius, as we can see, is just as pious and prone to report miracles as Evagrius, who wrote about the finding of the image a generation later,[31] and would have included the story had he known it, as he did the miracle of the True Cross at Apamea.

Other passages formerly misinterpreted can now be re-read, in particular the famous account of the sack of Antioch in 540. Procopius writes: 'When I write about such a great disaster and pass it on to posterity, my head spins and I cannot understand why God should want to raise up a man or a place and then cast him down and extinguish him for no apparent reason.'[32] Far from implying real scepticism, this is a statement of uncomprehending faith. Procopius goes on to say that God always does things for a good cause, even if humans cannot understand the reason. In this case the disaster was foretold, in Procopius' narrative, by a miracle – the standards of the troops spontaneously turned round.[33] But most important of all, Procopius shows in his treatment of this, one of the worst disasters of the reign, and one which as we have seen he went to some lengths to minimise in the *Buildings*,[34] that he considers a religious explanation entirely acceptable, and that not so much an explanation as a statement of blind faith.

If there is no real scepticism in Procopius' work, it is also unlikely that there is a real effort to reconcile the pagan concept of Tychê with divine providence.[35] Sometimes he uses the language of Tychê merely as a way of expressing his views on historical causation in acceptably traditional terms; it should not therefore be over-interpreted. He remarks in *Wars* Book VII that God had decided that Totila should prosper, and that consequently however much Belisarius seemed favoured by fortune, his plans were bound to be thwarted.[36] Up to this point Procopius seems to

---

image (ed. I. Guidi, *CSCO Script. Syri* III.14.1, Paris, 1903, trans., p. 11). The earliest certain reference to the miraculous image is in Evagrius, *HE* IV.37, from *c.* 590. Naturally by the tenth century, when the *Narratio de Imagine Edessena* (PG 113, 425ff.) was composed, the story had been much elaborated.

[30] II.26-7. The return of Chosroes to Edessa is however presented as a religious crusade – Procopius was not averse to such explanations as such.

[31] N. 29. The image is also mentioned in the Syriac hymn on the rebuilt cathedral of Edessa, but the date is uncertain (Averil Cameron 1980b, 9f.; McVey 1983).

[32] *Persian Wars* II.10.4.

[33] II.10.1f.

[34] P. 106 above. Of course, in laying the responsibility on God, he can divert attention from Byzantine neglect or incompetence.

[35] So Downey 1949. See also Elferink 1967, Evans 1971, 93f. Against: Veh 1951/52, 26. There is no warrant for Evans's supposition (pp. 99f.) that Procopius reflects 'the thought-world of Alexandria, and, we may conjecture, of Gaza'.

[36] *Gothic Wars* III.13.15-19. For the ending of the passage cf. *Persian Wars* II.12.30 (after Procopius' comment on the rider to Jesus's letter at Edessa). Neither ending should be taken at face value; when Procopius does interpose his own views, he likes to undercut them in some such way.

be relegating Tychê to the level of success in the world, whereas he attributes causative force to God; but then he goes on to write of 'fortune' thwarting the plans of those whom God wishes to fail, as if fortune is an instrument of God's will. As if to confuse us still further, he concludes the section with a typically deprecatory remark – 'whether this is so or not I cannot tell'. There is another such seeming harmonisation between the very different concepts of divine providence and Tychê in the *Vandal Wars*, where Procopius writes that before the battle of Ad Decimum he was moved to wonder at the way in which God manipulates events to their desired conclusion while men are left in ignorance.[37] God's purpose, he says, is to make a path for Tychê to bring about the appointed end. But we should not make too much of these passages. Procopius was no philosopher or theologian. He was feeling the constraints of working within a tradition of historical writing in which appeals to Tychê and direct statements from the historian about causation were canonical. Even the fifth-century ecclesiastical historians were not exempt from this obligation; but for Christians – or indeed simply for writers who in the natural order of things had to write about events in which Christianity played a large role and which were largely interpreted by contemporaries in a Christian light – there were obvious problems in fulfilling these expectations. It seems unreasonable to look for total consistency in Procopius' work, therefore. He can say that men call the power of God fortune,[38] because they do not understand it; he can write of the jealousy of fortune,[39] of 'fate',[40] or he can refer to 'some chance', using the same word in a dilute sense.[41] Probably most telling are those cases where in different passages he uses the same language interchangeably of Tychê and of God.[42] Procopius had a strong sense of the unexpectedness of events, as of the role of the irrational in history, and this led him, as we have seen, to give serious attention to the miraculous. But it also meant that he still found the classical conception of Tychê a useful one. He was not successful in developing a uniform philosophy of history. His thinking may even seem shallow, for he was far more interested in people and events than in theoretical analysis of causation. A man content to

---

[37] *Vandal Wars* I.18.2.

[38] *Gothic Wars* IV.12.33f.

[39] *Gothic Wars* II.8.1. Procopius uses the term *phthonos*, in fact standard in Christian texts for the Devil (Averil Cameron 19066 = 1981, I, 477). His terminology may appear superficially classical (cf. the frequent use of *to kreitton* and *to theion*), but must be judged in the total context of his work: see Rubin 1954, 60f. (full collection of references to Tyche etc.: ibid., 56-70). Rubin's instinct is right: 'Prokopios ist auch hier nicht unkompliziert sondern komplexer Spätzeitmensch', p. 70.

[40] *Vandal Wars* I.4.20 etc. Clearly this terminology, especially, as often, at the end of an episode, owes a stylistic debt to Herodotus.

[41] See *Gothic Wars* I.24.5-6.

[42] *Vandal Wars* I.19.25 (God) with *Gothic Wars* III.13.16 (Tyche); *Persian Wars* II.9.13f. juxtaposes God and Tyche.

see in barbarian treachery and the like an adequate explanation of Byzantine foreign relations has not given very much thought to the real causes of events. And there was always the problem of maintaining the balance between linguistic purity and conveying the whole truth. But if there is a 'real' Procopius he is to be found rather in the miracle stories and the touching acceptance of what God wills than in the elaborate but clumsy evocations of a classical Tychê, or the incongruous Herodotean tags.[43] We need only to reflect, first, that there are no philosophising passages about Tychê in the *Buildings*, and secondly, that the more elaborate attempts to 'harmonise' Tychê with divine providence (and they are few) are all directly concerned with Procopius' closest personal preoccupations – that is, they have all to do specifically with Belisarius or with Justinian and Theodora.[44] Far from being symptomatic of Procopius' real views, they are self-conscious and untypical.

There is, however, one area where Procopius does seem to emerge as a genuine critic of establishment Christianity – in his condemnation of doctrinal controversy and persecution. His is one of very few voices raised in late antique literature against the imperial preoccupation with correct belief. 'I will not even record the points of disagreement [between Byzantium and Rome on doctrine], since I think it crazy folly to enquire what the real nature of God is. Humans cannot even understand human things fully, let alone what pertains to the nature of God. So I intend to keep safely quiet about such matters, simply so that existing beliefs shall not be discarded. I can say nothing about God except that He is totally good and has everything within His power. But let each say what he thinks he knows about this, both priest and layman.'[45] This is the opinion of the believer, not the sceptic. But Procopius returns to the theme elsewhere. Justinian's taste for doctrinal controversy is a recurring feature in Procopius' critique; he can write in the *Secret History* that in his zeal for orthodoxy Justinian acted only 'under the pretext of piety; he did not think that putting men to death counted as murder unless they were on his own persuasion.'[46] Naturally the *Buildings* presents the other side of the case: 'finding that doctrine was at first wavering and tending

---

[43] For the latter, see e.g. *Persian Wars* I.24.31; II.8.14, 13.22; *Vandal Wars* II.13.22; *Gothic Wars* I.4.4. See Rubin 1954, 62. There is no obvious way to distinguish these as more or less meaningful than the whole repertoire of Herodotean imitations of a more trivial sort.

[44] So Elferink 1968, 134.

[45] *Gothic Wars* I.3.6. I am grateful to Geoffrey de Ste. Croix for letting me see a forthcoming paper from which the rarity of Procopius' attitude strikingly emerges, though a few passages in church historians indeed take the same view (Allen 1981, 60). It is important to note that here Procopius places a high priority on the maintenance of existing belief, as we would expect from his general insistence on order (pp.239f. below). In practice formal doctrinal disputations were a feature of Justinian's reign (see Guillaumont 1969/70, 46f.; Evans 1970, 149ff.; Brock 1981).

[46] *SH* 13.7. At *Gothic Wars* I.13.9f. Procopius expresses disapproval at Amalafrid's attempt to enforce Arianism on his wife.

inevitably towards plurality, he crushed all the pathways to error and set the faith firmly on one foundation'.[47] But in the *Wars* Procopius comes surprisingly close to the outspokenness of the *Secret History*, when he makes Arsaces, inciting Artabanes to revolt, say that Justinian is an easy target, sitting up night after night with a bunch of old priests discussing the Scriptures.[48] A little later in the same book he comes near to blaming Justinian directly for neglecting the war as a result of over-concern for doctrinal matters –[49] exactly the charge made in the *Secret History*. The bloodshed caused by Justinian's persecution of heretics runs through the *Secret History* too.[50] It is hard to imagine that if Procopius had fulfilled his promise to write elsewhere about these ecclesiastical matters he would have done so with any sympathy.[51] His hatred for the official policy of persecution probably had personal roots, and may have been less unusual than it now seems in a man of Procopius' class.[52] The many thousands who were 'converted' by Justinian's missionaries, and the smaller numbers who were themselves persecuted for their beliefs must have shared Procopius' opinions of imperial policy. A disinclination for theology, resentment against persecution when one risked being one of its objects are reactions that are entirely understandable in a sixth-century context, even if there are few surviving literary expressions of them. But equally, we must remember, they could coexist with acceptance of the basic Christian interpretation, and with approval of a policy of conversion. It would be politic to protect oneself in a work such as the *Buildings*. But Procopius and others, living in a split and ambivalent society, inevitably found that their mentality was ambivalent too. Christian/pagan is far too crude an antithesis to apply to most writers of the age, especially Procopius, in whose work there are so many gradations and many shades of opinion.

In fact we learn a good deal from Procopius about the importance of missionary activity in imperial foreign policy. He is perfectly aware that Justinian used conversion as a prime instrument in his relations with foreign peoples, and in the *Wars* he allows this theme to come through

[47] *Buildings* I.1.9.

[48] *Gothic Wars* II.32.9; cf. *SH* 12.30f. But these passages were all written when Procopius was at his most critical of Justinian (below, Chapter 11). At an earlier stage he was ready to take a more pragmatic view (n. 45).

[49] III.35.11; cf. *SH* 12.27; 18.29-30. See n. 48. Udal'cova 1975, 185 takes this indifference to theological dispute as a class feature in Procopius.

[50] *SH* 13.4f.; 18.30, 34; 19.11. It is part however of the rhetoric of accusation, and linked to the hostility to the war policy expressed especially at *SH* 18; it does not imply blanket disapproval of the reconquest policy and all that went with it (below, p. 140).

[51] *SH* 1.14; 11.33; 26.18.

[52] John of Ephesus, acting for Justinian, claimed to have denounced 'a mob of grammarians, sophists, scholastici and doctors' (Nau 1897, 481f.); for Justinian's religious policies in general see Thurman 1968. Agathias agreed with Procopius: *Hist.* I.7. See also above, pp. 92f. on Procopius' opinions about the Samaritans. Because of this critique, Bonfante saw Procopius as a heretic himself (Bonfante 1933, 283ff.), but see Veh 1951/52, 29.

very clearly. There may be some problems, for instance, in his account of early Nubia, but he is essentially correct in laying stress on the official conversion of the Blemmyes and Nobadae in the reign of Justinian.[53] It now seems possible that Christianity had already penetrated Nubia in the fifth century, since Christian silver has been found in fifth-sixth century tombs, but from Procopius' point of view, focussing on diplomatic connections and foreign relations at the inter-state level, the decisive move came when Narses, acting on official orders from Constantinople, dismantled the temples of Philae; once this symbolic gesture had been made, Byzantine missions could follow, and temples were steadily converted into churches. Doubtless the reality of Christianisation was much less tidy, but Procopius' black and white presentation is less over-simplified than merely conditioned by the necessary emphasis in a secular and diplomatic history.[54] On the other hand, in his short account of the Ethiopic conquest of the Himyarite kingdom in South Arabia, while paying due attention to the religious motives for the expedition (Christian annexation of the kingdom of the Jewish ruler who had martyred South Arabian Christians in Najran), he tells the story as though it was a local dispute. There is no hint of Byzantine help, or of the existing Byzantine involvement in this area.[55] We know a good deal about these matters from others sources, especially the Greek *Martyrium Arethae* and the Syriac *Book of the Himyarites*; but Procopius' interest is limited to the expeditions of Caleb the Ethiopian Negus and the establishment of Abraha;[56] he does not consider

[53] Nubia: Rubin 1954, 101 for bibliography. Blemmyes and Nobadae: Kirwan 1966 (discussing *Persian Wars* I.19.27); Engelhardt 1974, 31ff., 46f.; Hardy 1968, 36f.; Frend 1975a. Procopius' assumption that missions are appropriate activity for a Christian monarch: Veh 1951/52, 9.

[54] Kirwan 1966, 127f.; Frend 1975a, 10. The main source apart from Procopius is John of Ephesus, *HE* IV.6, 53, who describes the continuation of Justinian's policy later in the century. Procopius therefore records the first symbolic act in a lengthy process, and writes at a relatively early stage, when, seen through official eyes, the prognosis seemed highly favourable for the success of Justinian's efforts. For the Gospel book from Qasr Ibrim, possibly brought to Nubia during these missions, see Plumley 1976. Again, Procopius's account should not be over-pressed, as though he were trying to give a fully comprehensive history of the problem.

[55] *Persian Wars* I.19-20. On these matters see Shahid 1964, 1970, 1971, 1979; Sartre 1982; Engelhardt 1974, 27ff.; Avi-Yonah 1976, 237f.

[56] As usual, Procopius makes rather straightforward points, not aspiring to a full discussion of the highly complex network of alliances on the Arabian frontiers. He had not been as far south as this himself, and it is asking too much to expect from him a sophisticated awareness of all the problems of the area. Procopius shows little or no consciousness of the difficulties of maintaining the frontier south of the Euphrates (p. 104 above), and his vague and biassed awareness of the phylarchs of Palestine (he does not seem to know for instance of the journey of his 'Kaisos' – Imrulqays the poet – to Constantinople in c. 533: see *Persian Wars* I.20.9 and Sartre 1982, 173f.) must in part reflect the limitations of his information. In particular (unlike John of Ephesus) he is unconcerned with the important role played by the Monophysitism of the Ghassanids. Particularly unsatisfactory in this passage are Procopius' naive remarks on the diplomatic significance of the Palm Groves (I.19.8f.) and later his brief note of the embassy to Axum under Julianus (I.20.9f.; contrast the attention given to it by Malalas, p. 456).

the persecutions as such (though he makes his disapproval clear) or the church-building that followed. As a discussion of these complex relationships under Justin I and Justinian, Procopius' account is, in our terms, a disappointment. But for our present purpose it is interesting to see that he is led into this subject by the theme of conversion in foreign policy in the immediately preceding chapter on Nubia, and that he shows disapproval of military campaigns undertaken for motives of Christianisation or for the reinforcement of Christianity. It is similar when he writes of the Lazi and the Iberians, wedged on the east of the Black Sea between Byzantium and Persia. The Iberians were Christian, and thus provided a continuing provocation and excuse for invasion from the Persian side, simply a fact of life to Procopius.[57] He tells of Byzantine involvement with the Iberians and Lazi in the familiar terms of personality – the king of the Iberians, for instance, applies first to Justin I for the alliance;[58] the Lazi are motivated by bad experiences under individual Byzantine officers whom Procopius happens to dislike.[59] But Procopius never doubts that the religious affiliations of these peoples are a crucial factor in their situation as buffer between the two major states,[60] though it is oddly not Procopius who tells us that King Tzath of the Lazi had gone to Justin I in Constantinople and asked for alliance, which carried with it the obligation of conversion to Christianity.[61] In another place he makes the telling observation that the Lazic kings had made a habit of marrying Byzantine women of the senatorial class, and that Gubazes's maternal ancestry was Byzantine.[62] Procopius' world is one in which we are to believe that foreign peoples spontaneously asked for Byzantine protection, as he says the Heruls did under Anastasius (though only after their defeat); in this case Justinian merely completed the process by 'persuading' them to become Christian and, as Procopius puts it, to 'adopt a gentler manner of life'.[63] Naturally this approach is entirely disingenuous, for it emerges from Procopius' next remarks that the 'persuasion' actually took the form of an alliance with distinct and precise conditions attached, no doubt including the stipulation that they adopt Christianity. He cannot resist adding that conversion did not prevent the Heruls from mating with asses, or from remaining the most disgusting kind of creatures. Still, the defects of this and other passages have more to do with Procopius' own limitations and the temptation of the anecdotal than with any failure to recognise the working of imperial

[57] *Persian Wars* I.12.2-5.

[58] Ibid. For the theme (barbarian kings making personal application for conversion and alliance with Byzantium) see Engelhardt 1974, 80f.

[59] *Persian Wars* II.15.9 (John Tzibus); 6-8 (Peter). Abasgi: *Gothic Wars* IV.3.21; cf. *Buildings* III.6.9f.

[60] Cf. *Persian Wars* II.28.26-30.

[61] See Malalas, p. 414; *Chron. Pasch.*, pp. 614-15.

[62] *Gothic Wars* IV.9.8.

[63] Ibid. II.14.34-6.

diplomacy. We hear from Procopius something similar of the Huns (probably Onogurs) round the Bosporus, who, he says, had 'recently decided to become subjects of the Emperor Justin'.[64] He does not explicitly state that this involved accepting Christianity, but we know that it did from Malalas' story of the journey of their king, Grod, to Constantinople. Again strategic advantage and Christian missions went hand in hand.[65] For a more practical view of these missions and in particular their connection with the ordination of clergy, we must look to John of Ephesus, who conducted a major campaign himself.[66] But in a history like the *Wars* that kind of detail and emphasis was inappropriate. It remains surprising, then, how clearly Procopius does indicate the overall aims of Byzantine foreign policy, and their intimate link with the Christian missions.

We can see this quite clearly in the part of the *Buildings* which is in some ways the most interesting – Book VI, on North Africa.[67] Corippus' *Iohannis*, praising the campaigns of the Byzantine John Troglita in Byzantine Tunisia in the years 546-9, lays disproportionate emphasis on the paganism of the Berbers, and uses their supposed attachment to the oracle of Ammon and their horrid rites as a literary foil for the blameless Byzantines.[68] But Procopius too brings out the importance of Christianisation as an instrument of Byzantine control, as was made explicit in Justinian's legislation.[69] He does it differently, however. Whereas for Corippus the great oracle at Ammon is represented as still the very centre of Berber religion, for Procopius its pagan glories had already faded into the past. 'Even up to the time of Justinian' sacrifices continued, but now they have been totally replaced by a great church of the Virgin, a sign of Justinian's aim of saving souls as well as bodies, and the preserver of true doctrine.[70] The likelihood is that this church was already standing when Corippus wrote, probably in 549; the two writers have treated the same contrast of Christianity and paganism in quite different ways. There are other cases where Procopius emphasises the ease with which the pagan Berbers are said to have accepted Christianity: at Ghadamès the Moors were 'persuaded' 'very willingly' by

[64] *Persian Wars* I.12.8, cf. Malalas, pp. 431-2. Engelhardt 1974, 85f.

[65] See Beck 1967.

[66] See Stein 1949, 371f. Engelhardt 1974, 13f. John's own allusions to this: *HE*, Nau 1897, 481f.; *HE* II.44; III.36; *Lives of the Eastern Saints, PO* 18.861. He was deeply involved in the consequences of Justinian's religious policies, both in the eastern provinces and in Constantinople, where he spent much time, and writes about them in a manner totally different from Procopius, who for all his Christianity remained on the whole a detached observer on these issues.

[67] See below, Chapter 10.

[68] Below, p. 177.

[69] Cf. *Nov.* 37.6-8 (535).

[70] *Buildings* VI.2.21f. On Ammon see Bénabou 1974, 335ff. Whether the shrine was really as active in the sixth century as Procopius and Corippus suggest seems doubtful, however: see Averil Cameron 1984b.

Justinian to embrace Christianity.[71] At Boreum it is Jews who are
converted,[72] while at Lepcis, which received a church of the Virgin and
four other churches,[73] the local Gadabitani, 'being excessively devoted to
the so-called Hellenic impiety', were eagerly led to accept Christianity.[74]
Carthage and Septem were also the sites of churches of the Virgin,[75] and
a telling phrase about the latter brings out the mental association of
churches with civilisation: Justinian 'dedicated there a fine church to the
Theotokos, at the same time bestowing on it the beginnings of a city and
by it making this fortress impregnable to every kind of men'. The urban
centres which for Procopius spelled civilisation held two invariables –
churches and fortifications.[76] And as with his view of defence, his
conception of conversion was confrontational. He does not offer much to
the modern frontier historian, used to thinking in terms of ebb and flow,
small structures and interaction.[77] Instead, in his concept, the churches
and the defences work together, as at Sinai. We can see something
similar in his account of Resaina (Sergiopolis) in Syria, where the great
shrine of S. Sergius already stood, and which Justinian literally made
into a town by building fortifications and giving it a water supply,
houses, stoai and other buildings 'which usually adorn a city'.[78] Not
fortifications here, but the integration of religious centres in the very
centre of urban life.

It does at first sight seem surprising, compared with our other main
source for these missions, John of Ephesus, that Procopius seems to pay
so little attention to whether the conversions were to orthodoxy of
Monophysitism. In the case of Nubia, Procopius' account does not even
raise the issue.[79] Nor does he have anything to say on the real spread of
Monophysitism which was taking place in Syria and Mesopotamia since
the ordination of James Bar'adai and Theodore of Arabia at the request of
al-Harith the Ghassanid ruler (called Arethas in Greek).[80] It is hard
to believe that Procopius was entirely ignorant of this important
development; yet he did not choose to make it an issue in his criticism of

---

[71] *Buildings* VI.3.9-12.

[72] VI.2.21f. For Boreum (Bu Grada) see Goodchild 1951.

[73] VI.4.4. See Goodchild and Ward Perkins 1953, 1ff.; Kirsten 1961, 52ff.

[74] VI.4.12.

[75] VI.5.9; 7.16. It is an interesting question how successful this transplantation of the cult
of the Virgin actually was, since none of these churches has been investigated in terms of its
later history. See most recently Frend 1982, with n. 100 for the view that the Theotokos cult
was as successfully carried to Africa as Procopius implies; the material evidence however is
rather slight so far; see Duval 1982.

[76] See below Chapter 10, and above, p. 76 on Justiniana Prima. The first instincts of the
Byzantines in Africa are to start building.

[77] Cf. Trousset 1974; Fentress 1979.

[78] *Buildings* II.9.3-9.

[79] Above, p. 121.

[80] On Procopius' attitude to al-Harith, see n. 83.

Theodora.[81] In the *Wars* the subject was potentially awkward, for it involved a development that was parallel to, but also opposed to, official Byzantine orthodoxy, which now stressed the hope of concilation with Monophysites through the condemnation of the Three Chapters and the Fifth Council. Indeed that may be why Justinian was prepared to countenance Monophysite conversions in his name through the agency of John of Ephesus. From Procopius, however, we gain the impression that Byzantine missionary policy was smooth and harmonious; there is only the occasional hint here that bitter disputes were actually being conducted.[82] It is only partly that Procopius was deliberately leaving out the technicalities of ecclesiastical politics in the *Wars*, for as we have seen, the importance of Byzantine missions comes out clearly enough in other passages. The truth was that this Monophysite expansion in the east was an awkward matter in a work not openly critical of imperial policy.

The character of al-Harith himself also presented some problems. To the Byzantines this leader of the Monophysite Ghassanid Arabs was vital as a counterpoise to the pro-Persian Lakhmids under al-Mundhir.[83] Justinian had therefore elevated him over an unprecedented number of Arab tribes.[84] Other sources present him as a princely patron of Arab poetry, a noble leader of Monophysitism,[85] but Procopius is bitterly hostile. In particular he accuses him of treachery at the battle of Callinicum in 531 and lays on him the blame for the Byzantine reverse.[86] At an early state Procopius wrote an unflattering comment about him: 'Arethas was extremely unfortunate in every inroad and every conflict, or else he turned traitor as quickly as he could. For as yet we know nothing certain about him.'[87] The charge of treachery at Callinicum is a device used by Procopius to deflect blame from Belisarius, and we do not need an elaborate defence of al-Harith to see that he is exaggerating.[88] 'Treachery' is one of his favourite explanations in any case, as it was for Corippus also in the *Iohannis*.[89] But this is also one instance in which Procopius completely fails to bring out the true importance of the Ghassanids in the complex political and religious relations between

[81] Above, p. 79.

[82] For Monophysites and Chalcedonians in Nubia, for instance, see Engelhardt 1974, 57f.

[83] For these relations see Sartre 1982, 157ff.; on Procopius's presentation of al-Harith, Kawar 1957a, with Shahid 1971; Engelhardt 1974, 94-100.

[84] *Persian Wars* I.17.47.

[85] Kawar 1957a; For al-Harith's phylarchate, ibid., 84.

[86] *Persian Wars* I.18.36-7, and cf. II.19.26-46 (541). See below, Chapter 9.

[87] I.17.48.

[88] Christides 1970 defends Procopius, arguing that his attitude is merely one of standard Byzantine hostility to barbarians (which he certainly shared: see below, Chapter 13); but Kawar's position (see Kawar 1957a, 62, emphasising Procopius' hostility to al-Harith) vigorously restated by Shahid 1971.

[89] See Averil Cameron 1984b.

Byzantium and the peoples of the eastern frontier,[90] though it is not so easy to see why this is so, especially when he is in fact our main source for the career of al-Harith and the beginnings of the Ghassanid dynasty. Personal prejudice, obvious in all his remarks here, may be a sufficient answer. As always, he is more interested in the personal than the wider view.

It is worth looking further at Procopius' treatment of heresy, and especially Monophysitism, in the *Wars*. Often enough he will mention doctrinal dispute in a self-conscious way, as he does even in the *Secret History*: 'There are many rejected doctrines in all the Roman empire, which they call 'heresies' – Montanists, Sabbatians and all the other ways in which men's opinions can wander.'[91] This particular passage serves as an introduction to a long discussion of Justinian's attacks on heretics and pagans, one of Procopius' main complaints against him.[92] But why no mention of Monophysites or Nestorians, especially as the *Secret History* belongs to the height of the Three Chapters controversy? Procopius is very reluctant to name Monophysites at all, though he will refer to the doctrines of Chalcedon.[93] He states, for instance that Justinian and Theodora supported opposite religious policies, that is, that Theodora favoured Monophysites, though all he actually says is that 'they pretended to go opposite ways in the disputes'.[94] Yet he will devote a large amount of space to the problem of Arianism in the reconquered province of Africa.[95] Indeed the relations between Arians and Catholics in Africa are brought into the narrative as a major factor.[96] It is true that the sequence of events themselves dictated some discussion of Arians, and that Procopius is chiefly interested in the Arian factor as an explanation of the causes of the mutiny in the Byzantine army, or as a way of underlining the blessings of reconquest, which restored Catholicism. Yet there is nothing comparable even to this in relation to Monophysitism in the eastern provinces.

There might be several reasons for this reticence. One might be that when Procopius published *Wars* I-VII the Monophysites were a major factor in imperial policy, and a problem which Justinian had not solved. By the time he wrote the *Buildings* he could claim that Justinian had re-established orthodoxy and closed off all paths to heresy[97] – a statement which could be read as a reference to the Fifth Ecumenical

[90] See Kawar 1957b.

[91] *SH* 11.14.

[92] For Justinian's religious policies see Constantelos 1964-5; Thurman 1968; Alisavetos 1913.

[93] *SH* 27.3-25, on ecclesiastical affairs at Alexandria, also avoids stating the issue directly. Chalcedonian formulae in Procopius: Rubin 1954, 68.

[94] *SH* 10.15. See above, p. 78.

[95] See Chapter 10 below, and cf. *Vandal Wars* I.21.17f. (above, p. 114); II.14.21f.

[96] II.14.2f. (the revolt of Stotzas).

[97] *Buildings* I.1.9.

Council, unless it is simply an exaggerated claim in the panegyrical introduction. *Wars* VIII could be written without direct consideration of Monophysites, and in the *Secret History* they do not constitute one of the examples of Justinian's blood-lust towards heretics perhaps because in the late 540s, when the work was being planned, Justinian's policy towards them was one of attempted conciliation. To have dealt in detail with religious disputes would not have conformed to Procopius' plan for the *Wars*, while even in the *Secret History* Procopius says no more in relation to the Three Chapters affair than that Justinian was devoting all his time (in 549) to settling the disputes between the Christians.[98] This is the other reason why there is no direct discussion of Monophysitism. It is certainly not that Procopius was unaware of the bitter disputes leading up to the Fifth Council, for he knew perfectly well, for instance, that there were many influential Italians in Constantinople in about 550 trying to persuade Justinian of their views;[99] yet he mentions them in general only when they had some role in the course of the wars, like the Roman deacon Pelagius.[100] We would never guess from reading Procopius the depth of the involvement of the African bishops in opposing imperial religious policy, still less than they removed themselves almost in a body to Constantinople in 550, and that several of them died there where they had sought asylum.[101] Here again it is partly that he does not wish to go into these matters. But there is also the consideration that a revelation of the true discontent of the African bishops would have spoiled the impression that the Byzantine reconquest represented 'liberation' and not occupation. It remains odd that there is little or no direct discussion of Monophysitism by Procopius; but there is unlikely to be one simple reason. The very complexity of the structure of Procopius' works and the inclusion or exclusion of this or that subject is a useful reminder of how hazardous it is to expect him to have given us his whole and undistorted views on any one theme.

We are on surer ground, however, in considering the references in his works to the subject of imperial philanthropy.[102] It was not merely that Justinian, as his laws show, set great store by this,[103] but that Procopius too, while obviously unlikely to mention other Christian laws of Justinian, such as those on the regulation of clergy or the duties and recruitment of bishops,[104] makes imperial philanthropy a mark of a proper emperor, and assumes its importance without question elsewhere. He lists, for example, the guesthouses built by Justinian in Jerusalem,

---

[98] *Gothic Wars* III.35.11.
[99] Below, pp. 196f.
[100] Ibid.
[101] See Averil Cameron 1982, 45f.
[102] For this see Constantelos 1968; Boojamra 1975, and much in Patlagean 1979.
[103] E.g. *Novs* 6.6 (535); 59.7 (537); 80.4 (539); 120; 131 etc.
[104] See below, Chapter 9.

one of them for the sick poor;[105] then there was the *xenon* (hospice) of S. Sampson in Constantinople, between S. Sophia and S. Irene, rebuilt and enlarged by Justinian after it had been burned down in the Nika revolt, 'so that the sufferings of more wretched human beings could be relieved'.[106] Two more *xenones* were built by Justinian and Theodora opposite this one, in the palaces of Isidore and Arcadius.[107] Another is mentioned as having been restored, near the church of S. Panteleimon.[108] However ambiguous his treatment of Theodora's Convent of Repentance,[109] Procopius calls the *xenones* 'a most holy work'.[110] He was far less conscious of the increasing numbers of poor in the cities than the hagiographers, of course, and is quite ready to write disparagingly of 'the mob'. But even the right-wing Procopius reflects the truth that the endowment of philanthropic institutions, usually with specific Christian connections, was now an expected part of imperial largesse. The nature of urban experience had been changed by the establishment of official Christianity, and we can see this change even in the works of Procopius. Sometimes indeed he allows a little more direct insight: during the terrible attack of plague in Constantinople imperial funds were diverted for the burial of the dead, at any rate before there were so many dead to be buried that decent burial became a literal impossibility.[111] Procopius notes the tendency of many people to become religious during the plague, and their reversion afterwards to their former ways, but he is struck too by the real changes in the bearing and dress of the population: everyone stayed at home wearing ordinary clothes, and no one dressed properly to go out.[112]

The church's role in daily life does emerge from Procopius' work, even though it was in no way a direct subject. Some have thought that he is hostile to monks as such;[113] yet when he writes of the monks of Amida who had passed out from drinking when they should have been attending to the defences,[114] he writes as a typical man of the sixth-century east, for whom it was quite natural that monks should be involved in urban life.[115] His entire narrative of the Persian wars gives prominence to the role of local bishops in diplomacy and town leadership.[116] Procopius, who must have known the area, brings out both the religious element in the war

---

[105] *Buildings* V.6.25, and the list at V.9.34f.
[106] *Buildings* I.2.14.
[107] I.2.17.
[108] I.9.11.
[109] Above, p. 91.
[110] *Buildings* I.2.17.
[111] *Persian Wars* II.23.5-13.
[112] II.23.14-16; 20-21. See above, pp. 40f.
[113] See n. 18.
[114] *Persian Wars* I.7.22f.
[115] See Frend 1972; Seiber 1977; Susan Ashbrook Harvey 1981.
[116] See p. 163.

(Chosroes was intrigued by Christianity and anxious to demonstrate the superiority of Zoroastrianism)[117] and the way these towns worked. He does not make the role of bishops an issue,[118] but rather recounts the simple realities of emergency situations, when they naturally took charge. And though there is a difference here between the Persian narrative and the African and Italian ones, the reason for it lies not in any intention on Procopius' part, but in the natural demands of the different subject matter. In the east, Chosroes and his army made steady progress in 540 with demands on each town in turn; there is therefore a natural focus on diplomacy (not always successful)[119] and consequently on bishops and on the urban handling of crisis. In Africa, for instance, and in Italy too, it was more a matter of narrating battles and the progression of armies. But the relative absence of bishops and holy men from these narratives in comparison with the Persian wars should not be taken as a sign that Procopius had no knowledge or interest in their doings.[120] He was perfectly aware of their real importance and indispensability, but the narrative required fewer references to it.

When we look at the panegyrical description of Justinian's achievements at the beginning of the *Buildings*, we find Procopius listing his codification of the law in a rather interesting way.[121] Justinian, he says, took the body of law, which was complicated through unnecessary repetition and even contradictory, and by a thorough revision removed these defects. He passes then to Justinian's own legislation, saying that the emperor removed all possible reasons for conspiracy and enriched the poor, thus putting the state on a footing of prosperity. This is a strikingly inadequate assessment of Justinian's legislation, given its mass and its overwhelmingly Christian character. Procopius says nothing whatever about the legislation on the church, on marriage, on bishops and so on, though he does pick out for comment Justinian's measures for welfare and for the poor in general.[122] However, before jumping to conclusions about his lack of interest in the details of Christian living, we only need to remember the constraints of the literary and rhetorical aim of this prominently placed and highly wrought passage.[123] From the legislation

---

[117] Chosroes had married a Christian called Euphemia taken captive at Sura (*Persian Wars* II.5.28) and for her sake he ransomed the other captives from the city. But the famous chariot race at Apamea demonstrated his sense of competition between Persian and Roman culture (II.11.31ff.); cf. also II.26.2, with n. 30 above.

[118] Though Justinian often legislated about them: eg. *CJ* I.5.18; 4.26; *Novs.* 86; 128 etc.

[119] Below, pp. 161ff.

[120] In the *Vandal Wars* Procopius mainly wrote of the early phase of reconquest, in the 530s, and there the focus is much more on the deeds of the Byzantine army than it can be in *Persian Wars* II, where the subjects are Chosroes and the cities; when he did write of the later 540s he had good reasons to pass over the African bishops and their opposition to Justinian: see below, Chapter 10.

[121] *Buildings* I.1.10.

[122] On the legislation, see Boojamra 1975. Procopius' attitude to it in general: pp. 228f.

[123] P. 86 above.

Procopius passes straight to Justinian's military campaigns, to which he
gives only two lines, moving to a panegyrical comparison of Justinian
with Cyrus. In other words, this is a formal survey, not a cool judgment.
In the *Secret History* we see a very different Justinian, one not so unlike
the emperor who was prepared to launch into the heart of ecclesiastical
dispute with writings of his own.[124] We can also see from the *Secret
History* another important contemporary development, the increase of
church property by means of legacies. Two of Justinian's laws on the
subject appear here.[125] Procopius is of course hostile to Justinian's aims,
and concerned in this passage to show up the corruption of the church at
Emesa, but his underlying position is that of religious belief, for he says
that the abuse was finally stopped by 'some forethought from God'.[126]
The primary attitude here is of criticism of Justinian simply for excessive
legislation, and then allegedly for breaking and changing his own laws;[127]
for the conservative Procopius any innovation is a bad thing in itself.
Thus he disapproves of Justinian's measures against Jews, because they
fall into this category, not because he has any particular fondness for
Jews himself.[128] Altogether, his evidence on Justinian's legislation is
partial and meagre, but it is not so out of religious prejudice or lack of
sympathy with Christian rule; indeed, he will introduce a miraculous
explanation even when he is criticising Justinian's meddling in religious
affairs.

Certainly there are noticeable gaps in Procopius' work, if we are
looking for ·indications of contemporary religious developments. The
growing cult of the Virgin, for instance, though implied in the *Buildings*,
has no emphasis in Procopius' own statements or in the other works.[129]
The course of ecclesiastical politics is mostly left out, unless it impinges
on the military narrative. The impact of African and Italian clergy in
Constantinople in the late 540s is largely ignored, though Procopius was
there at the time, and certain remarks show that he understood its
importance. Naturally also there are great differences between the three
works in the extent and type of religious material which they include.
But even in the *Wars* Procopius' own main interest is in the personal, and
he is certainly less interested in Christianisation as a social and economic
process, or in the problems it created, than in the external details
whereby imperial policy was sometimes affected. He contrives even here
to make Justinian's theological interests seem trivial and peripheral,
while in the *Buildings* he is content to pass over the real motivating force

[124] For Justinian's writing, see Schwartz 1973. The emperor personally entered the lists in
the Three Chapters affair: Averil Cameron 1982, 47; see Pewesin 1937, 139f. See *SH* 27.3f.
[125] 27.33-28. 15. Cf. *Novs.* 9 (535) and 111 (541).
[126] 28.13.
[127] Cf. 27.33; 28.16.
[128] 28.16f.
[129] Above, p. 90 and despite Downey 1953b, 724.

behind Justinian's legislation. We cannot know what might have ensued had he actually written an ecclesiastical history – or even whether the apparent promise was an entirely serious one. In the extant works, though, his treatment of religious subjects seems to show a man uninterested in theology and out of sympathy with its contemporary importance, even though religious divisions were perhaps the single largest problem that Justinian had to face. Just as in his general interpretation of people and events Procopius tends to focus on the external and the personal, writing in clichés and content to reproduce stereotyped reactions,[130] so too when he does treat of religious matters it is often in the same vein. He was not temperamentally inclined to deal with religious history in a sensitive or subtle way, and for the most part he does not even attempt it. And added to this natural disinclination was his deliberate refusal to include major religious discussion in his political history – a choice which in fact precluded him from a fully effective analysis of contemporary history.[131]

But if Procopius was not much of a religious thinker, at least as far as we can tell from what he actually wrote, nevertheless a strongly Christian impression comes over from his work. It is shown in a mass of minor remarks, in the basic attitudes underlying all three works, and in major set pieces such as his discussion of the sack of Antioch. The only unusual feature in all this is his apparently genuine distaste for religious persecution and intolerance – though he was extremely intolerant himself in most of his attitudes, as we have seen already in his views on women and will see again and again.[132] Despite the obvious differences between the three works, however, his religious assumptions at this basic level pervade all three equally; all share the same constant assumption of the working of divine providence, the admission of the miraculous, the odd remarks which spring from a conventionally Christian background. It is therefore wrong in principle to decide on one or other of the works as representing his real views – to reject the *Buildings*, with its emphasis on the divinely inspired emperor, as obviously insincere, or to ignore the *Secret History*'s demonology as an embarrassing aberration or as something clearly not to be taken seriously. We must assume that Procopius, in his rather superficial way, accepted both the Christian framework of empire and its obvious antithesis of demonic control. In neither case was there a rationalism or real scepticism impeding his belief: this is a fiction of modern scholarship. The three works are joined by the most deep-seated assumption that the fundamental cause of everything is supernatural. Divine providence – or evil forces – dictates the course of events even when we cannot comprehend it. For Procopius

---

[130] Below, Chapter 13.
[131] Below, pp. 234f.
[132] Below, Chapter 13.

this is quite enough, and his simple acceptance of this framework prevents him from ever rising to the level of truly critical history.

Indeed, such an assumption was completely at odds with the kind of history that Procopius was trying to write. It seems that he was conscious himself of the traditional divide between political history (like the *Wars*) and ecclesiastical history as such, and that he made a deliberate effort to stick to the former. The extent of his commitment to the acknowledged norms of secular historiography will be discussed in the next chapter, and it is impressive. Even though in so many ways he does reveal himself as deeply influenced by Christian modes of thought – admitting miracle, assuming divine intervention, showing his acceptance of standard Christian attitudes to holy men and so on[133] – he nevertheless cast the *Wars* very firmly within a tradition which necessitated explanation in human terms, or at least, only in relation to 'fortune', and which saw no long-term inevitable purpose in human history. Such a tradition was poles apart from the linear view of history, dictated by God's providence, implied both in Christian chronicles and in church history. We see Procopius, therefore, wrestling (not very successfully) with the problem of causation within such a tradition. Not only was he attempting something that was inadequate, because of its self-imposed limitations of subject, to cope with the problems of his own time: he was also attempting something which did not completely mesh with his own ideas – for as we have seen, whenever he really tries to explain a great event, and especially a great disaster, he falls back on appeals to the incomprehensible divine will.

But he has also set himself apart from the polemic over pagan and Christian interpretations of history. Unfortunately, we have no idea whether or not he knew the recent work of Zosimus,[134] with its vehement attacks on Christian interpretations of history, but it seems highly unlikely, for, compared with Zosimus, Procopius' knowledge of past history is sketchy and his views mild. He has none of Zosimus' violent detestation of Constantine for making the empire Christian, and effectively abstains from the partisan views taken on the reasons for the decline of the western empire. Significantly, Evagrius bitterly attacks Zosimus at the end of the sixth century,[135] but uses Procopius'

---

[133] For the overlapping between secular and ecclesiastical history see Cracco Ruggini 1977, 1981. There is much within the *Wars* of the Christian historical themes emphasised by Thélamon 1981: thus the importance of signs of God's power, the influence given to individuals (cf. Cracco Ruggini 1979), the centrality of conversion, even though the *Wars* is neither 'une histoire sainte' nor 'une histoire exemplaire'.

[134] On the question of the reception of Zosimus's work see Paschoud, *RE* s.v. (1972).

[135] *HE* III.40f.; Zosimus was possibly known to him through Eustathius of Epiphaneia (on whom see Jeep 1882). Interestingly, Evagrius uses of Zosimus the language which Procopius applies to Justinian in the *Secret History: palamnaie daimon* (see p.58 above). Unlike Procopius, he writes from the standpoint of Christian history and can therefore afford to be completely uninhibited.

Wars without feeling any such need to argue against Procopius' stance. Certainly in its earlier parts, the *Wars*, like the *Buildings*, accepts the prevailing Christian ideology and applies it to recent history and to relations between Rome and the barbarians. It is not hostile to a more overt Christian history, merely neutral and comparatively uninterested. It has been assumed in this book, as elsewhere, that Procopius was not free to write exactly as he would have wished, and that is clearly in some sense true. But it does not mean that his Christian interpretations are to be taken as insincere simply for that reason, and it is fair to suppose that they do represent his own views. The fact is that we are far from understanding what it was and what it was not possible to write in sixth-century Constantinople, since there is no external evidence whatever either for the reception of the *Wars*, of which parts are after all highly critical, or for the fate of Zosimus' *New History*. I shall go on to argue that Procopius' choice of literary form hampered him from giving a completely successful contemporary analysis; but it was much more than just a matter of what to put in and what to leave out. He was trying to write a history without religious polemic and without taking up a position on the major divisive issues. How much this was decided for him by literary aims and how much it came from his own convictions is an issue that cannot be settled, except to say that the *Secret History* and the *Buildings* are composed entirely within a Christian context in which the basics can be taken for granted. In the *Wars*, then, Procopius was attempting a heroic task which could not quite succeed because of the lack of fit between the type of history it implied and the underlying assumptions with which Procopius approached the writing of it. It is not a Christian history, but those assumptions are indeed Christian ones.

CHAPTER EIGHT

The Historian of the Wars

After considering the *Secret History* and the *Buildings*, and seeing the continuities and indeed the weaknesses in Procopius' work, we are much better equipped to turn to his major achievement, the eight books of *Wars*. One of the problems in treating this work is that of coping with its sheer bulk and the variety of its subject matter. It will need therefore both detailed discussion of the separate sections, on the western wars, on Africa and on Italy, and general discussion of its main characteristics. For much of its span this is the only, and always the major, source. But we have seen enough already of Procopius' work to make it likely that there will be tremendous variation in scale and approach from section to section, and that we can only approach the *Wars* adequately through an analysis that brings out these differences. I shall try in this discussion, therefore, to bring out what I take to be the major lines of development and the characteristics of individual parts, so that the *Wars* too can be seen less as a monolithic and remarkable work, beyond criticism, than as an interesting and varied history, often brilliant, sometimes very weak, but recognisably part of the same discourse as the *Secret History* and the *Buildings*. This first chapter on the *Wars* will set out some of the general issues before we move on to consider the parts of the work separately.

Both superficially and in its general construction the *Wars* belongs to the long line of secular histories concerned with military events in the author's own day. Procopius refers to it as 'a description of the wars',[1] and arranges his material by winters and spring, 'the winter ended, and the tenth year came to an end of this war which Procopius recorded'.[2] The MSS. and Photius call it a 'history',[3] but Procopius' focus is quite definitely the wars of Justinian, not the general history of the period. It was to be a secular, political narrative, arranged mainly annalistically

---

[1] Cf. *Buildings* I.10.3. See Rubin 1954, 84 and cf. *Persian Wars* I.1.1 'Procopius of Caesarea wrote about the wars which Justinian, emperor of the Romans, waged against the barbarians in the east and west ...'

[2] *Gothic Wars* III.11.39; cf. II.2.38; 12.41 etc. But the *Persian* and *Vandal Wars* are dated according to the years of Justinian's reign.

[3] Photius, *Bibl.*, cod. 63; cf. *Suda*, s.v. Procopius. Evagrius, on the contrary, called it a 'work about Belisarius' (*HE* IV.12); cf. also Cedrenus, I, p. 649; Nicephorus Xanthopoulos, *HE* XVII.10.

and focussed on events (*une histoire événementielle*), which it would treat within the traditional framework of statements on causes, speeches, battle descriptions, ethnographical digressions and so on. In this choice there was nothing unusual, but Procopius' is surely the major achievement, and certainly the major surviving one, among the classicising Greek historians of late antiquity.[4] How much is specifically Thucydidean in its conception is harder to say, since there had been so many followers in the genre in the thousand years that separated Procopius from Thucydides, and there are certainly other influences at work – Arrian, for instance.[5] But Procopius' language is a network of genuine Thucydidean phrases and vocabulary, and the whole conception of the *Wars* shows that he owed more than just that to Thucydides, the original model.[6]

In this genre Procopius was supremely well qualified, for its highest form of authentication was always the claim of autopsy, and Procopius had participated himself in much of what he describes and was well placed to know about most of the rest. He sets out his credentials in the opening remarks: 'and he knew well that he (that is, Procopius) was highly capable of writing about these things, for the simple reason that he had been chosen adviser to the general Belisarius and was present at all that took place.'[7] He will occasionally put himself into the narrative, at times to add a corroborative remark, sometimes with a more substantial contribution.[8] The high spot of his own participation was the Vandal expedition, where he was present throughout, at the dispatch from Constantinople (when he records his own prophetic dream),[9] at the landing, at the dramatic entry into the Vandal palace. On the voyage to Africa he was assigned the task of collecting information in Sicily and met an old friend there from Caesarea.[10] When Belisarius retired to Sicily after his first successes in Africa, Procopius stayed behind with Solomon,

---

[4] There is much in the *Wars* of a geographical tendency, and Procopius' own arrangement of material led, e.g., Nicephorus Xanthopoulos to describe it as consisting of *Persica* and *Gothica* (*HE* XVII.10). But this was entirely to be expected: cf. Dexippus' *Scythica*. It did not undermine the concentration on military affairs; but see further the excellent article by Maria Cesa (Cesa 1982). Set in this context Procopius' 'digressions' (see below, Chapter 12) can be seen to play an important structural role in the work. For the 'classicising' genre see Blockley 1981, 1983.

[5] See pp. 216f. below.

[6] Language: Chapter 3 above.

[7] *Persian Wars* I.1.3. See Austin 1983.

[8] See *Persian Wars* I.12.24; 17.17; *Vandal Wars* I.12.3f.; 13.3; 14.3-4, 7-13; 14.15; 15.35; II.14.31, 41; *Gothic Wars* II.4.19-20; 5.2-4; 7.1, 12; 17.1-11; 23.23-8; 29.32; IV.22.8; 21.10. It is noticeable that unlike the account of the early years (up to 540), Procopius does not put himself into the narrative of the later 540s. His presence in Constantinople during the attack of the plague (*Persian Wars* II.22.9) is his last explicit entry into the text as a participant actor.

[9] *Vandal Wars* I.12.3f.; above, pp. 171f. Oral sources: II.13.29.

[10] Ibid. 14.7f.

whom he admired, and escaped with him to the Carthage ship-yards during the mutiny.[11] Later he was with Belisarius in Rome, and sent on a foraging expedition to Naples with Belisarius' wife, Antonina. So he knew Rome well, both the condition of the city and the people. He was still with Belisarius at Auximum in 539[12] and on the approach to this town claims to have seen in Picenum a baby that had been nursed by a goat.[13] But after 540 he seems to have been in Constantinople, and he probably did not go back to Italy.[14] The later parts of the *Wars*, or rather, the parts narrating the events of the 540s, do not bear the same traces of autopsy and even personal participation as the earlier ones. When Procopius was closely involved, his main task seems to have been to do with supplies, which might not have given him direct military experience, but did put him in a good position for gathering information about troop numbers and the like – though it does not follow that he is therefore necessarily to be trusted.[15]

Most of Procopius' information on the wars themselves, then, will have come from oral sources, when it did not spring from his own observation recorded at the time.[16] But for most of the substantial material in the *Wars* he fails to name a specific source.[17] Written sources normally come into play only for the sections where he diverges from his main theme, either for background historical information or for ethnographical sections.[18] Thus to assess the evidential value of Procopius' work we need if possible to examine the credentials of every individual passage, without carrying over preconceptions from other parts of the work. The difference, for example, between sections dealing with places where he had been himself and those dealing with matters he knew only from hearsay can be great, though even this distinction is far from constant. On the whole, like Thucydides himself, he covered his tracks well, and we know far too little about the quality of his information or the depth of his inquiries on individual points to make it possible to generalise with any confidence. The greater part of the *Wars* is the only source we have for the events it covers, and implies all the problems for the historian of

---

[11] II.14.39f. This personal experience must explain why and how Procopius was able to treat the mutiny in such detail, as well as his high regard for Solomon.

[12] *Gothic Wars* II.23.23f. (his speech to Belisarius).

[13] II.17.1f.

[14] Above, p. 189.

[15] Below, pp. 148f. Complete army lists for Africa: *Vandal Wars* II.16.3. He often does seem to know the disposition of individuals and units: e.g. *Vandal Wars* I.19; II.3.4, 19.1f.; 21.1, 24.2; *Gothic Wars* I.5.3; II.5.1f.; III.6.9 etc.

[16] Bury 1923, II, 420 n. 2 suggests that he began keeping notes, and conceived the idea of writing some sort of history, only after the first Persian expedition, sketchily narrated in *Persian Wars* I.12-22.

[17] When he does refer to an individual, named or unnamed, it is typically for some small or curious detail: e.g. *Gothic Wars* IV.21.10 'a Roman, ... a man from the senate', for an elaborate story about a prophecy concerning Narses.

[18] Chapter 12 below.

using a single source.

By writing an 'alternative version' in the *Secret History* Procopius has laid himself open to the charge of deliberate distortion or at the very least disingenuousness in the *Wars*, and there is certainly some truth in this accusation. The work is cool towards Justinian, and gets progressively cooler; its hero, in the early stages, was Belisarius, Procopius' patron. But Procopius' view of Belisarius changed drastically, and the *Secret History*, as we have seen, was begun as much as a tirade against Belisarius as against Justinian.[19] So the *Wars* is pervaded by Procopius' personal views of people and events, and however he defined its real purpose to himself, it was from the beginning inspired by his own strongly held opinions and enthusiasms or dislikes. We can in fact easily see the growing disillusion with Belisarius which set in as Procopius wrote of the years after 540; it reaches its peak with the publication of *Wars* I-VII in 550 and the writing of the *Secret History*, and although by 554 and *Wars* VIII Procopius seems to have recovered some of his old confidence, it was by now essentially too late. Procopius was not a scholar or historian for its own sake. He drew his inspiration from being in the heat of affairs, and his heyday was in the first decade of his association with Belisarius; so the *Secret History* went back first to that period, as the embittered Procopius looked back to find the seeds of his present resentment in the early years, and the final stages of the *Gothic War* were left for others to finish. In large part the attitude of Procopius to Justinian and his régime was filtered through his relationship with Belisarius; as the latter deteriorated, so did his view of Justinian. In both there was clearly some improvement by 554, but the fire had gone out of Procopius' work as a historian. As we shall see when we come to *Wars* VIII[20] the emphasis of the work was changed; it has a world-weary tone far different from the hot enthusiasm with which he had written of the first Persian expedition and the Vandal war.

There is both bias and criticism in the *Wars*, and sometimes also what can only be deliberate distortion. Much of the latter is indeed centred on Belisarius. We can see the depth of Procopius' feelings from his handling of Belisarius' return to Constantinople in 540 after his great success in Italy and his refusal of the Gothic offer of kingship. Procopius' disappointment and his continuing admiration show through in his dignified words: 'Against all their expectations, he refused them outright, saying that as long as Justinian lived Belisarius would not venture to usurp the royal name.'[21] When Belisarius reached Constantinople, Procopius says, Justinian's jealousy prevented any public celebration being held as they had over the Vandal victory in 534,

---

[19] Chapter 4 above.
[20] Pp. 140ff. below.
[21] *Gothic Wars* II.30.28.

yet everyone talked of Belisarius, and queued daily to see him go by, a tall handsome man who yet behaved with genuine modesty and humility.[22] A long eulogy follows of Belisarius' success as a commander which was combined with the utmost personal moderation and restraint. So long a series of praises, quite out of place in the context, obviously had a significant role in the book: they replace and balance the set piece in *Vandal Wars* II on the triumph allowed to Belisarius in 534 and now denied him.[23] Procopius quite deliberately compensates for and underlines the shabby treatment meted out to Belisarius by Justinian. He concludes the passage begun with the mention of Justinian's meanness and suspicion with the opinion that from now on other generals out for their own ends destroyed the empire by their bad decisions, whereas Belisarius continued to give unbiassed and noble counsel.[24] This artful (but here not damagingly distorted) construction is a good pointer to what we should look out for in Procopius' technique generally. In this case, Procopius' art has concealed the fact that Justinian now kept Belisarius in a demeaning position in Constantinople because he suspected his loyalty: the affection of the people is made to counteract the severity of the emperor's attitude, which naturally is given full rein in the *Secret History*,[25] written surely not much later, but when Procopius' attitude to Belisarius had turned from disappointment and protectiveness to real resentment.

Much earlier in the *Wars*, Procopius' treatment of the triumph celebrated over the Vandals in 534 is equally tendentious.[26] Though it was clearly intended to focus attention on Justinian, Procopius places all the light on Belisarius, and increases the effect of singularity by passing smoothly over imperial triumphs after Trajan and suggesting that this was the first triumph on such a scale for six hundred years. He then reinforces the effect by moving straight to Belisarius's consulship in the following year and caling that a triumph too.[27] There is a striking difference between this section in the *Wars*, where Belisarius is undoubtedly the centre of attention, and the description in the *Buildings* of the Chalke mosaic also celebrating Belisarius' victories, for there he is

[22] III.1.2-7.
[23] Cf. *Vandal Wars* II.9.
[24] *Gothic Wars* III.1.8-21 (eulogy); 22-4 (final remarks).
[25] Ibid., 9.23. See *SH* 4.1f., referring to the return from the second Persian expedition; cf. especially 4.16 'Belisarius went about as a private citizen in Byzantium, almost alone, always gloomy and melancholy, in continual fear of death by a murderer's hand' (the reversal of the eulogy in *Gothic Wars* III).
[26] *Vandal Wars* II.9. Cf. also John the Lydian, *De Mag.* II.2.6; III.55.3; Jordanes, *Get.* 307. Rubin 1954, 146 sees in Procopius' reference to emperors who have made war on barbarians a criticism of Justinian's armchair generalship. The six hundred years would go back to the Republic, but is likely to be a round figure only; Procopius has in mind the cessation of triumphs by private individuals after the Principate.
[27] II. 9.15. Whereas the triumphal procession was conducted 'not in the traditional way', but on foot (II.9.3), Belisarius' consular procession, also called a 'triumph', is said to be 'in

clearly a secondary figure to those of Justinian and Theodora.[28] Similar in their general ideas, and in their overall language and set of assumptions, the early parts of the *Wars* and the *Buildings* differ sharply in their political tone. Later in the *Wars* we can see Procopius at first excusing Belisarius for his disappointing performance in the east and in Italy after 540 – God prevented him from using his usual good judgment.[29] Of the year 549 Procopius could write that 'the barbarians were unquestionably masters of the whole west',[30] and when Belisarius returned in the same year from Italy to Constantinople he calls his arrival 'undignified', for he had achieved nothing. His claim that even so Belisarius was honoured by all in the capital[31] is hardly convincing after his sharp critique in the previous chapters. Though Belisarius is still kept before the reader,[32] Book VII ends with Totila in possession of Rome and the appointment of Germanus to the Italian command,[33] which was for Procopius, despite his approval of Germanus,[34] a symbolic rejection of Belisarius. The death of Germanus so soon after was enough of a reversal to make Procopius stop writing, if only temporarily.[35] It represented a severe blow to Byzantine hopes, after a steady decline in previous years. The command was put in the hands of a eunuch;[36] Justinian had spoiled the chance of success through his parsimony and suspicion, and was almost wholly involved with his ecclesiastical policies. The same year that saw the death of Germanus also witnessed the gathering in

---

accordance with tradition', since he rode in the curule chair; thus Procopius underlines the connection in his mind between the two occasions, all the more apparent because Belisarius now scattered the spoils of the Vandal war in place of the usual consular largesse. For consular processions, and triumphal language used of them, see on Corippus, *Iust.* IV.206ff. In fact consuls in classical times walked: cf. Ovid, *Ex Ponto* IV. 9.17f. The splendours of Belisarius' consulship were followed shortly afterwards by a law regulating such expenditure (*Nov.* 105, a. 537); Justinian's own consulship in 528 had been renowned for its extravagance (*Chron. Pasch.*, p. 617 Bonn), and Belisarius seemed set fair to rival it. The consulship itself was suppressed in 541 and held subsequently only as an imperial prerogative.

[28] *Buildings* I.10. 15f.

[29] *Gothic Wars* III.10.1; 12.1-10; 13.13 (Belisarius' weakness and difficulties); 13.15f. (God thwarts his plans).

[30] III.33.1.

[31] III.35.1, 3.

[32] By means of oblique references, e.g. III.35.23; 36.1, 16; 37.9.

[33] III.39.9-20.

[34] Cf. III.40.9 – a striking eulogy. Germanus' death would have been very fresh when Procopius wrote these words.

[35] *Wars* VII ends abruptly with the ignominious defeat of the Byzantine force sent out to Italy with Germanus' son Justin and John the Glutton among others (40.34f.). Many soldiers were killed, and the leaders only just managed to escape (40.41). Even though a minor reverse was subsequently inflicted on the Goths (40.44), the book (and thus *Wars* I-VII) ends with a stark impression of Byzantine failure, and there is no attempt to round it off with any sort of general conclusion.

[36] 40.35.

Constantinople of a large body of bishops to oppose imperial policy, and
the incarceration of Pope Vigilius, all of which,[37] though not directly
treated in the *Wars*, is reflected in the *Secret History*'s concentration on
the evils of Justinian's ecclesiastical policies. The *Wars*, which had been
begun with such high hopes, came to a stop in 550 on a note of anxiety
and discontent. When Procopius added another book a few years later,
even that broke off in the middle of the story, as though Procopius
himself had lost heart.

Even so, Procopius' criticism and disappointment was directed at
personalities and individual actions and policies, not at the imperial
system as such or the aim of reconquest. Like Agathias and others, he
blamed Justinian for the way he carried out the policy, and for his failure
to back his generals and bring the aim through to complete success.[38]
Ultimately he could only explain the failures in terms of an evil agency,
as he does in the *Secret History*, at a time when the situation looked
increasingly bleak. And the Justinian of the *Buildings* is more a symbol
of the imperial idea, in which Procopius had never failed to believe, than
an agent in the sense in which he appears in the *Wars*. As an individual
Justinian was for Procopius seen in intimate relation to Belisarius, as the
Secret History above all demonstrates with its intermeshing of the two
married couples. But as emperor he remained the embodiment of the
ideal of empire, to be understood only in relation to supernatural agency.

The motif of Belisarius, and Procopius' changing view of him, runs
though the *Wars*, as it begins the *Secret History*, but it is a mistake to see
the *Wars* only in relation to this theme, or to make Procopius exclusively
the spokesman of an 'opposition group' or the like.[39] We need rather to
trace the theme in detail and especially in its development, and to see
where and why it takes precedence over or gives way to other
preoccupations. Only sometimes does Procopius distort the narrative in
order to glorify or excuse Belisarius.[40] By the time of the writing of Book
VIII, he is both outspoken and disillusioned. He can write quite openly, it
seems, that 'the Emperor Justinian, who had been very negligent in his
conduct of the war before this, gave it remarkable support in its final
stages'.[41] Totila's death leads to the recapture of Rome in 552 by the
Byzantines, but Procopius reflects on Fortune's sport with men, for
Bessas, who had lost Rome, recaptured Petra in Lazica, while
Dagisthaeus, who had lost Petra, was now instrumental in winning back
Rome.[42] But the very recovery of Rome turned out for the worse, and it

[37] See especially Vict. Tonn., *Chron.*, s.aa. 550, 551.
[38] See Rubin 1960, I, 227ff.; Tinnefeld 1971, 21; Cesa 1981, 393 f.
[39] Rubin 1960, I, 178f.; against: Cesa 1981, 395.
[40] Most obviously in the narrative of the early part of the Persian war, appropriately for
an early period when Belisarius' ascendancy was yet to be fully established (see pp. 156ff.).
[41] *Gothic Wars* IV.26.7.
[42] IV.33.24.5.

seemed that all prosperity was destined only to be reversed.[43] We may see Procopius' growing disillusionment in the long account in Book VII of the conspiracy of Artabanes. He tells in detail how Artabanes, whose coup in Africa he recounts in the Vandal section,[44] was prevailed upon to join in a plot against Justinian,[45] and emphasises throughout the nobility of Artabanes himself and the justifiable grievances of the conspirators.[46] In a carefully placed speech one Arsaces is allowed to dwell on the vulnerability of an emperor who spends his nights discussing the Scriptures with nothing but a lot of old priests round him,[47] and even to claim that 'not one of Justinian's kinsmen will oppose you'.[48] The whole plot is told entirely from the point of view of the conspirators, and though it was unsuccessful, in that Marcellus, the commander of the palace guards, revealed it to the emperor, Procopius feels it necessary to defend Marcellus, whom he admires, for informing[49] and to suggest that Germanus, who just managed to escape implication, was in fact involved, by praising Marcellus for rescuing him while insisting simultaneously that of course Germanus was too upright for such an involvement.[50] Procopius must have got his information about this conspiracy from those who were at its heart, and he makes it clear enough where his sympathies lay. On the other hand, Procopius' narrative is shaped by other influences as well as the specifically political. Even in the account of the Vandal triumph, which is one of the most clearly engineered set pieces in favour of Belisarius in the whole work, we find Procopius veering off in the direction of the curious and the pathetic: the greater part of the narrative is taken up in fact by the theme of the Vandal spoils, including the treasure of the Temple in Jerusalem, and the pathos of the captured Gelimer. As so often elsewhere in the *Wars*, it is both highly selective and determined by Procopius' own curiosity and interest. Now, having been struck already by the sadness of Gelimer's suffering,[51] he returns to the theme in a memorably visual description of his obeisance before the magnificent tableau of Justinian and the

[43] VIII.34.1.

[44] *Vandal Wars* II.27-8.

[45] *Gothic Wars* III.31f.

[46] The honour in which Artabanes was held, even by Justinian: III.31.9. His discontent with Theodora's interference in his marital situation: 31.14f. Arsaces plays on this grievance: 32.8, as he does on the grievances of Justin the son of Germanus: 32.17f.

[47] III.32.9.

[48] 32.10.

[49] 32.23-4 (a lengthy eulogy of Marcellus' upright and abstemious character); he delays informing the emperor till the last possible moment (32.24, 40-1; cf. 42).

[50] 32.44f. Marcellus' evidence cleared him (32.47f.), and Marcellus' reputation grew as a result (32.50). Procopius clearly states that he took the blame on himself for the delay in informing the emperor, thus protecting Germanus (32.49). It was in fact Germanus whom the conspirators destined for the throne (32.38). Justin however is made to deny firmly that his father will take any part (32.21).

[51] *Vandal Wars* II.7, especially 14f.

Byzantine officials in the Kathisma,[52] while an antiquarian interest in the Temple treasures leads him into an aside about what Justinian now did with them.[53]

As for the critique of Justinian in the *Wars*, it is of course for the most part indirect, as it would have to be. But especially in the earlier narratives, it is less that he is critical (he gives Justinian full and personal credit for the idea of the Vandal expedition, indeed)[54] than that his concentration on the military sphere leaves little room for frequent reference to a civilian emperor. Similarly his follower, Agathias, gave little space to internal affairs or to political events in Constantinople.[55] It is mainly in the latter parts, as we have seen, that Procopius' attitude to the emperor turns sour, simultaneously with his consciousness of the sadness and the waste of Belisarius' return. It is difficult to know how this was received.[56] We should expect with extreme disfavour; but other writers seem also to have been able to express political criticism to a degree that is rather surprising.[57] Procopius clearly had to watch his step in a period when there were purges of pagans and intellectuals;[58] but it seems that more could be tolerated in secular historiography than we might have expected. At any rate, there is certainly no indication that Procopius suffered as a result of the *Wars*. He makes great play at the beginning of the *Secret History* of the claim that a work of that kind, if known, would mean death, and there of course we find a more direct and virulent attack. But the *Wars* was in parts critical too, if more obliquely.

Neither the eulogising of Belisarius nor the criticism of Justinian, then, are constant in the *Wars*. There is a constant shifting and development. But over and above Procopius' own personal views and inclinations, it seems that some degree of critical assessment of the leading agents, in this case including Justinian, was called for by the type of history which Procopius was writing, however surprising this may seem in the sixth-century context. It was predictable, too, that Procopius would see history so much in terms of personality.[59] But what is more disconcerting is his frequent resort to the banal and the repetitive when he does make specific judgments. Like Thucydides and many other historians before him, he often puts these judgments into the mouths of others. He makes Vitigis' envoys to Chosroes say that Justinian is 'a

[52] II.9.19-11.

[53] 9.6-9.

[54] See below, Chapter 10.

[55] Averil Cameron 1970, 124ff.

[56] Criticism of emperors: Tinnefeld 1971, Averil Cameron 1977 (= 1981, IX); of Justinian, Rubin 1960, I, 227ff.

[57] The violence of Evagrius' critique of Justinian (*HE* IV.30f.), not all deriving from Procopius, must indicate the depth of contemporary feeling; see Allen 1981, 194ff., Rubin 1953 (suggesting but not proving influence from the *Secret History*).

[58] Lemerle 1971, 68ff. and see above, pp. 22f.

[59] See pp. 229ff.

natural innovator, desiring things that do not belong to him and unable to be satisfied with the status quo'.[60] But the same sentiment appears more than once elsewhere, and it obviously represents Procopius' own view.[61] However, it is alarming to find him using the same critique of Chosroes, even to the preoccupation with theology that is one of his main complaints against Justinian.[62] The criticism is reducible to a set of formulae: treachery, innovation, parsimony, deceit and false piety. Both the greed and the blood-lust that are major themes in the *Secret History* are applied to Chosroes too. So Procopius' 'critique' of Justinian is not much better than abuse. Nowhere does he attempt a real analysis of imperial policy or a balanced discussion of Justinian's own contribution. But this is only what we should expect if we consider the banality of his comments on other people. His terminology, both of praise and blame, is cliché-ridden and repetitive: John the Cappadocian, for instance, is 'wicked', 'with no concern for God or man, greedy, a destroyer'.[63] In many cases the same phrases are applied indiscriminately to different people.[64] It is then less that he has a serious and sustained critique of Justinian, even in the *Wars*, than that he writes throughout from a set of fixed or stereotyped attitudes which in fact stood in the way of critical thinking. When we look more closely at individual passages to see what the political slant amounts to, it is often less a deliberate political bias that makes them seem inadequate than his own idiosyncratic taste and care for the curious, which seems to dictate the arrangement and content of individual sections just as much or more than any carefully sustained line of argument. None of this suggests that Procopius' political thinking was actually of a high order.

We shall see that the *Wars* demonstrates both the overall framework of acceptance of the imperial system and the objectives of reconquest that we find in the *Buildings* and the prejudice of the *Secret History*. The disapproval of all innovation which we have already noted pervades the *Wars*, and Procopius never asks whether or why these changes might have been necessary. In the *Secret History* he criticises the war policy of which he normally approves;[65] but he does not seem to realise that this war policy made necessary the financial measures which he so violently criticises. Thus Justinian is both criticised for keeping his generals short on resources, and for trying to raise the money to pay for their needs. On

[60] *Persian Wars* II.2.6.

[61] E.g. *Secret History* 6.21; 3.26; 18.12.

[62] Ibid. 18.28-30; *Persian Wars* I.23.1; II.9.8-12.

[63] *Persian Wars* I.24.12-15 (though John the Lydian, *De Mag.* III.57ff. presents a similar picture in this case).

[64] See p. 240 below. We badly need a concordance to Procopius; in the meantime see the examples given by Rubin 1954, 72f.

[65] *Secret History* 18.1f. But this is a critique of the effects rather than of the policy itself; moreover, Procopius' views changed over the period 533-50 (a factor insufficiently considered by Cesa 1981).

particular issues, the Nika revolt is treated in all three works, but in none is there any real attempt to analyse its causes; Procopius is content with prejudiced allusions to the 'rabble'.[66] Nor does he help us to understand the riotousness of the Blues and Greens. In the *Wars* he describes their conflicts as a prelude to his account of the revolt in 532, but just as there is no real attempt to find the cause of the revolt itself, so the factions feature only as the participants in a 'rivalry with no cause'.[67] Their activities are 'mad folly', a kind of 'psychological disease'.[68] In the *Secret History* their function in the work is to demonstrate yet again Justinian's tendency 'to throw everything into confusion';[69] they are a sign of topsy-turvydom, in hair-styles, dress and behaviour.[70] They do not need to be explained, for Procopius, because they so neatly symbolise that under Justinian everything was wrong, or indeed that there was 'no concern for God or man'.[71] We shall look in vain, therefore, for real information: 'The entire Roman empire was shaken from its foundation as if by an earthquake or a flood or as if every city had been captured by the enemy.'[72] In the *Wars* there is no point in looking for a real insight into the Nika revolt, because Procopius' very attitudes prevented him from discussing these events in a genuinely critical fashion. It would be charitable to think, from the fact that in the *Secret History* it is made the reason for Justinian's attacks on the senatorial class, that he was kept from revealing in the *Wars* the senatorial involvement that he knew to have been a factor by the need to present the whole affair in terms not too discreditable to the government, but that does not really convince, in view of the unflattering way in which Justinian himself is here portrayed;[73] more likely that the senatorial emphasis in the *Secret History* version is itself dictated by the formal requirements of the work – the need to make a transition to the theme of Justinian's attacks on the senatorial class which takes up a large amount of space in the next section. Procopius is full of indignation at the lot of the senators under Justinian, but he never seriously discusses their real potential or the role they did play in political life. 'The senate sat as if in a picture, with no control over its voting and no power of doing good.'[74] Their decisions or

[66] Cf. p. 227.

[67] *Persian Wars* I.24.4.

[68] Ibid. 1-6 (Procopius emphasises throughout his view that the rivalry of the factions had no cause, thus was inexplicable; the final straw is that women joined in too – 6); *Secret History* 7.1-21 emphasises their dangerous innovations, unnatural in dress and behaviour. Both these accounts are as hostile as *Buildings* I.1.20f., where Procopius openly calls the rioting in 532 a sin against God.

[69] 7.1, 6-7.

[70] 7.8; cf. 7.11 – their dress was unsuitable to their station. On disorder in Procopius, see below, pp. 239f.

[71] *Persian Wars* I.24.5 (and cf. 13, a similar expression used of John the Cappadocian). Lack of order: *Secret History* 7.6, 31, 39.

[72] Ibid. 7.6.

[73] See above, p. 69.

[74] *Secret History* 14.8.

wishes were ineffective, we are told, not because of any serious conflict between them and the emperor, but simply through Justinian's restless desire to interfere and upset.[75] Procopius writes himself from the position of this class; but his presentation of their position and their needs owes everything to blind prejudice and nothing to historical criticism.

There is in fact very little effort in the *Wars* at formulating a theory of historical causation or of explaining individual events. Certain major events – the sack of Antioch, the plague – demanded some attempt, but here Procopius resorts to general confessions of faith in the mysteries of divine providence.[76] Throughout the *Wars* he uses fatalistic Herodotean vocabulary ('it was fated to happened this way ...')[77] which, like his use of Tyche, seem more like decoration of the text than judgments to be taken at face value.[78] The work is peppered with accusations against Justinian of poor choice of personnel, inadequate support of the armies, poor discipline, lack of well-maintained frontier defences and so on,[79] but even these are less a matter of serious historical judgment than of personal attack on Justinian. There is also the possibility, in the section on Chosroes' invasions in 540, that Procopius has laid stress on the poor state of the eastern defences in order not to have to admit to the actual speed and effectiveness of the Persian army.[80] Similarly, the apparently heartfelt resort to supernatural explanation for the sack of Antioch may actually be a device for deflecting blame from the Byzantine Germanus.[81] The human reasons for the disaster are therefore minimised, and it is made to seem an act of God, which of course, since it was such a devastating blow to the Byzantine cause, Procopius could not explain. He does not comment on the economic consequences for the empire of the loss of such a major city and the deportation of so many of its inhabitants,[82] nor of the real danger of falling morale in Syria as a result (it was not so long after this that the Monophysite 'alternative' ordinations began);[83] and when in the *Buildings* he tells of the rebuilding of Antioch he is equally careful not to reveal that the restored city was actually reduced in size for lack of governmental funds.[84]

Nevertheless, if the level of political critique in the *Wars* is relatively low, there are certainly places where Procopius has carefully structured his narrative for partisan reasons. One such is the account of Belisarius'

[75] Justinian's attacks on senatorial wealth: 19.12; 26.16; 29.19f. Imperial scorn for senatorial dignity: 31.21f.　　[76] *Persian Wars* II.10.4f. See pp. 106f and 117f.

[77] See above, Chapter 3.

[78] Ibid.

[79] Bruckner 1986, 51-2.

[80] See below, Chapter 9. The reverse procedure (in the *Buildings*) was to exaggerate the extent of Justinian's building work so as to glorify the emperor: Croke and Crow 1983, 146f.

[81] See Downey 1938, 367f.; 1953; 533f., 539, 542f.

[82] Ibid., 546f. Cf. John the Lydian, *De Mag.* III.54.5f., commenting on the loss of tax revenue from Syria as a result of his disaster.

[83] Though see p. 160.

[84] *Buildings* II.10.2-25; see Downey 1961, 546.

campaigns in the east up to 532. For once we have another version for direct comparison.[85] It seems likely, moreover, that Malalas' account is based on official sources. It is certainly very different from Procopius, though not uniformly so. It is naturally briefer and less literary: whereas Procopius' account of the battle of Dara, Belisarius' first major engagement in the war and Procopius' own first experience of battle with him, is long and detailed, Malalas' is much more to the point, though exaggerating for public consumption the number of enemy losses.[86] Malalas gives only the barest outline of what follows, whereas Procopius has an interchange of letters between Belisarius and the Persian commander, with rhetorical set speeches.[87] In general, then, there are the obvious differences we would expect to find between a historical and a chronicle treatment, and Procopius gives much more prominence to Belisarius than Malalas. But a closer look shows that the matter is a little more complicated. Procopius is not uniformly fuller: he does not give by any means a full narrative after the battle of Dara, or include all details of the embassies in 530, though his version is much longer.[88] His narrative is shaped first by his own experiences more than by historical accuracy, and then by his admiration for Belisarius. In the account of the battle of Callinicum this takes the form of defending him, as we can see when again we compare his version with that of Malalas.[89] The latter seems to be drawing on the official notes, perhaps of Hermogenes, whereas Procopius lays all the emphasis on the role of Belisarius, and relegates Hermogenes to a minor place.[90] While Malalas says straightforwardly that the battle took place on Easter Sunday, Procopius makes this into an elaborate and melodramatic section on Belisarius.[91] Most of the men were fasting, and Belisarius is made to try to dissuade them from fighting on that day, but is forced to yield when his speech is greeted with catcalls. The battle itself was a Persian victory, and Malalas mentions dispatches from Hermogenes to Justinian, and has the Byzantines defending themselves for as long as possible, but with Belisarius retreating at an early stage and Sunicas and Sittas getting most of the credit for the stand.[92] In Procopius' version, on the contrary, the blame for the defeat is placed squarely onto al-Harith, and (as we

---

[85] Malalas, 452f. See Kirchner 1887, 10ff.

[86] *Persian Wars* I.13.12f.; cf. Malal., 453: Plan of the battle: Bury 1923, II, 83. Bury remarks (p. 82) that it is curious that Zachariah Rhetor does not mention Belisarius when he describes the battle (*HE* IX.3); but it is Procopius who has deliberately cast the limelight on to him.

[87] *Persian Wars* I.14.1-12; speeches: 13-27.

[88] See Kirchner 1887, 11f.

[89] I.18; cf. Malal., 460-7. See Rubin 1954, 100; Bury 1923, II, 86f.

[90] I.18.16f.

[91] Malal., 463.14; *Persian Wars* I.18.15f. The date was April 19, 531. See too Zachariah, *HE* IX.4. Full source references in PLRE III s.v. Belisarius.

[92] 464-5.

now see) onto the weakness of the men from fasting, which of course Belisarius is supposed to have noted and made a reason for waiting. Thus Belisarius is absolved from all blame for a premature retreat. Procopius does not mention that other sections of the Byzantine army fought on. And in Malalas al-Harith is carefully singled out from the other Arabs for standing his ground – the very opposite of Procopius' charge.[93] The aftermath of the battle is also instructive: Procopius conveniently distracts attention from this inglorious episode by moving quickly on to the Ethiopians and Himyarites, and when he does return to Belisarius, he says only that he was removed from the east to set out against the Vandals.[94] Malalas, on the contrary, says outright that he was replaced by Mundus.[95] In another place, Procopius reveals that he knew about the suspected recall, for he says that Justinian did not now reveal to Belisarius his ideas about an expedition against the Vandals, but let him think that he had been removed from office.[96] Since the Vandal expedition did not leave until a year or so after the battle of Callinicum, there may well have been a period during which Belisarius was out of favour; if so, Procopius has been at pains to conceal it in his account of Callinicum. Of course Malalas' version too is somewhat distorted: it presents the campaign as reported by the generals other than Belisarius, and its 'hero' is the Byzantine side as a whole. But Procopius' is infinitely more subtle, varied and artful.

For the vast majority of the *Wars* we have no such convenient control. Nevertheless those passages where internal evidence makes the conclusion possible, and where there is at least some external evidence, tend to show that the methods used here by Procopius are the rule rather than the exception. First-hand reportage meant here that he was deeply involved personally with much of what he wrote about, and that his narrative of those events shows all the passion and selectivity of one who felt deeply about his subject. These parts of the *Wars* are much nearer to partisan reporting than to history; they have the faults and the strengths of high-class journalism. In the sections which cover events known only at second hand, and where Procopius' involvement was correspondingly less, there tends to be less deliberate bias, but just as much personal idiosyncrasy. We have seen his writing shaped by his own curiosity, antiquarianism and personal attitudes, and this is obvious throughout as the more detailed discussions to follow will show. It is not hard either to find in the *Wars* most of the general faults of ancient historiography. Its ethnographical digressions, for instance, and the discussions of the early history of such peoples as the Vandals and the Goths, show Procopius in

---

[93] 464.
[94] I.19-20; 21.2. For the Ethiopians and Himyarites, see p. 121.
[95] 466.
[96] *Vandal Wars* I.9.25.

a much worse light than does the main narrative, for here he was using sources, written and oral, of very unequal value, and was usually in no position to put the material together with any real accuracy.[97] The very arrangement of his work, by theatres of operations, diminishes his chance of providing a convincing sense of historical causation, for it required inevitably that some events were recorded more than once, and that the overall connections and chronology were obscured.[98] In the matter of numbers, notoriously a weakness of ancient historians, but where Procopius might have been expected to have better information than most, we may suppose that many did come from his own battle diaries; yet he is commonly vague (deliberately so) about Byzantine losses, which have rather to be inferred from passing references or from the tone of speeches. Byzantine figures tend to be self-consistent and credible, where given, whereas his numbers for the enemy are massaged in order to show up the Byzantine ones more favourably.[99] This is noticeable above all in the *Gothic Wars*. Gothic losses alone in the first phase of the war in Italy are given as reaching 40,000, and Vitigis is said to have led 150,000 men against Rome in 537; yet the internal logic of the narrative would suggest that the whole Gothic army at the start of the war totalled no more than 30,000.[100] Procopius is far from unusual here, of course; indeed he is notable for the amount of credible information he does give despite this kind of manipulation.[101] His deficiencies, however, conventional though they are, sometimes tend to get overlooked in the general admiration for his good qualities. Another conventional element in the *Wars* is of course provided by the rhetorical speeches and letters scattered with considerable frequency though the text. Some may add to the characterisation of the individual concerned, or contain some genuine insight into the general conduct of the war, but most are little more than formal exercises of the kind that anyone of Procopius' background had been taught to compose as a matter of course.[102] Many contain a kernel of plausible or appropriate observation, decked out in extended rhetorical amplification, in the scheme *captatio benevolentiae*, factual kernel, moralising expansion.[103] There is not much characterisation, for all

---

[97] Below, Chapter 12.

[98] For the form of the work see Rubin 1954, 84ff.; Cesa 1982.

[99] See in particular Hannestad 1960.

[100] Hannestad 1960, 161f. At 180f. Hannestad suggests that this distortion was forced on Procopius by Belisarius. Numbers in the *Gothic Wars*: see also Thompson 1982, 77ff.

[101] Especially for the latter part of the Gothic war, after 540 (see Hannestad, 164f.). Here too, therefore, there is most exaggeration in the early narrative, when Procopius was most concerned to promote the cause of Belisarius (though hardly forced to do so – see n. 100).

[102] See Dahn 1865, 89f. A look through *Persian Wars* I reveals twelve speeches, five letters and one piece of dialogue (I.25.16-17). Most of the speeches in the *Wars* are either exhortatory or diplomatic, and both kinds often come in pairs, as before a battle; it is the same with pairs of letters.

[103] Ibid., 133.

Procopius' speakers, high and low, tend to use the same language and the same rhetoric. He is more interested in the sentiments expressed than the personality of the speakers, though he does sometimes deliberately include speeches that will illustrate the qualities he wishes to emphasise, for instance with Belisarius, whose speeches often illustrate his *euboulia* (good counsel).[104] Thus the speeches do relate intimately and thematically to the main text, like those of Thucydides;[105] their inspiration is intellectual rather than dramatic; but they are of course less successful than those of Thucydides because their rhetoric is so much drier and their sentiments so much more conventional. Presumably deliberately, Justinian is never allowed to speak directly in the *Wars*. He features in letters, brief and official, instead.[106] A good example of how artful Procopius can be on occasion is provided by the exchange between Belisarius and Justinian in Book V of the *Wars*, where Belisarius in Italy, hard pressed for men and supplies after the capture of Rome, writes at length to the emperor and with high rhetoric, in a letter that mixes hard argument with exaggeration and rhetorical commonplace, and ends on a note of sheer bravado: 'I know that I am destined to die for your rule, and for that reason no one can ever drag me away from here alive, but consider what kind of publicity such a death for Belisarius would bring to you.'[107] This outpouring, which can hardly have been sent in this form, occupies nearly half the chapter; Justinian's reply is reported in indirect speech in only one sentence. Here Belisarius' tactic achieves its objective, and the emperor acts, but the focus is not on the effect but the rhetoric itself. Incidentally, it is in this letter that Procopius has Belisarius claim that Vitigis' army amounted to 150,000 men, while the Byzantines were reduced to a mere 5,000. Probably he never meant his readers to take these figures seriously as a sober statement of the odds. In the main, Procopius' speeches are characterised by their heavy moralising. For instance, Totila before Perusia: 'We all fail sometimes', 'It is easier to win a good reputation by daring than by prudence', 'Nothing stays the same', 'Only God never makes mistakes'.[108] Procopius likes balanced pairs of speeches, another legacy of his rhetorical training. But they can at times also be vehicles for criticism, as when the envoys of Vitigis speak to Chosroes, or the Armenians put their case to him against Justinian.[109] An oblique remark, reported by Procopius with disingenuous ease, serves the same purpose: the Persian Mermeroes is said to have

---

[104] E.g. at *Persian Wars* II.18.5f.

[105] For this see Hunter 1973; de Romilly 1956. Procopius usually moves from speech to narrative with a phrase indicating the purpose of the speech in question.

[106] E.g. *Vandal Wars* I.16.13; *Gothic Wars* I.3.16; 6.22-5; 7.22-4.

[107] *Gothic Wars* I.24.1-21. Dialogue in the *Wars*: *Persian Wars* II.10.21f.; *Gothic Wars* II.6.4-36. Procopius attributes a speech to himself at 23.23-8.

[108] *Gothic Wars* II.25.4-24.

[109] *Persian Wars* II.2.4f.; 3.32-53 (especially 39).

claimed tauntingly that the Roman state deserved tears and lamentation for being so weak that it could not capture a hundred and fifty undefended Persians.[110] Occasionally the speeches of barbarians do carry a tone of authenticity.[111] But Procopius makes no pretence of claiming that they were authentic, or even that they were as close as possible to what was actually said. The tradition of rhetorical speeches in history was too strong for them not to be taken for granted as formal compositions in their own right. Thus it is hazardous to leap too readily to the obvious conclusion that the sharp criticisms of Justinian put into some of the speeches in the *Wars* reflect Procopius' real views, which he could not express directly. They do, of course, but at the same time they were required and expected as part of the form of the work itself.

The *Wars* is a work heavily constrained by a tradition which went back for a thousand years, and which had not been fundamentally challenged. While Procopius' *Wars* naturally shows many different and more recent influences, it follows both superficially and at deeper levels the pattern for contemporary political history laid down at its very beginning. It was a pattern which, especially in its later development, had some important characteristics and disadvantages that were shared by the *Wars*. Among these were its slight interest in economic and social factors, in this case extending to religious issues. The *Secret History* amply shows how sharp an observer Procopius was in these fields; yet the *Wars* alone would have left us in ignorance of very many major issues. Its focus is heavily military and political focussing on high-level diplomacy and personal relations between the ruler and his chief officials and generals. Convention precluded a real attempt to bring together this sphere and the religious one, even though at this period religion was a major issue of public policy. The author was allowed to include passages of religious or moralising tendency himself when commenting on events, but serious discussion of such issues was not appropriate. Obviously such constraints make it a dangerous business to look for an author's 'real' views. Again, the focus of the *Wars* is chiefly external; life in the capital is not fully described, with the exception of fully traditional set pieces like the plague description or the Nika revolt (the equivalent of *stasis* at Corcyra) where Procopius could be seen to be following classical precedent. Tacitus well defined the subject matter of this type of history, though he felt that in his *Annals* he could not approach it – it should consist of the record of glorious foreign wars and captured kings.[112] Unlike Tacitus, Procopius did have such subject matter, and he is at his best when he keeps to it.

---

[110] II.30.17.

[111] For example, the Utrigurs. at *Gothic Wars* IV.19.9-21. Totila is given a strikingly high number of speeches.

[112] Tacitus, *Ann*. IV.32. His own work by contrast was *in arto et inglorius labor*.

The *Wars*, then, has many built-in failings, by modern requirements. It was an odd type of work to write in the sixth century, and indeed Procopius was almost the last to try to do so. Yet Justinian's wars cried out for some such work; they were odd too in their chronological context. In fact Procopius was an excellent reporter rather than a historian. He must have conceived the idea of writing a record in the bright days of his service with Belisarius. He came to the *Wars* infused with patriotism and admiration, as a minor participant, not as a scholar or writer looking round for a subject. If he is not very good on reasons and causes, that is not very surprising, for he is much better at vivid description. But during the long writing of the *Wars* he became disillusioned and resentful, and the work turned into a record of such deep disappointment that it provoked a parallel 'true' account setting the record straight on those early and optimistic years. Thus the *Wars* is conceived on many levels. It changes, subtly or obviously, from section to section, and it is shaped overall by a highly limiting tradition. It can only be approached through the close analysis of individual parts.

CHAPTER NINE

Procopius and the Persian Wars

In the two books of the *Persian Wars* Procopius was writing of territory that he knew from his own youth and background – the world of the eastern provinces, especially Syria and Mesopotamia, where the inhabitants of ancient cities with cosmopolitan populations had seen the two empires of Byzantium and Iran alternately fighting and negotiating for centuries, and where some of the cities themselves had evolved a cultural amalgam of Greek, Semitic and Persian influences.[1] Writing of such places was not at all like writing of Italy or Africa, where the towns were an unknown quantity to Procopius, and their inhabitants Romans felt by the Byzantine government (and by Procopius himself) to need liberation from a barbarian oppressor. The war in the east was not fought against barbarians but against the only power which Byzantium recognised as nearly its equal. The quality of relations between Byzantium and Persia was therefore on an entirely different level, and we should expect to find this reflected in a corresponding emphasis on diplomacy in Procopius' work. But at the same time the early part of the Persian Wars differed from the rest of the work in having no glorious victories like the conquest of the Vandals or the entry into Ravenna in 540 to record, but a less spectacular achievement, won before Belisarius was at the peak of his recognition as Byzantium's greatest general. In these years Procopius' relation to Belisarius was new and enthusiastic; he was readier to defend his patron – and there was more need, for Belisarius was not yet always and overwhelmingly successful.[2] Not surprisingly, it is this section which forms the basis of the 'corrected version' of the *Wars* which the *Secret History* purports to be. So the record of the early campaigns on the eastern front is both more domestic in tone than other parts of the *Wars* and more vulnerable in general to charges of bias. There are profound differences when Procopius reaches the second expedition to the east after 540, for by now his anger is rising;[3] there is no less bias, but its focus is different. In these books taken together, there is more variety than in the other parts of the *Wars*. They contain, for example, the two major set pieces about Constantinople, on the Nika

[1] Segal 1955; 1970.
[2] See above, p. 146f. on Callinicum.
[3] Pp. 156f. below.

revolt in 532 and the plague in 542. The narrative itself takes the Persian war from 527 to 548, the death of Theodora. But because of the nature of his material Procopius did not have the same chance of describing great and unequivocal victories as in the *Vandal* or *Gothic Wars*. The Persian war was fitful; it could not end in decisive victory for either side, and indeed, much of Book II is occupied with Chosroes' incursions into Byzantine territory, more a matter for the local people than the Byzantine army, which indeed stayed in the background, powerless to stop the Persian advance. Indeed, a major set-piece of this section is the account of the crushing blow caused to Byzantium by the sack of Antioch, which the Byzantines were unable to prevent, and which therefore Procopius is under an obligation to explain.[4] Perhaps indeed the lack of a clear war narrative is what caused him to include in these books the two major sections on the Nika revolt and the plague;[5] he does not write on this scale about the capital in the rest of the *Wars*, where the subject matter in hand gave him a more sustained and engrossing story.

As in the *Vandal Wars* and *Gothic Wars*, Procopius prefaces his account of Byzantino-Persian hostilities with a long origins section about Persian history since the early fifth century.[6] As usual, too, its sources are uncertain and its quality uneven. Rubin supposed that Procopius knew Persian, imagining that it would have been necessary to him in his position under Belisarius at Dara; but he never claims direct acquaintance with Persian sources (contrast the proud emphasis of Agathias, who evidently felt that he was contributing something new, even via translation).[7] Anecdotes which may have come to Procopius orally are quite a different matter. So although he does seem to know a fair amount about the Iranian government, it probably came to him through a variety of sources, including western written sources already in existence. Take the opening story, according to which the dying Arcadius entrusted his son Theodosius II to the protection of the Persian Yazdgard.[8] This appealed to Procopius as a colourful tale and as a parallel to that of the proposed adoption of Chosroes by Justin I.[9] It may well have come to Procopius from a written source, since it is told also by Theophanes, apparently without reference to Procopius.[10] Agathias says the story was well known, but that only Procopius had put it into his history.[11] Typically, he adds that it is not surprising that this should be

---

[4] *Persian Wars* II.8-9.
[5] I.24; II.22.
[6] I.2-6. 7-11 discuss the Persian wars of Anastasius.
[7] Rubin 1954, 52. Agathias: *Hist.* II.23f.; IV.24f., on which see Averil Cameron 1969-70; Suolahti 1947.
[8] *Persian Wars* I.2.1f., followed by Agathias, *Hist.* IV.26, with elaborate discussion of this passage.
[9] I.11.6f.
[10] Theoph., p. 80 de Boor, and see Averil Cameron 1969-70, 149.
[11] Loc. cit. (n. 8).

so, that the learned Procopius had found something in an earlier work which he himself had missed, for Procopius had 'read all history'. In any event, Procopius' story comes from the Byzantine side: Arcadius is here praised and credited with divine inspiration, while Yazdgard, universally condemned in the oriental tradition, is commended for his general character and his loyalty to his promise.[12] Indeed, Agathias took over this favourable view of Yazdgard without realising that it conflicted with the Persian sources which he was generally following.[13]

From Arcadius and Yazdgard I, Procopius moves on to Peroz and his expedition against the Hephthalites,[14] where again Agathias provides a useful comparison. To this reign Procopius devotes a large amount of space,[15] and much of it is taken up with anecdotal material for which he does refer to what 'the Persians say',[16] though he has enlivened it himself with additional stuff (a speech, again said to have been reported by the Persians,[17] and ethnographic matter about the Hephthalites).[18] For the first expedition of Peroz, in which he escaped by a ruse from a humiliating position, caught effectively in an ambush by the enemy, Procopius mentions a Byzantine envoy called Eusebius who happened to be with the Huns at the time of the expedition,[19] and who was used by Peroz's entourage to try to persuade the king not to be so foolhardy. Probably therefore this story too came through western, not eastern, sources. The second encounter with the Hephthalites, in which Peroz and his army were so ignominiously lost through their own foolishness, is subordinated in Procopius' account to the anecdote of Peroz's pearl earring, said to have been removed by the king himself for safety and then sold by the Hephthalites to Cavadh;[20] Procopius now relates at quite disproportionate length the elaborate story which the Persians told of how Peroz had acquired this pearl in the first place.[21] He is more interested in the anecdote of the pearl and its origin than in the fate of Peroz himself, of which his version is tame in comparison with the very hostile Syrian and Armenian tradition, which seems to have influenced Agathias.[22] For the Persians the total defeat of Peroz and loss of the king himself, most of his sons and the entire Persian army was a terrible blow

[12] *Persian Wars* I.2.6; 8-9. For Yazdgard see Averil Cameron 1969-70, 150.
[13] The Persian tradition regarded Yazdgard as the 'sinner' for his mild attitude towards the Christians; Christian sources are correspondingly favourable.
[14] I.3.1f.
[15] I.3.1-4.35.
[16] I.4.17, 18, 22.
[17] I.4.22-6.
[18] I.3.2-7.
[19] I.3.8, 12.
[20] I.4.14-17. The story of the pearl is not in Agathias (see Averil Cameron 1969/70,153). Procopius treats it dramatically (see below), but it seems basically folkloric; for the pearl as symbol in Syriac literature see Brock 1983, 31.
[21] I.4.18-21.
[22] *Hist.* IV.27; cf. e.g. ps.-Josh. Styl., p. 8 and see Averil Cameron, loc. cit.

which needed to be explained away, especially as Peroz was a favourite of the magi. But Procopius is far more concerned to tell the curious anecdotes surrounding Peroz than to say much directly. His self-conscious 'criticism' is limited to the trivial observation that he does not think it likely that Peroz would have thought of his earring in such an extremity,[23] while most of his literary effort goes into the speech of the fisherman who promised to get the pearl for Peroz and was subsequently killed in the attempt.[24]

The early part of the reign of Cavadh is treated even more expansively than that of Peroz.[25] Cavadh was still on the throne when Procopius was first appointed by Belisarius, and presumably it was still possible to find out about recent history in general terms. But Procopius confuses Valash, the brother of Peroz who succeeded him, with Zamasp, who replaced Cavadh when the latter was deposed and imprisoned,[26] and he knows little about the real situation which led to Cavadh's downfall; he is more interested in reporting the supposed debate about whether or not the king should be put to death.[27] It is difficult to use Agathias' Persian excursus as a control here, since he himself in turn used Procopius extensively at this point.[28] But Procopius now interposes a long story about the 'Prison of Oblivion' which he explicitly ascribes to 'Armenian history', that is to written rather than oral sources, and which actually comes from Faustus of Byzanta.[29] He returns to the subject proper with Cavadh's romantic escape from prison, dressed in his wife's clothes, and refers to different stories circulating about this among the Persians.[30] The rest of the account of Cavadh's vicissitudes, his stay with the Hephthalites, his return and deposition and the blinding of Valash-Zamasp, is full of circumstantial local detail, despite the mistake of identity, and Procopius did no doubt derive this from talking to Persians. We should remember, though, that too sharp a distinction between 'Syrians' or Syriac-speakers and Persians is unrealistic; the eastern frontier towns of which Dara was the show-piece, were populated by a complex mix of peoples often as much influenced by Persia as by Byzantium. Procopius could have got the Persian history he does know from all kinds of people, not necessarily Persians from the Persian army. At any rate, at this point he reaches the outbreak of war between Persia and Byzantium, with the wars of Cavadh and Anastasius, and for that he draws very heavily, of course, on information from the towns in Byzantine territory most

[23] I.4.14-15.
[24] I.4.22-6.
[25] I.5.
[26] Cf. Agathias, *Hist.* IV.27.
[27] I.5.3-6.
[28] See Averil Cameron 1969-70, 156-7.
[29] Faustus, 130f. Lauer; see Haury, *Prolegomena*, xx.
[30] I.6.9.

affected by it. The siege of Amida was the first major episode,[31] and
Procopius' story about the local holy man obviously comes from the
townspeople, as must his account of the Amidan monks.[32] It would have
been easy for him to pick up the local stories, which included claims of
cannibalism,[33] but he used official Byzantine sources too for the list of
officers in charge of the army sent by Anastasius,[34] and perhaps written
ones.[35] A brief notice of the founding of Dara and a longer one of the
negotiations between Cavadh and Justin I about the adoption of
Chosroes,[36] followed by a short account of the involvement of both Persia
and Byzantium with the Lazi in Iberia[37] effectively brings the narrative
up to the appointment of Belisarius at Dara and of Procopius as his
assessor, immediately before the death of Justin and accession of
Justinian.[38]

Procopius' 'background' to the *Persian Wars* is, as we shall see, not at
all untypical of these sections.[39] It does not amount to much real history –
rather to a mixture of anecdote and notices taken from a variety of
sources, mixed in with a fair amount of literary dressing. There is little to
suggest the complexity of Byzantino-Persian relations in the past, and
the geography of Syria and Mesopotamia is taken for granted. If we
compare the narrative of Procopius for Anastasius' Persian war with the
other surviving sources, Joshua the Stylite and Zachariah of Mytilene,[40]
as well as with Marcellinus and John the Lydian,[41] it is clear that he has
selected the anecdotal and (naturally, for this is merely his introduction,
after all) telescoped the sequence of events. On Dara, he is noticeably
reticent, perhaps saving the theme for a later treatment where he could
lay greater stress on the Justinianic connection with the fort.[42] Procopius'
talent reveals itself best when he writes of what he knows well himself; he
is not well served by these introductory sections which use material
gathered from a variety of places. Once he gets into the main narrative,
the history acquires a different texture altogether.

The Persian war narrative moves in distinct stages from the early
battles of Dara and Callinicum through ethnographical set pieces, the
account of the Nika revolt and the departure of Belisarius for Africa, all

[31] I.7.1f.

[32] I.7.5-11, 22-25; cf. 30-1.

[33] I.9.18, 22.

[34] I.8.1-5.

[35] While Theophanes here presents an account from the Byzantine point of view,
Procopius' is closer to the eastern versions, whether through Zachariah Rhetor or Eustathius
(Rubin 1954, 90; Bury 1923, II, 11; Haury, *Prolegomena* to his edition, xix f. – Procopius'
debt to Eustathius).

[36] I.10.13-19, 11.1-18.

[37] I.12.1-19.

[38] I.23.24, 13.1.

[39] On which see Cesa 1982, 195f.

[40] See Bury 1923, II.8f.

[41] Marcellinus, s.a. 503ff.; John the Lydian, *De Mag.* III.53.

[42] Above, p. 107, on *Buildings* II.1.13ff.

in Book I, and covering a space of hardly more than three years, to the characteristic narrative of Chosroes' invasions in 540 and later, interposed with the campaigns in Lazica, the comings and going of Belisarius and the account of the plague in Constantinople.[43] Each of the two books has a major digression concerning Constantinople placed near the end, while the death of Theodora provides a conclusion to both.[44] Like the Vandal and Gothic sections, the first book of the Persian wars has a Byzantine victory to report (at Dara) but the nature of the war is quite different: this is not a 'reconquest' of land held by barbarians and reclaimed for Romans, but a continuation of a permanent state of hostilities between two great powers. It could not therefore offer Procopius the same high peaks as the other parts. Furthermore the pitched battles recorded in Book I belonged to the earliest period of Justinian's wars, when Belisarius was still making his way. We have seen how conscious Procopius was of the need to show Belisarius in the best light from Malalas' parallel account, and how far he took this aim, from the opening chapters of the *Secret History*.[45] But for the events in Book II he was not so obviously drawing on his own experience;[46] he depended on whatever information he could get. And Belisarius' position had changed, and with it Procopius' attitude towards him. There are accordingly distinct differences of treatment between the two Persian books.

Appointed *dux Mesopotamiae* in 527, Belisarius' first brush with the Persians was an ignominious failure, as also was a second attempt to build a fortress on the border at Mindous.[47] A comparison of Procopius' narrative with the other texts (Zachariah and Malalas) shows up a general confusion of chronology, as well as revealing that Procopius has turned two Roman defeats and two attempts to build on the border into one, possibly through inadvertence, but more probably to hurry on the narrative and deflect blame from Belisarius.[48] The first major engagement after his appointment as *MUM per Orientem* in 529,[49] when he commenced full-scale war with Persia, was the defence of the border fortress of Dara (June, 530), which resulted in a Roman victory. Procopius' account makes it clear that Belisarius and Hermogenes exercised a joint command, but when the Persians invaded Commagene, it was Belisarius who took the initiative.[50] In the battle of Callinicum

---

[43] Pp. 167. below.
[44] II.30 (AD 548).
[45] Above, pp. 146, 51f.
[46] Unless he went briefly to the east in 542: below, p. 163.
[47] I.13.5-8; 3.2f.
[48] See Rubin 1960, I, 264f., 487, n. 777; *PLRE* III s.v. Belisarius. In fact Belisarius had no success until the battle of Dara (below).
[49] I.13.9; Malal., 445.
[50] I.18; Malal., 461f. Belisarius yields to pressure to fight: I.18.12-25; cf. Zach. Rhet., *HE* IX.4. On Callinicum, see above, pp. 51f.

which followed, Belisarius' part may have been less than glorious; Malalas says he fled by boat, leaving Sunicas and Simmas to carry on fighting as long as they could.[51] It seems from his immediate replacement as MUM that this was the truth, and that Belisarius tried to extricate himself from blame by throwing it on to his men.[52] Very blatantly, Procopius defends Belisarius by pinning all the blame onto the supposed treachery of al-Harith.[53] Other little touches help the general impression: the emotional speech in which Belisarius tries to dissuade his men from fighting, according to Procopius.[54] But when Procopius suggests that Justinian deliberately allowed Belisarius to think he had been recalled when really he was wanted for the Vandal war[55] is going too far, especially as the Vandal war narrative itself implies that the African expedition had not been long in the planning when it was sent out in early summer, 533, although Belisarius had been in the capital for nearly a year (he was back in time to deal with the Nika revolt on Justinian's behalf).[56] When Procopius records the replacement of Belisarius by Sittas, he does so with the laconic 'so the Emperor Justinian had resolved',[57] surely implying his own indignation.

After this Sittas and Hermogenes (back from Constantinople as an envoy) were faced by a Persian siege of Martyropolis, which was proving hard for them, when news came that Cavadh was ill, and then that Chosroes had succeeded.[58] Both sides, for different reasons, desired a respite and eventually peace was made (531) – not a victory for Byzantium but merely a temporary lull, even though it was labelled the 'Endless Peace'.[59] Included in its terms was the stipulation that there be no Byzantine detachment in future quartered at Dara. So Procopius had no military success with which to end the book, rather the contrary. Instead, therefore, he offers an artful juxtaposition of plots against both Chosroes and Justinian.[60] That against Justinian is the great Nika revolt of January, 532, and the account of it stands functionally in Book I as the climax of Belisarius' achievement in these years, for it was he who led the government troops into the Hippodrome where the factions and people

[51] Malal., 464; according to Procopius, I.18.41-50, he dismounted and fought on foot until nightfall before escaping by boat.

[52] He was succeeded by Mundus: Malal., 466. After an enquiry he was himself recalled to Constantinople (I.21.2; *Vandal Wars* I.9.25; Malal., 466; Zach. Rhet., *HE* IX.6 (blamed for the defeats at Tanurin and Callinicum); Jord., *Rom.* 366; Zon., *HE* XIV. 7; Nic. Cal., *HE* XVII.12).

[53] See pp. 125.

[54] I.18.17-23.

[55] *Vandal Wars* I.9.25; cf. *Persian Wars* I.21.2.

[56] Nika revolt: (Jan. 13-18, 532): Malal., 475; Chron. Pasch., pp. 626f.; *Persian Wars* I.24.40f. Planning of Vandal war: *Vandal Wars* I.10.1.

[57] *Persian Wars* I.21.2.

[58] I.21.23f.

[59] I.22.17.

[60] I.23.1.

were gathered, and who put down the riot with a bloody show of force.[61] Loyal as ever, Belisarius supported the government side, and was followed by the faithful Procopius, who sympathised totally with the interests of law and order. It was Belisarius' loyalty now, rather than his conduct in the past, that induced Justinian to give him the Vandal command, whatever Procopius may imply elsewhere.[62] Predictably, Procopius makes the most of the appointment: he claims that when Chosroes heard the news of the proposed African expedition under Belisarius he regretted having made the peace, for he saw the power of Rome growing on all sides, and even ironically suggested that Justinian, owed him a portion of the Vandal spoils, for the Romans could never have hoped to win Africa if they had not first made peace with Persia.[63]

So Book I of the *Persian Wars* gave Procopius considerable scope for a favourable presentation of Belisarius. This was not the case with Book II. Procopius now has to deal with the events associated with Belisarius' second appointment in the east after his recall from Italy in 540, and the arrival of his wife Antonina, all of which is told from a very different angle in the *Secret History*.[64] Even in the writing of the *Persian Wars*, however, Procopius seems conscious of the vulnerability of Belisarius to criticism, for it is obviously with deliberate intent that he includes at the end of the Nika revolt account in Book I (out of chronological context) the story of how Antonina brought about the fall of John the Cappadocian.[65] While it follows on reasonably enough from the theme of Theodora's hostility to John and his subsequent fortunes after being deposed by Justinian, to appease the rioters, the story also gives Procopius the chance to praise Belisarius and clear him of all blame in the affair. According to Procopius, John was quite alone in being an enemy of Belisarius, out of pure jealousy at Belisarius' fame and esteem.[66] As usual in the *Wars*, the narrative is bland: Procopius says merely that Belisarius was expected to go to the east without Antonina, with no hint of intrigue or any personal difficulties, and he emphasises Antonina's extraordinary forcefulness without pointing any conclusions about possible implications for the character of Belisarius or for their relationship.[67] But it was artful to include the story at all at this point: no doubt in many quarters Belisarius represented the forces of repression rather than heroic generalship, and his position after Nika depended on the gratitude of the emperor whom he had saved from the hostility of men of his own class. In the *Secret History* Procopius naturally puts

---

[61] Malal., 476; *Persian Wars* I.24.44f.
[62] I.26.1; contrast *Vandal Wars* I.9.25.
[63] I.26.2-4.
[64] *Secret History* 2f.; see Chapter 4 above.
[65] I.25.11ff.
[66] I.25.12.
[67] I.25.13; for Antonina see Chapter 5 above.

things rather differently.[88] But here he has been able to divert attention
from this aspect of Belisarius' action and by jumping ahead
chronologically to remind his audience, as a counterweight, of his
preeminence in Italy in 540 and the reputation which he then enjoyed in
Constantinople. He uses the same technique as in the *Gothic Wars* when
he inserts an emphatic eulogy of Belisarius just at the point where he had
been recalled from Italy by the jealous emperor.[69]

When Procopius reaches this point in *Persian Wars* Book II (with
chapter 14), he relates in detail the siege and eventual capture of
Sisauranon,[70] which Belisarius achieved despite difficulties of equipment
and opposition from some of the Roman commanders on the spot; but the
aftermath was somewhat equivocal, for we are told here that he retreated
from Sisauranon in the face of general unease and illness among the
army. Even this Procopius turns into praise of Belisarius, by putting the
pleas of the troops into the form of a speech delivered by John the son of
Nicetas, beginning:

'Noble Belisarius, I do not believe that there has been another general like you
in the whole of time, either for good fortune or for valour. And this fame has
not only surpassed that of the Romans, but even that of all the barbarians.
You will best preserve this reputation if you can take us back alive to Roman
territory – for now our spirits are at a low ebb.'[71]

As at Callinicum, Belisarius, it is implied, was in the hands of his troops.
Clearly Procopius felt that a defence was necessary; at any rate, in the
Secret History he produces quite a different and hostile story – that at
just this point Belisarius heard of the impending arrival of his wife
Antonina, and returned posthaste to settle a private quarrel with her:
'The result of this move was that an accusation was levelled at Belisarius
by Romans everywhere of having sacrificed the most vital interests of the
state to his own domestic concerns.'[72] Here Procopius suggests that
Belisarius could have crossed the Tigris with his army and reached
Ctesiphon without opposition, even rescuing all the Roman prisoners
taken when Chosroes sacked Antioch in 540.[73] We are further assured
that the leaders of the Persian expedition to Lazica were so alarmed by
the news of the fall of Sisauranon that they urged immediate retreat, and
that although Chosroes attempted to stem the panic, he was forced to
yield; yet the psychological advantage thus won by the Byzantines was
thrown away when Chosroes failed to meet with the expected opposition

[68] The Nika revolt handled by Justinian so as to confiscate senatorial property: *Secret
History* 12.12f.; 19.12. No blame is attached to Belisarius however.
[69] *Gothic Wars* III.1.1-22; cf. II.30.1-2.
[70] *Persian Wars* II.16-19.
[71] II.19.36-7.
[72] *Secret History* 2.19.
[73] Ibid. 2.25.

on his retreat to Persia.[74] The treatment of this episode in the *Secret History* is so emphatic that it is easy to believe that Procopius was conscious of the need to produce a defence for Belisarius even when writing the *Wars*, and his deliberate introduction of Antonina in Book I makes us suspect that the artful narrative in Book II skates very much over the surface. This was the sum of Belisarius' stay in the east on this occasion; he was recalled again by Justinian and spent winter 541/2 in Constantinople.[75] So it was essential for Procopius, with only this rather ambivalent set of events to play with, to make the most of them.

But within a year news came that Chosroes had invaded Euphratensis, and Belisarius was sent once again to the east.[76] Again the events that followed allowed of differing interpretations. Belisarius avoided battle and secured the retreat of the Persian army by diplomatic means. In *Persian Wars* II Procopius extravagantly claims that this feat won Belisarius acclaim even greater than when he brought Gelimer and Vitigis captive to Constantinople.[77] But he also reveals that in fact the Roman troops were too few to risk a battle,[78] and in the *Secret History* we are told that Belisarius was thought cowardly or negligent for not pursuing Chosroes after the Persians had taken Callinicum on this occasion.[79] To make this diplomatic concession palatable Procopius had to resort to even more special pleading than usual. Another crisis during the same year involved Belisarius, stemming this time from the plague which raged in Constantinople and seized the emperor himself. And here too the *Wars* and the *Secret History* sharply diverge. According to the former, Belisarius was recalled now in order to fight the war in Italy,[80] a bland statement reminiscent of Procopius' description of his earlier recall after the battle of Callinicum.[81] The *Secret History* is far more circumstantial: the illness of Justinian naturally provoked urgent discussion about a possible successor, during the course of which Belisarius and Buzes were accused of having refused in advance to serve any new emperor appointed in their absence, whereupon a furious Theodora summoned them back to Constantinople; unable to prove any offence, she nevertheless had Belisarius dismissed and replaced by Martinus, and further undermined his position in various ways, by dispersing his *bucellarii*, forbidding his friends to associate with him and seizing his wealth.[82] The essence of this and of the further detailed

---

[74] Ibid.

[75] *Persian Wars* II.19.49.

[76] II.20.20.

[77] II.21.28-9; 26.46.

[78] II.21.18f., no doubt in large part due to losses from plague (n. 135 below).

[79] *Secret History* 3.30-1.

[80] *Persian Wars* II.21.34; *Gothic Wars* III.9.23; Jord., *Rom.* 377.

[81] Above, p. 158.

[82] *Secret History* 4.4-6, 13-15, 17.

description of Theodora's intrigues against him which follows in the
Secret History[83] finds some confirmation in Marcellinus' *Chronicle*,
where we are told that on his recall Belisarius 'in offensam periculumque
incurrens grave et invidiae subiacens rursus remittitur ad Italiam'.[84] It
may be Procopius' later resentment against Antonina and Theodora that
makes him claim that Belisarius wanted to go to the east but had his way
blocked by his wife, and that his recovery of his wealth was only achieved
as an indirect favour to Antonina by the empress,[85] but his stay in
Constantinople from 542-4 as a private citizen in reduced circumstances
probably has truth in it, and was doubtless a major contributor to
Procopius' growing disappointment, especially if Belisarius meekly
accepted it. Certainly his appointment in 544 as *comes sacri stabuli*
raised some eyebrows, and was followed by the campaign in Italy which
caused Procopius such pain.[86] Although he claimed that on this occasion
too Belisarius was given complete power to conduct the war,[87] it may be
that even this is an exaggeration to save his patron's face.

Thus the repeated praise of Belisarius in *Persian Wars* II for avoiding a
battle against Chosroes in 542 is there for a reason. Behind this short
excursion of Belisarius to the east, as with his earlier campaigns, lay a
whole background of intrigue, jealousy and accusation, which Procopius
wanted at this point to exclude from the *Wars* completely. But he could
not totally obscure the fact that Belisarius achieved little positive, or
that his actions were often at least ambivalent. With this material he did
his best, sometimes over-arguing, sometimes relying merely on artful
juxtaposition, or the chance of a well-positioned speech. But overall, the
two books of the *Persian Wars* are less successful in putting over the case
for Belisarius than either the *Vandal Wars* or the earlier parts of the
Gothic Wars; in large part this was due to the nature of the subject
matter itself. Much more here than in the other sections, we feel a sharp
discrepancy between the *Wars* and the *Secret History*; but a closer look
at both narratives reveals them as complementary rather than opposed.
Far from being a straightforwardly approving presentation of events, the
Persian Wars is a clever, self-conscious and artful composition.

These books are dominated not only by the figure of Belisarius but also
by the personality of Chosroes. Again we see Procopius reducing history
to simplified terms. He has no explanation for the hostilities other than
that in Chosroes, who came to the throne only after Procopius' own
appointment by Belisarius, the Persians had found a ruler who was
'unstable in character and an extraordinary lover of novelty'.[88] Such a

[83] 4.16, 20-1, 18-31, 37, 38.
[84] s.a. 545.3.
[85] *Secret History* 4.18-31, 38; 5.18.
[86] *Secret History* 4.39.
[87] *Gothic Wars* III.21.25.
[88] *Persian Wars* I.23.1-2. See too *Gothic Wars* IV.10.12 and above, p. 143. Chosroes
represents the denial of humanity: *Gothic Wars* IV.10.8.

man could only upset the existing order,[89] and indeed the 'most capable Persians'[90] rose against him, though without success.[91] With this first introduction of Chosroes to the action, Procopius sets him up as a foil to Justinian, not merely through the use of similar vocabulary, but also explicitly by situating these remarks on Chosroes here in the first book of the *Persian Wars*; he underlines the parallelism between the two rulers by saying that he will now relate the plots which each had to suffer.[92] The two characters are presented in exactly similar language and are put forth as parallels; they perform an explanatory role in the narrative of the *Wars*, no less than do Justinian and Theodora in the *Secret History*.[93]

Much of *Persian Wars* II is the catalogue of the incursions of Chosroes into Mesopotamia and Syria, the effect of these on the towns and their populations, and the dominating factor of Chosroes' own personality. For all that Procopius tried hard with Belisarius, it is Chosroes who steals the thunder. Many vivid episodes remain in the mind: his deception of the people of Sura and his delight in making them an example;[94] his subsequent offer to ransom the 12,000 prisoners to bishop Candidus of Sergiopolis merely for an I.O.U.;[95] his way of playing cat and mouse with the frightened towns and their envoys, usually their bishops; the abject terror inspired by his coming;[96] the terrible sack of Antioch which followed a misguided show of scorn from its inhabitants;[97] the unforgettable evocation of Chosroes conducting hippodrome races at Apamea and cheating.[98] Procopius writes of all this with great detail and plausibility, and with much local knowledge, which it would be much easier to explain if we supposed that he accompanied Belisarius to the east in 542. It is usually assumed that he stayed in Constantinople throughout that year because of his detailed plague description and his statement that he was there when it came to the capital in the height of spring.[99] But Belisarius' expedition was not dispatched until news arrived of Chosroes' invasion of Euphratensis, which took place in early spring,[100] and Belisarius was back in Constantinople before the end of 542.[101] Procopius could have seen the beginning of the plague in

---

[89] 'He was always filled himself with disorder and agitation and was reponsible for affecting others in the same way.'

[90] *drastêrioi* – a favourable word in Procopius' vocabulary (p. 240).

[91] I.23.3-11.

[92] I.23.1.

[93] See above, pp. 138.

[94] II.5.14-27.

[95] II.5.28-33.

[96] II.7.34-5 (Megas of Beroea).

[97] II.8.7.

[98] II.11.31-8.

[99] II.22.9, on which see Stein, *BE* II, Appendix X, p. 841. It raged in Constantinople for four months, though it was at its height for only three – II.23.1.

[100] II.20.1, 20-8.

[101] Above, p. 161.

Constantinople and composed his highly literary account of its effects on
the basis of information gathered later in the year. Certainly his detail
about the expedition of Belisarius in 542 speaks for close personal
involvement, and if he was there himself, he could also then have
collected the very detailed information about small-town personalities
and reactions during the invasion of 540 from talking to people on the
spot. It is true that there is nothing to suggest that he was out in the east
again to collect the information which he has on Chosroes' 544 invasion,
or about events in Lazica. Nevertheless, he tells of 540-2 in an altogether
more intimate and full manner. The story of Abgar of Edessa and the
letter of Jesus comes into this section, while by contrast the account of
the 544 threat to Edessa is lacking in the miraculous overtones found in
other versions;[102] this would need no special explanation if Procopius had
no first-hand knowledge of the 544 attack and was not in close touch with
sectional local accounts.[103] What he did know was that Chosroes' main
objective was to extract large sums of gold from the Roman towns, and
his whole narrative moves around the politics of these transactions.[104] as
his account of Edessa's experience in 544 well shows.

The focus on Chosroes as a personality helps Procopius gloss over the
uncomfortable fact that these towns could expect no help from Byzantine
troops. If Belisarius had too few men to risk a battle in 542, there were
also too few to defend these exposed towns or in any way protect them
from the Persians. The locals – and Procopius – knew that the only way
was negotiation, or rather, pleading, with Chosroes, if they did not have
substantial treasure to hand over. Some towns fared better in this game
than others, and some were saved by Chosroes' own caprice.[105] But by
casting the narrative in the shape of a drama in which Chosroes is the
main character, Procopius avoids the need for an explanation of the poor
state of Byzantine defence. In the case of Antioch, there was such a
defence, but the Byzantines only just arrived in time to stop all the
Antiochenes from running away, while it was thought that Ephraem, the
bishop, was only too ready to 'sell the city to the Persians'.[106] It is not
surprising that Procopius could only explain the disaster in supernatural
terms, for an explanation in human terms would have revealed the
deficiencies of Byzantine preparedness all too clearly. Procopius' vivid
account of the taking of the city makes it clear as it is that the Byzantine
soldiers were more of a hindrance than a help to the townspeople; only
the young men of the factions stood firm, against all expectation,[107] while

[102] II.12.6f. (540); II.26-7 (544). See above, pp. 116.
[103] See Averil Cameron 1980, 1983.
[104] Cf. II.27.46.
[105] Sura, Beroea, Antioch suffered; Hierapolis, Apamea, Edessa escaped. The weakness of
the available Byzantine forces: Liebeschuetz 1977, 498f.
[106] II.7.16.
[107] II.8.17 (Procopius' surprise).

the soldiers, spurred on by a false rumour that Buzes was coming to their aid, rode wildly to one of the gates and trampled on many of the inhabitants who rushed after them in the same vain hope.[108] This very incident was to be repeated in reverse soon after, when the city was entered by the Persians, for the soldiers now deserted it, pouring out through the one gate not in Persian control, while the factionaries, though mostly armed only with stones, met the Persians inside the city, thought themselves victorious and hailed Justinian as victor.[109] Antioch was taken and sacked by the Persians in an unexampled show of savagery which Procopius had yet somehow to accommodate within the logic of his narrative. He must acknowledge the major importance of this catastrophe, but can hardly not in so doing cast doubt on the whole Byzantine record. His way out of the dilemma is to resort to musings on the mysterious working of God and fortune,[110] while also attributing the disaster to the personal vengeance of Chosroes. Precisely here he inserts a statement of Chosroes' treachery, with an express connection drawn between Chosroes and Justinian.[111] Even without the distortion detected in the Antioch narrative by Downey,[112] it is evident how skilfully Procopius has moulded the material to cast blame onto personalities, and to avoid a realistic critique of the Byzantine dispositions in the east. An explicit statement of the nature of a major character in the narrative is here as elsewhere carefully placed to achieve a specific effect; but here also (as elsewhere) the detail of Procopius' own account undermines the artful suprastructure. Finally, the all too obvious failings of the eastern campaigns of 540 onwards, culminating in the sack of Antioch, must have been a major factor in changing Procopius' attitude from the simple enthusiasm of the early days to the weary disillusionment and then bitter resentment of the later period. It was now very clear that not even a Belisarius could extract victory from the logistics of the eastern frontier. This is the message of *Persian Wars* II, however much Procopius tries to soften its effect.

The real texture of events on the eastern front, then, has significantly affected the shape of Procopius' narrative. As we have seen, there is more openly Christian material here, and more of a sense of small-town life in this frontier area. Both are there because of the nature of Chosroes' incursions, a progress from one town to another, in the almost total absence of the Byzantine army. Perhaps because of this lack of opportunity to write major battle pieces, Procopius includes in these books not merely the account of the Nika revolt, which would not have

[108] II.8.17-19.
[109] II.8.25-9.
[110] II.10; see above, p. 106.
[111] II.9.8-13; see especially 8.11.
[112] Downey 1953.

fitted easily elsewhere, but also his description of the plague, which would have been equally at home in the *Gothic Wars*.[113] Neither fits the general subject, for both concern Constantinople, but they are major literary treatments comparable with Procopius' presentation elsewhere of, say, the entry into Carthage or the Vandal triumph.[114] At the same time, they were major misfortunes for the regime, and Procopius was faced with the problem of how he was going to work them in to the logic of his work. He does so, as we have seen, by utilising the parallelism between the two monarchs, Justinian and Chosroes.[115] While this does not save him from the implications of either the Nika revolt or the plague, it does reduce the problem of explanation to a more possible level, while their inclusion both balances the two books and gives Procopius the chance of traditional literary display.

Of the two themes, the Nika revolt offered the more awkward subject matter, and something of Procopius' embarrassment is suggested by the fact that he included it also in the *Secret History* and the *Buildings*, naturally very differently.[116] Quite apart from the problem of responsibility and causes, the affair showed up Justinian in a bad light, very early in the reign, and placed Belisarius in the position of leading the bloody suppression of the riot. Here Procopius blames the affair entirely on the Blues and Greens. Yet his explanation will hardly do: he cannot account for the actions of the factions except by referring to their general and 'incomprehensible' opposition to everyone outside their own group.[117] Procopius' responses are themselves irrational – one of the worst aspects for him is that women are involved,[118] the ultimate sign of disorder.[119] In fact his whole account here is inspired by the wish to defend order against chaos and irrationality.[120] At the same time, had he had a more adequate understanding of the revolt, it would have been difficult to express it in the *Wars*, where the logic of the work dictated that its implications for Justinian's rule be minimised, at least in this early placing. The subtle changes in Procopius' own attitudes, and the powerful constraints of what was actually sayable in the *Wars*, make it difficult to be fair to Procopius on matters of causation, since at any point he may not be writing what he really thinks. But though this account of Nika is prejudiced and superficial, it is also more differentiated than either of the other two. He does for instance here

---

[113] *Persian Wars* I.24; II.22. For the plague, see pp. 40f. above.

[114] *Vandal Wars* I.20; II.9.

[115] Above, n. 111.

[116] *Secret History* 12.12; *Buildings* I.20f.

[117] *Persian Wars* I.24.4.

[118] I.24.6; see p. 144 above.

[119] See Chapters 5 and 12.

[120] He would fit Barthes's definition of the writing appropriate to all authoritarian regimes: 'It is what might be called police-state writing: we know, for example, that the content of the word 'Order' always indicates repression.' (Barthes 1953/1968, 25).

distinguish genuine grievances held by the 'demos' against Justinian's ministers,[121] and it is the 'demos' who are here represented as hostile to the government, even if they are led by the factions.[122] The senators, here, are divided.[123] Procopius' own position is on the side of the government, or at least of law and order: he condemns the senators who followed Hypatius for behaving 'as a crowd usually does', and he presents Belisarius and Mundus as the only hope for the emperor.[124] This is exactly what we should have expected. Perhaps prudently, he nowhere attempts to analyse the source of opposition, and devotes his available space rather to the mechanics of the operation in which the crowd in the Hippodrome was overcome and Hypatius and Pompeius taken.[125] Again, he reduces a complex set of events to personalities. The implication is that once Justinian makes concessions about the hated ministers, the matter is over. Similarly, Theodora's famous intervention is for him ideal material for a rhetorical display.[126] Such interpretations are quite sufficient for Procopius. Here the Blues and Greens, on whom the first blame was placed, fade entirely out of the picture as the account unfolds, and he leaves the whole subject without further comment for a long story, out of context, of the eventual fall of John the Cappadocian,[127] part of Procopius' own personal preoccupations rather than integrally connected with the Nika account. We have seen him doing something similar in other set pieces, where he will leave the main subject and go off at a tangent on something which happens to interest him.[128] Here his account of the Nika revolt is a carefully external one, which largely avoids the issues at stake, and focusses on the brilliance of Belisarius, even in this inglorious engagement. Procopius says the affair ended in much evil (*kakon*) for the *dêmos* and the senate,[129] but he nowhere condemns the level of state violence in its suppression, or says that it was excessive (30,000 dead according to Malalas),[130] claiming that although there was much slaughter the defeat of the *dêmos* in the Hippodrome was 'glorious'.[131] His responses, in other words, are authoritarian and for 'law and order', even after making allowance for the need here not to be too critical of Justinian's régime.

With the plague description Procopius did not face the same problems of awkward political implications, and was more readily able to turn his

[121] I.24.17.
[122] I.24.22, 24.
[123] I.24.25.
[124] I.24.26f., 31, 40.
[125] I.24.42-56.
[126] Above, pp. 69.
[127] Ibid.
[128] See pp. 141f. on the account of the Vandal triumph.
[129] I.24.1.
[130] Malal., 476; John the Lydian, *De Mag.* III.70 says 50,000.
[131] I.24.53.

account into a literary display because of the obvious classical model.[132] He does so at great length and emphasis. There are certain similarities, all the same, between this section and the parallel set-piece on the Nika revolt. Here too he picks up the odd and the curious – the odd reactions of the victims, their hallucinations, the way they fell ill, the variety of forms taken by the disease, the difficulty of obtaining care, the bewilderment of the doctors and the general impossibility of forecasting either the course of the disease or its proper treatment.[133] And he is content, similarly, with an over-simplified explanation which will release him of the need to delve deeper into effects; here too it is the incomprehensible will of God, just as with the sack of Antioch. Indeed, he even says that men are fools to think they can explain such disasters by scientific means.[134] He is satisfied to say that we cannot understand it – and to leave it at that. This plague had extensive repercussions, and affected most of the empire;[135] it was probably a main cause in the problems of manpower and money which bedevilled Justinian's later years, and it caused an immediate financial crisis.[136] But Procopius limits it in the *Wars* to a discrete and literary excursus, as though to suggest that its effects could be equally easily dealt with, and as though it only affected Constantinople. And here he leaves out – surely deliberately, for it is emphasised in the *Secret History* – all but a passing reference to the fact that the emperor himself fell ill of it, not even telling the reader how serious was Justinian's condition or how he managed to escape death.[137] Whether we explain this as a careful attempt to minimise the plague's seriousness – he also leaves out here the constitutional crisis precipitated by the emperor's illness, and which resulted in the recall of Belisarius –[138] or as a symptom of Procopius' covert dislike of Justinian, it makes the plague account a less than adequate historical treatment. In fact, Procopius has sanitized the plague, as he has diminished the seriousness of the Nika revolt by blaming it on the incomprehensible folly of the factions.[139]

He is no more inclined in these books to give us any real analysis of the relations between Byzantium and Iran or the nature of the two empires. Although he is interested in the mechanics of diplomacy, he treats the Persians in general as if they differed from other barbarians only in scale of importance. Their fire-worship, for instance, merits only an

---

[132] See Chapter 3 above.

[133] II.22.10-14, 15-17, 18f., 23-7, 29, 33.

[134] II.22.1-5.

[135] Allen 1979; Mango 1982. In the short term, it was surely a main factor in Byzantine weakness on the eastern front from 542 (Teall 1965, 316f.) – yet Procopius does not draw the conclusion (see above), content as always to elevate personal factors to first place.

[136] Above, p. 42.

[137] II.23.20.

[138] Above, p. 42.

[139] I.24.1-6.

antiquarian comment, that it recalls the worship of Hecate by the ancient Romans,[140] and while he recognises the importance of religion as a factor in the war in Lazica, it is without any sense of the complex cultural intermingling of the whole eastern frontier region. The fourth invasion of Chosroes, directed at Mesopotamia, is said to be aimed not against Justinian but at the Christian God;[141] but the reasons which Procopius gives for it are reasons of personal spite, Chosroes having previously been foiled in his aim of taking Edessa (in fact he decided again to let the Edessans buy their freedom for a high price).[142] Similarly, Procopius sees the interraction of the Lakhmids and Ghassanids, under al-Harith and al-Mundhir, in terms of personal rivalries, not as reflecting the Byzantine and Persian attempts to maintain a balance of power in the frontier zone.[143] Such facile devices as he employs in the case of the role of al-Harith at the battle of Callinicum[144] make interpretation very much easier for Procopius, but of course preclude a real understanding.

Despite their high spots, therefore, the two books of the *Persian Wars* remain less than satisfactoy. The emphasis is often oddly placed, and from the *Secret History* we can see why. The Persian books end, for example, with the return of John the Cappadocian to Constantinople and the curious prophecy then fulfilled, not with the death of Theodora, which, like Justinian's illness in the plague excurses, is mentioned only in passing.[145] The years described in the *Persian Wars* were years in which Procopius was near to Belisarius, but when he also saw Belisarius' vulnerability revealed. The narrative of a war without great conquest or glory was therefore not going to be an easy matter, and we see Procopius often resorting to omission or bland over-simplification. On the other hand, the *Persian Wars* does not see the extreme disillusionment which Procopius came to feel and which is most evident in the *Gothic Wars*.[146] Nor did Procopius have to deal here with the depressing aftermath of great conquest, as in the *Vandal Wars*, where the high point reached with Belisarius' triumph near the beginning of the second book is followed by a far less edifying narrative of division in the Byzantine armies and severe threats from a different and less tractable enemy than the Vandals.[147] The tensions underlying the *Persian Wars* are of a more personal and partisan kind; but Procopius does not speak

---

[140] II.24.2. Persians as barbarians *par excellence*: Cesa 1981, 404. Payments to Persia as an extension on the grand scale of Justinian's subsidy policy: see *Gothic Wars* IV.15.

[141] II.26.2.

[142] II.26.12f.; 27.46. It was not surprising, faced with having to explain their unexpected escape, that the Edessenes evolved a story in which it came about through miraculous means, through a wonder-working icon.

[143] See for example II.28.12-13.

[144] Above, p. 125.

[145] II.30.49-54: return of John; 30.49: death of Theodora.

[146] Below, Chapter 11.

[147] Below, Chapter 10.

out so clearly as he was later to do. He was on the other hand more ready to defend and glorify Belisarius. So the *Persian Wars* consists of a narrative in which not all is told. More than the rest of the *Wars*, it was found wanting when Procopius came to write the *Secret History*.

CHAPTER TEN

Procopius and Africa

The *Vandal Wars* covers Belisarius' greatest victory. The campaign against the Vandals was pressed by Justinian himself against the judgment of everyone else, if we follow Procopius; yet it was crowned with amazing success and brought Belisarius to a dazzling peak of fame – the Vandal 'triumph' in AD 534, when Gelimer the Vandal king walked in chains behind his captor, and the consulship in the following year, whose opportunities Belisarius exploited to so great an extent that Justinian himself grew alarmed. In these years Procopius was close to Belisarius and accompanied him throughout. Not only therefore did he have personal knowledge of the great campaign, but he had not yet felt the disillusion that set in in the 540s. The two books of the *Vandal Wars* should then mark a high peak in Procopius' own experience and in his writing of the wars of reconquest.

In fact they record Byzantine incapacity as well as Byzantine triumph, and the difficulties as well as the successes of reconquest. A long 'origins' passage on the history of the Vandals[1] precedes the telling of the dispatch of the expedition, its victories and Belisarius' triumphant return to Constantinople, his victory celebration and his consulship.[2] But the rest of the second book is occupied by renewed and serious Berber warfare, mutiny in the Byzantine army, the excellent command of Solomon, cut short by his death in a minor engagement, the misconduct of Sergius, the plots of Areobindus and then his murder, followed by that of the rebel Gontharis, and finally the relatively successful campaigns against the Berbers of John Troglita.[3] Procopius ends the book on an exhausted and resigned note: 'So a certain degree of respite – late and with difficulty – was given to the remaining Africans, now few and reduced to beggary.'[4] It was in fact – though his disappointment did not extend to Belisarius, who had left in Africa in 534 and only returned once for a brief excursion

---

[1] *Vandal Wars* I.1-9, bringing Vandal history up to AD 533; see Chapter 12 below, pp. 208.
[2] I.10-II.9.
[3] The latter told also in Corippus' *Iohannis*, covering the years AD 546-9.
[4] II.28.52.

in 536[5] – a saddening experience. Procopius himself stayed longer in Africa than Belisarius, for when the mutineers seized Carthage he was with Solomon, and escaped with him to a ship with the help of one Theodore the Cappadocian, who sensibly forced them to eat first, though they were desperate to be off and join Belisarius in Sicily.[6] But this detailed narrative of the problems that followed in Africa up to 549, when *Vandal Wars* II breaks off, came to him indirectly, for he was with Belisarius in Italy from 535 to 540, and then in Constantinople in 542 and probably for most of the 540s. He takes up the African story again in *Gothic Wars* IV, though only briefly, to praise John for his successes against Iaudas and Antalas, but to add the final comment, deliberately to reinforce his earlier criticisms, that 'after all, the province had been deserted of men in the preceding campaigns and mutinies, and continued very much in the same condition'.[7] When he wrote the final book of the *Wars*, Africa was still enjoying the 'respite' provided by John Troglita, though it was not to be the end of Byzantine difficulties by any means.[8] The *Secret History*, written before John's achievement could have been fully recognised, pursues the theme of the depopulation of Africa much further. According to Procopius, five million dead, including Vandals, Roman Africans and Berbers, would not be a high enough estimate.[9] It is one of his prime examples of Justinian's 'blood-lust', his deliberate wish to exterminate existing populations.[10] But Procopius has a more serious criticism than this abuse: Justinian, he claims, 'made no plans to ensure that the resources of Africa could be secured for him by winning the firm loyalty of the inhabitants', instead recalling Belisarius too soon, imposing fierce taxes on the population, bringing in anti-Arian measures and failing to pay the troops. 'The result of all this was an outbreak of revolts that led to widespread destruction'[11] If we ignore the wilder claims (that Justinian wished 'to swallow up the plunder of Libya' and that he was deliberately trying to throw things into confusion), this is a far more solidly based critique of government policy in Africa than anything in the *Wars*, though there are hints there that point to it too. Procopius omits the Three Chapters affair, which did more than most things to enrage the Roman Africans;[12] but in the *Buildings*, where a substantial and detailed section is devoted to Africa, the role played by

---

[5] II.15.9f. After a minor victory over the rebels under Stotzas he was forced to return to Sicily on hearing of trouble in the army there: II.15.46-9.

[6] II.14.37-42. It was a result of the urgent pleas of Procopius and Solomon on reaching Sicily that Belisarius returned to Africa in 536.

[7] *Gothic Wars* IV.17.21.

[8] See Corippus, *Iust., Pan. Anast.*, 36f.; I.18f.; Stein, *BE* II.558f.

[9] *Secret History* 18.1-9, especially 8.

[10] For which cf. 18.27, 29.

[11] 18.9-12.

[12] See Averil Cameron 1982, 45ff.

religion in the ideology of reconquest comes over clearly.[13]

In writing about the reconquest of the province of Africa, therefore, Procopius encountered problems and contradictions which we can only appreciate fully by putting all three of his works together.

The theme of success and victory is the first to present itself in the *Vandal Wars*, after the lengthy introductory chapters. Belisarius' quick and unexpected victory gave Procopius easy material, which he heightens by emphasising the opposition encountered by Justinian in planning the operation.[14] As elsewhere, he represents the reconquest policy as a sudden whim which gets its impetus from the immediate situation.[15] A temperate speech by John the Cappadocian gives Justinian pause, but he is spurred on again by an eastern bishop who promises God's aid.[16] Procopius himself claims to have been convinced by a dream that the expedition would succeed: he saw a gift brought to Belisarius in his own house – the earth blooming with fruits, and Belisarius lying on it and eating the fruits and inviting the members of his bodyguard to do the same, as though they were lying on a bed.[17] The author features in the text, as one of Belisarius' party, and as one who had formerly been suspicious of the whole plan, but who was convinced by a divine sign. The effect of such an emphasis, underlined by the vivid account of the fleet's departure, sped on by emperor, empress and patriarch.[18] was to stress that the expedition had God on its side. Similarly, Procopius no doubt exaggerates Belisarius' fears while the fleet was still off Sicily in order both to make the final victory seem the more remarkable.[19] The old friend he says he met at Syracuse was able to produce a man just returned from Carthage who could assure Procopius that the Vandals had no idea of the approach of the Byzantine fleet, and indeed that their army had just left Carthage on quite a different errand. Procopius includes another portent as the fleet landed at Caput Vada, just three months after leaving Constantinople: water in large quantities gushed forth in arid Byzacena, and Procopius represents himself as assuring Belisarius that it was indeed a sign of success from God, as was proved, he says, by what later happened.[20] As if by magic, the Byzantines met no

[13] Above, Chapter 6.

[14] *Vandal Wars* I.10.2-6. The standard guide for the Byzantine military operations in N. Africa remains Diehl 1896; see however Pringle 1981, I.9ff. for a fresh account; Duval 1981; Durliat 1981.

[15] I.9.25-10.1; cf. *Gothic Wars* I.5.1. But this does not mean (Cesa 1981, 400) that Procopius was hostile to the idea as such.

[16] *Vandal Wars* I.10.7-21.

[17] I.12.3-5. Cesa 1981, 400f. concludes from I.10 that Procopius wishes to suggest the folly of the idea of reconquest, but the dream related here suggests the opposite.

[18] I.12.1-2.

[19] I.14.1-3, 7-13.

[20] I.15.34-6. Procopius seems to have been at his closest to Belisarius during this period: see I.14.3f., 15.

obstacle on their way to Carthage.[21] Even dangerous moments were
circumvented, Procopius suggests, by the unseen working of God.[22] And
when, at the battle of Ad Decimum, Gelimer had victory in his hands, it
was obvious to Procopius that it was through the hand of God that he
threw it away.[23]

The first high-point of this part of the *Vandal Wars* is Belisarius' entry
into Carthage,[24] prefaced by a lecture to his soldiers about the reasons for
the war and the care they must take not to harm the Africans, who were
all after all Roman.[25] With unforgettable drama, Belisarius entered the
palace and sat upon the throne of Gelimer; then he and his leading
officers, including Procopius himself, dined off the food prepared for
Gelimer and were served by Gelimer's household.[26] On that day, says
Procopius, Belisarius attained a peak of achievement greater than that
reached by any other man,[27] not least because no one was harmed and
there was such *kosmia* among the occupying soldiers that the people did
not even lock their doors. Yet another heavenly dream was now fulfilled –
the regular appearances of St. Cyprian, seen by many, promising that
one day he would avenge the seizure of his basilica by the Arians.[28] Now,
as the Arian priests made ready for the festival of St. Cyprian, the
Vandals were defeated at Ad Decimum; the Arians fled, and the
orthodox were able to enter the church and celebrate the festival with the
bright lamps and furnishings prepared by the Arians. There is no place in
the *Wars* more dramatic than this, or more striking in its juxtaposition of
the secular and the religious.

But the war was not over; Gelimer engaged the Byzantines again in the
middle of December, but was put to flight, taking refuge on Mt. Pappas
in Numidia.[29] He resisted Byzantine attempts to capture him for three
months and surrendered only when he saw the miserable sight of two
boys, one of them his own nephew, fighting over a morsel of bread.[30]
Typically, Procopius calls Gelimer's weakening 'giving way to feminine
feelings'.[31] But the pathos and vividness of this story, the Vandal boy at

[21] I.17.6.
[22] I.18.2-3.
[23] I.19.25.
[24] I.20.
[25] I.20.18-19.
[26] I.21.
[27] I.21.8.
[28] Above, p. 114.
[29] II.3. Procopius has a strong sense of the nobility and pathos of Gelimer's position; here
he says that for a long time the Vandals did not know that Gelimer had fled, and that when
they found out, the men lamented, the children cried and the women wailed, and everyone
else then fled headlong, heedless of property and of the unhappiness of their loved ones
(3.22).
[30] II.7.
[31] I.7.6.

first playing idly and then fighting in earnest with the Berber, is typical of his own treatment of this campaign, which is full of divine portents and curious anecdotes, and which so often draws explicitly on Procopius' own experiences.[32] After Gelimer's surrender, Procopius tells another such story: when the Vandal king met Belisarius at Anclae, a suburb of Carthage favoured by the Vandals, he laughed loud and long, causing some to think he had lost his wits. Those who knew him best, however, interpreted the laughter as meaning that after his experience of the extremes of human fortune, Gelimer found life worth only laughter.[33] Procopius ends with a new twist to his usual formula: 'As to Gelimer's laughter, let each pronounce as he sees fit, whether enemy or friend.'[34] But he was sure himself that there was something miraculous about the defeat of Gelimer, of the fourth generation after Geiseric, by a 'force of five thousand strangers who did not know where to lay anchor'.[35] Only one thing spoiled this sense of elation: Belisarius was accused by his fellow officers of plotting treason and replaced by Solomon with the choice of remaining in Africa or returning to Constantinople; Procopius got to know of the plot even though the accusers sent two separate messengers to Justinian, when one of them was detained in the fortress of Mandracium in Carthage and handed over his secret letter.[36] But at this stage such mischief could be allowed to be forgotten in comparison with the magnitude of Belisarius' success.

The high point of that success was represented for Procopius in the 'triumph' that was allowed to Belisarius in Constantinople.[37] Whereas in 540 he was denied it, now, despite the accusations, he was allowed to walk in solemn procession from his house through the city and into the Hippodrome to the Imperial Box, with Gelimer and his family following behind in chains with all the spoils of the Vandal war. When the procession reached the Kathisma, Gelimer, in his purple robe, looked round, saying 'O vanity of vanities; all is vanity', until like Belisarius he was forced to do obeisance, lying flat on his face before Justinian seated on his high throne. Procopius draws out the full piquancy of this meeting, when Justinian and Theodora gazed down on the descendants of Hilderic and the heirs of Valentinian.[38] The philosophical Gelimer would not give up his Arianism, and thus forfeited the chance of being made a patrician, but he and his family were given substantial estates in Galatia for an honourable exile.

---

[32] See n. 20.
[33] II.7.12f.
[34] II.7.16.
[35] II.7.18-21. Some of Procopius' best writing comes in these chapters, among the most dramatic in the *Wars*.
[36] II.8.6-8.
[37] II.9.
[38] II.9.13.

Naturally Procopius presents the occasion as a glorification of
Belisarius;[39] while in theory it was the triumph of Justinian, Belisarius is
at the centre of Procopius' account. There was justification, surely.
Belisarius was given the consulship for 535, and celebrated it with
overwhelming magnificence;[40] Procopius underlines its importance, both
at the beginning of the year and when he records how Belisarius spent its
end in Syracuse.[41] He could scatter for largesse gold and silver from the
Vandal spoils as he was carried on his curule chair by Vandal prisoners.
Some of this treasure thus passed into the hands of the common people,
who thought, or so Procopius claims, that they were experiencing a true
revival of ancient glories.[42] As a result Justinian may well have felt that
things had gone too far. But Procopius naturally presents this great
occasion as the culmination of the success of the reconquest. It was
commemorated again, no doubt many times; we know of the great
mosaic on the roof of the Chalke gate to the palace, which Procopius
describes in the *Buildings*,[43] and Justinian's woven funeral pall.[44] It was
an opportunity for Procopius to show Belisarius at the very height of
glory, and he does not miss it. Nevertheless, with this triumph Belisarius
passes out of the story of Byzantine Africa, apart from one short and
saving return.[45] And with his departure the theme of victory gives way to
one of strife and disillusion.

Even before this Procopius has to deal with the topic of Berber
hostilities, and the chapter in which he introduces this theme is in many
ways typical of his approach to the general situation in Africa. There is a
certain awareness of problems, of course: thus he lets us know that there
are as yet insufficient troops, with inadequate bases, to defend the
Roman towns;[46] taxes are to be imposed at once, and will be a burden to
the Roman population.[47] Already, therefore, there is the problem of
holding and organising the conquered territory. But his attitude to the
Berbers is trivialising: that they raid the towns is a sign of their
barbarian nature;[48] they are motivated by a prophecy made by their
women,[49] but restrained at first by the very presence of Belisarius.[50] The

[39] II.9.1-2.
[40] II.9.15. The extravagance of this consulship caused Justinian to legislate to curb such
excesses (*Nov.* 105, a. 536) though his own consulships in 521 and 528 had been notorious for
this (Marcell. Com., a. 521; *Chron. Pasch.* p. 617) and to end the consulship for private
citizens after 541 (see Cameron and Schauer 1981, *fin.*).
[41] *Gothic Wars* I.5.17-19; cf. *Vandal Wars* II.14.2f. (a rare forward reference to the *Gothic
Wars*).
[42] II.9.16.
[43] *Buildings* I.10.16f.; see p. 85.
[44] Corippus, *Iust.* I.276ff.
[45] *Vandal Wars* II.15.9f.
[46] II.8.21.
[47] I.e. the 'Libyans' (II.,8.25).
[48] II.8.10.   [49] II.8.12f.
[50] II.8.19 – more likely it was because of the presence of his bodyguard and the remaining

situation was indeed bad – a small party led by two of Belisarius' men was soon afterwards cut to pieces by a Berber band – but Procopius is typically more interested in supplying at this point a digression on the origins of the Berbers than an analysis of the situation.[51] It is not a good sign that, whatever the actual sources he draws on here, he seems to confuse Berbers with Carthaginians and Libyan with Punic.[52] As a Roman African himself, the poet Corippus, who came from one of these beleaguered towns, knew more about the Berbers than Procopius, but his attitude was if anything even more supercilious.[53] We should not then be surprised if Procopius' interest is caught chiefly by oddities like the disposition of the Berber camels, and the device adopted by Solomon to get over the antipathy of the Byzantine horses to the camels, or if he expands the encounter at Mamme with lengthy set speeches.[54] In the great conflict at Mt. Bourgaon which followed, he writes up the magnitude of the battle (fifty thousand Berber dead, not one on the Byzantine side), and adds the typical remark that Berber children were selling for the price of a sheep, so many were the prisoners taken.[55]

For Procopius the fight against the Berbers is a series of separate engagements; he makes no attempt to place them in an overall context, or to consider the long-term chances of the Byzantines in Africa. But by 535 the Byzantines were in trouble. Solomon had been unable to prise Iaudas from the Aurès, and was forced to retreat to Carthage, the Berber threat growing meanwhile. By the spring of 536 there was mutiny in the Byzantine army. Procopius gives three reasons for it: first, that the soldiers who had married Vandal women were unwilling to give up the land formerly held by these women's Vandal husbands into the Byzantine treasury for public ownership; secondly, that the many Arians in the Byzantine army were disaffected because of anti-Arian measures taken by the emperor against them – especially, though Procopius does not make the point, when they were as now in an Arian environment; and thirdly, that the matter was fomented by the arrival of four hundred Vandal troops destined to serve in the Persian wars but who had turned round and sailed back to Africa.[56] A planned attempt on Solomon's life in church at Easter failed, perhaps through religious scruples,[57] but the

---

Vandals, for on their departure they are said to have taken immediate steps to terrorize the Roman population – II.8.20.

[51] II.10.13-29 (the Berbers came from Palestine before the Phoenicians of Dido's day). It is in this passage that Procopius refers in his absurdly 'objective' way to Moses, a 'wise man' – II.10.13 (above, p. 35).

[52] See Rubin 1954, 53 on the question of Procopius' linguistic competence.

[53] See Averil Cameron 1982, 39ff.; 1984b.

[54] II.11.15-56.

[55] II.12.17-27.

[56] II.14.7-21. See Kaegi 1965.

[57] II.14.24 'whether in respect for the service going on in the church, or through shame at the reputation of the general, or even because some divinity (*theion*) held them back'.

mutiny grew; some laid waste land outside Carthage, while those still in the city gathered in the hippodrome, alienated one of Solomon's officers and killed another, after which they began to rampage through the city.[58] Procopius now tells of his own exciting escape with Solomon from the great church in the palace down to the quay and by ship to Belisarius in Syracuse.[59] A quick dash to Africa by Belisarius frightens the rebels and temporarily saves the situation,[60] but when the newly appointed Germanus arrives from Constantinople he finds that two thirds of the Byzantine troops are with the rebels (now under the leadership of a member of Martin's bodyguard called Stotzas).[61] After preparation Germanus was ready to engage the rebels at Scalae Veteres,[62] and inflicted a great defeat, though Stotzas himself was able to escape to Mauretania.[63]

Only at this point does Procopius allow himself a general comment, when Solomon has been restored to the African command and Germanus recalled; it is both non-committal and entirely pro-Byzantine. Solomon, he says, ruled Africa with moderation and security; he dealt wisely with possible rebels in the army, expelled the remaining Vandals and recruited more Byzantine troops, fortified the African cities and preserved 'the laws'. The result of all this, Procopius blandly continues, was that under him Africa was prosperous and strong in revenue.[64] But these remarks, already so vague as hardly to be informative, are also entirely disingenuous. The fact is that Solomon's rule lasted only a few years; he was killed at Cillium (Kasserine) in 544,[65] by which time the benefits of his régime can hardly have been apparent. Stotzas was still alive and the Berber threat only temporarily stilled. We find a similar glossing of the difficulties of these years in Corippus' *Iohannis*. Both writers do their best to pass over the more deep-seated problems and suggest that all was well in the best possible world, even if there were a few small military difficulties.[66] But Corippus, as an African himself, would have felt the effects of the Byzantine arrival, in the form of heavy taxation, military mobilisation and increased warfare; his defence of the Byzantine cause can only be an attempt to persuade his fellow-Africans of the blessings of a régime which they now doubted profoundly.[67]

[58] II.14.30-6.
[59] Ibid. 37-42.
[60] II.15.9-49.
[61] II.16.3.
[62] II.17.
[63] II.17.35.
[64] II.19.3-4. Solomon's second governorship (AD 539-44) saw the consolidation of the Byzantine policy of building fortifications and disposing troops in Africa: see Pringle, I, 54ff. But Procopius does not draw the connection between taxation and defence, nor hint at the elaborate provisions now laid down by Justinian (*CJ* I.27.1-2, AD 534).
[65] I.21.19-28; Corippus, *Ioh.* III.413-33; Vict. Tonn., a. 543.
[66] See Corippus, *Ioh.* III.320-36; cf. III. 289-90. See Averil Cameron 1982, 38.
[67] See Averil Cameron 1984b.

Procopius is not so specific in his aim, or so personally involved. He does admit some of the problems, such as that of increased taxation, but only at the level of set pieces like the assessment of Solomon's good government here or the final summing-up of Byzantine rule in Africa in the 550s in the last book of the *Wars*.[68] For most of the African narrative itself he simply concentrates on the military events, without much attempt to set them in a wider context.

This narrative offered him ample scope. He can now recount the disaster involved in the appointment of Solomon's nephew Sergius, in 534/44, beginning with the unfortunate incident when Sergius' haughty demeanour led to the slaughter of a delegation of the Louata from Tripolitania.[69] The death of Solomon followed, and by various turns Lorbus unnecessarily paid a large sum to the Louata to leave the city alone, while Hadrumetum was entered and sacked by a Berber army including Stotzas.[70] There were not enough troops in Carthage to relieve it, and its bishop could only do so by trickery,[71] which, however, when known, incited the Berbers to terrible reprisals.[72] Procopius now abandons the pretence of putting a favourable case for Byzantium and admits that the Berbers have it all their own way, and even that Byzantines from the army were deserting to them in significant numbers.[73] There was worse to come, for Justinian's solution, as always, being to send out a new commander, Areobindus now arrived, only to be slaughtered himself as he clutched the Scriptures and begged for mercy in a bid for power by Gontharis.[74] With this dismal catalogue Procopius approaches the end of his *Vandal Wars*, but there was still the slaughter of Gontharis himself to relate, by a faithful band of Byzantine officers led by Artabanes.[75] At last a victory of sorts could be hailed for the emperor in Africa,[76] and all who were loyal, hearing the cry, burst into the houses of the rebels and killed them as they slept or ate, or while they gazed in horror at their assailants. After this the campaigns of John Troglita, told by Corippus at such length, are a mere pendant following the return of Areobindus at his own request to Constantinople.[77]

---

[68] *Gothic Wars* IV.17.20-1 (undercut however by the concluding remark of the chapter: Africa was peaceful after the campaigns of John Troglita, AD 546-9, 'but the country remained for the most part depopulated because of the earlier wars and uprisings' – cf. *Secret History* 18.4f.).

[69] *Vandal Wars* II.21.1-22.

[70] II.22.20; 23.14.

[71] II.23.21.

[72] II.23.27.

[73] II.23.30-1.

[74] II.24.1-2, 14; 26.29-33.

[75] II.28.1f., 35f.

[76] II.28.36-7.

[77] II.28.42-52. For the comparison between Procopius and Corippus see Partsch, ed., xvf.; Pringle, I, 33f.

Procopius deploys much of his usual dramatic skill in writing of the disasters that befell Africa after its initial 'conquest', and in the *Vandal Wars* he does not blame Justinian directly for mismanagement, leaving the sharp critique for the *Secret History*. The account here ends on an elegiac note: 'Thus a sort of respite came to the surviving Romans.'[78] But in 553/4 Procopius could still maintain an optimistic view of John's campaigns.[79] Nowhere in the Vandal books does he attempt to assess the chances of the Byzantines in dealing with the new enemy, encountered after the too-easy conquest of the Vandals, nor to set the Byzantine occupation in economic or geographical context. For the truth was that the great Vandal victory was only a curtain-raiser to a longer and more arduous struggle with the Berbers, made worse by serious and prolonged disaffection in the Byzantine army and command itself. Procopius could minimise this to some extent by presenting it purely as a matter of personal politics, as he makes the Berbers into examples of barbarian *perfidia*, but he could not turn the latter part of *Vandal Wars* II into anything other than a shameful record of Byzantine failure. Thus Procopius had a difficult task, of combining two very different types of material – the optimistic record of an amazing success, in which he was himself at hand to record all the odd little details and prophetic signs, and the sad and shaming aftermath, hardly counterbalanced by the campaigns of John Troglita, which he could not even find the enthusiasm to recount in detail. Nor are the later parts enhanced by the blatant omission of the real background to Byzantine government, or of the violent opposition in Africa to Justinian's Three Chapters policy. Something of the real defensive situation in Africa comes out from the *Buildings*, as we shall now see, but it is impossible to believe that Procopius was really unaware of the problems when he wrote the latter part of the *Vandal Wars*. Like Corippus, he did his best to gloss it over, but even he could not gloss over the sorry record of the military events.

There is then very little in the *Vandal Wars* about Byzantine fortifications in Africa or the stationing of soldiers and the effect of this on the general military situation – only a few asides or casual references.[80] But in Book VI of the *Buildings* Procopius devotes a detailed section to precisely this topic. In the context of the *Buildings* as a whole, this is one of the most polished parts, and the knowledge that Procopius had been present in Africa himself has led scholars to assign it a high level of credibility. As usual, there are few external checks for Procopius' information, and archeology can rarely provide information of sufficient exactitude to set against the written record; rather, Procopius' data are inevitably taken as the starting point.[81] Unfortunately, excavation of the

[78] II.28.52.

[79] *Gothic Wars* IV.17.20f.

[80] For these questions see Pringle, I, 55f.

[81] Croke and Crow 1983; Averil Cameron 1982. For the state of the subject see Duval 1981, 531f.

fortresses of Byzantine Africa has up to now been limited, and still barely allows generalisation, while many sites known to the great Charles Diehl have now deteriorated to the point where their ground plans are no longer visible.[82] Nevertheless we should be cautious in using Procopius' information, above all in view of the subtle complexity of the *Buildings* itself. Book VI on Africa is no more a straightforward collection of reliable information than the other parts of the work which have already been examined.

As usual, there are no direct indications given as to how Procopius gathered his information, and we are left to suppose that much of it must have come through first-hand observation, though that cannot be true for the whole, since, for instance, Procopius himself was in Constantinople during the years of Solomon's highly praised administration when he tells us that many works of fortification were undertaken[83] Not enough attention is usually given to the development of the Byzantine building effort in N. Africa, and a closer concern for its stages would help in reading this section of the *Buildings*. During the years covered in the *Vandal Wars*, i.e. as far as 550/1, there cannot have been a steady and consistent policy, as leadership changed and the Byzantine governors were faced with internal and external military threats. These short-term needs were not necessarily the same as those of the longer-term defence of the province. But the *Buildings* does not do much to clarify this development. Rather, it presents a timeless, and also an over-schematised picture of the Byzantine building.

The section on Carthage itself is perhaps a special case. Here Procopius is very clear, and seems moreover to place this extensive building programme in the context of the immediate post-conquest period.[84] It seems likely enough that the buildings named here dated from the first phase of building: churches, including one to the Virgin in the palace, and one to a local saint, outside; *stoai* beside the 'maritime *agora*', a bath named for the Empress Theodora, a fortified monastery called Mandracium, and, most important, the repair of the walls and construction of a ditch. With the exception of the wall-rebuilding, however, archeology has so far been unhelpful in assessing Procopius' claims. The wall rebuilding was undertaken immediately by Belisarius

---

[82] See now Pringle 1981, I, 131ff.; for the epigraphic record, Durliat 1981. The whole question of the impact of reconquest on the economy and society of N. Africa is ripe for new treatment, but Procopius is not interested in such matters, and would present them in strictly imperialist terms if he were.

[83] AD 539-44; above, p. 14. Similarly the elaborate description of Dara at *Buildings* II.1.4-3.26 describes the fort at secondhand, for Procopius knew it only in 530 and before (Croke and Crow 1983).

[84] *Buildings* VI.5.1-11; of this account, 1-7 contains general material about the Vandal conquest, 8-11 specific data about Carthage. Clearly the date of the *Buildings* ought to provide a secure *terminus ante*, but Procopius was selective about what he included – see n. 98.

and seems well confirmed on the ground;[85] the Mandracium monastery, though not identified archeologically, was soon put to use as a prison,[86] and the *stoai* are credible in view of the extensive Byzantine refurbishing of the harbour revealed in recent excavations (but not mentioned by Procopius),[87] while the naming of the bath again points to an early date.[88] The church of the Virgin, however, may have existed already;[89] if so, Procopius' phraseology is distinctly misleading. In general, his account of Carthage is oddly brief – why leave out the work at the harbour, so important for Byzantine control? We simply do not know how much else he has omitted, nor the extent to which building was 'official'. Other parts in the African section are expanded for purely literary reasons, as with his description of Caput Vada,[90] where he draws on his narrative of the *Vandal War*, where he had made this the site of a programmatic miracle, and then describes the new city in a lengthy passage full of literary stereotypes but without solid data. Lepcis Magna and Hadrumetum are also both given comparatively 'literary' treatments. Lepcis comes first, following an ethnographic treatment of the Berbers round Cidame,[91] and receives even more space than Caput Vada. Procopius paints a vivid picture of how the great city had been almost buried in sand and deserted of its inhabitants. We do not have to take this literally, however, for he goes on to describe how the wall was rebuilt enclosing a smaller city area, five churches founded including a great one to the Virgin, and the palace of Septimius Severus restored, as well as new baths built, and it was certainly used as a base of operations during the re-occupation.[92] Procopius claims that shortly before the Vandal war, though still in the reign of Justinian, the Louata had raided Lepcis and emptied it of people;[93] he decorates this with a story of Berber prophecy which we would be right to regard as a picturesque detail, since it is hardly likely that Lepcis was literally deserted.[94] It would be all too easy to take his statements out of context and fail to realise that his language is both stereotyped and exaggerated. The case of Hadrumetum is rather different, for here Procopius' attention has been caught by the

[85] Cf. the results of the British excavations on the Avenue Bourguiba site; Hurst 1977, 256f., Hurst et al. 1984.

[86] Vict. Tonn., s.a. 555. Also the name of a harbour: *Vandal Wars* I.20.14.

[87] One of the two other main sites excavated by the British team in the UNESCO Save Carthage campaign, 1977-8 (Hurst 1977; full publication forthcoming).

[88] I.e. its connection with Theodora (d. 548); cf. also VI.4.14. (Vaga).

[89] See Averil Cameron 1982, 33, n. 34, and cf. *Vandal Wars* II.14.37. See Duval 1982, II, 617, with 760 on Byzantine imperial initiatives in religious cult in Africa.

[90] VI.6.8-16; cf. *Vandal Wars* I.15.31f.

[91] VI.3.9-4.13. For the Phoenician origin of the Berbers cf. *Vandal Wars* II.10.13f.

[92] Pringle 1981, I, 208f.; *Vandal Wars* II.21.2-15.

[93] VI.4.6.

[94] VI.4.7f. The Louata, after this raid, were encamped near the city when they saw a flame rising from it, though it was deserted; their soothsayers prophesied that the city would soon be populated again.

piquancy of the situation of the inhabitants, and he devotes his notice more to them than to a straight record. Hadrumetum, a large and flourishing city on the coast of Byzacena, with the status of metropolis, had had its walls razed by the Vandals so that it was totally exposed to Berber raids. The citizens did the best they could, fortifying their own houses with broken bits from the walls,[95] but their situation was desperate, and when the Byzantines rebuilt their wall and gave them a fort as well, they were so overjoyed that they renamed the city Justiniana.[96] For once in the *Buildings* Procopius allows us to see how things were actually achieved – through self-help, which we may assume accounts for very many of the small fortified buildings that are to be seen in the towns of Late Roman Africa. He nevertheless twists the story to suit his theme: after the Byzantine building, the people of Hadrumetum could afford to forget about Berber attacks completely, he claims – though Corippus' *Iohannis* makes it clear that Byzacena was far from safe.[97] The appropriate response of the Roman Africans to their new Byzantine rulers is defined by Procopius as 'gratitude', which begs many questions about the true impact of the reconquest.

If Procopius handles these set passages in so complex a way, what of the more 'factual' sections, especially the list of fortifications? He gives a series of names and places and many statements of what seems like clear fact. Yet there are too many omissions for the simple assumption that he was working from official lists;[98] if he did so, he has abbreviated or taken from them only selectively. From Byzacena, for example, he names only Hadrumetum and Caput Vada of the coastal towns, both of them in set descriptions, and then passes straight on to the inland region; but here too only four sites are mentioned.[99] But it is on Numidia where his evidence is more problematic.[100] At first a literary description of the Aurès,[101] his account then gives a *terminus post* for Justinian's building in this region – after Iaudas and the Berbers had been driven out, that is, after the campaigns of John Troglita, 546-9. We have no reason to believe that Procopius was in Numidia himself on any occasion, and he was certainly not in Africa as late as this. He must then be drawing on lists kept in Constantinople, not on personal knowledge. If the *Buildings* dates from 554, these lists could well be lists of projected rather than

[95] VI.6.1-5. At *Vandal Wars* I.16.9. Procopius tells the same story of Sullectum.
[96] VI.6.6-7. Cf. Corippus, *Ioh.* IV.75; Pringle, I, 199f. Similarly Carthage: VI.4.8.
[97] Averil Cameron 1982, 38-9.
[98] For a list of known forts and indication of whether or not they are mentioned by Procopius see Pringle, I, 305ff.; II, 523. Cities: ibid., I, 121ff. Procopius's admission that his list is incomplete: *Buildings* VI.7.18f. (from lack of space or lack of knowledge). Most will have been built after he left Africa in 536. For discussion see Pringle I, 80f. and for the inscription (again 'official'), Durliat 1981.
[99] Mamme, Thelepte, Cululis, Aumetra.
[100] VI.7.1-11. See Averil Cameron 1982, 35f.; Desanges 1963.
[101] VI.7.1-7.

completed work. Procopius tells us that the province of Numidia now under Byzantine sway was larger than the area previously ruled by the Vandals.[102] But it is not easy to extract from this section a real sense of the geography of Byzantine Africa.[103] The material is arranged geographically, moving westwards from Egypt, Cyrenaica and Tripolitania through Byzacena and Proconsularis to Numidia and ending with Septem.[104] But Procopius makes little effort to delineate the borders of Byzantine rule, nor to locate the places he does mention within a general logic of defence. It is rather as though he has done his best to present some dry material as interestingly as possible, by anecdote and selection. Certain themes are stressed – those of the furtherance of orthodoxy by church building[105] and of the blessings of Byzantine rule.[106] But over and above these needs was the simple problem of how to make the subject matter more interesting. This is very different from a real attempt at giving a full or critical discussion of the areas included.

Procopius' knowledge of the province of Africa, then, is probably more limited than one would at first sight suppose. He does not give us many indications of his own movements in the province, and there is in fact no reason to think that he had travelled extensively. What really interested him was the course of the military campaigns, and the various anecdotes that he had picked up while in the province. In the *Buildings,* where we might expect fuller documentation, there is instead a surprisingly high degree of reference back to the *Vandal Wars*;[107] to this we must add the rhetorical adornment, so that while he does undoubtedly convey genuine and useful information as well, it is not easy to rely absolutely on any individual statement.[108] In addition to the stress on the 'gratitude' allegedly felt by the local population, it is assumed that the fortifications were all built 'against' the Berbers, so that they would not 'overrun' Roman territory.[109] Thus Procopius operates even here with a simple opposition between the Roman or rather sub-Roman population of the towns and the barbarian Berbers. In fact there must have been a much higher degree of assimilation between these groups than Procopius or the Byzantines in general were prepared to realise. In the towns, especially, the population must have been very mixed.[110] But Procopius uses the opposing terms 'Libyans' and 'Moors'. He assumes a rigid demarcation

[102] VI.7.9. Contrast *Vandal Wars* II.20.30 and see Duval 1970.
[103] See Duval 1970 and Averil Cameron 1982, 35f.
[104] VI.7.14.
[105] E.g. VI.2.18f., 23; 4.11; 6.9f. See Chapter 7 above.
[106] VI.4.6. – the arrival of the Byzantines saved Lepcis from complete capitulation to the Berbers. The whole tone is panegyrical (cf. e.g. VI.4.6f.; 5.7).
[107] VI.4.6; 5.9.
[108] VI.7.9 for example (see n. 102).
[109] VI.6.17.
[110] See Averil Cameron 1982, 36.

between the two groups and implies, though without discussion, that Byzantine territory was to be marked off by fortifications which would divide Roman from Berber[111] – an anachronistic idea which ignores the all too obvious presence of Berbers all over the province in the heart of Byzantine territory, even close to the major towns of Byzacena. It is clear from the *Vandal Wars* that this is how Procopius thinks himself, though occasionally he allows another side to show through, as when the Byzantines, just landed in Africa and newly on the road to Carthage, proceed with extreme caution towards the city of Sullectum; as it turns out they are well received, but Belisarius was by no means certain of their reception.[112] A little later Procopius makes a telling comment: 'Belisarius so won over the Africans by his restraint and generosity that from now on he advanced as if in his own country – the local people did not hide away for themselves or try to conceal anything, but offered goods for sale and supplied whatever other services to the soldiers that they wished.'[113] This is not exactly the joyful acceptance among one's own people that Procopius elsewhere suggests. On arrival Belisarius had already had occasion to remind – or perhaps tell – his men that the population of the towns was of Roman origin, and hostile to the Vandals; the people must therefore be treated well, or they would transfer their hostility to the Byzantine army.[114] Some of his soldiers had already been plundering the crops from the fields of the Roman Africans. And Belisarius had to repeat the lesson with great force when the army was about to enter Carthage, explaining to the men why Justinian had gone to war: they should do no harm to those whose liberation was the reason for the war itself.[115] Even so, a crowd of Carthaginians who lived near the harbour came to him and complained that Byzantine sailors had stolen their goods on the previous night while the fleet lay at anchor.[116] This rather spoils Procopius' emphatic claim that the entry into Carthage was a miracle, for the total lack of outrage or rough behaviour, and without even any disruption to work or hitches in billeting and rationing.[117] We are also told that Gelimer made considerable headway in bribing Roman farmers to kill any Byzantine soldiers who came their way and take the heads to him;[118] Procopius takes some pleasure in pointing out that most of those killed in this manner were not soldiers but slaves and attendants who had ventured into the villages in hope of gain, so that when Gelimer believed he was paying for the heads of Byzantines he was really only getting their

[111] See Fentress 1979; Trousset 1974.
[112] *Vandal Wars* I.16.9-11.
[113] I.27.6-7.
[114] I.26.3-6.
[115] I.20.18-20.
[116] I.20.22-3.
[117] I.21.9-10.
[118] I.23.1-4.

menials; the implication none the less is that the invading army did mistreat the local population and that the latter was naturally not well disposed to it.

Procopius, then, was well aware of the official justification for the expedition, according to which it was to liberate the Roman Africans from their Vandal masters, and as we have seen, he was himself in favour of it after the dream in which he thought he received a divine intimation of victory;[119] the miracle of the water at Caput Vada, which he repeats in the *Buildings*,[120] confirmed him in his belief that the endeavour was righteous. But he had little sympathy with the Roman Africans for all that; they do not merit even as much description as the Berbers, and they feature in the *Vandal Wars* chiefly as a factor to be treated with caution. For the Berbers of course he has no sympathy whatsoever,[121] and no interest in their relations with the existing Roman African population or in how the previous situation was thrown out of balance by the arrival of the Byzantines. In the *Secret History*, of course, the emphasis is entirely different: Africa is a prime example of Justinian's destruction, and Vandals, 'Libyans' and Berbers are thrown together without differentiation as his victims,[122] indeed linked with the numbers of Byzantine soldiers who also fell in Africa. But Procopius here gives a telling reason for this destruction: Justinian 'took no steps to tighten his hold over the country and made no plans to ensure that its resources should be secured for him by winning the firm loyalty of the inhabitants'.[123] He imposed heavy taxes, took over the best land, introduced fierce anti-Arian legislation and neglected to pay the troops. 'The result of all this was an outbreak of revolts that led to widespread destruction.'[124] All these items are mentioned in the *Vandal Wars*, but the lesson is explicitly drawn only in the *Secret History*. In the early part of the war narrative, at least, Procopius is still favourably enough disposed to the régime to soft-pedal the adverse effects of reconquest. But as we have seen, the later parts, ending as they do with hasty praise of John Troglita, give the bland statements in the *Buildings* about the gratitude of the local population a hollow ring.

Unlike the *Persian Wars*, with its rich sense of the small eastern communities and the pressures of a border existence, or the *Gothic Wars*, with its interest in Rome as a historic centre, its awareness of the individual members of the Roman aristocracy and their still intimate

---

[119] Above, p. 114.
[120] Above, n. 90.
[121] The same applies to Corippus: Averil Cameron 1982, 1983. *Vandal Wars* II.10.27f. gives a very sanitized version (from the Byzantine side) of the situation of the Berbers vis-à-vis the Vandals and the Byzantines.
[122] *Secret History* 18.5f.
[123] Ibid. 9
[124] 18.11. Tax assessments: *Vandal Wars* II.9.25.

links with the eastern government in Constantinople, and its feeling for
the heroic stature of Totila, the *Vandal Wars* concentrates very much on
the Byzantine army and its officers themselves. We are never made
aware of the Roman Africans as individuals: except for Reparatus, the
bishop of Carthage, not one is mentioned by name.[125] Procopius' scorn for
the African Junillus is perhaps typical of his attitudes in general.[126] For
Gelimer he has that admiration for the noble barbarian that could
coexist with a contempt for barbarians en masse, but he has not taken
the trouble to show the relations of Vandals and Romans in any kind of
convincing manner. Nearly all the focus is on events and personalities in
the Byzantine force itself, whether Belisarius, who is at the centre of the
first half of the narrative, Solomon, who wins respectful praise from
Procopius even though they had been forced to flee together from
Carthage, the noble Germanus, who stayed too short a time, or the less
attractive figures of the confused decade or so after the reconquest –
Stotzas, Gontharis, the aged Athanasius, the feeble Areobindus or even
the dashing Artabanes. There are many memorable scenes in these
books: the entry into Carthage, Gelimer's surrender, Belisarius'
'triumph', the flight of Solomon and Procopius, the deaths of Areobindus
and Gontharis. Here, in these stirring events, and with these conflicting
personalities, lay Procopius' interest, not in Africa as such or its
economic and defensive problems. If he is less good in these books in
terms of historical analysis, or even fullness of detail, than elsewhere, the
pace and excitement of much of the narrative would in his own view more
than compensate.

---

[125] Reparatus: *Vandal Wars* II.26.31.
[126] Junillus: *Secret History* 20.16f. and see p. 231 below.

CHAPTER ELEVEN

Procopius and Italy

Procopius went to Sicily and Italy with Belisarius on his first campaign, in 535, not long after the latter's consular inauguration.[1] Within a few years, Procopius and Belisarius had been in all three fronts of war – the east, N. Africa and Italy. In 535, Belisarius, who was still consul, was able to take Sicily without difficulty and enter Syracuse in triumph on the last day of his year of office.[2] By December of 536 he had besieged Naples and entered Rome.[3] Throughout the great siege of Rome by the Goths in 537/8 Procopius was present, and employed on tasks such as gathering food and reinforcements from outside.[4] This siege, lasting for over a year and ending in a Gothic withdrawal, is one of his great set-pieces in the *Wars*. He was still with Belisarius when the Franks invaded Italy and turned on the Byzantines in 539, and at the siege of Ravenna in winter, 539/40. It was now that certain Goths offered Belisarius the throne, which according to Procopius he steadfastly refused,[5] entering Ravenna in May, 540 in the name of Justinian.[6] When he was recalled to Constantinople shortly afterwards, Procopius went with him, and was deeply emotionally involved in the rights and wrongs of the situation.[7] It marked a major turning point in his historical thinking and in his attitudes to Belisarius and Justinian. It is doubtful whether Procopius went back to Italy after this. He may have gone briefly to the east in 542[8] and he may have been in Rome in 546, as has

---

[1] So *PLRE* III s.v. Procopius. His presence in Carthage at Easter, 536 (*Vandal Wars* II.4.39-41) will then have been probably in the course of a mission from Belisarius in Sicily. When Procopius and Solomon then fled to Sicily from the rebels, Belisarius launched a brief campaign in Africa (II.15.10f., 46f.), from which, returning to Sicily, he received orders to proceed to Italy (*Gothic Wars* I.7.26).

[2] *Gothic Wars* I.5.17-19.

[3] He entered Rome on December 9, 536 (*Gothic Wars* I.14.14); for the other sources see *PLRE* III s.v. Belisarius.

[4] *Gothic Wars* II.4.1-2.

[5] *Gothic Wars* II.29.17f.

[6] II.29.29f. The date: Agnellus, 62.

[7] He claims at *Gothic Wars* II.30.1-2 that he was recalled in order to campaign in the east but admits that he had been accused of planning rebellion; cf. also *Persian Wars* I.25.11. But the placing of his eulogy of Belisarius at the beginning of *Gothic Wars* III (above, pp. 138f.) is clearly a conscious attempt to clear Belisarius of suspicion.

[8] Above, p. 164.

been thought from the fullness of his account of that year.[9] But there is only one explicit hint – the story allegedly told him by a Roman senator when he was in Rome[10] to the effect that one day a eunuch would destroy the ruler of Rome, a prophecy which Procopius thought fulfilled when Narses was sent out in 551.[11] But he need not have heard the story in 546; it seems that he had heard it long before, since he writes that at the time it was regarded as ridiculous; only later did events prove it true.[12]

So it remains unproven that Procopius went to Italy a second time with Belisarius, and indeed the tone of his narrative changes very strikingly when he writes of the second Italian expedition. From the lively engaged writing of the first books of the *Gothic Wars* the mood changes to one of increasing sadness and disappointment. Belisarius, whose reputation had reached an apogee for Procopius in his masterly handling of the entry to Ravenna in 540, achieved nothing on his second expedition to Italy, and Procopius, while still under the spell of his hero, became steadily more saddened, and more and more openly critical.[13] The change shows itself in the texture of his prose. Instead of vigorous descriptions of action we have short lapidary sentences conveying the bare and unflattering facts.[14] The third book of the *Gothic Wars* (*Wars* VII) is pervaded by a mounting gloom and criticism; Procopius was already preparing the full blast of his rhetoric for expression in the *Secret History*, where he writes of this second expedition of Belisarius with extreme bitterness.[15] In *Gothic Wars* III the critical tone is all the more perceptible for being couched in restrained terms:

> At this moment in the war the barbarians gained total mastery over the west. For the Romans the Gothic war came to this, though they had been victorious at first, as I have previously related, that not only did they lose many men and much money to no gain, but also let Italy slip and had to watch Illyria and nearly all of Thrace plundered and wantonly destroyed by the neighbouring barbarians.[16]

The first seven books of the *Wars* end on a serious note, with the sudden death of Germanus and Justinian's efforts to retrieve the situation for the Byzantine side. It was an odd place to end what had started as a glorious record of reconquest: but Procopius was tired and depressed. He could not continue the *Wars* in that mood, and indeed the *Secret History*, which allowed him to say in detail what he had to pass over in the public

---

[9] Cf. *Gothic Wars* IV.16f.; see Rubin 1954, 26.
[10] IV.21.10.
[11] IV.21.16-17.
[12] Ibid., 17-19.
[13] Above, pp. 138f.
[14] *Gothic Wars* III.27.1, 12; 28.4, revealing how Belisarius was starved of reinforcements.
[15] *Secret History* 5.1-7.
[16] *Gothic Wars* III.33.1.

work, shows us how he felt.

But by the time of the writing of *Wars* VIII, in 554, Procopius had apparently come to terms with the worst of his disappointment and reached a more subtle understanding of the politics of reconquest. The old optimism had gone. It had been shown that the way was to be hard at best, and Procopius now had to face the fact that the final slow victory in Italy would not go to Belisarius. He could now see heroic stature in Totila; for the first time in the *Gothic Wars* Procopius tells the events with real sympathy for the losing side. Teias attains the same respect:

> Now I shall describe a battle worthy of great fame, and bravery which Teias revealed on the present occasion, inferior, I believe, to none of the so-called heroes.[17]

The death of Totila is told as movingly and with as much sense of tragedy as anything else in the *Wars*,[18] preceded as it was by his splendidly barbarian war-dance:

> He was wearing armour plentifully covered in gold, and the decoration on his cheek-plates as well as on his helmet and spear was of purple – indeed a wonderful display of regal splendour.[19]

How to present the changed circumstances of the later parts of the *Gothic Wars* posed new problems for Procopius. There was no such literary opportunity as that presented by Belisarius' splendid achievements in 540. Some, it is true, found a temporary hope in the birth of a child to Germanus and Matasuntha, who might continue the legitimate Gothic line after the gap since the death of Vitigis.[20] But Procopius was more realistic. He was not tempted to minimise the problems of the Italian campaigns between 540 and 550, nor did the presence of Italians such as Cassiodorus in Constantinople just when he was finishing *Wars* I-VII sway him from his entirely Byzantine-centred point of view. There are both similarities and differences between the *Getica* of Jordanes and Book VII of the *Wars*, works so close chronologically.[21] But Procopius did not deviate, even in *Wars* VIII, from the gloomy picture painted in the latter part of I-VII.

After the release of *Wars* I-VII, then, he did take up the story again in a

---

[17] IV.35.20.

[18] IV.32.22-30.

[19] IV.31.17f.

[20] Jordanes, *Get.* 314. The interpretation of the political message and intention of the *Getica* has produced a spate of recent works, partly directed at attacking the thesis of Momigliano (1955, 1964, 1973) that it reflects a revision of Cassiodorus's *Gothic History* made by Cassiodorus himself in 551, but also taking a broader view: thus Bradley 1966; Wagner 1967; Baldwin 1979; O'Donnell 1979, 271f.; 1982; Croke forthcoming; Markus forthcoming; Alan Cameron forthcoming; Barnish 1984. See though *JRS* 71 (1981), 184f. and further below.

[21] *JRS* 71 (1981), 185.

final book (*Gothic Wars* IV or *Wars* VIII), in which he drew together all the fronts covered in the previous seven. It is impossible to know how the first instalment had been received, and indeed, it would be natural to think that contemporaries too were struck by the critical tone of the later parts. The *Buildings* has often been assumed to have been a response to an imperial commission; yet it could as well be a bid for just such patronage after the completion of the *Wars*.[23] In fact, *Wars* VIII breaks off without finishing its subject; Procopius did not go on to relate the ending of the Gothic war, carried to its conclusion by Narses – that was left to Agathias to narrate, twenty years later. Again we did not know why this was so. It could well be that the theme of reconquest had become so tarnished in Procopius' eyes that with the eclipse of Belisarius and the tragedy of the death of Germanus he responded to pressures to update his work as far as 553, but had not the heart to continue beyond that. The exact relation between the *Wars* and the *Buildings* must remain a matter for speculation, since the available evidence is too slight to permit anything more; I would suggest that it does not much matter anyway. Whatever Procopius' reasons for writing the *Buildings*, he had already in *Wars* VIII substantially altered his original conception of his theme, and had reached a more differentiated view of the wars of reconquest, with room – as there had not been in the beginning – for sympathy for both sides. It is interesting to find that even here, where Procopius was not, so far as we know, drawing on personal experience, he can none the less tell a convincing and detailed story, if without the anecdotal element that is so strongly present in *Gothic Wars* I and II.

The early Italian books show Procopius' curiosity and love of marvels being given full reign. Especially when he was in Rome in 537, he was picking up whatever intriguing detail he could. He claims, for instance, to have read the Sibylline books in their entirety, and assures his readers that he knows that they are impossible to understand before the event because they are arranged so randomly that one cannot be sure of the reference in a given case until experience has revealed what it is.[24] This is a comment on the attempt by some 'patricians' in Rome, presumably senators, to draw from one of the oracles the lesson that the siege would not continue beyond July;[25] Procopius can quote the oracle in Latin and must have read the books in Latin if indeed he did read them. He now

---

[22] *Getica* belongs early in 552 (see conveniently O'Donnell 1982, 239f.); the narrative of *Gothic Wars* III ends with winter 550/1, and Marcellinus' *Chronicle* was continued also in 550.

[23] The evidence for an imperial commission is in fact slight: *Buildings* I.3.1 'we must begin with the churches of the Virgin Mary, for we know that that is also the wish of the emperor himself'. I.1.4 may seem to suggest that Procopius has received some favour for which he is now expressing gratitude, but could as well be a general statement about panegyric.

[24] *Gothic Wars* I.24.33-7.

[25] I.24.28-31.

comments that everyone was proved wrong, for the siege actually lasted a year, and there was indeed another Gothic king to come. But Procopius was clearly well aware of currents of speculation in the city among the Roman aristocracy itself. Some senators were sent away from Rome when Pope Silverius was deposed under suspicion of treachery;[26] other Romans tried secretly (but unsuccessfully) to close the doors of the temple of Janus.[27] The latter occurrence leads Procopius to describe the location and appearance of the temple in some detail, but also to note that there was no inquiry, since very few knew of the attempt. The shape of the city and its environs comes over clearly from Procopius' narrative: Ostia;[28] the gates and bridges;[29] the walls, rapidly repaired in 546.[30] The Italian narrative, in fact, is much more firmly an urban narrative than those in the Persian or African sections, and Procopius seems more aware himself of the undercurrents and divided loyalties among the local population than he is in the other narratives.

Undoubtedly Procopius was strongly influenced here by a feeling of nostalgia for Roma as the ancient city and seat of the empire – the very symbol, therefore, of the ideology of reconquest – and the present home of the senatorial aristocracy of the west. The story of Rusticiana, the wife of Boethius and daughter of Symmachus, illustrates Procopius' consciousness of the sharp irony and the reversals inherent in the juxtaposition of barbarian Goths and high-born Romans. With other Roman ladies, Rusticiana was reduced in 546 to such destitution that she had to beg bread from the Goths; most were only too ready to kill or rape any women they could find, but Rusticiana and her fellow high-born ladies were saved by the intervention of the noble Totila.[31] Procopius is struck by the *peripeteia* that had befallen Rusticiana: the wife and daughter of consuls, she who had always given of her wealth to all who asked was now forced to dress in the clothes of slaves and peasants and to beg for herself, even from the very enemies of Rome. He does not add at this point that she who had escaped the onslaught of Theodoric was now herself at the mercy of the Goths, but a little later he does bring up the deaths of Boethius and Symmachus when he says that she had put her wealth at the disposal of the Byzantine army and destroyed pictures of Theodoric himself.[32] Procopius is using the story of Rusticiana to symbolise the brutality of the relations of Goths and Romans; he deliberately recalls the deaths of Boethius and Symmachus which are elsewhere presented in

[26] I.25.23.
[27] I.25.18-26.
[28] I.24.4-18.
[29] I.19. For Rome at this time see Llewellyn 1970, 52ff.; Krautheimer 1980, 62ff.
[30] III.24.1-7.
[32] *Gothic Wars* III.20.27f.; see Averil Cameron 1979b (= 1981, XIV).
[32] III.20.29.

similarly stark moral terms.[33] For Procopius these executions represented
the sole blot on the virtue of Theodoric and were to be explained as due to
the influence of malicious informers; inevitably, then, he would be struck
by the pathos of Rusticiana, Boethius' widow and Symmachus' daughter.
We see him in both places viewing Roman-Gothic relations in simple
dramatic and moral terms. But if his presentation of the political
situation in Italy is simplified, at least there was an element present in
the Italian campaigns that was absent from both the African and the
Persian, and which demonstrably did have some influence on Procopius.
In Italy there remained a powerful group of Roman aristocrats who had
retained, indeed even increased, their hold on the traditional offices in a
complex relation to the Gothic rulers and to distant Constantinople.[34]
The interests of these people, many of whom also had extensive estates in
the east,[35] were not necessarily to be simply identified with those of
Byzantine reconquest. On the other hand, they were able to exercise a
strong influence on Justinian's policies, especially when some of them
travelled to Constantinople itself, and they were taken very seriously by
the imperial government.[36] Procopius was certainly in touch with some of
these people, though the extent of his connections with them remains
problematic.[37] In Africa, by contrast, there was no such powerful Roman
aristocracy surviving in the sixth century, while in the east, leading
laymen were insignificant in comparison with the increasing prominence
of bishops and other clergy. Each narrative, therefore, reflects in its
emphasis the specific conditions of the area it describes; in the *Gothic
Wars* the role of clerics which is so noticeable in the Persian books is
much less emphasised, its place being taken by a stress on secular
tradition, above all of course in Procopius' accounts of Rome itself.

The paradox was that the Gothic war, which after all resulted in
victory for the imperial side, brought the destruction of this great Roman
aristocracy in Italy.[38] Two decades of constant war, and successive sieges
of Rome, ravaged their Italian properties. Byzantine victory, especially
in 540, raised their hopes to a peak that was recognised by the consulship
of Basilius in 541, the last consulship to be granted by Justinian.[39] But

[33] *Gothic Wars* I.1.32-9. Procopius sees none of the possible complexities, representing
the motives of these supposed informers as stemming from the simple jealousy of 'wicked
men' at the reputations of Symmachus and Boethius. See Matthews 1981, 35f.; Chadwick
1981, 63ff. ('Procopius, writing wholly without a theological *parti pris* ...'); Moorhead 1978.
Certainly Procopius shows no hint of the view (Chadwick, 67f.) that Justinian may have
connived at the executions as a convenient way of fomenting discontent against Theodoric.

[34] See Cameron and Schauer 1982, *fin.* But different views were taken: Wickham 1981,
21ff.; Moorhead 1983.

[35] Sundwall 1919; Hardy 1931, 1968.

[36] Ibid.; O'Donnell 1979, 131f.; Moorhead 1983, 589f.

[37] See below.

[38] Brown 1984. Rome after the siege of 546 and the consequent destruction by Totila was
reduced to a shadow. Further below, n. 132 and see Wickham 1981, 26f.

[39] Cameron and Schauer 1982.

the years that followed brought a reversal: there was no settlement in
Italy, and the terrible conditions of the siege and capture of Rome by
Totila in 546 made it clear that there could be no place in Italy for these
families, at least so long as the war continued. They could now function
neither politically nor financially in Italy. The representatives of several
of the great families, who had preserved their wealth on an extraordinary
scale through the hard times of Gothic rule, now left for Constantinople,
and once settled there (where they exercised a significant cultural
influence) they did not return to the west.[40] They included Decius and
Basilius, the last consul.[41] as well as Cethegus.[42] It was probably now that
Cassiodorus made his way to Constantinople,[43] and possibly Rusticiana
too.[44] When Cassiodorus returned, it was of course to a different Italy and
a different life,[45] while Rusticiana's family carried on the Italian presence
in Constantinople that was still very much to the fore in the reign of
Maurice when Gregory the Great was there as papal legate.[46] The story of
the Italian aristocrats therefore moves to the east. But these were the
lucky ones. Others, like Olybrius and Orestes and Maximus, could only
attempt to take refuge in the Roman churches,[47] or were captured while
trying to escape from Rome in 546.[48] Procopius does not present his
Gothic narrative in a way that could do justice to the social, political and
economic importance of these families. Nevertheless he could not fail to
be aware of them as a group, and must have drawn some of his
information from them. In his account of the first siege of Rome he quotes
their opinions and comments on their attitudes, as we have seen,[49] and
when he describes the siege by Totila in 546 he can detail at length the
feelings of the Romans, who send to Bessas and Conon claiming that they
are regarded neither as Romans, as relatives or as political allies, but
quite simply as enemies,[50] an accusation which Bessas and Conon are

[40] Sundwall 1919, 104f.; Stein, *BE* II.618, n. 1.

[41] *Gothic Wars* III.20.18 (winter 546).

[42] Letter to Vigilius (550), *PL* 69.49; cf. *Gothic Wars* III. 35.9 where Cethegus is clearly
meant. Cethegus certainly left in 546/7; cf. III.13.12. See Moorhead 1983, 584f.

[43] So *PLRE* II s.v.; O'Donnell 1979, 106f., has him leaving with Belisarius and Vitigis in
540, but see *JRS* 71 (1981), 184.

[44] There is no evidence for this Rusticiana after 546, but her descendants kept their ties in
both Rome and Constantinople: see Averil Cameron 1979b, 225f. (her grand-daughter, also
Rusticiana, who corresponded with Gregory the Great and had ties in Rome as well as
married children in the east).

[45] Again, the date of his departure from Constantinople is not fixed. After the Pragmatic
Sanction (554) and thus after the Fifth Ecumenical Council is a fair guess but no more
(O'Donnell, 136); see Moorhead 1983, 585f.

[46] Homes Dudden 1905, I, 154f.; Stein, *BE* II.618; Brown 1984.

[47] *Gothic Wars* III.20.19.

[48] III.26.11-14.

[49] I.17.12.ff.; cf. 18.28, 34, 39f.; 20.7; 23.5. Nevertheless, Thompson 1982, 100ff. is quite
right to emphasise that Procopius presents these issues from the Byzantine perspective
throughout.

[50] III.17.1-8, especially 5. Pro-Byzantine sentiments in 544: Arator, *de Act. apost.*
I.1070-4, cited by Moorhead 1983, 591.

forced to see is justified. He is interested too in the fates of various Roman senators after the siege.[51] whether he was himself present in Italy in 546 is, however, doubtful; several Italians, including the deacon Pelagius, were going to and fro between Italy and the east in these years[52] and would have been an obvious source of information. Procopius was certainly in touch with the Italians who now came to Constantinople, or at least was very conscious of the pressure which they could exert on the imperial government. He claims that 'the Italians who were there' in 548/9 pressed Justinian hard to try to recover Italy, among them Cethegus, patrician and ex-consul, who had come to Constantinople 'for his very purpose'.[53] Justinian's reply at this stage was lukewarm; he had ecclesiastical matters much on his mind with the Three Chapters affair reaching its height.[54] But in 550, with the ill-fated appointment of Germanus, the Italian lobby achieved some success. Despite the reverse caused by Germanus' death, the Byzantine side was indeed to go on to win. But by then Procopius' attention was focussed elsewhere; he had lost whatever sympathy and enthusiasm he had once had for the Byzantine cause in Italy, and the Totila who had been responsible for the sufferings of these Roman aristocrats in 546 can emerge now even more clearly (for his magnanimity to Rusticiana had already been noted) as a doomed but noble leader.[55]

When Procopius wrote of the taking of Rome by Narses two years later, the prelude to the victory over Teias at Mons Lactarius which is the last episode related in the *Gothic Wars*, and marked by Procopius more as the occasion for Teias' noble bravery than as a great Byzantine victory, he showed that his pessimism and despair at the fate of Rome continued unchanged. Starkly juxtaposed with the statement that Narses sent the keys of Rome to Justinian, marking its fifth capture during his reign, we read:

> Then indeed it was most plainly shown that when men are doomed to disaster even what seem to be successes always end in destruction, and that when they have got their heart's desire such success may bring ruin in its train. Thus for the senate and people of Rome this victory proved to be still more the cause of ruin.[56]

The immediate consequence, now related by Procopius, was the killing of any Romans they met by the Goths as they left the city, and of others by

---

[51] See n. 48.
[52] Cf. III.16.7f.; 21.18.
[53] III.35.9-11. Policies of Vigilius: Moorhead 1983, 589f.
[54] See Averil Cameron 1982, 45ff.
[55] See p. 201.
[56] IV.34.1-2; cf. 33.27. The passage is cited by Ure 1951, 172f., who rightly comments (p. 173) that after such disillusionment Procopius may have been glad to turn to a different kind of enterprise altogether in the *Buildings*.

the barbarians in the Roman army as they entered it; finally, all the three hundred noble Roman children taken as hostages by Totila were put to death by Teias. Nothing, then, in the intervening period had caused Procopius to revise the sense of gloom with which he had written of Belisarius' failure,[57] and the restraint of his closing remarks in *Gothic Wars* IV, the last words of the whole eight books of the *Wars*, underlines his bitter disappointment. From the optimism of the Vandal conquest, which he had come to believe was divinely inspired, however ill-advised it seemed at the time to others, his attitudes to Justinian's wars had come full circle to his final disillusion.

During the years 551-2, however, there were several Italians in Constantinople who might, one would have thought, have influenced Procopius' thinking. In fact it is extremely difficult to trace the contact. Romans like Pelagius, or the men in Belisarius' entourage who returned with him from the second Italian expedition in 549 could well have been Procopius' informants, without supposing that he had himself been in Italy after 540. But the prominent Italians, including Cassiodorus, now living in Constantinople are more problematic from our point of view. Cassiodorus himself was in 551 either revising his *Gothic History* to take account of the new Byzantine offensive under Germanus, or else living in pious retirement.[58] At any rate, the *Getica* of Jordanes, written in this year, ended with a short-lived hope of reconciliation focussed on the birth of a posthumous child of Germanus and the Gothic Matasuntha, widow of Vitigis.[59] According to Jordanes, the marriage was part of Justinian's general plans. But Procopius gives a clear and different reason: Germanus thought that if Matasuntha accompanied him to Italy as his wife, the Goths would be unwilling to take up arms against her out of respect for Theodoric and Athalaric.[60] The objective is not reconciliation but conquest, as ever. There is indeed a similarity between Procopius and Jordanes in that both seem to see the capture of Vitigis as the decisive Byzantine victory in the war.[61] But Procopius did not share the

[57] Ibid.: he returned to Constantinople in indecent haste, never having disembarked onto the land of Italy in five years, but spending the whole of this time like an exile, wandering from one port to another – which made it easier for the enemy to enslave Rome. No sooner had he left but Perusia fell. Procopius' next comment (35.3) that on his arrival in Constantinople he was still honoured for his previous successes does nothing to counteract the negative impression given by the opening sentences. See also *Secret History* 4.42-5; 5.1-3.

[58] O'Donnell 1979 opts for the latter, but see *JRS* 71 (1981), 184f.

[59] See n. 20 above. O'Donnell 1982, however, points out that the overall attitude of the *Romana* and the *Getica* of Jordanes is equally pessimistic, if in a different way: all secular glory must prove a phantom in relation to the heavenly life. The remarks at the end of the *Getica* are then not in tune with the message of the rest. But even if this was Cassiodorus's view of human history, it was certainly not that of Procopius.

[60] *Gothic Wars* III.39.15.

[61] Cf. III.1.1-32 (the panegyric of Belisarius, carefully inserted to carry the reader's mind back to his achievement in 540). See however n. 128 on Totila.

point of view which could represent that victory as still effective.[62] He had admired Totila from the beginning and knew that he was a worthy enemy, legitimate or not.[63] The expedition under Germanus might mark a new beginning, but the situation that gave rise to it was, in Procopius' eyes, grave in the extreme.

Thus he took an altogether more realistic view than that represented in the concluding chapters of the *Getica*.[64] He admired Germanus[65] and regarded his sudden death at Serdica as a disastrous blow for the Byzantines.[66] But he analyses his motives dispassionately: according to Procopius, Germanus was determined to win the maximum glory from his command, so that he could be called the man who saved both Italy and Africa for the empire,[67] and this was exactly why he married Matasuntha,[68] as the first step to this 'glory'. His objective, in Procopius' eyes, was 'victory over the Goths'.[69] Nor was Procopius in any doubt as to what the main aim should be: it ought to be to crush the Goths entirely. His criticism of Justinian, therefore, is that the emperor failed to take strong enough action, and failed to put his intentions into practice. Instead of sending an army while Totila was besieging Rome yet again, he had merely appointed Liberius and told him to stand by:

> If he had fulfilled this intention, I believe that Rome would be his; that the reinforcements sent from Byzantium would have been able to join the soldiers already there and would have been saved, and that he would have prevailed over the enemy in the war.[70]

There is no doubt of Procopius' opinion, nor of what he thought the Romans in Constantinople wanted: he represents Pope Vigilius as importuning Justinian to get on with the war,[71] Cethegus as having come to Constantinople for that very purpose. There is no mention in Procopius of the posthumous child who according to Jordanes was to offer hope to both peoples.[72] Procopius' view of Germanus and the

---

[62] *Get.* 313. The *Getica* moves straight from the capture of Vitigis in 540 to the marriage of Germanus and Matasuntha ten years later and the subsequent hopes of the child (313-14); there is no hint of the difficulties of the intervening years and no mention of Totila.

[63] III.2.7; IV.32.28-30.

[64] *Get.* 315 'this glorious race (i.e. the Goths) yielded to a more glorious prince and surrendered to a more valiant leader, whose fame shall be silenced by no ages or cycles of years; for the victorious and triumphant emperor Justinian and his consul Belisarius shall be named and known as Vandalicus, Africanus and Geticus.'

[65] *Gothic Wars* III.40.9.

[66] III.40.1-8.

[67] III.39.11-12.

[68] III.29.14.

[69] III.39.11.

[70] III.36.5-6.

[71] III.35.9-10.

[72] *Get.* 314.

marriage is as calculating as that of Germanus himself as reported by him.

We do not know, then, whether Procopius knew Cassiodorus in Constantinople, still less Jordanes, whoever he was. He certainly knew of Italians in the capital as a powerful pressure group, and we know that the Cethegus whom he singles out was like Vigilius a friend of Cassiodorus.[73] But his own point of view is firmly eastern. He regards the Goths as barbarians, though clever ones, and the Roman aristocrats as having natural ties with Constantinople. His realism shows in his comment that Theodoric was 'nominally a tyrant, but in practice a true king'.[74] As so often, he writes plainly even about the most sensational events. He relates the story of the executions of Boethius and Symmachus mainly in order to tell of Theodoric's repentance.[75] It is a kind of folk-motif: Theodoric seems to see the head of Symmachus in a large fish served up to him at dinner, and in his terror, consults his doctor, confesses his wrong and soon afterwards dies from remorse at this, his one and only offence against his subjects. Though Procopius describes Boethius and Symmachus as aristocrats, leaders of the senate and ex-consuls, and as philosophers and defenders of justice, generous to the distressed and to men of great reputation,[76] all this is strictly ancillary to the anecdote about Theodoric that is his main interest. He is in fact as vague in writing about Boethius and Symmachus as he is about other Roman aristocrats; their dramatic function here is to illustrate the tragic flaw in Theodoric. Similarly the restoration of their property to their descendants by Amalasuntha, the daughter of Theodoric, is presented more as a sign of her nobility than as an important event in its own right.[77] Procopius has an outsider's interest in the Roman aristocracy. He was probably not close enough to the group of high-born Italians in Constantinople in the late 540s to have absorbed their particular political views, and despite his own admiration for Theodoric and, later, respect for Totila, he did not share the Gothic longings of the end of Jordanes' *Getica*.

Procopius could not have used the *Getica* when he wrote the sections on the origins of the Goths, but the relation of Jordanes' work to his own is an intriguing problem; one of Jordanes' sources, the *Chronicle* of Marcellinus, which was itself probably continued in just these Italian circles in Constantinople that we have been considering,[78] was certainly

[73] Above, n. 42. Markus (forthcoming) rightly cautions us, however, against too hasty assumptions that these Italians were either close associates or united in their views. Similarly Moorhead 1983.

[74] *Gothic Wars* I.1.29.

[75] I.1.32-9; n. 33 above.

[76] I.1.32-3. Note that Symmachus is not here described as a historian (see below) but as practising philosophy.

[77] I.2.5.

[78] Momigliano 1964, 250. For the origins sections in Procopius, see Chapter 12 below.

available to him. Had he used Marcellinus, there might be implications
for Procopius' views of fifth-century Roman history, in view of the
influential thesis of Ensslin, developed by Wes, that Marcellinus
depended on the lost *Roman History* of the very Symmachus whose head
Theodoric thought he saw in the cooked fish.[79] But there are no certain
indications of use of Marcellinus by Procopius, and the similarities have
been explained otherwise.[80] It seems more likely, in fact, that
Marcellinus used eastern sources himself,[81] and that is certainly the
impression given of himself by Procopius throughout. He writes as an
east Roman; in his account of western history in the fifth-century his
viewpoint is strictly that of Constantinople. Like other eastern writers,
he sees AD 476 as a turning point.[82] But though he regards the
establishment of Theodoric's rule as marking the restoration of good
relations with the east after tyranny, he is careful to underline
Theodoric's deference towards Constantinople, and his favourable image
of the government of Theodoric and his house does not prevent him from
portraying the intervention of Justinian in Italy as entirely justified. On
this view, eventual Byzantine victory would entail the restoration of
legitimate rule.[83] But after all, Procopius is not a philosophical historian.
He treats these events, as others, more in terms of the anecdotal and the
personal than with real political analysis; what really matters to him is
Theodoric's fairness and popularity with both Goths and Romans, to
which theme the story of the deaths of Symmachus and Boethius, told at
such excessive length but without any real consideration of its political
significance, is a mere pendant, while the narrative of Amalasuntha and
her aspirations for Athalaric is turned into a stereotyped display of
'barbarian' as opposed to 'Roman' manners.[84] Whether or not he used the
Latin *Chronicle* of Marcellinus, then, Procopius' account of the end of

[79] Ensslin 1959; Wes 1967.
[80] I.e. by reference to a common eastern source. See Croke, forthcoming; Markus,
forthcoming for the eastern sources of Marcellinus. There is little to suggest that Procopius
made use of extensive Latin sources.
[81] Argued by both Croke and Markus against Ensslin and Wes; see too O'Donnell 1982,
236f.; Varady 1978.
[82] See *Vandal Wars* I.7.15; *Gothic Wars* I.1.2-8 (Odoacer deposed Augustulus and
established a *tyrannis*). The notion of 476 as a turning point also appears in Evagrius,
possibly from Eustathius of Epiphaneia (Evagrius, *HE* II.16), and in the Byzantine
chronicle tradition; see Croke 1983b, and in general Momigliano 1973; Cracco Ruggini 1978;
Cesa 1981, 399.
[83] *Gothic Wars* I.1.9f. Theodoric is effectively given power by Zeno (I.1.9), and does not
assume the title *Basileus* (I.1.26). I cannot agree with Cesa 1981, 399f., who sees the praise
of Theodoric and Amalasuntha as implying criticism of Justinian's Italian war. Veh
1950/51, 17ff. on the contrary emphasises Procopius' view of Justinian as emperor of the
'Romans', with all its implications of legitimate reconquest.
[84] Theodoric's praises: I.1.27f.; Symmachus and Boethius: I.1.32f.; praise of
Amalasuntha: I.2.3; education of Athalaric: I.2.6f., cf. especially 11f., 19. Naturally the scale
of the narrative broadens as Procopius reaches the moment of Justinian's intervention; all
the same, the personal and anecdotal elements are given enormously more space than the
political analysis.

Roman imperial rule in the west is typically his own, moulded more by his taste for story and anecdote about individual personalities than by Roman political ideology.

But if there is not much explicit discussion by Procopius of the Gothic situation as such, either in the past or at the time of writing, there is nevertheless a wealth of detail and nuance in his actual narrative.[85] His account is often more revealing than he himself may realise. Thus the upper classes among the Goths, or some of them, were ready, we are told, to sell out their people to Byzantium, and even to accept Belisarius as emperor, while the common people seem to have been untouched by Romanisation and unswervingly hostile to the Byzantine armies.[86] This distinction is embedded in Procopius' narrative rather than consciously pointed out by the writer. His own expressed views of barbarians and their proper treatment by Byzantium are rather simple: give in to them and they will never cease to take advantage.[87] Yet there are many instances mentioned in the *Gothic Wars* of Byzantine soldiers deserting to the Goths,[88] especially during Belisarius' second expedition, when success seemed to have deserted the Byzantines. The conditions in the Byzantine army of which Procopius complains in the *Secret History* – failure to pay the troops, lack of reinforcements or even of provisions – are clear even in the *Wars*, and Procopius gives ample evidence of the discontent of the Byzantine soldiery. He knew, too, that many Italians were less than enthusiastic about the arrival of the Byzantines. At Naples there was a reluctance to admit them that was later seen to be amply justified, when Byzantine troops took part in a general rampage of killing and destruction.[89] Procopius does not say directly that the citizens were opposed to the Byzantines, and he minimises the degree of destruction so far as he is able, but he cannot gloss over the situation altogether and in fact deals with it by presenting the opposing arguments in a set of formal speeches,[90] thus removing them to some extent from the hard actuality of the main narrative. The Romans were in an equally awkward position. They could hardly keep Belisarius out; yet once they

---

[85] Well brought out by Thompson 1982, 77ff.

[86] Ibid., 95ff.

[87] I.1.4; II.14.28-9.

[88] Thompson 1982, 98f. ('in no other war of ancient history, so far as I know, do we hear of anything like so many deserters'). Some examples: I.17.7; 18.7; 25.15-17; 28.4 (all from the early days when Belisarius's reputation was at its height; there are more from the second campaign).

[89] I.10.29, 34; Thompson 1982, 100f. Procopius represents the Byzantine action as 'liberation' (I.10.35), as generally with his presentation of the wars of reconquest (cf. *Vandal Wars* I.16.9; 20.20), but many signs, especially here in the narrative of the taking of Naples, show that the attitude of the local population was equivocal at best.

[90] *Gothic Wars* I.8.7f. (Neapolitan envoy); 12f. (Belisarius); 29f. (pro-Gothic speech of Pastor and Asclepiodotus). I.8.7-42 therefore constitute a formal debate on the subject of Neapolitan reactions to the arrival of Belisarius.

let him in with his army they faced a certain siege.[91] Nor did present
support of the Byzantines help them later when Rome was taken by
Totila in 546 and 550.[92] Procopius does his best to show the Romans as
loyal to the imperial cause, but, like Tacitus, he does not fail to include
details which tell against his contentions.[93] In the same way he records
the profiteering of the Byzantines, who sold corn at high prices to the rich
during the 546 siege, and allowed many of the civilians to leave the city
for a price after the terrible hunger and deprivation of the siege, only to
die by the wayside or at the hands of the Goths.[94] The leading Romans
were tossed from one side to another with no certainty of an end, but in a
war 'fought between barbarians on the one side and civilised men on the
other', 'the Italians chose civilisation'.[95] This was also Procopius' view.
But the irony is that in the last siege of the war his sympathies lay on the
side of Totila. The unforgettable war dance performed by Totila before
the battle of Busta Gallorum was for Procopius a strange yet glorious act
by a leader soon to meet with a death unworthy of his nobility of
character,[96] rather than another example of the uncivilised barbarity of
the Goths which in the end educated Italians could only reject.[97]
Similarly, it was for Procopius a galling blow that the final victory in
Italy was won by Narses and not Belisarius, by a man whose ability he is
forced to admit[98] but who would for him always be the wrong choice.[99]

Particularly in the earlier part of the Italian war narrative, then, it was
to be expected that Procopius would at least present things from the
Byzantine point of view. He can make Belisarius claim, for instance, that
the Goths had not been defeated through their own lack of courage or
shortage of men, but simply by the superior leadership of the
Byzantines.[100] Whether or not Procopius has actually distorted or
falsified facts so as to glorify the Byzantine side is difficult to establish
with certainty, except perhaps on the numbers of enemy dead, which
seem to be distorted on any calculation.[101] We should also beware of
taking the narrative of the *Wars* too much at face value. Many factors,
including convention and didacticism as well as political bias, may have
influenced both content and form. Thus it seems odd that Belisarius
should seem to have known nothing of Gothic equipment and military

[91] I.14.4 – they feared they would suffer the same fate as the Neapolitans.
[92] The harsh treatment of Romans by Totila: III.20.16ff. The city was deserted (20.19);
21.21f.: Totila upbraids the senators for their support of Byzantium.
[93] Thompson 1982, 102-4.
[94] III.17.25.
[95] Thompson 1982, 109
[96] IV.31.18f.
[97] Thompson, 108-9.
[98] II.13.16.
[99] IV.21.6f. (denigrating the choice of Narses).
[100] II.18.14.
[101] Above, pp. 149; Hannestad 1960; Thompson 1982, 80.

techniques, or even of those of the Vandals, and that Procopius should
have to fill in the gaps.[102] In fact this apparent ignorance is part of the
rhetoric of the *Wars*; it allows the author to include direct didactic
sections on arms and tactics which are there because Procopius wants
them there, not because Belisarius was really totally devoid of military
intelligence. The *Wars* operates within an elaborate rhetoric of military
history in which 'factual' detail is often deceptively carefully structured.
Things are certainly not always what they seem. Thus when Procopius
ascribes to Totilla the desire to meet the enemy in pitched battle instead
of operating through siege warfare and attrition[103] it is not at all obvious
that this was in fact Totila's wish; the final battle in which Totila himself
was killed was just such a pitched battle, and it was disastrous, not least
because Totila's tactics were exactly those calculated to give the
Byzantine mounted archers most advantage.[104] In fact Procopius was not
well-informed on Gothic aims: he does not explain why the Goths
invested so much in a naval conflict in 551, nor why Totila was diverting
his forces to Corsica and Sardinia.[105] Nor is he sure about the reasons for
Totila's policy of destroying urban fortifications, ascribing it to the desire
to force the Byzantines to come out into open battle; he does not consider
what conception of the future the Goths could have had in an Italy where
even Rome might be razed to the ground.[106] The speeches, therefore, are
the least reliable indicators of real argument and real policy, even when
put into the mouth of Belisarius.

As for the main narrative, however, and especially for the portions
where he was not himself in Italy, it is difficult not to admire Procopius'
grasp. As we have seen, he was sent himself more than once on special
missions,[107] and is usually presumed to have had excellent information.
But his actual range of informants was perhaps more limited than is
often supposed. By far the most frequently mentioned group in the
Gothic Wars are the members of the 'bodyguard', the *doryphoroi*.[108]
These men are often known to Procopius by name; they are used
individually for special tasks or delicate missions, without much
differentiation of task.[109] Surely they are the source of much of the
factual detail about engagements and movements of Byzantine troops,
and individuals like these must have provided most of Procopius' data
for the sections where he or Belisarius were not personally present and
when (presumably) he no longer had immediate access to military

---

[102] Thompson, 77f., 80.
[103] III.25.11.
[104] IV.32.6f.
[105] IV.23.29f.; 24.31f. See Thompson, 86-7.
[106] III.22.6f.: Totila plans to raze Rome completely in 546; in fact he reduced the walls
and then was persuaded by a letter from Belisarius not to do further damage.
[107] II.4.1; cf. 17.10.
[108] I.18.14; 27.4, 11; 28.23; 29.20; II.2.16; 5.18; 8.3.
[109] Or else are singled out among those killed in battle: I.18.14 Maxentius.

records. Of the Italians, there are three groups singled out. First, and most numerous, are the members of the Roman senate, mentioned at times collectively but often named as individuals; a few passages suggest that Procopius had talked to them personally.[110] When they are named, it is usually with one name only in the Greek manner. Then there are the priests, including bishops.[111] They are not so prominent here as in the *Persian Wars*, not only because of the strength of the secular aristocracy in Italy, but also because the anecdotal or miraculous material in the *Gothic Wars*, unlike the corresponding element in the *Persian Wars*, tends to focus on pagan survivals and mythology (the temple of Janus, the Sibylline books, Aeneas' ship).[112] Thus the very subject matter here tended to minimise the role of bishops and clerics; it would perhaps be premature to conclude from that they did not figure large among Procopius' informants. The third category to be explicitly mentioned (far less frequently) is that of rhetors,[113] who occasionally have a part to play as prominent men in their cities. Procopius sees the situation in terms of restricted, but highly predictable, categories, and it is presumably from these groups that he drew his information. Notable Goths might be named as individuals, particularly in the course of military set pieces, but are not envisaged as a clearly distinguishable group. Procopius' view is both class-based and eastern. It is also the view of someone closely involved with the military actions themselves. By far the most vivid writing comes in the description of the first siege of Rome, when Procopius was present himself with Belisarius.[114] The latter is at the centre of the narrative, boldly escaping into the city, posting the inhabitants on the walls, keeping his head in danger, confident of success and too excited to eat.[115] Procopius could pick up intriguing details – the taunts of the Goth Vacis, who reproached the Romans for preferring Greeks unable to defend themselves, when the only Greeks they had seen before were actors and mimes and thieving sailors;[116] the mischievous

[110] III.22.20 (patricii); 26.11 (senators, Clementinus, a patrician, Orestes the consul, AD 530); 20.18-19 (Decius, Basilius, patricians; Maximus, Olybrius, Orestes 'and some others'); 20.27 (senators begging bread like Rusticiana); 9.7f. (Totila writes to senate); 13.12 Cethegus, patrician and *princeps senatus*); I.4.15 Liberius and Opilius, senators); 6.2 (Theodatus and senate); 25.13-15 Belisarius expels some senators including Maximus, then restores them); 26.1-2 (Vitigis orders killing of senators, but Burgentinus escapes with Reparatus); IV.22.2 (Totila divides senate between Rome and Campania).

[111] I.6.13 Rusticus; 14.4 etc. Silverius; 25.13; III.15-16, 35 Vigilius; II.7.35 Datius; III.16.7, 20.23 Pelagius; I.26.2 Reparatus.

[112] I.25.18f. (Janus); 24.28f. (Sibylline books, quoting in Latin); IV.22.7f. (Aeneas' ship). See too I.24.22f. (dissolving mosaic of Theodoric). IV.22.5f. is an interesting (if touristic) comment by Procopius on the traditional patriotism of Rome, which had preserved so many ancient monuments intact through all the barbarian threats.

[113] I.8.22; III.21.18.

[114] I.14ff.

[115] See I.18.34-43; Antonina and his servants could only with difficulty persuade him to snatch a mouthful.

[116] I.18.40.

actions of the Samnite children, which foretold victory for Belisarius;[117] the complaints of the Romans under siege conditions;[118] Belisarius' laughter at the approach of the ridiculous Gothic siege towers and the bewilderment of the Romans.[119] Many touches like this, as well as a wealth of topographical detail,[120] bring the siege to life more vividly than any other episode, and it is enlivened with anecdotes and explanations rising from Procopius' own keen interests.[121] Procopius can quote Belisarius' words when he finally explains why he had been so confident on the day when he had actually been put to flight by the Goths[122] and noted the awkward situation in which he found himself when Romans Byzantines thought he had been too cowardly to risk his army.[123] The events of this siege take up a whole book, and the raising of the siege, the siege of Auximum and events leading to the entry of Belisarius to Ravenna and the capture of Vitigis take us up to the end of Book II. Procopius can thus end Book II of the *Gothic Wars* on the climactic note of Belisarius' capture of Vitigis, the extraordinary offer of the Goths and his noble refusal; followed by his sudden recall. Thus he gets maximum effect by beginning Book III with his arrival in Constantinople, and his overwhelming prestige then, contrasted with Justinian's failure to grant him a triumph.[124] By contrast with these opening books, however, Book

---

[117] I.20.1-4.

[118] I.20.5.

[119] I.22.2

[120] Even in the shabby state indicated by Cassiodorus' *Variae* (Krautheimer 1980, 65) Rome impressed Procopius with a deep sense of its history and traditions, and we get more of a feel for its physical shape and appearance than for any other city mentioned in the *Wars*, including Constantinople.

[121] Cf. I.15.4f., an excursus on Beneventum, commenting on the tradition of the teeth of the Calydonian boar and moving on to the story of the Palladium of Rome. We imagine Procopius as a tourist – an image of the Palladium was still on view in the temple of Fortuna 'even in my day', in front of the Egyptian-looking Athena which also attracts his attention (I.15.11f.). Here he inserts a rare comment (for the *Wars*) making a specific contrast between Roman and Byzantine beliefs about the Palladium: I.15.14 'the Byzantines however say that the Emperor Constantine buried this statue in the Forum named after him' (i.e. the Forum of Constantine in Constantinople, supposedly under the 'Great Statue' of Constantine on a porphyry pillar (see Dagron 1974, 39; Malal., p. 320; *Chron. Pasch.*, p. 528; Cameron and Herrin 1984, 242f; 263f.). These are not the words of one who had thought deeply about the notion of *translatio imperii*.

[122] I.27.25-9. Procopius was presumably among the friends who asked him about this. Belisarius replied that he realised at that moment the difference between the two armies – that the Romans and their allies were experienced mounted archers, while the Goths were weak in this area; see Thompson, 1982, 77-8. The difference was forcefully demonstrated by the manoeuvre tried by Vitigis (I.27.15-19).

[123] I.28.3.

[124] II.29.17-30.30; Belisarius slandered to Justinian by some of his officers and subsequently recalled: II.30.1f.; praise of Belisarius on his return to Constantinople:III. 1.1-22; Justinian displays the treasure of Theodoric only to the senate and not to the people, and refuses Belisarius a triumph: III.1.3; Procopius follows this with his lengthy defence of Belisarius.

III tells a dreary story, and though it ends effectively, as it begins, with a panegyric (of Germanus this time),[125] the panegyric is in fact an obituary; though the book concludes with a modest Byzantine success, imperial policy was in tatters and reduced to makeshift expedients.[126] The three books solely devoted to the Gothic war represent, therefore a climb to a high peak (end of Book II), followed by a decline. When Procopius broke off and made public *Wars* I-VII there was no triumphant note to sound as a climax, as there had been in 540, and he was a long way from claiming lasting Byzantine victory or from preaching rapprochement with the Goths.

So it is a mistake to look to Procopius for complex analyses of the Gothic situation. His narrative is personal, and his very assessments of character, tending to the repetitive and simplistic,[127] are a pointer to his black-and-white views. The variation he employs in terms for the Gothic rulers seems to indicate his pragmatism too.[128] It does not follow however that because some sections are provably deficient in exact reporting we can throw out his evidence altogether. W. Goffart, for instance, has lodged a sharp attack on Procopius' evidence about Odoacer and the allotment of one third of Italian land to barbarians.[129] He concludes, on the basis of the correct observation that Procopius often distorts and makes mistakes, especially in his 'origins' sections, that it is impossible to know when to believe him: 'There is no scientific way to extract nuggets of fact from basically dubious but unique information.'[130] Precisely, for the *Wars* is, if nothing else, a literary work: it cannot be approached through 'scientific' methods. And the vulnerability of some parts is by no means enough to show that Procopius is always wrong. Goffart needs, for his own argument, to discredit the evidence of Procopius, but this is not the way to do it. For just as Procopius' excursuses and 'origins' sections are not all good, so certainly they are not all bad.[131] The *Gothic Wars*, as much as any other part of Procopius' work, shows that a close analysis of the structure of individual sections,

---

[125] III.40.9.

[126] III.40.44; cf. 40.10 (Justinian's reaction to the death of Germanus). The appointments which followed: O'Donnell 1981, 66f. (Liberius, in his eighties, was already en route for Sicily; further on Liberius, Wickham 1981, 22f. and see Cantarelli 1915).

[127] See Chapter 13 below. In these books, the recipients of Procopius' approval are often praised for their *dikaiosynē* (I.1.27 Theodoric; 33 Boethius and Symmachus; I.2.3 Amalasuntha; I.8.21 Antiochus; II.13.17; III.40.9 Germanus). Soldiers, equally, are invariably *drastērioi* (see p. 240 below and cf. I.2.25; 3.1; 27.4; IV.31.11).

[128] See Thompson 1982, 74; Jones 1962. Thompson rightly recognises that Procopius' usage varies (between *tyrannos, rex* and even *basileus*) according to changing circumstances and the demands of the argument at a particular point in the *Wars*. Since there is no real consistency, therefore, it is hard to know whether to press his final comment on Totila, where he calls him simply *basileus* (IV.26.4).

[129] Goffart 1980, 62ff.

[130] Ibid., 69.

[131] See Chapter 12 below.

without prejudice overall, is the only way to arrive at any fair estimation of the credibility of his evidence. There will be many instances, where he is the only witness, where we simply cannot go further. But at all costs we must avoid judging the issue on the basis of generalisations about Procopius' work as a whole.

It is in these books of the *Gothic Wars* that we see the full development of Procopius' point of view. He may not have had a very nuanced understanding of the situation in Italy, but it was here that the Byzantines encountered the greatest and most prolonged difficulties of the reconquest policy, and in telling the story of these years Procopius had a more complex subject than in either the Vandal or the Persian books. It was on this front that the Byzantine armies suffered most from lack of support and resources; here that their own leaders failed them and here that they had to overcome a new and serious threat, even after the capture of Vitigis which must at the time have seemed like the final stage in the war. Here more than elsewhere in the *Wars*, Procopius had to adapt himself to a changed and unexpected situation, and here the connection with the *Secret History* reaches its closest point. Eventually the Gothic war did end in victory for Byzantium, and a settlement to match that made for Africa nearly twenty years previously.[132] Procopius did not record it. Had he done so, it would not have been with the same savour and enjoyment with which he wrote of the Vandal conquest, or of the thrilling events which followed not long after it in the first siege of Rome.

---

[132] The Pragmatic Sanction of 13 August, 554: *Nov.*, app. 7.1; Stein, *BE* II.613ff. This was the effective end of the senatorial aristocracy of the west, though the legislation in fact sought to protect them; many, as we have seen, had gone to the east and stayed there (Stein, 617f.), and the position of those who remained yielded before the increased importance of the military and the church (Brown 1984).

CHAPTER TWELVE

Times and Places

Only after analysing the texture of Procopius' work in general, therefore, and especially that of the *Wars*, is it possible to move with confidence to the question which has in fact dominated most of the earlier discussion – the deceptively simple one of Procopius' credibility. In practice this must be the hardest issue of all to face adequately, since so little of his information can be checked directly against other sources. Yet here we have a writer who gives us voluminous material on *Realien*, geography, topography and the recent history of little known areas outside the empire. It is impossible not to use Procopius and impossible not to rely on him. But at least now we can avoid the trap of assuming for him a blanket accuracy and reliability which he may well not have in individual instances.

Procopius' apparently firm and reliable information on Justinianic building is easily shown to be highly vulnerable and his overall picture to be misleadingly clear-cut. It is not so much deliberate falsification for political or panegyrical ends that has shaped his presentation (though it is certainly not absent) as the overriding influence of the writing itself. He was not, in any of his works, producing a fact book for future historians, but, in each case, a complex narrative with many subtle requirements. In this light we can now turn to an aspect of his work which has given rise to some of the sharpest disagreements and most obvious misunderstandings.

It was required of a writer of history in Procopius' manner to include various kinds of digressions, especially about the peoples of the areas where the conflicts took place, and he duly preceded his war narratives with histories of the relevant peoples and places.[1] These sections, however, have proved extremely difficult to deal with, partly because of the general lack of literary sources for much of this material, but also because of the highly charged atmosphere in which the debate has been

---

[1] *Persian Wars* I.2f. (not so much an ethnographical excursus as a history of Persia in the fifth and sixth centuries); *Vandal Wars* I.1-8 (again a general history of the Goths and Vandals since AD 410); *Gothic Wars* I.1-4 (Italy from the time of Theodoric). Other excursuses in the *Wars* are more precisely ethnographic: see in general Cesa 1982; Emmett, forthcoming. Agathias followed the pattern with lengthy sections on the Persians and the Franks, both claiming contemporary information (Averil Cameron 1968, 1969-70).

conducted, especially in the case of the history and character of the early Germans. Procopius' information on the early history of the Vandals, therefore, which precedes the *Vandal Wars* proper, makes a good starting point, since it has recently been the subject of a lively attack in the course of a discussion which brings out well the failure of most scholars to appreciate these sections on origins for what they really are.[2] To quote: 'Modern historians value these chapters of background very much, for ethnographic information is rare, and Procopius' historical introductions are chiefly about the otherwise badly documented fifth century. Our books accord a place of honor in his testimony on these subjects and hinge some very important notions upon his word alone.'[3] We must now therefore take these introductory chapters in the full context of Procopius' method overall, and link them with other ethnographic or geographic sections, getting away from the usual approach of seizing on individual statements out of context. It is hard enough to use information from 'digressions' in ancient historiography in any case;[4] but here there is the additional difficulty that Procopius' own technique as a writer has been so powerful in influencing the shape of what he says. I am less concerned here, then, with the truth or falsity of individual statements (that belongs to the next stage of discussion) than with trying to establish how Procopius went about gathering his material and shaping it into literary form.

Let us begin then with the sketch of Gothic migration which Procopius has placed at the beginning of the *Vandal Wars*.[5] On this the conclusion of Goffart is that 'although wholly admirable from a literary standpoint, Procopius' sketch is misleading history, carried along by anachronism, telescoped chronology, *suppressio veri* and outright legends'.[6] Indeed, the whole opening of *Vandal Wars* I (chs. 1-9) forms a highly wrought introduction to the narrative of Belisarius' campaign, covering the entire history of the Vandals from the beginning to the reign of Gelimer. It is far from clear what literary sources Procopius used; needless to say he has covered his tracks, and Rubin's assumption of Priscus is not proved.[7] It is surely mistaken, however, to suppose that he was following a single source; this section like other comparable ones bears all the traces of literary reshaping and characteristic stylistic touches. Nor can we

---

[2] Goffart 1980, 62ff. For the nature of these 'origins' sections see p. 64 n. 14.

[3] Ibid., 63.

[3] Ibid., 63.

[4] Digressions as part of the rhetoric of history: Emmett 1981; 1983; forthcoming. Cesa 1982 (in an extremely useful discussion) identifies three types of excursus in Procopius, geographic, historical and ethnographic, emphasising their integral relation to the narrative.

[5] *Vandal Wars* I.2ff.

[6] Goffart 1980, 66 with n. 17. Further on this excursus: Bachrach 1973, 44ff.

[7] Rubin 1954, 128; against Priscus: Goffart, loc. cit. and see Cesa 1982, 195f., 204f.

assume, with Rubin, that when Procopius says 'it seems to me' or the like, he is really marking out an original opinion. To judge from parallel passages in Theophanes and Nicephorus Callistus, Procopius has reshaped his material;[8] but we should probably go beyond that and admit that he used sources other than Priscus. In fact not all of this material can have come from Priscus.[9] We cannot say, in the present state of our knowledge, whether Procopius was drawing direct on Priscus or on, say, Eustathius of Epiphaneia. What is certain, though, is his own bold and selective presentation of the material. In the account of the fifth-century invasions, the Huns are casually passed over and Attila only said vaguely to have led a 'great army of Massagetae and other Scythians' and to have gained power after the death of Aetius.[10] This is more the approach of a mid-sixth-century writer than what one would expect from Priscus. The latter section of the introduction offers even less indication of source; from chapter 8 onwards, we can no longer use Theophanes to clarify the matter, for at this point Theophanes, like Evagrius, begins to rely on Procopius himself.[11] Again, however, we can see the personal approach of Procopius: he is concerned now to present a set piece on the contrasting characters of the various Vandal kings – the persecutor Huneric, the mild Hilderic, with his general known as the Vandal Achilles,[12] the overwhelming Gelimer. And this is all part of a smooth transition to the main narrative, beginning in chapter 10, through an exchange of royal letters.

The conclusion to be drawn from these chapters is that Procopius was primarily interested in putting together a smooth and artistic introduction. Where he can, he shapes the plain historical narrative to convey personal opinions or lessons which he wants to inculcate. His 'origins' are strictly tailored to the demands of his main narrative. It is therefore dangerous in the extreme to take isolated statements out of their context and treat them as though they must be literally true. But equally, we cannot assume that because Procopius is proved wrong in some cases, he must always be wrong, or conversely that because he is

[8] Rubin, loc. cit.

[9] For discussion see Blockley 1981, 115f. and for Priscus Haury, ed. rev. Wirth, I, vii-xix. Common derivation from Priscus explains some of the similarities between Procopius and Jordanes's *Getica*, but the use may be indirect in both cases. Further, Blockley 1983, 379f.; 391 (especially n. 112).

[10] I.4.24, 29. Procopius on the Huns: also *Gothic Wars* IV.5.

[11] Rubin 1954, 134. Evagrius: direct knowledge of Priscus, Allen 1981, 240f.; use of Procopius, 9f.; Tricca 1915. Evagrius certainly also used Eustathius, perhaps the intermediary for Procopius.

[12] I.9.2. Cesa 1982 points out (196f.) that if Procopius was in a sense continuing Eustathius's narrative, which ended with the year 502/3, his decision to begin these books with a historical excursus starting much earlier than that seems all the more deliberate, not mere antiquarianism but aimed at setting out his own views; see too Cesa 1981, 398f. But there was also the literary consideration. Further, it was precisely now that 'origins' myths were being developed, as we can see from Jordanes on the Goths: Reynolds 1983.

often reliable he must always be so.

Another such passage for comparison is his treatment of the origins of the Franks in the *Gothic Wars*.[13] There are three relevant passages, commenting both on the state of the Franks when they invaded Italy in 539 and outlining their origins, much as he does for the origins of the Goths; a study of these passages is most instructive for Procopius' methods. We might best begin with the sections on Theudebert's army,[14] where we are on the firmest ground, and here there are several points to be made, quite apart from what Procopius actually says and whether or not it is credible. In writing of the Franks, then, probably in the late 540s, Procopius was dealing with a people who had, in the eyes of Byzantium, broken faith, ignored the obligations laid on them by Byzantine subsidies, and gone all out for their own interests. The expedition of Theudebert in 539 turned on the Byzantine army, to Belisarius' incredulous indignation, and followed up this treachery by grabbing whatever land it could.[15] Procopius was with Belisarius in 539; he shared his sense of outrage and was still smarting from it when he wrote *Gothic Wars* I and II. In addition to this hostility to the Franks, there was his own prejudice against barbarians as such which he shared with most of his contemporaries. Nor is there anything to make us believe that he actually knew much about the Franks. These sections were probably written before the arrival of the Frankish embassy to Constantinople in *c.* 550.[16] We must presume that Procopius was using oral sources, but we have no idea what those sources were, nor whether they were at all reliable. Certainly he had no conception of the importance of Clovis, or any inside information about the Franks before Theudebert. Further, though he was present in Italy at the time of Theudebert's invasion, he was not present at the engagement with Byzantine troops.[17] Thus his general statement that the Frankish army consisted mainly of infantry, which has been so much debated, may well derive simply from a general assumption about barbarian armies.[18] Taken as a whole, the passage is a complex mixture of reliable reporting and vague prejudice. When Procopius says blandly that the Franks are the most treacherous race of

---

[13] *Gothic Wars* I.11.29ff.; II.25; IV.24-5. In general on Procopius' material on the Germans: Ditten 1975.

[14] II.25. Procopius' hostile presentation of Theudebert is strikingly at odds with the favourable views of Marius of Avenches and Gregory of Tours: see Collins 1983, suggesting that Theudebert's expedition was a response to requests for aid from Milan.

[15] Or so Procopius claims: see Collins 1983, 31-2, warning against too readily taking Procopius' words at face value.

[16] For which see *Gothic Wars* IV.20.10; see Bury 1923, II, 258, n. 4; Thompson 1980, 501; see below.

[17] II.23.23f.; 25.13-15; Procopius himself was with Belisarius.

[18] II.25.2-3; see Bachrach 1970a, with Benedicty 1965, 56, 73 on the *topos* of barbarian infantry.

all[19] he is no more reporting an objective fact than when he says that the invading army numbered 100,000.[20] The details here about Frankish weapons, then, may be partly literary, and certainly depend on hearsay; it is clearly unsafe to take them as certainly reliable. We can see, in fact, how far Procopius has overlaid his evidence with emotion from the letter which he now includes, supposedly sent by Belisarius in protest to Theudebert: its chief themes are *hybris* and treachery.[21] Perhaps then we ought to interpret the section on Frankish origins[22] in the light of this presentation of Theudebert, and to take it less seriously than many modern scholars have done. It is after all merely latched on to a passing reference to the Franks in a general introduction to the *Gothic War*.[23] In general, however, it has been made to bear far more weight than is reasonable. The mysterious 'Arborychi', for instance, apparently a mistake of Procopius rather than the result of a textual corruption,[24] most probably simply arose from a mishearing of 'Armorici'. When he assures us that both the Franks and these Armorici were Christian at the time of their alliance,[25] we can have no idea of the credentials of his statement, which is unsupported by other evidence and not open to confirmation from within the *Wars*. The account in general is curiously externalised, quite unlike the detailed knowledge which Agathias seems to have had a generation later.[26] Procopius actually had very little information. He did not know that the Visiogoths were defeated and Alaric killed at Vouillé,[27] and typically launches into speculation about the whereabouts of the treasures of the Temple at Jerusalem rather than keeping to the main theme.[28] Above all, we cannot use a single statement in such an account to discredit or confirm the rest.

If we now turn from the allusions to the Franks in *Gothic Wars* I and II to the statements about them in Book IV, we find Procopius' attitude much changed. In 539 he had been enraged by Frankish duplicity; but as time went on and he became increasingly disillusioned with the Byzantine cause, he came to see the invasion of 539 as representing not so much Frankish treachery as everything that was wrong with Justinian's subsidy policy. At the beginning of the war Justinian had written to the

---

[19] II.25.2. For the stock theme of barbarian treachery see Cesa 1981, 403; 1982, 211f.; Averil Cameron 1982, 38f.

[20] Ibid. For comparison with Agathias' treatment of the Frankish army, see Averil Cameron 1968, 129f.

[21] II.25.20f.

[22] I.11.29ff.

[23] I.11.28-9.

[24] I.12.13f. See Thompson 1980, 502.

[25] I.2.15.

[26] See Averil Cameron 1968.

[27] See I.12.33f. But for a defence of Procopius against Lot 1930 see Bachrach 1970b, 23f.

[28] I.12.42f.

Franks claiming their support on grounds of common orthodoxy against the Arian Goths, and giving them gifts with the promise of more.[29] Yet they invaded Italy, confounding the Byzantines by attacking *both* sides. For Procopius now this perfidy seemed a perfect illustration of the dangers of subsidies. Even after receiving subsidies, he wrote in the *Secret History*, barbarians would overrun imperial territory and encourage others to terrorize the emperor into paying them to go away.[30] By 553/4, when the last book of the *Wars* was finished, he could attribute the success of Theudebert's invasion in 539 also to Byzantine neglect,[31] not a factor admissable earlier. There was good reason for a Byzantine change of tack also because Theudebert was now dead, and the new king might be more amenable. Thus the way was open for a version of the events of 539 which removed some blame from the Franks and admitted Byzantine responsibility. Ambassadors were sent, and Procopius gives us a pair of speeches, that of the Byzantine Leontius and that of the Frankish ruler Theudibald.[32] The Byzantine tone is strikingly conciliatory; Leontius states the Byzantine grievances against Theudebert but avoids carrying any blame on to Theudibald, asking him simply for help against the Goths. To which Theudibald replies that the Franks and the Goths are friends, and that Theudebert did not deprive the Byzantines of anything, for they had already lost those lands to the Goths – he can even add that the Byzantines should have helped the Franks. The present Byzantine request is evaded by the promise to send ambassadors to Constantinople. Now the Franks, approached also by Teias, refuse formal alliance with either side, keeping their own counsel and plotting to see whether they could get hold of Italy for themselves.[33] Thus Procopius allows a different view of the Franks to emerge, and one seen more nearly in their own terms. He knew well now that the Franks held the balance.

The speech of Theudibald here is one of the mischievous compositions in which Procopius puts his own criticism of the Byzantine government.[34] In the earlier passages about the Franks he took a hard pro-Byzantine line. Now Byzantine attitudes and needs have changed, and Procopius too is ready to allow himself a more differentiated view of the relations between Franks and Byzantines. Even so, it is a view which owes its being to Procopius' personal approach. Theudibald's lively reply could hardly represent what was actually said, and does not tally with his documented epistolary manner.[35] The interpretation given therefore to

---

[29] I.5.8f.

[30] *Secret History* 11.5-6.

[31] *Gothic Wars* IV.24.7.

[32] IV.24.12-24; 25-30.

[33] IV.34.17f.

[34] Compare the speech of Arsaces, III.32.8-11.

[35] See Averil Cameron 1968, 123.

Procopius 'on the Franks' needs to bear many different factors in mind.

Far from being made up of discrete lumps of information, waiting to be dug out by modern scholars, Procopius' digressions and 'origins' passages are complex, subtle and varied. The text is many stages removed from the simple transmission of information. It has been shaped by literary aims, personal opinion and wider changes in Byzantine policy; moreover, references to the same people in different parts of Procopius' work need always to be considered in the light of their placing within the work and its development. The level of credibility in the *Wars* is thus far more variable than has usually been admitted, even within a single passage. Since we are so often without controls in other sources, the problems of interpretation are obvious.

Another good – and difficult – example is provided by Procopius' passages about Britain. There are two main ones, one a part of the 'origins' section that opens *Vandal Wars* I, the other a digression in the last book of the *Wars*, leading on from a passing reference in the main narrative.[36] There is just enough plausible detail, among the hearsay and the personal comment, to qualify as serious evidence, with sufficient distortion to make its interpretation highly problematic. And quite apart from their value or otherwise for the history of sub-Roman Britain, these passages are very instructive for our understanding of Procopius. They should be taken closely with those already discussed.

In the 'origins' section in *Vandal Wars* I, Procopius tells of the revolt of Constantine in 407; after its suppression in 409, the Romans could hold on to Britain no longer, and it was then ruled by 'tyrants'.[37] This statement has been endlessly debated, for Procopius is the only author to say so explicitly that Roman rule now ended.[38] There is no such clear statement in western sources, save for allusions in Bede to the cessation of imperial rule after the sack of Rome by Alaric (AD 410).[39] Zosimus puts the emphasis rather differently: the Britons drove out the Saxon invaders and then set themselves up independently of Rome.[40] In this context Honorius is supposed to have written to the Britons telling them that they must defend themselves.[41] Clearly Procopius' bald statement does less than justice to a very tangled situation. Roman rule is unlikely to have come to such an abrupt end; more likely it petered out gradually, as soldiers ceased to be paid from imperial funds, while the situation in

---

[36] *Vandal Wars* I.2.31f.; *Gothic Wars* IV.20.
[37] I.2.38.
[38] The controversial question of the end of Roman rule in Britain has been much debated; cf. the series of articles by Thompson (1977, 1979, 1980, 1982a), with Kent 1979; Johnson 1980; Bartholomew, Welsby 1982; Wood 1984, to mention only the most recent. Procopius' 'tyrants' are pressed in association with Gildas' 'proud tyrant' to refer to Vortigern by Johnson 1980, 115.
[39] *HE* I.2; V.24.
[40] *New History* VI.5.
[41] VI.10. See Thompson 1982a.

Britain became more and more fragmented.[42] But if Procopius has oversimplified, so he has been taken too literally by historians. 'We can date with extreme precision the end of Roman rule in that island. It ended in 409.'[43] In fact there is no need to interpret Procopius' words so rigorously. He simply says that Rome could not henceforth regain control of Britain, and this is not incompatible with there having followed a confused spell during which some Romans remained, without effective overall Roman control. Procopius does not say explicitly that the army was withdrawn. Nor does it necessarily follow that Roman contact now ceased permanently, for the Britons themselves seem to have made overtures for aid against the Picts and Scots to Aetius between 446 and 452.[44] If that aid was not forthcoming, it does not mean that the Britons thought they had been abandoned for ever by Rome. But this too is compatible with Procopius' bare statement. In the longer term the Saxon revolt of *c.* 455 may have seemed a more drastic cut-off point than the events of 409;[45] but after all, Procopius was not seeking to give a complete account of Britain in the fifth century, and there was no reason why he should say more than he did. That the British sources did not on the whole see 409 as the vital date does not mean that Procopius was wrong; but neither was he attempting to say the last word.

The other passage on Britain demonstrates all too clearly how little Procopius and his generation really knew. At *Gothic Wars* IV.20 he writes of an island, Brittia, lying not more than 200 stades opposite the mouth of the Rhine, between Bretannia and Thule. Bretannia is to the west, off the coast of Spain, 4,000 stades from the mainland, while Brittia is to the north, off the coast of Gaul, Thule being still further to the north. Brittia is inhabited by three peoples, the Angles, the Friesians and the Britons, who are so numerous that each year some migrate to the Franks and are settled in their territory;[46] some Angles were included in a recent delegation from the Frankish king to Justinian.[47] A little further on Procopius claims that horses were unknown to Brittia; so much so that when its representatives have to ride for some embassy or other (that just mentioned?) they have to be mounted and dismounted by others since they cannot do it for themselves.[48] The references to Brittia lead Procopius into a full-scale digression.[49] The island was divided by a wall,

[42] See e.g. Wood 1984. For the archeological evidence see Fulford, in Casey 1979; Reece 1980.

[43] Thompson 1982, 216.

[44] Gildas, *De Excidio Britanniae* 20.1. See Thompson 1979, 215ff.

[45] Wood, 1984. Gildas lays heavy stress on the ills of this period (but for his faint awareness of the historical end of Roman rule see Thompson 1979, especially 214).

[46] IV.20.8. The wide-reaching conclusions drawn from this passage do not seem justified: see Thompson 1980, 500.

[47] IV.20.10.

[48] IV.20.29-30. But Jordanes, *Getica* II.15, alludes to British horses.

[49] IV.20.42ff. On this section see Burn 1955; Chadwick 1976, viii; Thompson 1980, 504ff.

effectively separating the temperate parts from the uninhabitable. Procopius is clearly intrigued by this wall, but he has no idea that it was built by the Romans, nor any sense of Brittia as a former Roman possession. He now moves to the famous story, which he hesitates to believe himself, but which was attested by 'countless people', that it was the home of dead souls. Many people had told him that the inhabitants of an island off the coast of Brittia, instead of paying tribute to the Franks, acted as escorts of the dead. In their houses at night they hear a mysterious summons, go down to the beach in response to a compulsion which they do not understand, and embark on strange vessels which they row to Brittia, able to land without difficulty, though in their own boats it is next to impossible. On their return journey their boats are lighter, though they themselves never saw a passenger.

Whatever we make of this strange story, from which after all Procopius carefully dissociates himself, it does contain certain possibly historical details – the suggestion of Frankish domination at least – and if we are to believe Procopius, it was widely disseminated. In the *Secret History* Procopius claims that Justinian squandered money on subsidies as far afield as Britain,[50] and at *Gothic Wars* II.6.28, in a speech with the dramatic date of AD 537, he makes Belisarius magnanimously offer the Goths Britain, 'long subject to Rome' – a splendidly ambiguous phrase.[51] There seems to be a considerable degree of confusion, then, in Procopius' references to Britain. In *Gothic Wars* IV the island with the wall can only be Britain;[52] yet everywhere else he calls Britain Bretannia, a name here given to a place firmly distinguished from Britain, and perhaps rightly identified by Thompson with Armorica, i.e. Britanny.[53] If that is correct, Procopius' is our earliest suggestion of the name. But that does not save him from having failed to realise that Brittia here is the same as what he calls Britannia elsewhere. It is equally hard to know what to make of the 'countless' informants from among these ferriers of the dead. As for the Frankish domination, perhaps it is only a mistake.[54] He might well have got some information from the Angles in the Frankish embassy which he mentions himself; but the curious mixture of fantasy and history in his account betrays his ignorance. Britain was a far-away place about which Procopius had little hard information, merely vague suppositions and common stories. He is quite capable of using the name to add verisimilitude to the accusations in the *Secret History*, but that should

[50] *Secret History* 19.13.

[51] Sceptical: Thompson 1980, 505 n. 32. Ward 1968 believes that these passages do indicate contact between Britain and the east.

[52] IV.20.42. Against Bury's view that Procopius could not have identified this miraculous island with the well-documented former Roman province (Bury 1906, 83) see Thompson 1980, 498f., who defends Procopius. Gildas, after all, a close contemporary and a British writer, can completely mistake the date of the wall (*De Excidio*, 14).

[53] Thompson 1980, 499f.

[54] IV.20.10.

not lead us to take even those references literally.[55]

These passages about Britain, which have so vexed historians, show all too clearly the limitations of Procopius' approach and the extreme difficulty of pressing single statements. That is a lesson to remember.

It is equally hard to decide whether or not Procopius used earlier authors direct, and to what extent. Take the case of Arrian. It is a curious paradox that the only time that Procopius actually cites Arrian by name is on the fortress in Lazica called Cottiaeum, a detail which does not correspond to anything in Arrian's surviving work;[56] the passages in the *Wars* which do clearly depend on Arrian's *Periplus* do not name the source explicitly.[57] Thus there is ample scope for disagreement as to his exact debt to Arrian.[58] There is no consensus as to whether his digressions on Transcaucasia are based mainly on autopsy, oral or written sources, or when, if at all, Procopius ever went to the region himself. But again it is instructive to look at the way in which the main excursus (*BG* IV.1.7-6.61) is presented. The whole section is a polemic against earlier writers, called 'the ancients'. An example of their errors, according to Procopius, is that they say that the Colchi or Sanni were neighbours of Trapezus, to which he objects that these peoples were not the same, and that they did not live next to Trapezus.[59] Only then does he admit that there might have been some changes in the intervening period.[60] Presumably these 'ancients' are Xenophon and Arrian,[61] though since Arrian mentions Xenophon too there is no need to suppose that Procopius used the former direct. There are other signs of Arrian in this section, on the name Apsarus and on the Zechi.[62] But Procopius does not make things easy for us by spelling out his sources. He justifies his enterprise in terms of history versus myth.[63] A few touches suggest

[55] Above, n. 51. See also Wood 1984, 24f., taking seriously *Gothic Wars* II.6.28 and emphasising Procopius' view, shared with other eastern writers, of a distinct break in continuity in the west in the fifth century. For Procopius Britain was a far-away and fabled place.

[56] *Gothic Wars* IV.14.48.

[57] IV.1.7-6.61. See Pekkanen 1964 (Procopius only knew parts of Arrian's *Periplus* and did not depend on him throughout). Other sections dealing with Transcaucasia: *Persian Wars* I.10.1-12; 12.2-3; 15.20-5; II.29.14-26.

[58] I am grateful to Everett Wheeler for letting me see parts of his dissertation arguing (against Pekkanen, for example) that Procopius used Arrian direct and that IV.14.48 comes from Arrian's *Alanica* (possibly also IV.2.24-6). John the Lydian also knew Arrian's *Alanica* (*De Mag.* III.53), though perhaps indirectly (so Wheeler) and Arrian is cited by Malalas, p. 399, and Evagrius, *HE* V.24, no doubt also indirectly.

[59] IV.1.7-10. The whole tone is self-consciously literary; Procopius follows the standard arrangement of the *Periplus* tradition (Schnayder 1950), adding his own flourishes. Note that although he promises a different plan in Book IV (IV.1.2), in practice he divides his material here too entirely geographically, and includes a good deal of straight geographical subject matter.

[60] IV.1.11.

[61] Cf. Arrian, *Peripl.* II; Xen., *Anab.* IV.8.22.

[62] IV.2.16; Arrian, *Peripl.* VI.2; IX.3-5; X.3. Zechi: IV.4.2; Arrian, *Peripl.* XVIII.3.

[63] IV.1.12-13.

contemporary knowledge, though not necessarily Procopius' own: a tomb survives 'to my own day'; 'the inhabitants say'; the physical description of Apsyrtos and so on.[64] In other words, Procopius is self-consciously 'correcting' early accounts of the area from modern knowledge (though despite his dismissal of 'myth' he several times appeals to mythology himself). But the interplay between literary sources and other kinds of material including Procopius' own speculation is complex. He explicitly cites Strabo 'and others' on the Amazons, only to provide a rationalising explanation which in turn could perhaps derive from Arrian,[65] but to which Procopius gives his own assent[66] – I myself also believe that things happened something like this and that the Amazons fought with men, judging from what has happened in my own day'; he claims that in the Hun invasions women's bodies have been found among the fallen.[67] He can also add his own comments when he comes to the Tetraxite Goths,[68] who came to Constantinople asking for a new bishop in 547/8; Procopius hardly knows whether they are Arian or not, as their beliefs are so loose (an interesting comment in view of his often expressed disapproval of doctrinal rigidity), but they were useful to Justinian in his policy of knocking barbarian heads together (of which Procopius heartily approves), for they lodged information against their enemies the Utigurs. After this Procopius turns again to polemic, on the subject of the river dividing Europe and Asia, which according to some was the Phasis and others, including Arrian, the Tanais.[69] Arrian had quoted Aeschylus for the opposite view, and Procopius duly picks up the quotation.[70] His own 'quotation' from Herodotus comes direct from Arrian. But he adds that the *Prometheus* reference comes at the beginning of the play, whereas Arrian had merely quoted the lines. It seems unlikely however that Procopius had consulted Aeschylus; he does not quote the line itself, which would have been to the point. In any case, the polemic continues: he refers in the next section to 'these [writers] who know about these things' and then to the opposite argument, and he concludes the long excursus with a story about Aristotle. We can fairly conclude that Arrian is the main authority behind this passage, but typically, Procopius does

---

[64] IV.2.11, 12, 14.

[65] IV.3.6.

[66] IV.3.8.

[67] IV.3.7; on Amazons see also below, p. 241. A standard *topos* in the repertoire of misogynists like Procopius (see Chapter 5) it was said also of the Avars in the siege of AD 626 (Nicephorus, p. 21 de Boor). Procopius' views on women in the factions: *SH* 17.25: above pp. 144, 166.

[68] IV.4.9-13.

[69] IV.6.1-15. Cf. Herod. IV.45.2; Arrian, *Peripl.* XIX.1; *Anab.* III.30.8-9, citing Aeschylus.

[70] IV.6.15, from the *Prometheus Luomenos.* Pekkanen 1964, 48 argues that Procopius uses Aeschylus direct. As Wheeler points out, however, Procopius merely summarises, whereas Arrian quotes the Aeschylean passage. This excursus is one of Procopius' most literary, yet it remains infuriatingly hard to pin down its sources exactly.

not say so explicitly, and he constructs the whole in an artful literary manner, moving easily from personal comment to hard information and back again.

There is certainly a good deal of material in Procopius' ethnographic excurses which derives from general prejudice about barbarians. Not only was he no friend of barbarians himself, but his presentation is inevitably coloured by the strong tradition of ethnographic writing about barbarians which connected their supposedly typical characteristics with the climate of their homelands. It would be a mistake to try to pin down a distinct source of these ideas for Procopius; rather, they form a complex which had been part of the general cultural apparatus in a direct line back to Herodotus and the Hippocratic corpus.[71] Echoes of this tradition assert themselves with great frequency, for instance in Procopius' assertions about Frankish reliance on infantry,[72] but its influence can most clearly be seen in the five main excursuses, and especially in that on the Slavs in *Gothic Wars* III.[73] Needless to day, the latter is also necessarily a major document for Slavic prehistory. Scholars using it however need to be especially sensitive to the operation of these hidden assumptions.

But it is more than a half-conscious absorption of traditional attitudes: Procopius was also deliberately imitating classical authors, especially Herodotus, and the line between stylistic imitation and incorporation of content is a fine one.[74] Herodotean phraseology is combined with certain motifs recognisable from other ethnographic texts; thus the problem is to know whether, in the absence of a control, Procopius was drawing on real information. It is a real methodological dilemma. Most scholars, naturally not wishing to forego the data, recognise the ethnographic clichés, yet persist in supposing that Procopius had access to good information from the chatty barbarians he is supposed to have met while in the Byzantine army.[75] But a few examples show how tricky the problem actually is. Religion, for instance, is often a theme in ethnographic writings, yet one of the most suspect in terms of accuracy. In Procopius we read that the Sclavenes sacrifice to rivers and spirits; similarly with the people of Thule.[76] Like the Goths and so many other northern barbarians in the literature, Procopius' Sclavenes have yellow hair[77] and tend to wear trousers.[78] They fight like the Franks and the

---

[71] See Benedicty 1963, 1965 and in general Averil Cameron 1968, 111, 129f., 134f. Barbarian *apheleia: Gothic Wars* IV.3.18f.; 4.11.

[72] Above, p. 210.

[73] *Gothic Wars* III.14.21-30; cf. also *Persian Wars* I.3.2-7 (Hephthalites); *Vandal Wars* I.2.2-6 (Goths); *Gothic Wars* II.14.1-7 (Heruls); 15.16-26 (Thule).

[74] See Chapter 3 above; Benedicty 1965, 52f.

[75] Benedicty 1965, 60f., and his conclusion at 77-8.

[76] *Gothic Wars* III.14.24; II.15.23.

[77] III.14.27; cf. *Vandal Wars* I.2.4 (Goths).

[78] III.14.26.

Britons as infantry.[79] More interesting than these standard features are Procopius' comments about character and political organisation: the northern peoples were thought to be wild, full of unbridled *thumos* (spirit) because of the influence of the northern climate, and to tend for similar reasons towards depravity and lack of control.[80] So the Tetraxite Goths are characterised by *apheleia* (simplicity) and *apragmosynê*[81] (idleness) and the Sclavenes will not accept a ruler but live by *dêmokratia* – not a favourable word in Byzantine sources.[82] By contrast the Hephthalites are distinguished as more civilised than other Huns by the fact that they live under one ruler and follow a lawful constitution; because of this Procopius can say that they are as good as the Romans or the Persians,[83] that is, that they have transcended the quality of barbarism. The opposite of this is called a 'brutish' way of life. So these sections are made up of stock themes, enlived with fabulous stories like the one about the newly delivered mothers hanging their babies in skins from trees and feeding them on marrow instead of human milk,[84] or how the Heruls dispatch the sick by sending a stranger to kill them after tying them in trees, and then burning them, trees and all.[85] Mixed with these two elements are Procopius' own comments, the whole in a rather Herodotean dress.

Perhaps we should return at this point to the *Buildings*, where in addition to the kinds of influence operative in the *Wars* there is also a panegyrical aim. The handling of Procopius' evidence on the Balkan sites in Book IV is particularly tricky, though it has often been accorded a high level of credibility. Procopius seems to be giving such clear-cut and unequivocal information that it appears churlish to disbelieve him, especially when there is no other literary evidence and there are so many archeological sites to date. Yet we have seen already how subtly distorting Procopius' presentation can be, even in the highly finished section on Africa.[86] It might well seem that the unadorned lists in Book IV, naturally explained as deriving from official sources, would be more reliable, being uncontaminated by Procopius' literary intentions,[87] and clearly these lists are in some sense vital evidence for buildings, topography, toponymy and language in the Balkans area, though there is little agreement as to what kind of sources they represent (an official

---

[79] III.14.25; see above on the Franks and IV.20.29-30 for the Britons.
[80] See Benedicty 1962, 8; 1965, 54f.
[81] *Gothic Wars* IV.4.11.
[82] III.14.22; see Benedicty 1962, 8; 1965, 54.
[83] *Persian Wars* I.3.5.
[84] *Gothic Wars* II.15.20-2.
[85] II.14.1-7.
[86] See Chapter 10 above.
[87] *Buildings* IV.4.3; 11.20; above, p. 86. Thus despite lip service to Procopius' 'panegyrical intentions' (pp. 13, 213), Velkov 1977 in fact accepts them without qualms (pp. 95, 118, 127, 131).

map, reports kept by provincial governors, records from government archives or even lists of projected rather than completed projects).[88] In fact, very few of the names on the lists can be identified with existing sites; those that can seem to show, as we would have expected, that the fortifications lay along the military road system.[89] It is less clear whether they were really all the work of Justinian, as Procopius claims; current work increasingly suggests that the major fortification took place at an earlier date, and that Justinianic building sometimes in fact represented a retrenchment.[90] It is unlikely, too, that Procopius knew the area himself. Even on Justiniana Prima, Justinian's birthplace and an acknowledged showpiece, his account is curiously vague, high on rhetoric but lacking in detailed description.[91] There is no attempt either to describe the physical detail of the city or to locate it in its geographical context; yet we might have expected this site above all to have featured in an official archive. Turning to Greece, we encounter the same tendency to regard Procopius' very vague remarks as fundamental.[92] He tells us that before Justinian the cities of Greece were almost totally unprotected, yet the original Isthmian wall, probably built in the fifth century, perhaps in the last years of Theodosius II, evidently withstood the Cutrigur invasion of 540, to judge from a passage in *Persian Wars* II.[93] We would never have supposed that a substantial wall stood as late as this had we only the statement in the *Buildings* that the old wall had 'to

[88] Obviously the lists are important for the linguistic history of the area (Skok 1935; Beševliev 1967, 1969 (Latin original), 1970 (with much further bibliography) and it is unlikely that Procopius collected the information himself. But beyond that, and in the absence, in most sites, of epigraphic evidence identifying the existing site with one of those listed by Procopius, there is room for much speculation as to what the lists actually represented. For an orientation see the works cited, with Beševliev 1966; Velkov 1977; Hoddinott 1975, 241ff.; Poulter 1983, 94ff.; Browning 1975, 89ff.; Velkov 1983. Procopius' sources and methods have been extensively studied in Poulter's unpublished London PhD. dissertation (London, 1983), stressing the complexity of the problem, the probable variety of Procopius' sources and the extent of Anastasian building in these areas. At any rate it is rash to apply the 'evidence' of Procopius too literally for the identification of sites.

[89] See Pülhorn 1977, 450.

[90] See Poulter 1983, 97 (Capidava, Nicopolis). Previously, Procopius' panegyrical account had often been taken at face value and urban continuity assumed until *c.* 600. But this view imposes Procopius' 'evidence' on the interpretation of the physical remains. For an example see Velkov 1977, pp. 213, 232.

[91] IV.1.19f.; see above, p. 94. Procopius is again accepted by Velkov 1977 (p. 215). The vagueness of much of Book IV (cf. 2.23f. on Greece) suggests that Procopius was not very interested in the area covered, or else that he was working in haste; contrast the sections on Syria and Mesopotamia. IV.4 and 11 should be taken in conjunction with V.9, which Downey suggests comes from Procopius' 'working notes' (Downey 1947, 172f.). See also Perrin-Henry 1980. Of IV.11 Poulter writes 'as the two lists cannot ... be regarded as providing a reliable geographical progression, only those sites otherwise attested can be even generally located' (PhD. thesis, Appendix VI). I am grateful to Andrew Poulter for letting me see these sections.

[92] IV.2.22-3.

[93] *Persian Wars* II.4.11; see Hohlfelder 1977, 173f. Other building in Greece by Justinian: Daly 1942.

a large extent already collapsed'.[94] In the *Secret History* Procopius goes to the opposite lengths, claiming that Justinian undertook no building in Greece whatsoever.[95] We ought therefore to be cautious before accepting the lists in *Buildings* IV.4 and 11 too much at face value. In the first instance, the introduction to the chapter is the purest padding, to fill out the obvious fact that Procopius can offer no personal knowledge of the area.[96] It does indeed seem likely that these lists derive from some source other than Procopius himself, and probably from an 'official' list, whatever that term may mean. But we have only the word of Procopius that these forts are Justinianic, or that they were all actually completed. Elsewhere he demonstrably enhances the efforts of Justinian in comparison with the extensive work completed by Anastasius, and the epigraphic record from the lower Danube would suggest that Anastasius' effort there was as great as if not greater than that of Justinian.[97] It must be at least a strong possibility that Procopius has exaggerated Justinian's building activity in the Balkans as he has in other regions, and that these imposing lists are a less sure guide than has been thought. The African section of the *Buildings*, where Procopius omits a number of fortresses known from epigraphic evidence to be Justinianic and of a suitable period in the reign, is enough to show the difficulty of discovering his principles of selection.[98] As for the lists in Book IV, they may represent Procopius' raw material, but we cannot know how far he has already digested it, or how far he intended to alter it in a more finished work. Above all, we do not even know what kind of raw material it may have been.

Scholars have been ready to credit Procopius, partly simply on the strength of his reputation, with an extensive reading of earlier sources and an equally extensive knowledge of languages.[99] In view of the range of information he provides which is otherwise unknown, and the sheer scope of his curiosity, such trust is understandable. His evidence on Armenia, for example, stands comparison with the Armenian tradition, though it is not without mistakes, nor is it proven that he knew Armenian.[100] But we should not assume too readily that he knew Persian simply because he uses Persian names and titles,[101] or that he knew Gothic from the same

---

[94] IV.2.27-8.

[95] IV.2.27-8.

[95] *Secret History* 26.33. Both the *Buildings* and the *Secret History*, therefore, convey distinctly misleading impressions.

[96] Among other signs of haste or ignorance (n. 91) might be Procopius' complete omission of churches, in contrast with the other books.

[97] See e.g. Velkov 1958; Barnea 1960, 1967.

[98] See Chapter 10, Durliat 1981, 7ff.; Pringle 1981, II, 523. For Book V see too Downey 1950, 265.

[99] In general see Rubin 1954, 31ff., 37ff.; Schwyzer 1914.

[100] Adontz–Garsoian 1970, ch. 6. Armenian: Rubin, 1954, 52.

[101] Schwyzer 1914, 307ff.

argument.[102] Even Syriac is a matter of doubt. A 'Levantine origin' is not
proof enough that he knew it.[103] Certainly on grounds of general
probability he might have known some Syriac, coming from Caesarea
and having travelled in Syria and Mesopotamia; but his outlook was
firmly that of the Byzantine élite, and his sense of identification with the
people of the eastern provinces did not extend to identifying himself with
their culture as distinct from the culture of Constantinople. When he
gives an opinion about the conversions in Caesarea it is to distance
himself from his fellow townsmen.[104] His own definition of culture, which
in his view distinguished civilised men from barbarians, was the high
culture of Byzantium. Even Latin, which he must have learnt from his
legal training, evoked in him an ambiguous reaction, at once the object of
linguistic curiosity and yet to be avoided by a Greek writer with
pretensions to high style.[105] We have already discussed the connections
which Procopius may have had with the many Latin-speaking émigrés in
Constantinople who arrived just as Procopius was finishing the *Wars* and
writing his other works: it is hard to prove much direct contact, and it
seems unlikely that Procopius has used the Latin sources available in
more than a cursory way, if at all. A comparison of the surviving *Getica* of
Jordanes with Procopius' sections on the origins of the Goths does not
make it probable that the latter had used Jordanes' source, the *Gothic
History* of Cassiodorus,[106] nor does there seem to have been a direct
connection between his work and the *Chronicle* of Marcellinus.[107] Above
all, Procopius' views were his own.[108] His greatest strength is in his
personal observation and the collection of contemporary material for a
subject in which he was deeply involved, not in the historical or
ethnographical excursuses, where his approach is often anecdotal and
impressionistic. Procopius was extraordinarily energetic and determined
in the pursuit of interesting or useful information, but he was not a
scholar. He was a practical man, curious for detail and keen to work it
over with his own highly idiosyncratic imagination.

---

[102] Rubin 1964, 51 ('*a priori* wahrscheinlich').

[103] Ibid., 53.

[104] *Secret History* 11.24f. Rubin (loc. cit) tries to argue on the contrary from his
'sympathy' with Samaritans and Jews. Procopius' whole orientation is strikingly different
from that of his contemporary and fellow-Palestinian, Cyril of Scythopolis (see Flusin
1983).

[105] Rubin 1954, 51. John the Lydian, a writer of more practical bent, had no such
inhibitions, and regarded knowledge of Latin as essential to learning (*De Mag* III.29.,1,
41.2f.). Theophylact's probable lack of Latin: Whitby 1982.

[106] Above, pp. 196; Svennung 1967, 194ff.

[107] Above, p. 199.

[108] See Chapter 13 below.

Part III

CHAPTER THIRTEEN

The World of Procopius

For a writer of the sixth century, Procopius is as remarkable for what he leaves out as for what he does have to say. It is a curious paradox that the major historian of Justinian, judging by volume as well as quality, leaves many areas of contemporary life unexplored. Some are hinted at only to be denigrated,[1] but most are left out because they simply do not fit their rigid framework of military history which Procopius has imposed upon the *Wars*. It is Procopius' own view of what is important and what suitable for inclusion that has had most effect, and which has made his work seem most deceptively classical. On one level, then, Procopius is notable for the powerfully traditional conception of history displayed in the *Wars*, so restricted a conception in the context of sixth-century Byzantium that he needed a *Secret History* and perhaps also a *Buildings* even to approach the rounded view of which he was capable. But at a deeper level, all three works present certain uniform characteristics, modes of thought or terms of expression which transcend the barriers of genre or intention. We must now look both at the self-imposed restrictions in Procopius' work and at these underlying unities.

In the first place, the *Wars* makes no attempt to integrate the reconquest narrative into a general perspective of Justinian's policies. First, the recognition of the fact that the bulk of the *Wars* was finished by 550/1, while Justinian himself reigned until 565, is a necessary step towards realising that Procopius' evidence is heavily slanted towards the earlier part of the reign. In the nature of things, the *Wars* is not a history of Justinian, but of the reconquest. It would be for others to write of the difficulties of Justinian's later years.[2] But even for the parts which Procopius does cover, the vision is narrow. When, in the *Secret History*, it is extended beyond the military, it is only to distort and trivialise. Above all, the great Fifth Ecumenical Council, which opened in Constantinople on 5 May 553,[3] is left completely out of consideration,

---

[1] For example, imperial pomp and ceremonial: *Secret History* 30.21f.

[2] Those who date the *Buildings* and even the *Secret History* as late as 559/60 cannot explain the lack of allusions in this very politically aware author to events and policies of the later 550s.

[3] Stein, *BE* II.660f. The *Buildings*, less constrained by the restricted conception of the

though the political and theological debate surrounding it formed the essential background for much of what Procopius does consider his subject matter. Indeed, though it did not fall strictly within the time-span of *Wars* VIII, the antecedents to this Council were of such importance that a history, even a military history, which leaves them out altogether must seem very one-sided. Not only were there complex preparations for the Council itself, but it was preceded by some years of theological and political polemic (the two can scarcely be separated), and by the movement of many interested parties to Constantinople.[4] As it is, the Italians who shared in this movement are only a shadowy presence in the *Wars*, while the African narrative is, as we have seen, seriously diminished by the simple omission of the major problems caused there by Justinian's Three Chapters decree and the active part taken in the opposition to it by the African bishops.[5] These omissions are quite deliberate: Procopius makes the famous claim that he intends to deal with ecclesiastical affairs elsewhere,[6] thus, if we can take this at face value, accepting that ecclesiastical and secular history must still be kept separate. But the loss to the general quality of Procopius' interpretation caused by this decision was a major one. Even in the *Secret History*, where sectarian persecution is a central theme, the politics of the Council are totally ignored, and in the *Wars* Procopius' choice meant that he inevitably failed to bring out the close connection that actually existed between Justinian's ecclesiastical policies in the 540s, the presence of so many influential westerners in the capital, and the general situation leading up to the Council itself, with the prospects for consolidation of the reconquest, whether in Italy or Africa or the east. It is not simply that these were matters that concerned Constantinople (in Procopius' eyes) and might not then seem relevant to the war proper, for he did choose to include the Nika revolt and the plague, both accounts centred on Constantinople. The decision to exclude the Council and nearly everything connected with it was implied by Procopius' conception of secular, above all military, history, just as his decision to include the Nika revolt and the plague was dictated by good literary precedent.

Other works of the period give quite a different impression of priorities, and emphasise the narrow limits within which Procopius worked in all three of his works. To find the links which do exist between Procopius' thinking and that in different sorts of contemporary texts, we must look

---

Wars, can afford to include Justinian's religious policy among the list of his achievements (I.1.6f.), but it does so only in general terms.

[4] See above, p. 126f.; the *Life* of the patriarch Eutychlius written after his death in 582 (*PG* 86.2, 2273-2390) provides much evidence for the stage-management of the Council.

[5] Ibid.

[6] Above, p. 36.

under the surface;[7] on the face of things, Procopius' work is poles apart from the actual thought-world of Constantinople in this period. The crucial years when Procopius himself was writing – in Constantinople, as far as we can tell – were dominated for most people by the furious theological battles through which the government sought to bring the churches into line. Week by week the regular homilies filled the minds of most of the population with a heady mixture of Scriptural analogy, elaborate and argumentative analyses of the Gospel narratives, and their application to daily life.[8] Only the faintest trace of all this filters through in Procopius' works, even in the emphasis on churches in the *Buildings*, which is largely formal and externalised. Procopius' church services, except for the processions in the frightened towns of Syria and Mesopotamia in the face of the Persians,[9] are big public occasions, not familiar everyday events; he does not allow us to feel the atmosphere of ordinary liturgical practice, nor indeed the imperial ceremony which was also now part of the regular experience of the capital.[10] Although there are some similarities between Procopius' work and contemporary or near-contemporary chronicles, such as that of Marcellinus, the differences are often as striking. He has subjected his material to a rigid selection and limitation of focus, dictated by the traditional demands of high literature as well as by his own fiercely personal political views; but this limitation has finally prevented him, even in the three works considered as a whole, from reaching a rounded view of the period he covers.

He was limited too by his élitist assumptions, which reinforced his generally black-and-white view of the world. The people, for instance, often prominent in events recorded in the chronicles, feature in Procopius' work in a derogatory role, as 'the rabble', or as trouble-makers – even, paradoxically, in the *Secret History*, where one of the grounds for åttack on Justinian is his alleged elimination of so great a part of the population of the empire.[11] Procopius sees himself as speaking for an élite, often called simply 'senators', meaning above all the land-owning classes, but also including professionals like himself, doctors, teachers and lawyers.[12] He gives the impression that they all shared his views and

---

[7] See Chapter 2 above.

[8] See MacCormack 1982.

[9] Above, pp. 115, 163.

[10] See Averil Cameron 1979, 6ff.

[11] *Secret History* 18. 'Rabble' vocabulary: *Buildings* I.1.20 (Nika revolt); *Gothic Wars* III.32.27 (speech of Arsaces). Elitism: *Persian Wars* I.24.8 (Nika revolt); II.6.7. On the people: Veh 1951/52, 14f.; cf. 15 – the people have no positive role in the state, they are merely the object of government. Cf. *Secret History* 26.17: class structure of the Byzantine state.

[12] Rubin 1953, 20f. Particularly important: *Secret History* 12.12. Procopius constantly uses class language (Rubin, 21). Identification with the *eudaimones: Secret History* 12. 12f.; cf. 26.17. Uncomplimentary language of the lower classes: 26.18.

formed a homogeneous group. Clearly he was wrong in this simple view, but this class as a whole did invite upon itself the full blast of Justinian's purges, again during the years when Procopius was writing.[13] It was not easy for a critic of the régime, pagan or not, to live in Constantinople in the 540s, and Procopius knew the pressures well: writing of the laws against heresy, he says that the 'country people' found the idea of renouncing their beliefs blasphemous and that many preferred suicide to conversion, while among the Samaritans the sensible ones yielded.[14] The three works are full of underlying and surface statements which show a basic acceptance of Christianity, but they also show hostility to the authoritarian form in which it was practised by Justinian. Procopius writes as someone who knows what it is like to live without freedom and who has learned what it is safe to say.[15] On the other hand, except in religious matters he was entirely traditional in his élitism; he despises the rabble and identifies himself easily with the well-to-do, not so much a dissident as a disgruntled partisan.[16] Nor is he an intellectual or an idealist; he sees compromise as the best policy when faced with persecution, and scientific and philosophical speculation he considers a waste of time.

There is equally little sense in these works either of the effects of Justinian's enormous programme of legislation or of the administrative (and still less the economic) problems of the empire. Though in the *Buildings* the codification of the law falls within the scope of the general panegyric at the opening of the work, it is left out in the *Secret History* and largely ignored in the *Wars*. Justinian's own laws are presented as indicative of meddling with the status quo:

> When Justinian ascended the throne it took him a very little while to bring everything into confusion. Things hitherto forbidden by law were one by one brought into public life, while established customs were swept away wholesale, as if he had been invested with the forms of majesty on condition that he would change all things to new forms.[17]

Every law must have a bad motive – if not sheer meddling, then the looting of the wealthy,[18] just as in Procopius' view Justinian's economic policy was characterised by overspending and the squandering of subsidies on barbarians.[19] Procopius does not address himself to the

[13] See Lemerle 1971, 68ff.; Stein, *BE* II.369ff.; above, p. 22.

[14] *Secret History* 11.21f.

[15] *Secret History* 1.1-3.

[16] *Secret History* 11.40 associates the *eudaimones* and the senatorial class; Procopius writes with evident sympathy. Cf. also 23f.; 26.16f., with Cesa 1981, 393f.

[17] Ibid. 11.1. (Penguin trans.).

[18] 13.20; 14.20; cf. 29.17f., with 27.30.

[19] See Gordon 1959. Subsidies: 8.5-6, 31, cf. 9.3, 5; 19.13-15. On the heavy Byzantine payments to Persia see *Gothic Wars* IV.15. Procopius would rather see an active war policy at whatever cost than 'inglorious' diplomatic manoeuvres; his reactions are patriotic rather than practical.

problem of how the expensive reconquest policy was to be maintained, but is content to criticise the sluggish conduct of the war and the inadequate provisioning of the armies.[20] Naturally the *Secret History* both trivialises and exaggerates the bad side of Justinian's policies – the heavy taxation of Africa after the reconquest is presented merely as an example of the emperor's alleged passion for confusion and chaos.[21] But the *Wars* is hardly better in terms of the level of its explanations. Procopius is as satisfied here as in the *Secret History* with personality both as a sufficient and a proximate historical cause[22] and makes hardly any attempt to indicate more than the narrowest political or economic context for his military narrative.

The case of Justinian himself is particularly instructive. Though so fundamental to all three works, the emperor never emerges from them as a real person. Paradoxically, this is partly exactly because Procopius does include elaborate descriptions of his character, for these descriptions are expressed in such extreme polarities and in such a highly literary manner as to be devoid of real meaning. The few circumstantial remarks are buried in a welter of phrases of art: Justinian had a plumpish aspect with an amiable round face, but really he was like the notorious emperor Domitian ...[23] 'not one thing more need be mentioned, I think, regarding the character of this man', only the fact that he had married Theodora;[24] his manner was affable, his piety famous, like his asceticism, but for Procopius all these are simply shams, concealing his real greed, lust for destruction and desire to cause constant turmoil. 'His prolonged vigils, privations and painful efforts were undergone with this object alone – always and every day to devise for his subjects bigger calamities for him to crow over.'[25] Justinian is a caricature. Occasional touches of realism show through, but they are greatly out-numbered by the signs of the sheer hostility of Procopius, which reveals itself in repeated assertions of the emperor's true motives or wishes, usually without any supportive evidence. And far from setting to rights the distortion of the *Wars* and *Secret History*, the portrait of Justinian in the *Buildings* is merely the converse of that in the other works, showing Justinian as the stereotyped model Christian ruler, inspired by God with special insight, but not described in realistic personal terms.[26] The emperor is fundamental to all three of Procopius' works. He is seen as the fount and instigator of all policy, and is credited with maximum personal responsibility for events, whether for good, as in the *Buildings*, or for evil, as in the *Secret History*. In the *Wars* too he is central to the articulation

---

[20] *Secret History* 24.
[21] 18.10-12.
[22] Above, Chapter 8.
[23] *Secret History* 8.12f. See p. 57.
[24] 10.3.
[25] 13.32.
[26] For a modern eulogy along these lines see Gerostergios 1982.

of the historical narrative. In this attitude to the emperor Procopius did
not essentially differ from other contemporary thinkers,[27] and there is no
need to deny the fundamental seriousness of his approach to the imperial
role on the grounds of the sharp criticisms of Justinian in his work.
Again, personality as such is central to Procopius' understanding of
history, not just the personality of Justinian,[28] and it was understandable
that he should lay this stress on the emperor. But the terms in which
Justinian is actually presented to us remain at the level of the stereotype.

It is the same even with Belisarius. Throughout the earlier part of the
Wars, he is made to carry a weight of symbolism which even there is
sometimes forced and which fails to convince before Procopius himself
has given it up. As Procopius eventually admits, the *Secret History* was
necessary to redress the distortion of the *Wars*, especially the earlier
sections. Thus Belisarius was at first for Procopius a hero figure, and
when the glamour wore off he could only turn to total denigration, as he
did with Justinian and Theodora. And if history was seen by Procopius
through individuals, the range of individuals perceived as important was
severely limited. Others of Justinian's generals earn his praise and
admiration – Narses, Germanus, Solomon, Artabanes – though they do
not hold the stage for long. They too tend to be described in clichés.[29]
Men at the centre of affairs merit attention only when their action is
strictly relevant to the wars, while others receive a large amount of space
in accordance with personal prejudices of Procopius.[30] He does not name
consuls as a matter of course, or bring out the political interaction
between the Italian aristocrats and the eastern court, except in simple
terms of 'urging on' the war policy.[31] As a whole the *Wars* restricts the
range of personality it admits as severely as its subject matter. With the
Secret History more personal details are possible, if only to illustrate
Procopius' theme of Justinian's spite and greed. Thus Liberius, sent as
Augustalis to Alexandria to settle an ecclesiastical situation displeasing
to Theodora;[32] Procopius knew Liberius as a highly honourable man, and
writes in some detail of his sad manipulation by Justinian when over
eighty to replace Germanus in Italy in 550,[33] but he includes this
important figure here purely to illustrate the machinations of Theodora.
Procopius hardly brings out the real political significance of men like
Liberius, who was an Italian who had been praetorian prefect of Italy

[27] Below, Chapter 14.
[28] On this as a wider development in late antique historiography see Cracco Ruggini 1979,
1981.
[29] Below for the restriction of Procopius' vocabulary.
[30] Typical here are Vigilius, John the Cappadocian (above, pp. 69f.), Silverius: given full
attention only when Procopius wishes to tell some particular story, not in proportion to
their actual significance.
[31] Above, p. 193.
[32] *Secret History* 27.17f.
[33] *Gothic Wars* III.36.6; 39.6f.; 40.12f.; cf. also I.4.24.

under Theodoric in the last years of the fifth century before moving over
to the service of Constantinople.[34] Indeed the only way he is
distinguished by Procopius from other Roman senators and patricians is
by praise of his moral character, and later by comments on his extreme
old age and lack of military experience.[35] Another to receive personal
comment is the African Junillus, who succeeded Tribonian as quaestor in
542, mentioned by Procopius only as an illustration of the unsatisfactory
way in which Justinian handled the office, in which Procopius, trained in
law, shows a rare interest.[36] But Junillus receives only scornful criticism,
for greed and ignorance of the law, but mainly for his poor Greek: 'When
he did his best to pronounce a Greek word he moved his subordinates to
scornful laughter.'[37] This is sheer prejudice: the man was an African and
his native tongue was presumably Latin. He was the kind of man
Procopius must have met in Vandal Africa; these vicious comments
suggest Procopius' lack of sympathy with the natives of the provinces
through which he swept with Belisarius' victorious army. Certainly we
would never guess that Junillus was also interested in theology and in
touch with the African bishops in Constantinople.[38] Even Tribonian
scarcely emerges from Procopius' work as a credible character; he is
criticised for greed (the usual blanket accusation) but commended for
intellectual polish and dissembling.[39] Nowhere does Procopius even
consider whether there might have been serious intentions behind the
legislation framed for Justinian by Tribonian, nor whether Tribonian
merited the calls of the mob for his dismissal. As almost invariably, the
motivation of events and the depiction of such characters as are involved
is seen in his Nika revolt narrative in the most stark and oversimplified
terms. There is little difference, when it comes down to it, between the
articulation of events as presented in the *Wars* and the more obviously
exaggerated *Secret History*.

Procopius' forte lay not in character but in action. His mind did not
naturally turn to the visual. The three set-pieces in the *Wars* which
concern Constantinople – the Nika revolt, Belisarius' triumph and the
plague – are all descriptions of events. There is little sense in the *Wars* of
the variety of terrain over which the wars were fought, or of the physical
appearance of the key places or cities, except in cases like Edessa and
Antioch where it was strictly relevant to the military narrative.[40] We are

[34] See O'Donnell 1981, emphasising Liberius' piety.

[35] *Gothic Wars* III.39.7.

[36] *Secret History* 20.16f.

[37] 20.17. Latin was the access language to the bureaucracy of which Procopius
disapproves. Proclus, an earlier quaestor, earns his approval for the conservative and
aristocratic qualities whose absence he deplores in Junillus and Tribonian: *Persian Wars*
I.11.12.

[38] See Averil Cameron 1982, 46; Kihn 1880; Honoré 1978, 238-39; Guillaumont 1969-7, 47.

[39] *Persian Wars* I.24.16; 25.9. John the Cappadocian criticised for ignorance: ibid. I.24.12.

[40] Edessa: *Persian Wars* II.12; 26f.; Antioch: II.8f. (see below).

not told what it was like to be in Carthage, except incidentally, when Belisarius enters the Vandal palace and eats Vandal food, or when Procopius and Solomon escape, and even then the palace and the harbour are left strictly to the imagination.[41] Rome seems at first sight to stand out for its physical description in the *Wars*, but this too is chiefly incidental to the siege narratives.[42] When Belisarius enters Ravenna, the culmination of his early success in Italy, Procopius emphasises the miraculous ease with which the Goths accepted their fate, but passes over the entry itself, and even the capture of Vitigis, in laconic understatement, with no word for the glories of Ravenna itself or the obvious pictorial scope of the occasion; here was an opportunity for a descriptive passage of the first order, based on the great churches and monuments of Ravenna, capital of Theodoric, but Procopius does not take it.[43] In most of the narratives of great occasions in the *Wars*, Procopius' attention is caught by irony, by the moral of the episode, or by the curious detail, but the scene itself is left to the imagination. Take for instance the great sack of Antioch in 540, where Procopius describes the reactions of the population, especially the tragic irony by which some were trampled in their panic by Roman horses, and the incident when two well-born Antiochene women jumped into the Orontes with their faces veiled rather than suffer the humiliation threatened by the Persian soldiers;[44] he stresses the miracle of the turning of the standards, and reflects at length on the meaning of the catastrophe, but does not focus on the sight of Antioch itself, one of the greatest cities of the empire, or on the scene of carnage when the city was taken.[45] When he turns in the *Buildings* to the theme of the rebuilding of Antioch, it is in the well-worn clichés of late antique urban description.[46] Here his treatment is rhetorical rather than pictorial, focussing on ideas; Procopius' attention is on human action, but less for its own sake than for the lesson which it can be made to yield. Because of this approach in general we are deprived of a visual sense of Constantinople or of the parts of the empire in which military action took place. Even in the *Buildings*, where a different treatment was called for, Procopius only partially escapes into a

[41] Above, Chapter 10.

[42] Nevertheless there is more detail about Rome than anywhere else; above, p. 192.

[43] *Gothic Wars* II.29.32f.

[44] *Persian Wars* II.8.35; cf. 17-19. The account is notable for its human detail, not its visual description.

[45] I.10.1f., 4f. The taking of Antioch and deportation of the citizens: Downey 1961, 544f.

[46] *Buildings* II.10.19-25. For this aspect of Procopius's city descriptions see above, pp. 94, 102. Significantly, he plays down the Persian damage in the *Wars* narrative but emphasises it in the *Buildings* (II.10.20). All the same, he has little beyond generalities to contribute about the rebuilt city (for which see Downey 1961, 546ff. (cf. 547 'the account ... must be viewed ... primarily as one of a number of passages in a panegyric, in which accuracy and fullness of detail were necessarily sacrificed to considerations of literary technique'; yet when he chooses, as on Dara, Jerusalem or Sinai, he can be entirely specific).

more detailed approach;[47] often enough his descriptions rely more on
rhetoric than on observed detail, and are more concerned to draw lessons
or point reasons than to describe faithfully, a very important observation
to bear in mind in the interpretation of the work.[48] Procopius conveys the
ideas behind Justinian's building policy (or at least, how it was meant to
seem) more successfully than he does the appearance of the finished
works, as we can see even in the famous description of S. Sophia in
Constantinople.[49] Procopius' account is technical, but it often lapses into
vague rhetoric without conveying either the precise look of the building
or its atmosphere, so that his account compares badly with that of Paul
the Silentiary a decade or so later.[50] This deficiency might be ascribed,
supposing a late date for the *Buildings*, to the difficulty of writing about
the church convincingly without mentioning the collapse of the dome.[51]
It should rather be connected, however, with Procopius' habitual
methods, for while panegyrical set-pieces involving military dispositions,
such as the description of Dara,[52] were entirely congenial to him, he did
not often embark on precise *ekphraseis* of specific buildings. This
description is unique in Procopius' work both for subject matter and
length. Clearly S. Sophia required a very special treatment, but it was
not so clear that Procopius was the man to do it. There are indeed a few
memorable descriptions in the *Buildings* – the church of the Holy
Apostles, the Nea in Jerusalem, and, for all its problems, the monastery
of Sinai.[53] But all have special features which made them remarkable to
Procopius, and are less aesthetic descriptions than records of *curiosa*.
Very few of the many other churches mentioned in the work are described
at all; when a sentence of comment is added, it tends more often to be an
allusion to the purpose of the building, or its effect, than to its
appearance.[54] The purpose of the *Buildings* itself was, after all, to be
more a political panegyric of Justinian than a repository of aesthetic
ekphrasis, and so we find Procopius constantly turning from visual to
rhetorical elaboration. The most memorable effect of Book I, the section
on Constantinople and the most artistically finished part of the work, is
atmospheric rather than descriptive – the evocation of the watery
freshness of the city familiar to this day;[55] but as a description even of the
Justinianic building in the city the book must be termed a
disappointment.

---

[47] As on the Chalke mosaic (I.10.15f.).
[48] Particularly true of his account of the fortified monastery on Sinai (V.8), where he has
been criticised for the wrong reasons (above, pp. 96).
[49] I.1.20-65; Mango 1972, 72ff.
[50] Translated in Mango 1972, 80ff. (much longer and more detailed).
[51] I owe this suggestion to L.M. Whitby.
[52] *Buildings* II.1-3. The technique is entirely different (Croke and Crow 1983).
[53] I.4.9-24; V.6.1-26; V.8.
[54] Above, p. 100.
[55] Above, p. 101.

The oeuvre of Procopius is in some ways highly individual. His responses may be conventional to the genres within which he worked and to the milieu of his professional life, but they are not all straightforwardly representative of the society in which he lived. Partly because of the narrowness of his own perceptions, but partly too because of the restraints which he imposed upon his work, he presents only a very partial view of the world, one which many, perhaps even most, of his contemporaries would have found unfamiliar. Those who followed him in the next generation to write military history could no longer convincingly restrict their range so drastically, and for Theophylact Simocatta in the reign of Heraclius it was clear that a real history must include at least ceremonial imperial occasions as well as campaigns on the field.[56] This adaptation might have enabled secular history in the high style to survive for longer, had it not been for the demise during the later seventh and the eighth centuries of the level of education which it required, and which was still available to Procopius and his contemporaries.[57] For Procopius, however, there were still severe problems inherent in reconciling a traditional view of military and imperial history with the contemporary world in which he lived and wrote. He still had the technical equipment for such an enterprise, but it was already incapable of doing complete justice to contemporary political realities.

The most noticeable problem lay simply in the handling of Christian material, not merely because such subject matter, however central it might now be, did not fit easily into the kind of secular history that Procopius wrote, but also because most other contemporary literature accepted an overwhelmingly religious approach with unembarrassed ease. I have tried to show that Procopius shares far more of this conceptual apparatus than has been realised. Even so, it was difficult for him to integrate ecclesiastical with political and military subject matter, and he could not discard the idea that the two types of material must be kept distinct.[58] There was an awkwardness at the level of historical causation too, for whenever Procopius tries to grapple with causes, as secular historiography required, he tends to fall back on a pietistic appeal to the will of God and to express distaste for speculation.[59] There is too much contradiction in Procopius' statements to ascribe to him a consistent theory of causality,[60] but it is beyond doubt that although he parades 'reasons',[61] he retains overall a theology of divine intervention,

---

[56] E.g. *Hist.* I.1 (accession of Maurice); 10 (marriage of Maurice); 12.12 (consulship of Maurice). Similarly, the *Chronicle* of Malalas, more open to the realities of political life than Procopius, allows for the importance of ceremony especially in relation to diplomacy.

[57] Wilson 1983, 60f.; Mango 1982, 80, 136f.

[58] Above, n. 6.

[59] Pp. 29, 40, above.

[60] As Downey 1949.

[61] E.g. *Persian Wars* II.22.1.

which brings his history much nearer to ecclesiastical history than appears on the surface. Neither the *Wars* nor the *Secret History* (and of course not the *Buildings*) seeks explanations in human terms, which may be why Procopius is content with such a superficial analysis of character. For if the ultimate answer lies with the divine, there is no need to look further for human agencies than to individual personality, and yet that too is important in the end only as an instrument. In a way the case of Belisarius illustrates Procopius' problems in this area as well as in others. He had originally cast Belisarius in the role of hero, and that was easy so long as he was successful. Later, however, the fading of that success needed explanation, and here Procopius alternates between ascribing it to Belisarius' own failings of character, to his dependence on the whims of Justinian or to the divine will using him as a tool.[62] Procopius did not succeed in reconciling a theory of causes, required by his self-chosen style of historiography, with one of divine intervention, or in locating the place of character within this theory, though he gave it a particular prominence. He was, I would suggest, deploying within – and against – the formal historiography of the *Wars* a notion of causality which owed far more to standard Christian writings than to the classical models to which he aspired. This above all led him into the inconsistencies that have so often been noted. It is those who have been unwilling to acknowledge this aspect of the *Wars* who have had most difficulty with the interpretation of the *Secret History*, where Procopius had to reconcile somehow the fact of an autocratic and (he believed) evil ruler with that of a beneficent divine plan. But once we have realised the true extent of supernatural causality in the *Wars* it becomes much easier to accept that the same writer can turn in the *Secret History* towards invoking the demonic as an explanation for evil in the world. Procopius was less constrained here by formal requirements, and resorts more openly to supernatural explanations. In the *Buildings*, of course, the conventions of imperial panegyric allowed him to be completely open about divine intervention in human affairs. In a sense, then, the two briefer works allowed Procopius to express more clearly a view of God and man which caused him some problems in the *Wars*. But the common view that these works are essentially opposite to the *Wars* rests on a misunderstanding of the latter, and in particular on the false assumption that the *Wars* is a fully secular work conceived in a spirit of 'rationalism'.[63]

There were problems, then, in handling this kind of history, and Procopius made things more difficult for himself by choosing to arrange his material by theatre of operations rather than chronologically. Such a choice made it difficult for him to attempt an overall view of the wars or the reconquest policy, and it cannot be said that *Wars* VIII, tacked on at

[62] *Gothic Wars* III.13.16.
[63] Above, pp. 112.

the end, redresses the balance. Procopius does not try to absorb the picturesque or stirring incidents that he loves into a general theory of the wars and their progress, and indeed it would have been difficult for him to do so while he was still restraining himself on crucial issues. The *Wars* is after all unfinished in the sense that it does not carry through its subject to the end. But even in the course of the work Procopius allows judgments on the shape of events to emerge from the narrative itself rather than through direct statements of his own; two good examples are provided by Belisarius' second Italian expedition and the ill-fated attempts in 550 to retrieve the situation, and the dreary catalogue of Byzantine attempts to control their own army and deal with Berber attacks in Africa after the first flush of victory.[64] He works through omission and juxtaposition rather than by authorial utterances. But of course this is much dependent on the difficult question of when Procopius began writing, how he conceived the *Wars* at the time, and how it developed during the composition, and, perhaps especially, whether he went back over the first seven books as a whole in the light of his attitudes in 550/1 when he made them public. In fact it is unlikely that when he began Procopius could have had an overall conception of the work in terms of philosophy of history. He must have formed the idea of writing a history of the wars early on in his association with Belisarius, and kept a diary to that end; but he could have had no idea then that he would be led into such deep political waters or that the situation – and his own reading of it – would change so much. The *Wars* as first conceived by Procopius was then to be a record of military campaigns, focussed round the figure of the general Belisarius, in whose train Procopius was and who provided him with access to the material, written in high style and classicising manner. By the time of the African campaign it must have become apparent that there was a large theme available to write about. Perhaps the early diaries were not so full as the notes which he now took and that might account for the evident distortion in the early Persian sections in favour of Belisarius.[65] Perhaps, too, he did not begin the actual writing of the history until after he returned with Belisarius in 540;[66] Belisarius had declined with accustomed nobility the Gothic offer, but it was not yet clear how much of a reversal of fortune there was soon to be – the situation changed as Procopius wrote. It does not however follow from the passages in the Persian and Gothic sections which can be dated to the year 545, that Procopius intended to publish the work in that year, as some have thought.[67] It would not have been a natural stopping place, and

---

[64] Above, pp. 189; 177.

[65] See Bury 1923, II, 420 n. 2; Rubin 1954, 81.

[66] The earliest datable references belong to 545 (*Persian Wars* I.25.43; *Gothic Wars* I.24.32; II.5.26-7).

[67] Bury, loc. cit.

Procopius cannot have thought, even if he had brought his narrative up to the time of writing in 545, that the reconquest was over or matters settled. It is clear from these passages, however, that he was writing the different sections simultaneously, or at least the Persian and Gothic ones. If he had stopped writing in 545 he would not have expressed the degree of criticism which developed during the later 540s and which found its expression above all in *Wars* VII, relating the achievements of Totila and the second Italian expedition of Belisarius. The most important year for Procopius was perhaps 540. It saw Belisarius at the peak of his achievement, but it revealed his unquestioned loyalty to Justinian even when he was badly treated by him. The same year saw the sack of Antioch, a disaster for which Procopius can find no human explanation, followed only two years later by the plague, which also seemed to Procopius like the incomprehensible work of God. The events which followed during 542, when Belisarius was sent to the east, had begun before 545 to undermine the optimistic view with which Procopius had followed Belisarius on campaign, and the next years were to see the development of new and troubling themes. By 545 Procopius was already experiencing the disappointment that was to change the nature of the *Wars* and burst out in the *Secret History*.

So the subject matter of the *Wars*, and with it Procopius' own reactions, was changing as he wrote. This did not make it easy for him to convey a well thought-out theory of the process of the reconquest. It is an attractive thought that he failed to finish the record of the Gothic war for reasons of this kind: it was one thing to write a panegyric, that is, to turn in quite a different direction, another to take up the *Wars* again where *Wars* VIII leaves off and record the victories won after nearly twenty years not by Belisarius but by Narses. *Wars* VIII, then, is itself not the end. There was more to come, and Procopius left it unrecorded. But *Wars* VIII does claim to tie up the ends left on all three fronts by *Wars* I-VII. Yet although Procopius still has the energy to write ethnographical digressions, and to recount the war in Lazica in some detail, to write of the antique splendours of Rome and the final battle and death of Totila and then that of Teias, he has lost his sense of exhilaration. This is no longer the glorious advance of Roman power, even though Procopius saw the hand of God in Narses' success.[68] Justinian made a shameful peace with Persia, criticised by clear implication here,[69] and even the recovery of Rome by the Byzantines is seen by Procopius as the cause of still worse suffering for the senate and the people of Rome, no splendid and glorious victory but the bringer of a tragic irony.[70] The summing-up of the whole war narrative written by Procopius does not end with the real end of

---

[68] *Gothic Wars* IV.33.1.
[69] IV.15.12.
[70] IV.34.1-8.

Byzantine effort in Italy and the establishment of Byzantine rule, as in Africa, but with the deaths of the two Gothic leaders. Procopius now sees the tragedy of war and its complexity: the other side can show nobility, and the people on whose behalf all this is supposed to be taking place, the Romans themselves, are seen to be the losers. Since 530 the subject matter has changed dramatically. Then it was possible to think in terms of unadulterated victory, and to see the position in simple black and white. The great African victories reinforced that impression, and Belisarius' own achievement reached a peak in 540. But twenty years of war and twenty years of writing have brought Procopius to a much sadder and profounder realisation, one which does not cohere at all well with the early parts of the *Wars* or with the work as he originally conceived it.

The true importance of this chronological perspective on the *Wars* has seldom been realised, even though the dating of the works is still a central concern, for most of the considerable effort expended has been to try to 'reconcile' Procopius' three works in terms of his own personality, and specifically his critique of Justinian. Part of the aim of this book has been to protest at this over-simplified linear conception of the relation between the works and to show that in fact they form a conceptual unity. But there is also too little realisation of the complexity of the *Wars* itself, even though its basic chronology was long ago established by Haury.[71] It is not possible to take passages at random as indicative of Procopius' 'attitude' when the subject is connected with his developing view of the war or the people concerned in it. We can do that for his more general ideas, but the political views of the *Wars* must always be approached through a close analysis of the context and the place of the passage in the development of the work as a whole.

But the question remains: did Procopius go over the earlier sections with the intention of giving his work an overall unity of conception? So far as we can tell, there is no sign that he did. Except in a few cases it is usually hard to know when a given passage was written, so that it must remain a possibility that some key passages were added at a later date than the original composition. But the narratives of the early and more splendid years up to 540 are probably based on contemporary notes, and little intrudes to spoil the optimistic tone. The early *Vandal War* narrative, up to the time of Belisarius' triumph, is not sullied by hints of later problems, while the early Persian sections are not merely lacking in criticism but slanted hard in favour of Belisarius; when Procopius wanted to counter what he had written earlier he wrote a different work altogether. Both the *Persian Wars* and the *Vandal Wars*, in their later sections show a less glorious side, and the criticism mounts to its height in *Gothic Wars* III. But it seems that the earlier parts were allowed to

[71] Chapter 1 above.

stand, and correction left for the *Secret History*. The latter thus provides a crude corrective for the early parts of the *Wars*, but *Wars* VII, written while Procopius was feeling most disappointed, showed that a very different kind of war narrative was a possibility. By then, however, it was not a serious option to go back and revise the *Wars* from the beginning, and he allowed the whole to be made public in 550/1 as it stood.

At the best of times, Procopius lacked a profound philosophy or a deep understanding of human nature. Since in addition he did not interest himself in the aftermath of reconquest or the longer-term problems of controlling these territories, we should not be looking for deep insights into the reconquest policy as such or its progress. Procopius did not choose to go back and rewrite the early narrative so as to bring out his final understanding of what it had been for, perhaps simply because he still felt, despite his anger against Belisarius, that those were glorious days and that the glory could and should have continued. But it was a grand gesture to end his whole history with the deaths of the Gothic leaders rather than with the sense of Roman victory: 'At this point a notable battle and valour not inferior to that of any of the so-called heroes shall be recorded – that shown by Teias on this occasion.'[72] The ending is low-key, not worthy of twenty years of Byzantine struggle, and it is Teias who dominates the final pages as Totila had dominated the narrative before that. Procopius allows the sadness and pride of Gothic defeat to stand at the centre of the stage, and does not even underline the fact that the Byzantines had at last achieved what they had been trying to do for two decades. He would not have written this way at the start of the war.

Nevertheless there are some themes that can with justice be said to pervade his work as a whole. Mostly they have to do with preserving the established order, and for Procopius the established order includes a strong demarcation between civilised people and barbarians. There are of course some distinctions: barbarians as individuals could make their way to the top of the Byzantine army, and often did, sometimes winning Procopius' approval,[73] while the Gothic descendants of Theodoric are regarded as on a higher level than the tribes relegated to the ethnographical digressions.[74] Naturally Persians were regarded as essentially civilised in the diplomatic sense, even though much play can be made with their 'barbarian' natures.[75] And room is always made for barbarian royalty as the object of pathos or admiration, if not fear as with

---

[72] *Gothic Wars* IV.35.20.

[73] *Persian Wars* I.18.38; *Vandal Wars* I.11.9; 18.13; *Gothic Wars* I.5.2 (Mundus); 6.2 (Bessas); 17.17; II.1.21 etc.

[74] P. 218.

[75] Respect for Persia: *Persian Wars* I.16.1; II.10.13, 14; I.3.5. Critique of Chosroes: II.9.8; 11.26; *Secret History* 18.26.

Chosroes.[76] Nevertheless Procopius operates with a strong sense of
borderlines, which makes his judgments easy.[77] Barbarians are to be
brought within the Byzantine orbit, by diplomatic means including
conversion, or if necessary by war;[78] they are treacherous,[79] though
sometimes useful as buffers against a greater evil,[80] and there is no doubt
that right is ultimately, with God's aid, on the Roman side. There is
nothing in the critique of the *Secret History* to suggest that Justinian's
policies against barbarians were wrong in themselves; Procopius simply
uses their results to attack Justinian.[81] The *Secret History*, in fact, starts
in this respect from the same premises as the *Wars*, and is even more
firmly based on another of Procopius' most deep-rooted demarcations,
that between the well-to-do, often but not wholly identified with the
landowning senatorial class, and the rest of society, to be condemned as
unworthy of serious attention.[82] Procopius is fond of sweeping
condemnation; he sees the world as full of individuals and whole sections
of society who can be dismissed as 'wicked',[83] implying besides moral
condemnation that they can also be ignored politically. Those
Byzantines outside military circles who are praised are usually members
of the élite like Procopius himself. People are assumed, like Justinian, to
act from simple motives, often greed or the reverse, and tend to be
described in a restricted terminology,[84] which contributes to the feeling
of sameness created by the linguistic texture especially of the *Wars*.
Similarly Procopius holds to certain assumptions, or rather, prejudices,
about women,[85] which equally hamper his capacity for convincing
historical analysis. Throughout his work he operates with a strong moral
divide between 'good' and 'bad'. His chief criticism of Justinian (as of
Chosroes) is that he is constantly 'stirring things up', that is, creating
disorder when order prevailed.[86] The Nika revolt then can simply be

[76] Gelimer: *Vandal Wars* II.7; 9.11; Theodoric: *Gothic Wars* I.1.27-28; Totila: ibid.,
III.2.7; Chosroes: *Persian Wars* II.9.8 (cf. the similar language of Gelimer, *Vandal Wars*
I.9.7).

[77] Similarly with his views on women: Chapter 5 above. Everything is black-and-white for
him.

[78] See in general Veh 1950/51, 23-5.

[79] Pp. 176f., 218 above. See especially *Vandal Wars* II.8.9f. (Berbers); and II.4.29f.
(Procopius' patronising assumption that it is remarkable for a Herul not to be treacherous
and drunken).

[80] E.g. *Gothic Wars* I.5.9 (the Christian Franks against the Arian Goths).

[81] Especially *Secret History* 18.1f. (the wars and consequent loss of human life a sign of
Justinian's demonic nature).

[82] Above, pp. 227.

[83] *Ponêroi, miaroi*, usually in the superlative (Rubin 1954, 72).

[84] See Rubin 1954, 73f. Favourite words of praise: *drastêrios* (*Persian Wars* I.6.19; 8.5;
17.40 and very often); *sunetos, sunesis* (I.15.3; 17.40; 24.18 and very often, commonly with
drastêrios or *andreios, andreia*); *agathos ta polemia* (I.5.30; 6.15; 18.38; 20.10 etc.). These
standard terms are often combined, even in descriptions of major characters (cf. *Gothic
Wars* III.2.7 (Totila); 40.9 (Germanus); I.1.27 (Theodoric)).

[85] Above, Chapter 5; Fisher 1978, 297ff.

[86] Rubin 1954, 75; above, p. 59.

ascribed to the zeal of the factions for disorder,[87] thus releasing Procopius from the obligation of providing a more subtle analysis, though one can see from the *Secret History* that even he found the disorder explanation unsatisfactory.[88] This over-strong opposition between order and disorder stems from a rigid and conservative approach to change, and Procopius' conservatism has often been noted. It needs to be firmly said, however, that this conservatism, and Procopius' criticism in general, is often based merely on prejudice, as much in the *Wars* as in the *Secret History*. The same man wrote the two works, and, in part at least, at much the same time. The same prejudices underly them both.

Procopius' great strength was as a reporter, in the impressive verve and persistence with which he recorded events over a period of more than twenty years, and the powers of observation and vigour with which he could describe great scenes of action. He was more a reporter than a historian, better at the narrative of events than at the analysis of causes or the delineation of motive, and better at telling a good story with a highly personal point of view than at sifting out different versions. When pushed into the discussion of causes which the *Wars* obliged him to include, he was content to appeal to the inscrutability of God. Nevertheless the energy and passion of the *Wars* and the *Secret History* would be remarkable at any date. They have established Procopius as an independent, if prejudiced, observer, but above all as a keen, efficient and voluminous reporter. On these qualities, especially, his reputation rests.

---

[87] *Persian Wars* I.24.6; cf. *Gothic Wars* II.29.34. Given his attitudes, and his devotion to order, it is not surprising to find Procopius trying to rationalise the Amazons (the most extreme example of topsy-turvydom) into women unwillingly dressing in their dead husband's clothing, forced to fight for their lives (*Gothic Wars* IV.3.6f.); some things strain his credibility too far. He justifies his interpretation by appealing to current Hunnish practice (IV.3.8).

[88] Above, Chapter 4.

CHAPTER FOURTEEN

Procopius and Sixth-Century Political Thought

However oversimplified some of Procopius' views may seem, he was writing during a reign which provoked an unusually high level of theorising about the political order and the role of the emperor, and he was far from immune to such ideas. The same restless activity on the part of Justinian which Procopius so deplored stimulated new thinking, if not new conclusions, about the proper role of a Christian emperor, and the relation of the ruler to his subjects. While he wrestled in three different works with these issues, others addressed them more directly, or found, like him, that they formed the natural subject even of quite unexpected works. It was a reign that saw violent contradictions, rapid change under the guise of restoration, new strains on the state alongside existing problems. Worries about these things inevitably tended, in this centralised political system, to concentrate on the person and function of the emperor; whether they are formal treatises supportive of the system, or the critical remarks of contemporaries at the end of the reign, the range of Justinianic writings touching on this subject shows that Procopius was not alone in his preoccupation with the place of Justinian within the political framework, and that the tensions and contradictions within his work correspond to similar problems felt by others. We shall see that far from being the isolated critic usually assumed in modern books he shared, through his three works, the full range of contemporary reaction. In particular, the *Buildings*, once it is taken seriously, falls into place as part of the contemporary rhetoric of approved political theory; to dismiss it as mere insincere flattery is to fail to realise that it is the logical counterpart of the *Secret History* – the one implies the other.

Among the Justinianic writers who dealt with the subject of the emperor's role and function, John the Lydian is one of the most interesting – a civil servant in the office of the Praetorian Prefect and author of three extant learned works besides a lost panegyric of Justinian and a history of the Persian war.[1] Of these, the *De Mensibus*, a work on

---

[1] *De Mag.* III.28.4-5 (if the history was ever written – John does not say so explicitly). There was also a panegyric on Zoticus, the praetorian perfect under whom John served.

the calendar, and the *De Ostentis*, on portents, do not directly deal with the political structure or with Justinian, but the *De Magistratibus*, a treatise on the regalia and history of Roman magistracies, is conceived within a philosophical and theoretical framework which has much to say about the contemporary situation.[2] Like Procopius, John was a provincial from Philadelphia in Lydia, who entered public service through his talents and came quickly to the fore through the patronage of an influential man; like Procopius again he had an early success in a quasi-legal capacity, but engaged also in literary work which, in the manner of the day, brought him commissions for panegyrics. Like Procopius, his experience was mixed: after initial success under Anastasius and Justin I, he greeted the administrative innovations of Justinian, especially in his own office, with dismay. He supported the wrong man in the Nika revolt,[3] but although he retired for a time from the *officium* into a life of letters, he kept or gained imperial favour and finally retired only in 554 after forty years of service.[4] Finally, again like Procopius, he combines many assertions of support for Justinian in the *De Magistratibus*, just as one would expect, with a surprisingly obvious critique of contemporary policies and conditions.[5]

There is every likelihood that John and Procopius knew each other, though there is no direct indication that they did. Both were in Constantinople for most of the 540s, when intellectuals were being scrutinised for their loyalty,[6] and when Justinian was on the look out for reliable panegyrists and official historians. It would seem that John may have been writing the *De Magistratibus* at about the time when Procopius was writing the final book of the *Wars* and the *Buildings* (he had started it much earlier, while Procopius was working on *Wars* I-VII and the *Secret History*).[7] Like the *Wars*, this work of John's is uneven in coverage, according to how much access he had at different times to bureaucratic records. It has a marked emphasis on the early years of the reign (the Nika revolt, the Vandal triumph, the first prefecture of John the Cappadocian), so that when he was writing in the 550s, with the caution of a man only too well aware of the constraints on total frankness, he was looking back, like Procopius, on more then twenty years of Justinianic rule, over a period of setbacks as well as achievements.

---

[2] For John see chiefly Carney 1971. Note also the Berkeley dissertation of M. Maas (1982); Bandy 1982; Tsirpanlis 1974.

[3] For John's career, see *De Mag.* III.25, with Carney II, 3; Phocas, briefly praetorian prefect in 532, died in Justinian's purge of pagans in 546: *De Mag.* III.72-6. He is also praised by Procopius, *Persian Wars* I.24.18; *Secret History* 21.6.

[4] *De Mag.* III.30.10.

[5] Carney 1971, II, 164f. offers a number of interesting tables comparing the attitudes to Justinian expressed by John and by Procopius.

[6] Cf. *De Mag.* III.28.3 'since fortune was, as she had not heretofore, exhibiting displeasure towards men of letters ...' (Carney's translation).

[7] So Čarney 1971, II, 11f.; but see Stein 1949, 839-40: Bandy 1982, xxxiiiff.

Whether John knew the *Secret History* must remain a mystery, but he surely knew the *Wars*. In any case, the extent to which the two men worked within a shared code is immediately striking. John was writing an antiquarian study, not a history, but he treats his subject throughout in a historical perspective, and statements of historical causation are as natural to him as the analysis of decline (he shares Procopius' conservative and élitist attitudes). Fortune often makes an appearance,[8] along with God;[9] yet no one has yet tried to analyse the 'scepticism' of John the Lydian. Indeed John is highly conscious of the active participation of the Devil in human affairs.[10] The uncertain and demonic present is seen by him against a backdrop of the reassuring and stable past,[11] and Justinian's principal characteristic, his indefatigability, comes dangerously near to being openly equated with the kind of innovation and change which John generally so deplores.[12] There are two Justinians in John's work, as there are in Procopius': the 'good father', most gentle and kind,[13] who is likened to the 'good' emperor Trajan[14] and contrasted with the Domitian with whom Procopius in the *Secret History* has so disingenuously compared him,[15] and then the other Justinian, implicit rather than explicit it is true, but who was after all responsible for the decline which John notices in all public services, and for the devaluation of letters, even as he promoted literary men of whom he approved,[16] and whose wars necessitated taxation at a level impossible to realise.[17] John and Procopius alike direct their anger at individual ministers, though each is aware of the implication that Justinian himself must carry responsibility for the bad situation; John's elaborate attempts to absolve the emperor of blame serve only to draw attention to it.[18] Again like Procopius, John found the Nika revolt hard to deal with. While he sympathised with the hatred felt against John the Cappadocian

[8] *De Mag.* II.2.7; 7.3; 10.2; 12.1; III.40.1; 42.1-2; 45.3; 46.1; 55.1.

[9] III.69.1; 76.2, 8-9.

[10] III.12.1 'the Devil has pared off and taken all the good qualities away from us'; 57.1 'the evil power'.

[11] John's consciousness of change: Carney 1971, II, 157ff. Maas 1982 has studied John's conception of 'restoration' as a desirable end.

[12] See *De Mag.* II.15.3; III.55.1 (Justinian); II.28.1; 68.3 (innovation). Conversely, Justinian's good qualities are praised inasmuch as they recall the 'good' emperors of old: II.28.3; 53.4 (Trajan), cf. 28.1 [Justinian] 'in his eagerness to preserve everything that was of use for the commonwealth and aiming to summon back all of the lofty authority of the form it had possessed of old ...'

[13] I.6.2; 8.2; II.8.2.

[14] N. 12 above.

[15] II.19.3; see above, pp. 58f.

[16] Decline: III.11.1f.; 12.1; 14.1; 18.1; 38.1; 39.1; 43.1f.; 44.1; 68.5. Promotion of literary men: III.28.4ff.

[17] III.56.2.

[18] See III.69.2 (on the evils of John the Cappadocian): 'the emperor, gentlest of souls, knew nothing of these happenings'; 69.3: 'the emperor, being a good man and slow to requite evil, was in the toils of a perplexing situation that was impossible to resolve.'

and rejoiced in his fall, and gives an account of the antecedents of the riots in realistic terms, pointing out the urban over-crowding resulting from an influx of poverty-stricken country-dwellers and the subsequent over-reaction of the city authorities,[19] he could not go further without seeming to cast blame too overtly on Justinian, and so merely records the casualties (set at 50,000 as against Malalas's 30,000)[20] without further comment. Phocas, who replaced John the Cappadocian and whom our author praises so fulsomely,[21] did not last long, though as John's work breaks off at this point we do not know how John would have coped with the fact that he was replaced as early as October, 532, by John the Cappadocian himself.[22] Like Procopius in the *Buildings*, John here saves the reputation of the emperor in the Nika revolt by appealing to the divine aid by which he was able to restore the devastated city.[23] Finally, the class bias of both writers is the same: both belonged, in Carney's phrase, to the sub-élite,[24] so many of whom had suffered in Justinian's administrative reforms, and who bore the brunt of the heavy taxation. Neither doubted that aristocratic values and property were under attack from Justinian, or that they should be preserved. The short-lived Phocas so admired by John was a rich aristocrat out of sympathy with the Justinianic regime and thrust into power only when the emperor was compelled to remove his own choice, John the Cappadocian. Neither of our writers had any time for the common people. Each of them, consequently, displays in his work all the tension of having to describe in panegyrical terms an emperor whose policies ran totally counter in their view to the interests of their class and the values to which they clung.

Allowing for the natural differences between the military man and the civil servant,[25] John and Procopius approach the political structure of their contemporary world in essentially the same way, through the same categories and in the same terminology. In the formal parts of their work, where conformism was essential, they seem to endorse the conventional view of the ideal emperor as 'moderate', specially protected by God, merciful and gentle like a father to his subjects, but also victorious, like the good Trajan. 'Restoration' is a note struck by both authors: if there is mismanagement and inefficiency, or burdensome taxation, the emperor's role is to put things to right and restore the traditional virtues.[26] Of course much of this can be attributed to panegyrical convention;[27] but

[19] III.70.1-2.
[20] III.70.5.
[21] See especially III.76.
[22] Stein, *BE* II, 463, 784.
[23] III.70.6f.
[24] Carney 1971, II, 166; cf. 175.
[25] On which see Carney 1971, II, 163ff.
[26] III.1.1; cf. *Buildings* I.1.6; II.6.6; IV.3.24.
[27] Hence modern attempts to find irony in the language of the *Buildings*: above, p. 87.

there is no reason to think that either Procopius or John failed to subscribe to the general theory of imperial rule that was now standard, even though they both found Justinian himself wanting. But John's attitudes are more complex than those of Procopius, since he had himself been the recipient of favours from the emperor,[28] while at the same time Justinian had sanctioned the changes in the prefecture which John so deplored, restored the hated John the Cappadocian, fought wars which emptied the treasury and reduced tax-payers to impoverishment. While John must try to dissociate these charges from the emperor himself, as we have seen, his defence is often unconvincing. In these authors we find the same features in imperial character or policy made the object of both praise and attack. The discourse within which Justinian could be evaluated was extremely limited, and it is the very aspects singled out by John for comment that are condemned in the *Secret History*: the emphasis on the role of Theodora in bringing down John the Cappadocian, Justinian's encouragement of literature, his asceticism.[29] It is hard to believe that John was unaware of the alternative view. Indeed, in the passage about Theodora, though the empress is praised, Justinian does not emerge creditably, for it is implied that he was not only ignorant of what was going on but also unable to do anything concrete about it. As for Justinian as patron of the arts, John himself says that men of letters were no longer honoured, and deplores the decline of scholarship in the *officium* of the Prefect.[30] Justinian's restless activity and his abstinence ('he neither gets complete relaxation in sleep nor does he touch solid food')[31] were evidently notorious, and linked in the public mind. Abstention from meat and personal asceticism, always a sign of the philosopher or the saint, and thus a token of exceptional power for good or in this case for ill, led Procopius apparently to go much further and see Justinian as actually demonic.[32] But John too is ambivalent: he makes this theme part of another defence of Justinian, evidently against the criticism that he took too much on himself. John complains that other emperors have been idle, so that Justinian's constant activity, which is somehow linked with his asceticism ('How could this emperor be idle, since he neither gets total relaxation in sleep nor does he touch solid food?'), must be good. Further, John says, he needs to be active, because the common people cause so much trouble.[33] So John is not so much

---

[28] *De Mag.* III.28.4, 29.1f.

[29] Carney 1971, II, 167ff.

[30] III.29.1; 30.9; 47.1 (patronage); III.28.3 (disfavour to men of letters); II.12.2, III.42.2; 68 (decline of Latin).

[31] II.15.2-3.

[32] Above, p. 56.

[33] II.15.2. The trouble caused by the people is attributed to 'discord sent from God' – cf. Procopius on the Nika revolt (p. 91). And Justinian's role is to counteract the 'indolence' of previous generations (see too III.55.1).

praising as justifying Justinian's restlessness and well-known asceticism, and the straightforward statement elsewhere of Justinian's indefatigability, where it is seen as beneficial,[34] must be read with caution, remembering that this very feature is central to Procopius' attack on Justinian and indeed also to his depiction of the character of Justinian's enemy, Chosroes.[35] Asceticism, therefore, usually a claim to virtue, is here subtly associated, and not only by Procopius, with the constant activity that both authors evidently regard with suspicion, and the very features which form the basis of a favourable assessment of Justinian can equally be turned to his discredit.

Both John and Procopius, therefore, seem to display a tension in their presentation of the emperor, and while their areas of concern may differ (John is not concerned with Justinian's religious policies or with his alleged neglect of the army), both seem broadly to accept the imperial structure while criticising its individual representative, and remaining attached to the ideal of a liberal and educated élite on whose freedom and traditions the emperor should not encroach. This high value set on Roman tradition and aristocratic life was not incompatible with a general acceptance of Christian causality encompassing the demonic as well as the divine. Procopius and John are opposed to most change as such, regarding it as a sign of tyranny to innovate[36] and seeing in antiquity a guarantee of moral stability.[37] Neither is much concerned about a real historical analysis of change (though there is more of this in John than in Procopius); when they give explicit causes, they tend to write in terms of Fortune or divine (and often incomprehensible) will.[38] Their interpretation of recent history tends to work through personality, on the bad side, John the Cappadocian, Peter Barsymes, Justinian and Theodora, on the good, Belisarius, Peter the Patrician,[39] the prefect Phocas. When Justinian receives praise, it is in traditional terms, for 'restoration' of the laws (but not for his own legislation), for reconquest, for fortification.[40] Neither, accordingly, has time for the constructive aims of his legislation, and when they mention it at all, it is usually to inveigh against the notion of 'interference' and 'meddling'.[41]

By and large, John the Lydian and Procopius both represent the continuation of senatorial historiography, if now in diluted form, and

---

[34] III.55.1.

[35] Above, p. 162.

[36] See II.19.9 (Domitian) and cf. I.3.3f.; II.1 on tyranny; *Secret History* 8.26; 11.1-2; 18.12; 30.21.

[37] *De Mag.* pref., 5; III.22.2-3; 68.3; *Secret History* 6.21; 14.1.

[38] John: above, n. 8; Procopius: above, p. 59.

[39] Peter the Patrician: *De Mag.* II.26 (praised for supporting tradition).

[40] Ibid. III.1.1-4, to be compared with *Buildings* I.6f. Cf. *Buildings* I.1.15 'like a gentle father'; n. 13 above. For 'restoration' cf. especially *De Mag.* III.1.1 'he maintains and as it were holds together ancient institutions which are crumbling away through age'.

[41] *Secret History* 27.33ff.

reveal through the contradictions in their work the tensions in Justinianic society itself. They do not express in simple form the opposition of a class out of sympathy with the prevailing government,[42] for it is clear enough from their works that there was wide divergence of opinion within the élite itself. John and Procopius themselves shared a good many basic assumptions and habits of mind with contemporaries who put less store on classical tradition and literary skill. But they do not seem to have been able to resolve their criticism into a coherent explanation of change and causality; they used instead an uneasy mixture of critical concepts and appeals to the miraculous, and allowed material to stand in their works which was contradictory to the main schema. These men lived in a period of rapid change, characterised on the surface by a much-advertised 'restoration' of Roman imperialism, yet which in their view also stemmed from dangerous innovation. Neither successfully reconciled his approval of Justinianic restoration with his disapproval of Justinianic innovation. They could not explain why the policy of restoration, of which they thoroughly approved, had met with increasing difficulty and brought adverse consequences, except through personality, starting with the personality of the emperor himself and then extending to his ministers, who could be accused of 'ruining' their offices; the only other explanation which they can offer is case in terms of appeals to Fortune, the influence of demons, or the incomprehensibility of the divine will. No doubt a part of this failure in explanation resulted in Procopius' case at least from the attempt to apply the manner of classical historiography to a transformed world, and part from the habit of a firmly rhetorical education which impeded original thinking.[43] But the difficulty also arose from the problem within this society itself of finding conceptual tools to explain the contradictions of the present crisis. If there was to be an adequate explanation at all, it would not come from the conservatives and traditionalists like John and Procopius.

As we have already seen, it is too easy, and misleading, to divide Justinianic culture and thought into 'classicising' authors like Procopius and 'popular' ones like Malalas.[44] Even in political thought there was room for a different approach, such as that of the curious treatise *On political knowledge (peri politikês epistemês)* often ascribed to the *magister officiorum* and diplomat Peter the Patrician.[45] Unlike the pious

---

[42] See further Cesa 1981, 393f. with n. 19.

[43] Hence the continual deployment of stereotypes without compensating analysis. Carney 1971, II, 174f. comments on the 'biassed selectivity' with which both John and Procopius present Justinian.

[44] Chapter 2 above.

[45] See Mazzucchi 1978, 1982; Fotiou 1981; Pertusi 1968; Dvornik 1963, II, 706-11; Valdenberg 1925. The work survives in fragmentary state on palimpsest (see Mai 1827, II, 571ff.; Mazzucchi 1982 prints a fuller text, see Behr 1974).

and conventional Mirror for Princes by the deacon Agapetus,[46] this work
is a theoretical treatise with a recognisable pedigree, through Cicero's *De
Republica* back to Plato's *Republic*. It certainly belongs to the sixth
century[47] and must be the treatise in six books mentioned by Photius,[48]
We have only parts of books four and five, dealing with military matters
and 'political knowledge'; unfortunately for us, book three, apparently on
kingship, is lost.[49] Even so, the existing work, truncated as it is, offers
some interesting points of contact with Procopius and John the Lydian,
even if it is not by Peter the Patrician.[50] Photius tells us that it discussed
a mixed constitution known as 'Dicaearchan', and this was confirmed
with the discovery of a new folium.[51] Thus there is in it a clear
dependence on classical material. Similarly, the military section is oddly
literary, written more in terms of Athens and Sparta than with
contemporary reference.[52] When the author emphasises the need to
restrain the lower classes, and their general subservience to their rulers,
who alone need political knowledge,[53] this too looks like familiar classical
material. But it is striking to see an emphasis on the senate, placed
second only to the ruler, and termed 'the best men' (*hoi aristoi*).[54] the
emperor's role, we learn, is to be above politics, so that it is the officials
(who are the *aristoi*) who need political knowledge.[55] At once this seems
reminiscent of John the Lydian and Procopius, and a possible reflection
of the senatorial revival in the sixth century, the very quarter from which
opposition tended to come.[56] The first of the 'laws' laid down for the ideal
state is also significant, for it concerns the lawful proclamation of the
emperor, who must be chosen by God and the citizens,[57] a formulation

[46] See below.

[47] The enemies of the state are still the Persians: Peroz of Persia is said to belong to the
not too recent past; the disputants, 'Menodorus' and 'Thomasius' (Menas and Thomas,
Phot., *Bibl.*, cod. 37, described as patrician and referendarius), are probably the Menas
praetorian prefect 528-9 (Mazzucchi 1978, 246) and perhaps the Thomas quaestor 528-9,
purged as a pagan 529 (Malal., p. 449); there is no Thomas known as a referendarius. For
the date of writing see below.

[48] *Bibl.* cod. 37. See Fotiou 1981 for the identification.

[49] The topics of books 1-2 and 6 are also unknown.

[50] See below.

[51] Behr 1974.

[52] The anon. prefers infantry to cavalry; but for sixth-century heavy cavalry see Proc.,
Persian Wars I.1.2, and on the realistic emphasis on cavalry in the *Strategikon* of Maurice
see Bivar 1972, 287ff. Of course, it was standard in works about kingship and political
theory to draw one's illustrations from classical literature, but this seems to be going
further than most. Mazzucchi 1978, 242; 1982, xiii, seeks to date the work before 535 on the
basis of its complaints about cavalry (39f., 48), but fails to realise the literary quality of
these sections. Equally, the complaints could belong in the context of Justinian's latter
years.

[53] V. 105f. (references are to Mazzucchi's edition).

[54] V.18.

[55] V.54f.

[56] Beck 1966.

[57] V.17.

remarkably apt in view of the development of inauguration ritual in the
early sixth century aiming at expressing just that paradox.[58] It could be
read as an affirmation of the right of the senatorial aristocracy (whose
interest is protected in the next 'law') to have the major say in the choice
of emperor; we might remember that on Justinian's death in 565
members of the senate moved quickly to put their own candidate on the
throne.[59] Interestingly the work moves on to the choice of patriarchs –
curious, it would seem, in a work which generally prefers a philosophic
emphasis to a Christian one. But once again this choice of subject reflects
contemporary reality; in 565 the major ally of the senators promoting
Justin the *curopalatês* was the patriarch. In the politics of sixth-century
Constantinople, senators could not have their own way without the
alliance of the patriarch, and this work recognises that political reality,
both here and when it goes on to concern itself with all patriarchs (and by
extension bishops).

While all this is very different, then, from the critique of John the
Lydian and Procopius, the treatise has certain things in common with
them, notably a certain senatorial or aristocratic bias and a guarded
attitude towards the emperor. If there is nothing in it to offend Justinian,
neither is there much to please him, as the author minimises his role in
political affairs and enhances that of his officials. The monarch, as seen
here, has two duties: imitation of God and the familiar obligation to be
like a father to his people.[60] But beneath him power is to be exercised by
his ministers in an ideal harmony.[61] Certain passages read like a warning
to the emperor to heed the interests of the *aristoi*.[62] Thus, while we
cannot put an exact date on this work, it does seem to be written in the
interest of the senatorial élite. It could belong to the early years, in the
context of the Nika revolt and the bitterness which must have followed
its suppression,[63] or to the later period, when there was a general
atmosphere of discontent and a regrouping of the senate round Justin. In
fact the patterning of the work on Cicero and Plato suggests that the time
of writing was later than the dramatic date (the opening of the reign) –
thus that it was written late in the reign when the emperor seemed to be
disregarding the *aristoi* even more obviously than before.[64] The last year
of Justinian's life had seen the deposition of one patriarch and a
replacement who aligned himself with some members of the senate, a

[58] See Nelson 1976.
[59] See Averil Cameron 1976, 131f.; 165f. Corippus' *In Laudem Iustini* is a defence of this
senatorial initiative.
[60] V.45.19, 198. Father: 132.
[61] V.54f. On the concept of lawful kingship in the treatise see Fotiou 1981, 539ff.
[62] V.16f.
[63] Following the connection made by Procopius in the *Secret History* (12.12f.), Fotiou
1981 dates the work before 532.
[64] For the plots against Justinian in his latter years, see Cor., *Iust.* IV.348ff.; Theophanes,
p. 235f. Bk V ends with a comparison of Plato and Cicero on the ideal state: V.209, cf. 48.

grouping nicely supported in the 'laws' put forward in this work.[65] On this basis, the work could be laying down a prescription for the next reign, though one that had been firmly dictated by experience under Justinian.

The other most striking feature of the treatise is its Platonism.[66] It is entirely written in the Platonic language of *epistêmê* and *doxa*, with analogies with medicine in the manner of Socrates and overt allusions to Socrates and Plato.[67] Certain of the author's assumptions, while not inconsistent with Christian views, are more reminiscent of the *Republic*, for instance, the view that justice amounts to giving all their due, that the lower classes must be led by their superiors, that government is a matter of knowledge. It was not calculated to appeal to an emperor who saw Platonist philosophers as potentially subversive and forbade them to teach. But Platonism was also a strong element in the thought of John the Lydian,[68] and Agathias showed that one could be a Christian historian and yet know and admire Plato.[69] More important for us is the fact that this work grapples with the problems of political authority at a serious level and without resorting to the crudely personal attacks found in both John and Procopius. Whether it is to be ascribed to the august Peter seems rather doubtful, however. The only basis for the identification is the assumption that this work is the *Peri politikês katastaseôs* ascribed to Peter in the *Suda*, and represented by several extracts in the *Book of Ceremonies* of Constantine VII Porphyrogenitus.[70] Those extracts, however, are so different in kind from our text that the identification can hardly be regarded as even probable. They may or may not be part of the work which John the Lydian seems to say Peter wrote on the office of the *magister officiorum*,[71] but in neither case is there anything to connect them with the present treatise.[72] The anonymous

[65] V.17-21. For the exile of Eutychius and his replacement by John Scholasticus see Averil Cameron 1976, 131, 164; the latter was intimately involved in the choice of Justin II as emperor, with the quaestor Anastasius and leading senators.

[66] See Praechter 1900; Valdenberg 1925. Knowledge of Latin too: Juvenal, Livy, Cicero, Seneca, Cato. The author is proud of his Latin (p. 608).

[67] E.g. V.13f (medicine); 208f. (Socrates).

[68] This is obvious, though it is less easy to point to an exact source; see Maas 1982, 149ff.

[69] *Hist.* II.28f. on Chosroes' pretensions to understand Plato and the ill-fated journey of the Athenian philosophers to Persia. For Platonism in this period as practised by Christians and pagans see the important work of Sorabji 1983.

[70] Stein, *BE* II, 728; see *De Caer.* I, chs. 84-95, with Bury 1907.

[71] *De Mag.* II.25.3.

[72] Especially not if *katastasis* means 'ceremonial' (so Alan Cameron 1976, 252); the anon. treatise is described as being about *epistêmê*. More significantly, though, the anon. treatise is quite different, more literary and philosophical altogether, than the very detailed and precise chapters in *De Caer.* Against authorship by Peter, Mazzucchi 1978, 245f. Peter's learning is extravagantly praised by John the Lydian, *De Mag.* III.26-6, but his connection with the present treatise remains unproven. Mazzucchi 1978, 247 suggests that Thomas himself elaborated the dialogue on the basis of a real conversation; surely unlikely, especially in view of the gap in Plato's *Republic* and Cicero's *De Republica* between dramatic date and time of writing (n. 64). See too Alan Cameron 1966 on Macrobius.

author remains a mystery, but even in its mutilated state the work shows
that scholarship and thought had not been extinguished, and that there
were less partisan ways of looking at the same problems addressed by
Procopius.

In fact the defensive air of certain passages in the treatise, like John
the Lydian's attempts to justify Justinian, allows us to see that the
source of the emperor's authority, his relation to God, was a matter of
contemporary dispute. The deacon Agapetus accepted wholeheartedly
the Eusebian concept of imitation, according to which the emperor was
God's vice-gerent on earth, whose first duty was to make his kingdom an
imitation of heaven.[73] It was a doctrine taken for granted by almost all
theorists since Eusebius, from Augustine to our anonymous, and it is
colourfully expressed at the inauguration of Justin II in Corippus'
panegyric.[74] But it was a doctrine which rendered justified dissent
impossible; doubtless this is why Corippus revives it so emphatically for
Justin, whose claim to the throne was somewhat ambiguous.[75] Under
Justinian, when so much hostility was simmering, we would expect the
doctrine to be questioned, and so it was, it seems, by the Alexandrian
John Philoponus, who actually argues in one of his works against the idea
that the ruler is the image of God on earth. Taking the opposite line from
Augustine, for whom justice (which included paying due respect to
God) was inherent in the very concept of a state, John argued that
government was not a matter of nature but of convention, and that the
text 'God made man in His own image', used by Theodore of Mopsuestia
to expound the nature of Christian monarchy, refers to all men, not
specifically to kings, meaning rather that all men have free will and are
thus distinguished from the animals, not that kings are the images of
God on earth.[76] Thus while there may be leaders set up by divine law in
the animal kingdom (such as queen bees), men make their own political
systems and appoint their own rulers. In the context of John's work this
is an argument of only passing importance. It is not the voice of freedom
against authoritarianism, for John is not discussing political theory as
such, but Biblical exegesis, and the argument used here is strictly
secondary in the economy of the work, an *ad hominem* thrust at
Theodore of Mopsuestia. We should not press it too much. But the

[73] On Agapetus (*PG* 86.1, 1163-86): Henry 1967, with Dvornik 1966, II, 712ff., Downey
1960, 49ff. Eusebius: Baynes 1933 (= Baynes 1955, 168-72). Further on political theory
under Justinian: Rubin 1960, I, 168ff., offering however a too schematised division of
authors into 'naive Jasager' and 'der Ring des Opposition'; on this view Procopius'
Buildings is no more than 'seine Konzession' (pp. 175f.).

[74] Cor., *Iust*. II.426-8.

[75] See Evagrius, *HE* V.1f. for a violently hostile view of Justin's claim.

[76] *De Op. Mundi* VI.16, p. 263 Reichardt. I owe this point to G.E.M. de Ste. Croix (see de
Ste. Croix 1981, 634, n. 79; Dvornik 1966, II, 711-12). Zosimus had indeed inserted remarks
against monarchy (I.5.2-4; see Paschoud 1975, 1ff., de Ste. Croix, ibid.), but Procopius was
not opposed to monarchy as such, only to a 'bad' emperor.

discussion does suggest that Biblical authority was sought for the Eusebian doctrine, and that different views might be taken.

In their different ways, Procopius, John the Lydian and the anonymous writer were all critical of the régime as it worked in practice. In an obvious sense, writers had to be careful what they wrote: Procopius' *Secret History* remained unpublished, John's criticisms, where they affect the emperor himself, could only be implied, the anonymous states his case for harmony between the emperor and the senate in the subtlest terms. Yet sharp criticism was tolerated of recently dead emperors, as we see in the case of John of Ephesus and Evagrius on Justin II and Agathias on Justinian. John the Lydian records an outspoken lampoon against Anastasius during his lifetime supposedly posted up on his statue in the Hippodrome,[77] and it is clear that there was a good deal of such writing. So the *Secret History* is a less isolated phenomenon than it appears.[78] Nevertheless, at official and public level, most writers accepted the Eusebian doctrine of Christian rule and wrote in a justificatory manner about the regime itself and about political theory in the wider sense.

These writers ranged from Cyril of Scythopolis and Agapetus to Paul the Silentiary, and their works fall into several different categories.[79] The only one specifically addressed to the theory of government is Agapetus' *Ekthesis*, the work of a deacon of S. Sophia written in the form of a set of precepts for Justinian, arranged as a pious acrostic.[80] It is a veritable mine of Eusebian language: the emperor must be an image (*agalma*) of piety; he must be impassive and unmoved; he must imitate God and be slow to anger; he is like an eye for the world, and men are his limbs,[81] his kingdom is 'fortified with mercy', and a ladder to heaven for himself. God gave him his kingdom and he must in turn be the servant (*doulos*) of God.[82] Agapetus turns Plato on his head: kings should be philosophers and Justinian a philosopher-king, but true wisdom is fear of the Lord.[83] It was Agapetus' work, which made no claims to originality, that became popular and gained a circulation which lasted to the fifteenth century and beyond.[84] It was perhaps another of the contradictions of the reign that a work so thoroughly eastern and non-classical in its literary

---

[77] *De Mag.* III.46.4.

[78] Timotheus of Gaza, for instance, wrote a *tragoedia* against the *chrysargyron* tax (Suda, s.v.); Evagrius's hatred for Justin II is noted above (n. 75); the 8th-c. *Parastaseis* can refer to emperors as *pornoi* (c. 41, Averil Cameron and Judith Herrin 1984, 227) and mentions verse invective (c. 80); for iconoclastic lampoons see Gero 1973, 113ff. In general, Tinnefeld 1971.

[79] For Cyril see *V. Sabae* 74 (panegyric of Justinian), and in general Flusin 1983.

[80] Above, n. 73.

[81] *C.* 46; cf. Cor., *Iust.* II.178ff.

[82] *Cc.* 61, 68.

[83] *C.* 17. Agapetus refers to the idea of philosopher-kings as a theory of 'one of the ancients'. Contrast the Platonism of John the Lydian and the anonymous (see above).

[84] Ševčenko 1978.

affiliations should have emerged in the early years when the emperor was pushing forward with his most 'Roman' policies, seen by John the Lydian as a restoration of the Roman past. At the same period, Romanos, also a deacon of S. Sophia, was pouring out an amazing series of liturgical hymns in which at times the imperial and the divine liturgies became enmeshed in an elaborate assimilation of the emperor with Christ.[85] It was understandable that the entry of Christ into Jerusalem should have been treated with the imagery and overtones of an imperial *adventus*, but Romanos carried the assimilation to its furthest point:[86] the shouting of Hosanna called to mind the acclamations at familiar imperial occasions, and the theme of the Christlike ruler found expression in a liturgy which the Byzantine emperor themselves enacted.[87] In Romanos' *kontakia* the emperor is not only linked to Christ through ideas and imagery but also brought into the whole sacred drama of redemption history, where he rubs shoulders with Adam, the first man, whom Christ will call up from Hades.[88] With these elaborate public hymns we are on the edge of a large shadowy area of popular ideology and belief, in which the emperor of the day could be imaginatively linked with the whole world of the apocrypha and their rococo elaborations of the Gospel narrative.[89] Sometimes Romanos took an explicitly contemporary and political theme, as in the *kontakion* 'On earthquakes and fires', dealing with the rebuilding of S. Sophia after the Nika revolt.[90] Justinian appears in it both as the spokesman of the people in prayer and as the chosen instrument of God for the rebuilding of S. Sophia and S. Irene. The destruction itself is present as the chastisement of God on a people who turned from folly to wickedness,[91] the rebuilding as a sign that they were none the less favoured by God above the Jews, whose Temple was never rebuilt.[92] After only one day the imperial couple, Justinian and Theodora, were already planning the rebuilding with the help of God.[93] As pious rulers they were enabled to rebuild the whole city and wipe out the memory of the sin. Even more interesting is the conclusion, in which Romanos links in liturgical thanksgiving 'the imperial couple, the citizens and the priests' and then prays that Christ will preserve the city, the churches and the rulers.[94] It was a powerful juxtaposition, and one

[85] Above, p. 26.

[86] Topping 1977.

[87] E.g. *De Caer.*, p. 638; see Ostrogorsky 1956.

[88] Adam: Romanos, *Kont.* 16 refrain; pp. 116ff. Maas-Trypanis ('On the Entry into Jerusalem').

[89] Above, p. 56f.

[90] Maas-Trypanis no. 54; see Topping 1978.

[91] P. 467 Maas-Trypanis.

[92] P. 470. Contemporary homilies likewise give a prominent place to the notion of Christian superiority to Jews: see e.g. *PG* 86.1.525H.

[93] P. 470.

[94] P. 471.

more natural in the context than Procopius' careful exclusion of the church from a major role in the *Wars*.

Romanos' *kontakion* refers to the rebuilding of S. Sophia begun in 532,[95] but in December 557 part of the dome collapsed after an earthquake, and Paul the Silentiary, author of many love poems in the Hellenistic style and close friend of Agathias,[96] wrote the official poem for the second rebuilding of the church by Justinian.[97] The re-dedication went on from Christmas Eve, 562, to Epiphany, 563. Much of Paul's poetic *ekphrasis* consists of architectural description, much longer than that in the *Buildings* of the first church of Justinian,[98] but this material is set firmly within an ideological and liturgical framework in which the emperor's role is central. As in Romanos' *kontakion*, the emperor plays the obvious part of rebuilder, but there is a further and much fuller development of imperial themes than in Romanos' case. Thus the subject of the church is embedded within a panegyric of Justinian, drawing on the standard imagery used by Agapetus: the emperor's mercy, his gentleness, his calm, his piety.[99] Paul combines contemporary imperial and religious ideology with rhetorical devices, as when he inserts a dialogue between Justinian and the personified Constantinople in the manner of Claudian's personifications of Rome.[100] But for us the most striking feature of the work is perhaps the great stress laid on the unity of emperor and patriarch, both at the beginning and end of the poem.[101] They are near equals, in different spheres. The emperor is linked specifically with the patriarch, not with the church in general as in the case of Romanos. By the end of the reign, Justinian was perhaps emphasising a more priestly and liturgical side to his imperial image,[102] and that is certainly how he appears in Paul's poem. But we must remember that this side of Justinian had been present from the beginning, obscured only in the works of conservative and classicising writers like Procopius.

Justinian's own laws also show us a side of Justinian which Procopius and John the Lydian preferred to overlook – when they were not attacking it. Like the letters of Constantine, the *Novels* of Justinian seem to bear the imprint of a distinctive personality, and it is tempting to believe Procopius when he claims that Justinian often wrote them himself and read them aloud in public, just as Constantine harangued

[95] According to a later source, 23 February, thus immediately after the suppression of the Nika revolt: Stein 1949, 457.
[96] See Averil and Alan Cameron 1966; Alan Cameron forthcoming.
[97] Above, p. 10.
[98] *Buildings* I.1.20-78.
[99] Especially *H. Soph.*, pref., 145f., 921f. For similar terminology in Latin see Averil Cameron 1976, 192 on Cor., *Iust.* III.309.
[100] *H. Soph.* 220f.
[101] 82f., 959f., 978f.
[102] See Averil Cameron 1979b.

his court with his own sermons.[103] As Tony Honoré points out,[104] the
earliest measures of Justinian's reign included savage attacks on the lax
and the deviant, especially among the clergy. Viewed from the throne, it
was the desire to clean up contemporary society and to mark the purge
with his own name that motivated Justinian's rapid moves to codify the
laws, just as much as any hope of 'restoring' the past. Again to quote
Honoré, 'Justinian is conscious of living in the age of Justinian'.[105] The
law commission worked with amazing speed; the *Code*, already
underway in 528, and the *Digest* by the end of 530, were both finished by
534, years during which the Nika revolt was successfully put down and
represented to the public as a sin duly punished, and the government
vindicated by extraordinary and unhoped-for victory in Africa. To
Justinian these dramatic events, like the completion of the *Digest*,[106]
seemed a genuine proof of God's saving providence, a view to which even
Procopius inclined.[107] But it is the *Novels* rather than the *Code* that
reveal Justinian's attitudes and aims. John the Lydian might represent
his intention as the restoration of tradition, but Justinian was more open:
it was to preserve or restore right belief.[108] This above all explained and
necessitated all else: it made the reconquest of the Arian-ruled western
province a duty, it called forth measures against pagans, heretics and
deviants, and it made an unblemished clergy a priority, for with that 'we
believe that we shall hold firmly the things we now have, and obtain the
things that have not yet come to us'.[109] The scheme was all-inclusive, the
reconquest only part of a wider programme which aimed at a kind of
Christian moral rearmament. In the 530s Justinian brought in a whole
series of laws relating to marriage and the family as well as to provincial
and civil reorganisation. He envisaged a comprehensive programme
which would win him the approval of God and thus guarantee him
success: in 536 he writes that his victories up to now give rise to the hope
that God will grant victory in the future, but this hope is intimately
connected with his resolve to bring back all these peoples to a better
state, by the help of God, an aim which he declares himself ready to
pursue by the utmost endeavour, whether it involves sleeplessness,
fasting or any other ordeal.[110] The labours and asceticism viewed with
suspicion by Procopius and recognised as needing explanation by John the
Lydian thus seem to have been a conscious part of Justinian's
programme for himself, a way of securing divine approval. His aim was

---

[103] *Secret History* 14.3-4; cf. Eusebius, *Life of Constantine*, IV.29, 55.
[104] Honoré 1978, 15.
[105] Ibid., 16.
[106] See Honoré, 19.
[107] On the Vandal victory, see Chapter 10 above.
[108] See the study by Michael Maas (Maas 1982), and for the prefaces, Hunger 1964, 49ff.
[109] *Nov.* 6 (a. 535).
[110] *Nov.* 30.11.2 (a. 536).

not a return to the Roman past but the achievement of *kosmia* and *taxis*, both dependent on pleasing God.[111] He claims it as his duty to see that those 'entrusted to him by God' should live a decent life.[112] This might involve correction by the emperor: if the prefect, for example, does not prosecute wrongdoers, he will encounter the judgment of God, followed quickly by punishment by the emperor.[113] The legislation of earlier emperors on second marriage is not good enough for Justinian; he 'does not shrink' from adding his own, or even from correcting his own earlier legislation.[114] God has exalted Jerusalem over other cities by making it the site of the resurrection of His Son; so it is the emperor's duty to reflect the same preeminence in his legislation.[115] When the church has anathematised heretics, the state too ratifies the decision, 'so that divine and human affairs should be placed in complete accord by right (orthodox) decisions'.[115] It is exactly the thinking of Augustine: since the earthly kingdom should mirror the heavenly, it is the state's duty to legislate for the correction of its people.[117] Justinian's notion of his duty was very positive, unquestioningly interventionist, much to the distaste of Procopius and John.[118] It certainly struck his subjects forcibly, both in its ideological application and in the strong military and policing measures needed to carry out Justinian's aspirations. He knew – so did his subjects – that he was not like other emperors; he condemned his predecessors for sloth, and knew that in his case success was the reward of industry and application to duty.[119] He was determined to undo the damage that had been done and make his conception of a Christian state a reality.

It was not easy to live under Justinian unless you shared his views, and contemporaries were forced to review their ideas about what Christian monarchy was or ought to be. There were many who could not accept the emperor's style or his formulae, from well-known intellectuals like the Athenian philosophers to the thousands killed in the Nika revolt. Since too this was a time of great disasters, from earthquake to plague, both the pious and the sceptical were driven to look for explanations. For some it was simple: the plague, like the Nika revolt, was the result of God's anger.[120] But others fell into confusion, like John the Lydian, who seems to endorse a physical explanation for earthquakes, and yet ascribes them

---

[111] *Nov.* 31.
[112] *Nov.* 77, pref. (a. 535).
[113] Ibid., fin.
[114] *Nov.* 22, pref. (a. 536).
[115] *Nov.* 40 (a. 536).
[116] *Nov.* 42, pref. (a. 536).
[117] Cf. *Civ. Dei* V.24 (duties of a Christian ruler); 26 (praise of Theodosius); Brown 1964. Constantine had felt the same way about the Donatists.
[118] See above.
[119] *Nov.* 41.1.2; *CJ* I.5.16.3.
[120] Malalas, p. 482; cf. Evagrius, *HE* IV.29 and see Allen 1979, 20.

in the same passage to the will of God, and who elsewhere claims to have been convinced of the truth of divination by the comet which predicted the Persian invasion of Syria in 540.[121] Procopius was thrown into bewilderment by the sack of Antioch and the transportation of its citizens to servitude in Persia;[122] he too could only ascribe it to the will of God. In Alexandria, the Christian philosopher John Philoponus argued against Simplicius in favour of a Christian theory of matter which took as its starting point the creation of the world by God.[123] But in his later work he was more willing to synthesise Christian ideas with Aristotelianism, while still retaining a Scripture-centred view of the universe.[124] Intellectual debate during the reign therefore found itself preoccupied with the relation of the Christian God to the world, and with the place of the emperor at the point of contact. It was a debate carried on in the fields of historical causation, physical theory and political thought, and stimulated by a particularly acute juxtaposition within a short period of time of staggering success and natural disaster on a vast scale, of forceful and interventionist imperial policies and personal attacks amounting to persecution. Above all, this was a time when there were still real and important differences of opinion. The very force which Justinian found necessary is a token of how far his ideal Christian state still lay from realisation. Undoubtedly, however, Justinian's own measures, combined with the strain placed on the state by over-ambitious wars together with massive depopulation through plague,[125] were beginning, by the end of the reign, to make Byzantium more nearly the overwhelmingly Christian and monolithic society that it was later to become. It is impossible to conceive of a Procopius at a later date.

If then political thinking under Justinian was part of a wider debate about the nature of the world and the relation of earth to heaven, the underside of that debate is represented by two further works, the *Christian Topography* of John Philoponus' fellow-Alexandrian Cosmas Indicopleustes, which we have already considered,[126] and the *Celestial Hierarchy* attributed to 'Dionysius the Areopagite', and probably of the early sixth century.[127] Both these works take a very concrete and pious view of the universe that is the equivalent in physical terms of Agapetus' theory of the relation of the earthly ruler to God. There is no room here for disputes about the earth's purpose: it is to be as nearly like heaven as possible, in a fixed order ordained by God and subject only to His will. The only kind of government that could cohere with such a physical

[121] *De Ostentis* 53, pp. 348f., 350; 1, p. 273 Bonn.
[122] Above, p. 106.
[123] Sambursky 1962, 154f.
[124] Ibid., 174; Sorabji 1983, 202.
[125] Above, p. 167f.
[126] Above, pp. 27f.
[127] Roques 1954.

universe is a theocracy, as Justinian now wanted.[128] The ps.-Dionysian world-view was already widespread in the sixth century, and was to become even more influential with the works of Maximus Confessor in the seventh.[129] But already it underlay the common idea that churches, for instance, had a symbolic meaning,[130] and it lent itself perfectly to the growing significance attached to icons, the physical representations on earth of the higher realities in heaven. Already the emperors of the sixth century were seen as the *imagines* of God,[131] and it was natural for them to ally themselves with the cult of the icons of Christ and the Virgin, also the images of the divine on earth.[132] For in such a way, as the *kontakia* of Romanos could bring the emperor into the liturgical drama, so the earthly authority of the emperors was imbued with divine authentication. In the regular round of imperial processions and ceremonies they were actually to be seen enacting a religious role and embodying in their own persons the unity of church and state. When Justin II decorated the new throne-room with a mosaic of Christ above the throne on which the emperor sat, he was simply making explicit a symbolic connection as real for Justinian as for himself and his successors.[133] Little survives, as it happens, of Justinianic art, and that little tends to emphasise themes of victory and military conquest.[134] Such was the ironic result for an emperor whose reconquest policy sprang, as his own laws claimed, from his sense of duty towards God.

Very little of this mode of thought seems to come through in the works of Procopius, except perhaps for the *Buildings*, which is so often merely dismissed out of hand. He distances himself in his writing from contemporary views of the world by the lack of a Scriptural dimension in his works. Whereas Malalas, for instance, has set the reign in the long progress of Biblical and Christian history, while Marcellinus, in his Latin *Chronicle*, consciously followed in the tradition of Eusebius, through the Latin of Jerome,[135] and while Romanos draws constantly on Old Testament imagery and example, Procopius has excluded Scriptural, and especially Old Testament, material from his works almost entirely. It no more fitted his kind of history than did matters to do with the liturgy, which often find a place in Malalas or Marcellinus. Yet this lack of a dimension shared by most contemporaries made it far more difficult for Procopius to operate a convincing theory of historical causation. We have seen that he does often appeal to the miraculous, or to the

---

[128] See Runciman 1977; Ahrweiler 1975.
[129] See Beck 1959, 436f.
[130] So Cor., *Iust*. IV.264ff., especially 290ff. with Averil Cameron 1976, 207; McVey 1983.
[131] Cor., *Iust*. II.428.
[132] Averil Cameron 1979a.
[133] Lavin 1962.
[134] For exploration of these themes see Averil Cameron 1975 (= 1981, VI).
[135] See Croke forthcoming.

intervention of divine Providence in history, but because he sets these passages in a history whose texture is largely classicising they have tended to lose conviction and to appear merely trivial or escapist. This very basic dichotomy in his work between his cultural aspirations and his actual assumptions is typical of the welter of contradictory views and attitudes held by his contemporaries.

But Procopius did share with many of them the assumption that the emperor of the day was somehow in a special and unique relation to God, and therefore that he carried within himself a quite exceptional potential to influence the course of human events. The presentation of Justinian in the *Secret History* is the logical outcome of such a view: if an emperor was really so destructive as Procopius felt Justinian to be, there was literally no other way of explaining him, while keeping to the general theory, than by supposing that he was actually inspired by the Devil. Many authors could more easily retain their general view of the emperor's special role while criticising individual emperors, as we see with Evagrius and John of Ephesus. But that is because their feelings were never quite so deeply stirred as were those of Procopius, for whom mere criticism were not enough to do justice to the enormity of Justinian's wrongs. The reign of Justinian called forth a ferment of questioning, by its very extremes, about the nature of the state and the emperor's place within it. In the context of Byzantine culture, these questions involved the central issues of Christian history and philosophy, as well as the capacity of classical literary genres to deal adequately with the contemporary order. It was unlikely that an individual response to these very basic issues would be either comprehensive, or entirely self-consistent. So Procopius both shared the attitudes of others and stood aside from them. He was no great thinker. But we can see that the terms within which he conducts his critique, and frames his praise in the *Buildings*, are the terms of contemporary thought, not just his own peculiar ideas. He was not just some embittered aide ready when cast off to turn his pen for gain to praise those he had just secretly vilified,[136] but a recognisable member of the complex society of the mid-sixth century. His violence of opinion and drastic changes of front spring directly from the dramatic changes and warring elements within that society, and reflect something of the variety of responses to which they gave rise among his contemporaries. If he stands apart from them, it is for his real skill as an observer and a writer, not for the originality of his views.

---

[136] This was essentially Gibbon's view. See Hunger 1978, I, 295 against Irmscher ('Opportunist') and Udal'cova ('nüchterner Karrierist').

Conclusion

We owe to the works of Procopius most of the responsibility for the abiding conception of Justinian's reign as one of the peaks in Byzantine history. In the Byzantine Dark Ages, when Procopius' works were not read, there was equally little tendency to look back to the reign as a great age. When the *Wars* began to be read again, Justinian's reputation immediately rose. It was a help that Procopius' classicism made his writing a model for later writers of high style.[1] But the subject matter itself and the scale on which Procopius treated it gave to Justinian's reign a prominence conceded even by those who like Evagrius themselves detested the emperor. In modern times the *Wars* provided material for differing interpretations of the end of antiquity, and the discovery of the *Secret History* welcome ammunition in the church-state controversy to some, embarrassing contradiction to their existing image of Justinian to others.[2] More recently Procopius' works form the underpinning, acknowledged or not, of books ranging from sensational novels to serious histories of the period. It was not just that Procopius wrote voluminously about great events; his characters – Justinian, Theodora, Belisarius and Antonina above all – seem to have attained a life of their own, from the medieval Belisarius legend[3] through the appearance of Justinian in Dante's *Paradiso*, remembering his general Belisarius,[4] to the innumerable poems, plays, romances and novels about Belisarius and Theodora from the sixteenth century to the present day.[5] Some of the

---

[1] Rubin 1954, 317f. (Anna Comnena, Niketas Choniates, John Cinnamus).

[2] On all of this, see Mazzarino 1959/1966, 92ff., with 82ff. (the use made of Procopius by Leonardo Bruni Aretini in 1441, who translated the MS. brought to Italy by Giovanni Aurispa in 1423 and passed the *Gothic Wars* off as his own work). By the time Alemanni discovered the *Secret History* in the Vatican Library in 1623, the debate centred on the relation of Justinian to the papacy; the *Secret History* thus aided those who, like Alemanni, saw Justinian already as the wicked enemy of the Popes.

[3] Rubin 1954, 319f.

[4] VI.10ff.

[5] Belisarius: Rubin 1954, 321f., a large number dating from the seventeenth century. In the Latin tragi-comedy 'Belisarius' by the Jesuit J. Bidermann (1666) Procopius appears as a character, together with a large cast of soldiers, senators, Vandals and so on, and with allegorical representations of Fortuna and Virtus. Another genre is the military memoir: Chassin 1957, following Lord Mahon, 1829. As a curiosity see the protest against over-valuation of Belisarius in the 1882 Lothian Prize Essay by George (Lord) Curzon, 41f. Theodora: Chapter 5 above and see Rubin 1954, 323f.

great scenes and stirring episodes have passed into the general consciousness, even though Procopius has not found a Shakespeare to do full justice to them.[6]

Thus the *Wars*, and, in a quite different way the *Secret History*, have contributed to an enlargement of the events and characters described in them. Justinian and his contemporaries have come to be seen as larger than life, the reign as a supreme effort at the restoration of Roman glory on the eve of the coming of Islam and the Dark Ages, or else as a vain attempt by jaded imperial arms to hold back the new vigour of the Germanic nations.[7] Whatever the view, Procopius has provided the material.

Most of these interpretations, however, have rested on too facile a reading of Procopius, whether he has been seen as a source of actual information too easily presumed reliable, or as a biassed partisan of Belisarius. The problem has been thought to lie in the relation of his three works to each other, or to the development of his own career, not in the nature of the works themselves. And their superficial differences have generally received more attention than their substantial similarities. At the same time, Procopius, as a classicising writer of recognisable and familiar military history, has been detached from his Byzantine background, a mistake which makes it unnecessarily difficult to explain those parts of his work which are not so reassuringly classical in appearance, while giving a false sense of support to the conception of the reign of Justinian as marking a 'classical revival'. As Procopius is a writer of such overwhelming importance for the period, and so often our only source, it is essential that his work be analysed as closely as possible in order for us to avoid falling into these rather elementary traps. The three works must be taken both singly and together and made to reveal their inner coherence and the principles on which they are constructed. As we know next to nothing about Procopius himself except from his writing, it is better to begin from that, while at the same time linking it to other contemporary works. This process, as we have seen, makes Procopius himself seem at once more ordinary, in his contemporary context, than he has usually appeared, and more unusual, in seeking to operate within so restrictive a framework as that chosen in the *Wars*. It also shows all three of the works to be highly complex and subtly differentiated, so that it is no use approaching any of them as though there is one simple straightforward key to its exposition.

In interpreting Procopius, then, there must be an interplay between two complementary techniques – that of recognising the unity of the works and the underlying ties between them, and that of giving full

---

[6] Rubin 1954, 121.

[7] As Procopius was claimed by Grotius to support his idealised view of the early Germans (Mazzarino 1959/66, 99-103).

weight to the variety within each individual work, which is a variety of method, reliability and authorial attitude. In particular there is considerable change and development within the *Wars* from part to part, in relation to the subjects treated and the time of writing.

Even then we are still left with the problem of using the evidence of a single source for most of the subject matter covered by Procopius. But at least that single source can be approached without prejudice.

The result of such an approach may seem to diminish the achievement of Procopius, and indeed in terms of power of historical analysis there is much to suggest a negative assessment. It is not that the sober and rational historian of the *Wars* for some unaccountable reason launched into venomous attack in the *Secret History* and servile flattery in the *Buildings*, but rather that similar interpretative weaknesses are to be found in all three works. Procopius did not have a profound view of the political situation, or an overall historical vision. His attitudes to the reconquest policy in general, insofar as it was a policy and not simply a piecemeal progression of smaller objectives,[8] are favourable, in a simplified way. He has little to offer by way of positive suggestions for alternative economic and social policies, and his usual posture is one of blind reaction. But in the *Wars* we can see, I would suggest, a conventional thinker grappling with a difficult set of changing circumstances, with developments unthought of in the early years with Belisarius, and with consequences of the wars unforeseen by their supporters. Procopius' attitudes changed drastically during the writing of the *Wars* as the implications and the problems of Justinian's policies became apparent; it is not surprising then if there are untidy ends and seeming contradictions between different parts. Into this overall framework we must slot the *Secret History* and the *Buildings*, works for which we cannot now know the exact circumstances of writing, but whose genesis is entirely explicable in general terms. Between them, they convey, even within the limitations of Procopius' intellectual horizons, a far more complex view of the state of the empire than the early parts of the *Wars* alone would have suggested. The man who was writing in the early 550s was very different from the man who had taken those early notes, or even from the man who had started writing the *Wars* a decade or so before. Thus there is no single political 'view' held by Procopius,[9] only a shifting set of perceptions and opinions within an overall range. To be aware of this fluidity is to come near to understanding the works themselves.

In so far, then, as it is possible to write of 'Procopius' rather than of the

---

[8] Brown 1971, 152; Honoré 1978, 18-19; Croke, 'Justinian and the ideology of reconquest'.

[9] The interesting paper by Maria Cesa (Cesa 1981) argues on the basis of a unified view (opposition to reconquest) which does not sufficiently take into account this degree of change and development.

Procopius of this or that passage in his works, we find here a man out of his depth. Feeling himself a representative, in some sense, of the small landowning classes of the eastern empire, in other words of traditional society, and an upholder of the traditional military values of Rome, he cannot see the enormous social and economic problems caused by the military policies which he approves, or the need for centralisation and strong government in order to carry them out. His criticisms are the criticisms of prejudice. New laws are seen as dangerous innovation. Subsidies, essential to diplomacy in themselves, but still more so to keep things quiet on one front while war was being waged on another, are seen as an unworthy betrayal of Byzantine might. The Nika revolt, indicative of dangerous emotions beneath the surface in Constantinople, is dismissed as the work of rabble or the inexplicable 'disease' of faction rivalry. The emperor himself, like his Persian counterpart, is presented as a stereotype villain or, when it suits, a new Cyrus; Theodoric, when he does not interfere with his subjects (the one glaring exception is trivialised into a personal anecdote) as a model of justice. All these attitudes are conventional in the extreme, and made more so by Procopius' deliberate choice, in all three works, of seeing his subject matter through classical spectacles, taking his parallels from antiquity and voicing his criticisms in a limited and cliché-ridden vocabulary. Nor, although his admiration for Totila and Teias came to match that which he had expressed for Theodoric, did he transcend the conventional categories of Roman thinking about barbarians. The Persians were different in many ways from the Goths or Huns often described in conventional terms by Procopius,[10] but his remarks in *Gothic Wars* IV.11 about the Persian embassy in Constantinople in 550 breathe all the indignation and contempt which he felt for the posing and the pretensions of the envoy and his train, and anger which Justinian's condescension towards them aroused in him. The five-year truce agreed with this embassy at cost to Byzantium of an enormous annual payment is different in Procopius' eyes only in scale from the regular payments to lesser barbarians, and his hostility comes clearly through despite the affectation of his language.[11] Chosroes features large in the narrative of the *Wars* because his was a personality to match Justinian's But Procopius does not progress towards a view of the necessity of coexistence between Byzantium and Persia any more than his admiration of Teias and Totila leads him to favour the Goths as a whole. If the *Buildings* is any sign of Procopius' own attitudes, as I have argued that in some sense it is, it must show that the notion of the glory of Rome, expressed in militarism and military defences, was as much still a part of Procopius' mental equipment as it had ever been, however far from the reality of

---

[10] For the latter see above, Chapter 12.
[11] *Gothic Wars* IV.15.5-7; 12-13.

frontier defence in the 550s.

But if his responses to the world around him were conventional, none the less Procopius brought to his writing exceptional vigour and ambition. He may be vague on military terminology and geographical description, and prone to the personal anecdote, but the whole enterprise of the *Wars* was astonishingly bold, a conception on the grand scale. In his introduction he claims that the events of these wars were greater than any before.[12] It was more than just a bow to classical models. Procopius formed his whole conception of the *Wars* on the basis of secular analytic history. He was trying consciously to write a modern Thucydidean history of Justinian's wars, a task for which he was (in theory at least) ideally well qualified. His history was to be true and useful, based on evidence and personal observation; it would eschew myth and analyse the causes of events.[13] It would focus on foreign and military policy, and deal with great and stirring deeds. It would not point an obvious religious lesson, but would reveal the changelessness of human nature. It would explain the origins and habits of the peoples who featured in it, and would present its author's views on situations and events in the formal rhetoric of dramatic speeches. Its pure, careful language would thus be a reflection of its very essence, and of the claims of Procopius himself to follow in this long tradition.

It proved more difficult than he had realised. It was hard enough to write in such a way of any wars in the sixth century AD, when this choice of form meant the omission, except incidentally, of so many of the factors that were now crucial in determining political events. But Procopius' own views, and his own position, also changed. The reconquest policy that had begun so spectacularly brought enormous problems that called forth unpalatable solutions as it dragged on beyond all expectation, and Belisarius fell short of his early glory and failed to seize the opportunities Procopius now wanted him to take. The *Secret History*, undreamt of when the *Wars* was begun, was the only way by which Procopius could express the disappointment and resentment that even he could not put into his public work, while the *Wars* itself, though it had gone very far in criticising the policies of the late 540s, petered out with its task unfinished.

Justinian's reign, at least in its early phase, provided unique and plausible subject matter for such an endeavour. Even then it was hard to insist on this traditional and secular conception of history when most of Procopius' contemporaries were unselfconsciously writing in Christian

[12] *Persian Wars* I.1.6f.
[13] Truth: I.1.5; usefulness: I.1.1; evidence and witness: I.1.3, cf. *Gothic Wars* IV.6.9: rejection of myth: ibid. 1.12, 2.30, 22.31-22; history will teach future generations: *Persian Wars* I.1.1-2. The purpose of history, claims Procopius, is not to show the relation of God to the world, or demonstrate God's providence, but to teach men lessons about human nature and human situations.

terms. Procopius did not succeed – though he tried very hard – in keeping such traces out of his own work. But progressively, indeed surprisingly soon, he found it impossible to make the available subject matter fit the confines of the *Wars*, and the result was the *Secret History*. The ambition of Justinian, and the magnitude of the successes and disasters that occurred during his reign, made possible the *Wars* and called forth the *Secret History* and the *Buildings* But no one after Procopius would attempt quite so restrictive a formula or in so doing find themselves forced into the writing of alternative and apparently contradictory works. That was the product of the extremes to be found in the reign of Justinian, and it is ironic that Procopius, the lover of order, should have been forced into such seeming topsy-turvydom.

A remarkable achievement when taken together; taken singly, noble failures, or at least only partial successes. Procopius could not achieve the full expression of his thought about the contemporary situation in any one of his three works, but put them together and they are powerful indicators of the contradictions inherent in the age of Justinian.

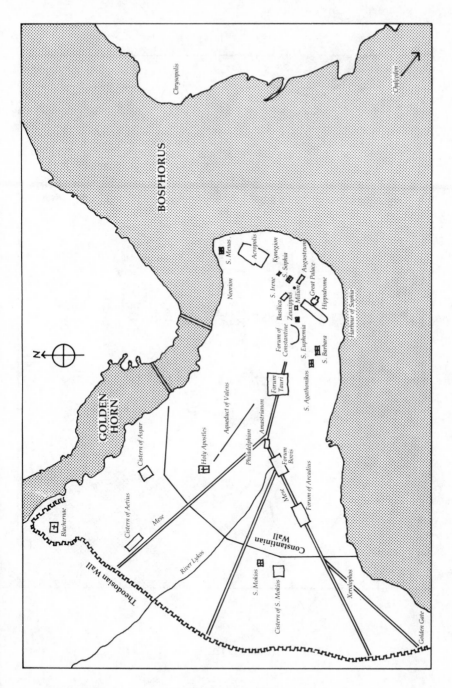

1. Constantinople

Chrysopolis

Chalcedon

BOSPHORUS

S. Menas

Acropolis

Neorion

Kynegion

S. Irene

S. Sophia

Basilica

Milion

Augusteum

Forum of Constantine

Zeuxippos

Great Palace

S. Euphemia

Hippodrome

S. Barbara

Harbour of Sophia

Forum Tauri

S. Agathonikos

GOLDEN HORN

Aqueduct of Valens

Amastrianon

Holy Apostles

Philadelphion

Forum Bovis

Cistern of Aspar

Forum of Arcadius

Mese

Constantinian Wall

Blachernae

Cistern of Aetius

Mese

River Lykos

S. Mokios

Cistern of S. Mokios

Theodosian Wall

Xerolophos

Golden Gate

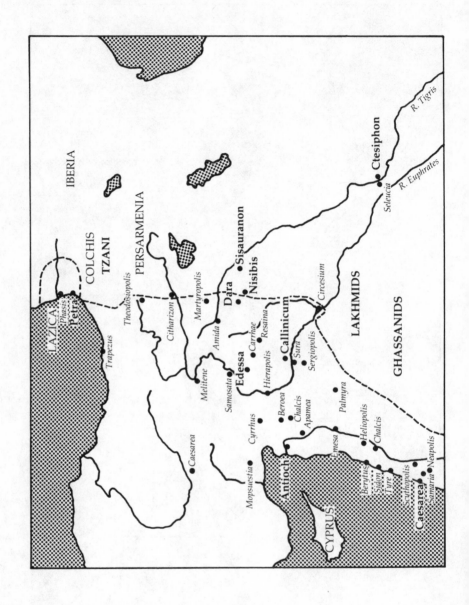

2. Map to Illustrate the Persian Wars

3. Carthage and Environs

4. Italy during the Gothic Wars

Bibliography

ADONTZ, N., 1970. *Armenia in the Period of Justinian*, trans. and rev. N. Garsoian, Lisbon

ADSHEAD, Katherine, 1983. 'Thucydides and Agathias', in Croke and Emmett 1983, 82-7

AHRWEILER, H., 1975. *L'Idéologie politique de l'empire byzantin*, Paris

ALEXANDER, P.J., 1967. *The Oracle of Baalbek: the Tiburtine Sibyl in Greek Dress*, Dumbarton Oaks Studies 10, Washington D.C.

ALISAVETOS, H., 1913. *Die kirchliche Gesetzgebung des Kaisers Justinian I*, Berlin

ALLEN, P., 1979. 'The "Justinianic" plague', *Byzantion* 48, 5-20

— 1981. *Evagrius Scholasticus the Church Historian*, Spicilegium Sacrum Lovaniense 41, Louvain

ARCHI, G.G., 1970. *Giustiniano legislatore*, Bologna

ARMSTRONG, G.T., 1969. 'Fifth- and sixth-century church building in the Holy Land', *Greek Orthodox Theological Review* 14, 17-30

ATHANASSIADI-FOWDEN, P., 1981. *Julian and Hellenism*, Oxford

AULER, A., 1876. *De fide Procopii Caesariensis in secundo bello persico Iustiniani I imperatoris enarrando*, Diss. Bonn

AUSTIN, N., 1983. 'Autobiography and history: some later Roman historians and their veracity', in Croke and Emmett 1983, 54-65

AVIGAD, N., 1977. 'A building inscription of the Emperor Justinian and the Nea in Jerusalem', *Israel Exploration Journal* 27, 145-61

AVI-YONAH, M., 1954. *The Madaba Map*, Jerusalem

— 1975. *Encyclopaedia of Archeological Excavations in the Holy Land*, Jerusalem

— 1976. *The Jews of Palestine*, Eng. trans., Oxford

BACHRACH, B., 1970a. 'Procopius, Agathias and the Frankish military', *Speculum* 45, 435-41

— 1970b. 'Procopius and the chronology of Clovis's reign', *Viator* 1, 21-32.

— 1973. *A History of the Alans in the West*, Minneapolis

BAGATTI, B., 1952. *Gli edifichi antichi di Betlemme*, Jerusalem

BAGNANI, G., 1954. *The Arbiter of Elegance*, Toronto

BAKER, G.P., 1931. *Justinian*, London

BALDWIN, B., 1977a. 'Four problems in Agathias', *Byzantinische Zeitschrift* 70, 295-305

— 1977b. 'Malchus of Philadelphia', *Dumbarton Oaks Papers* 31, 91-107

— 1978a. 'The career of Corippus', *Classical Quarterly* 28, 372-6

— 1978b. 'Menander Protector', *Dumbarton Oaks Papers* 32, 101-25

— 1979a. 'Leontius Scholasticus and his poetry', *Byzantinoslavica* 40, 1-12

— 1979b. 'The purpose of the *Getica*', *Hermes* 107, 489-92

— 1980a. 'Priscus of Panium', *Byzantion* 50, 18-61

— 1980b. 'Olympiodorus of Thebes', *L'Antiquité classique* 48, 212-31

— 1980c. 'The date of the *Cycle* of Agathios', *Byzantinische Zeitschrift* 73, 334-40.

— 1981. 'Physical descriptions of Byzantine emperors', *Byzantion* 51, 8-21

— 1982. 'An aphorism in Procopius', *Rheinisches Museum* 125, 309-11

BANDY, A.C., 1982. *Ioannes Lydus. De magistratibus reipublicae Romanae*, Philadelphia

BARKER, J.W., 1966. *Justinian and the Later Roman Empire*, Madison

BARNEA, I., 1960. 'Contributions to Dobrudja History under Anastasius I', *Dacia*, n.s. 4, 363-74

— 1967. 'Nouvelle contribution à l'histoire de la Dobrudja sous Anastase I^e', *Dacia*, n.s. 11, 355-6

BARNISH, S., 1984. 'The genesis and completion of Cassiodorus' *Gothic History*', *Latomus* 43, 336-61

BARTHES, R., 1968. *Writing Degree Zero*, Eng. trans., New York

BARTHOLOMEW, P., 1982. 'Fifth-century facts', *Britannia* 13, 261-70

BAYNES, N., 1933. 'Eusebius and the Christian empire', *Mélanges Bidez*, Brussels, 13-18 (= *Byzantine Studies and other Essays*, London 1955, 168-72)

BECK, H-G., 1959. *Kirche und theologische Literatur im byzantinische Reich*, Munich (I. Müller, *Byzantinische Handbuch* II.1)

— 1965. 'Zur byzantinischen Mönchschronik', in G. Bauer, *Speculum historiale*, Munich, 188-97

— 1966. 'Senat und Volk von Konstantinopel', *Sitz. Bayer. Akad. der Wiss., ph.-hist. Kl.*, heft 6, Munich

— 1977. 'Christliche Mission und politische Propaganda im byzantinischen Reich', *Settimane di Studi del Centro italiano di studi sull' alto medioevo* XIV: 'La conversione a cristianesimo nell' europa dell'alto medioevo', Spoleto 14-19 April, 1966, Spoleto, 654ff.

BEHR, C., 1974. 'A new fragment of Cicero's *De Republica*', *American Journal of Philology* 95, 141-9

BENABOU, M., 1974. *La Résistance africaine à la romanisation*, Paris

BEN-DOV, Meir, 1977. 'Found after 1400 years – the magnificent Nea', *Biblical Archaeology Review* 3.4, 32-7

BENEDICTY, R., 1962. 'Die Milieu-Theorie bei Prokop von Kaisareia', *Byzantinische Zeitschrift* 55, 1-10

— 1965. 'Prokopios' Berichte über die slavische Vorzeit. Beiträge zur historiographischen Methode des Prokopios von Kaisareia', *Jahrb. der österr. Byantinistik* 14, 51-78

BEŠEVLIEV, V., 1966. 'Les Cités antiques en Mésie et en Thrace à l'époque de haut Moyen Âge', *Études balkaniques* 6, 207-20

— 1967. 'Zur topographie du Balkanhalbinsel in Prokops Werk 'De Aedificiis'', *Philologus* 111, 267ff.

— 1969. 'Die lateinische Herkunft der Kastellverzeichnisse bei Prokop', *Hommages à Marcel Renard* I, Brussels, 94ff.

— 1970. *Zur Deutung der Kastellnamen in Prokops Werk 'De Aedificiis'*, Amsterdam

BIONDO, Biondi, 1936. *Giustiniano primo principe e legislatore cattolico*, Milan

— 1966. 'Giustiniano (nel XIV centenario della morte)', *Studi Romani* 14, 249-61

BIRABEN, J.N. and LE GOFF, J., 1969. 'La Peste dans le Moyen Âge', *Annales E.S.C.*, 1484-1510

BIVAR, A.D.H., 1972. 'Cavalry equipment and tactics on the Euphrates frontier', *Dumbarton Oaks Papers* 26, 273-91

BLOCKLEY, R.C., 1975. *Ammianus Marcellinus. A Study of his Historiography*

and Political Thought, Brussels
— 1981. *The Fragmentary Classicising Historians of the Later Roman Empire. Eunapius, Olympiodorus, Priscus and Malchus*, ARCA Classical and Medieval Texts, Papers and Monographs 6, Liverpool
— 1983. id., vol. II (ARCA 10)
BLUMENTHAL, H., 1978. '529 and after: what happened to the Academy?' *Byzantion* 48, 369-85
BONFANTE, P., 1933. 'Il movente della Storia Arcana di Procopio', *Bull. Ist. Dir. Rom.* 41, 283-7
BOOJAMRA, J.L., 1975. 'Christian *Philanthropia*: a study of Justinian's welfare policy and the Church', *Byzantina* 7, 345ff.
BRADLEY, D.R., 1966. 'The composition of the *Getica*', *Eranos* 64, 57-79
BRAUN, H., 1885. *Procopius Caesariensis, quatenus imitatus sit Thucydidem*, Diss. Erlangen
— 1894. *Die Nachahmung Herodots durch Prokop*, Progr. Nürnberg
BRIDGE, Antony, 1978. *Theodora: Portrait in a Byzantine Landscape*, London
BROCK, S.P., 1981. 'The conversations with the Syrian Orthodox under Justinian (532)', *Orientalia Christiana Periodica* 47, 87-121
— 1983. *The Harp of the Spirit: eighteen poems of Saint Ephrem*, Studies supp. to Sobornost 4, London
BROWN, Peter, 1964. 'St Augustine's attitude to religious coercion', *Journal of Roman Studies* 54, 107-16
— 1981. *The Cult of the Saints*, London
BROWN, T.S., 1984. *Gentleman and Officers: imperial administration and aristocratic power in Byzantine Italy, AD 554-800*, British School at Rome, London
BROWNING, R., 1975. *Byzantium and Bulgaria*, London
— 1978. 'The language of Byzantine literature', in S. Vryonis Jr., ed., *Byzantina kai Metabyzantina* 1, *The "Past" in Medieval and Modern Greek Culture*, Malibu, 103-33
— 1983. *Medieval and Modern Greek*, 2nd ed., Cambridge
BRÜCKNER, M., 1896. *Zur Beurteilung des Geschichtschreibers Prokopius von Caesarea*, Ausbach
BULLIET, R., 1975. *The Camel and the Wheel*, Cambridge, Mass.
BURN, A.R., 1955. 'Procopius and the island of ghosts', *English Historical Review* 70, 258-61
BURY, J.B., 1889. *History of the Later Roman Empire (395 AD to 800)*, I-II, London
— 1897. 'The Nika riot', *Journal of Hellenic Studies* 17, 92ff.
— 1906. 'The Homeric and the historic Kimmerians', *Klio* 6, 79-88
— 1907. 'The ceremonial book of Constantine Porphyrogenitus', *English Historical Review*, 22, 209-27; 417-39
— 1923. *History of the Later Roman Empire from the Death of Theodosius to the Death of Justinian*, I-II, London
CAMERON, ALAN, 1966. 'The date and identity of Macrobius', *Journal of Roman Studies* 56, 25-38
— 1969. 'The last days of the Academy at Athens', *Proceedings of the Cambridge Philological Society*, n.s. 15, 7-29
— 1970. *Claudian*, Oxford
— 1976. 'Theodorus *Triseparchos*', *Greek, Roman and Byzantine Studies* 17, 269-86
— 1977. 'Some prefects called Julian', *Byzantion* 47, 42-64

— 1978. 'The House of Anastasius', *Greek, Roman and Byzantine Studies* 19, 259-76
— forthcoming. *The Greek Anthology: From Meleager to Planudes*, Oxford
CAMERON, ALAN and AVERIL, 1964. 'Christianity and tradition in the historiography of the Later Roman Empire', *Classical Quarterly*, n.s. 14, 316-28
— 1966. 'The *Cycle* of Agathias', *Journal of Hellenic Studies*, 86, 6-25
CAMERON, ALAN and SCHAUER, DIANE, 1982. 'The last consul: Basilius and his diptych', *Journal of Roman Studies* 72, 126-45
CAMERON, AVERIL, 1965. 'Procopius and the Church of St. Sophia', *Harvard Theological Review* 58, 161-3
— 1966. 'The "scepticism" of Procopius', *Historia* 15, 6-25
— 1968. 'Agathias on the early Merovingians', *Annali della Scuola Normale di Pisa*, ser. ii, 37, 95-140
— 1969-70. 'Agathias on the Sassanians', *Dumbarton Oaks Papers* 23-4, 1-150
— 1970. *Agathias*, Oxford
— 1976. *Flavius Cresconius Corippus, In laudem Iustini minoris libri quattuor*, London
— 1977. 'Early Byzantine *Kaiserkritik*: two case histories', *Byzantine and Modern Greek Studies* 3, 1-17
— 1979a. 'A nativity poem from the sixth century AD', *Classical Philology* 79, 222-32
— 1979b. 'Images of authority: élites and icons in late sixth-century Byzantium', *Past and Present* 84, 3-35
— 1980a. 'The artistic patronage of Justin II', *Byzantion* 50, 62-84
— 1980b. *The Sceptic and the Shroud*, Inaugural Lecture, King's College London
— 1980c. 'The career of Corippus again', *CQ* 30, 534-9
— 1981. *Change and Continuity in Sixth-Century Byzantium*, London
— 1982. 'Byzantine Africa: the literary evidence', *Excavations at Carthage VII, University of Michigan*, Ann Arbor, 29-62
— 1984a. 'The history of the image of Edessa: the telling of a story', *Okeanos. Festschrift I. Ševčenko, Harvard Ukrainian Studies*, 7, 80-94
— 1984b. 'Corippus' *Iohannis*: epic of Byzantine Africa', *Proceedings of the Liverpool Latin Seminar*, 167-80
CAMERON, AVERIL and HERRIN, JUDITH, eds., 1984. *Constantinople in the Eighth Century: the Parastaseis Syntomoi Chronikai*, Columbia Studies in the Classical Tradition, Leiden
CANTARELLI, L., 1915. *Il patrizio Liberio e l'imperatore Giustiniano*, Studi Romani e Bizantini, Rome
CARNEY, T., 1971. *Bureaucracy in Traditional Society: Romano-Byzantine bureaucracies viewed from within*, Lawrence, Kansas
CASEY, P., ed., 1979. *The End of Roman Britain*, Oxford.
CASEY, P., 1984. 'Justinian and the limitanei', *Festschrift J.C. Mann*, forthcoming
CAVALLO, G., 1978. 'La circulazione libraria nell'età di Giustiniano; in G.G. Archi, ed., *L'Imperatore Giustiniano. Storia e Mito*, Giornate di studio a Ravenna, 14-16 Oct. 1976, 201-36
CESA, MARIA, 1981. 'La Politica di Giustiniano verso l'occidente nel giudizio di Procopio', *Athenaeum* n.s. 59, 389-409
— 1982. 'Etnografia e Geografia nella visione storica di Procopius di Cesarea', *Studi classici e orientali* 32, 189-215
CHADWICK, H., 1981. *Boethius*, Oxford

CHADWICK, NORA, 1976. *The British Heroic Age*, Cardiff

CHASSIN, L.M., 1957. *Bélisaire, généralissime byzantin (504-565)*, Paris

CHERF, W.J., 1982. 'Carbon-14 and Prokopios' *de Aedificiis'*, *Eighth Annual Byzantine Studies Conference*, Abstracts, Chicago, 44-5

CHESNUT, G.F., 1973. 'Fate, fortune, free will and nature in Eusebius of Caesarea', *Church History* 42, 165-82

— 1975. 'Kairos and cosmic sympathy in the church historian Socrates Scholasticus', *Church History* 44, 161-6

CHRISTIDES, V., 1970. 'Saracens' prodosia in Byzantine sources', *Byzantion* 40, 5-13

CHRISTOU, P., 1971. 'The missionary task of the Byzantine Empire', *Byzantina* 3, 279-86

CLAUDE, D., 1969. *Die byzantinische Stadt im 6. Jahrhundert*, Byzantinisches Archiv 13, Munich

CLOVER, F.M., 1982. 'Carthage and the Vandals', *University of Michigan, Excavations at Carthage VII*, Ann Arbor, 1-22

COLLINS, ROGER, 1983. 'Theodebert I, "Rex Magnus Francorum",' in P. Wormald, ed., *et al.*, *Ideal and Reality in Frankish and Anglo-Saxon Society, Studies presented to J.M. Wallace-Hadrill*, Oxford, 7-33

COMPARETTI, D., 1925. 'Maldicenze Procopiane I: Giustiniano equiperato a Domiziano', *Raccolta di scritti in onore di Giacomo Lumbroso*, Milan, 58-72

CONSTANTELOS, D.J., 1960-61. 'Philanthropy in the age of Justinian', *Greek Orthodox Theological Review* 6, 206ff.

— 1964-65. 'Paganism and the state in the age of Justinian', *Catholic Historical Review* 50, 372-80

— 1968. *Byzantine Philanthropy and Social Welfare*, New Brunswick, N.J.

COURTOIS, C., 1955. *Les Vandales et l'Afrique*, Paris

CRACCO RUGGINI, L., 1977. 'The ecclesiastical histories and the pagan historiography: providence and miracles', *Athenaeum* n.s. 55, 107-26

— 1978. 'Come Bisanzio vide la fine dell' impero d' occidente', in *La Fine dell'impero romano d'occidente*, Ist. di Studi Romani, Rome, 71ff.

— 1979. 'Potere e carismi in erà imperiale', *Studi Storici* 3, 585-607

— 1981. 'Il miracolo nella cultura del tardo impero: concetto e funzione', *Hagiographie, cultures et sociétés IVᵉ – XIIᵉ siècles*, Paris, 161-204

CROKE, B., 1983a. 'Marcellinus and Dara: a fragment from his lost *de temporum qualitatibus et positionibus locorum'*, *Phoenix* 37

— 1983b. 'AD 476: the manufacture of a turning point', *Chiron, 81-119.*

— forthcoming. 'Justinian and the ideology of reconquest'

— forthcoming. 'Cassiodorus and the *Getica* of Jordanes', *Classical Philology*

CROKE, B. and EMMETT, ALANNA eds., 1983. *History and Historians in Late Antiquity*, Sydney

CROKE, B., and CROW, J., 1983. 'Procopius on Dara', *Journal of Roman Studies* 73, 143-59

CROW, JAMES, 1981. 'Dara: a late Roman fortress in Mesopotamia', *Yayla. Fourth Report of the Northern Society for Anatolian Archeology*, Newcastle-upon-Tyne, 11-20

CRUIKSHANK DODD, E., 1961. *Byzantine Silver Stamps*, Dumbarton Oaks Studies 7, Washington D.C.

CURZON, GEORGE, 1883. *Justinian*, Lothian Prize Essay, Oxford

DAHN, F., 1865. *Prokopius von Cäsarea*, Berlin

DALY, LLOYD W., 1942. 'Echinos and Justinian's fortifications in Greece', *American Journal of Archeology* 46, 500-8

DAUBE, D., 1969. 'The marriage of Justinian and Theodora: legal and theological reflections', *Catholic University of America Law Review* 16, 380-99

DAY, A.A., 1958. *The Origins of Latin Love Elegy*, Oxford

DE GROOT, A.W., 1918. *Untersuchungen zum byzantinischen Prosarhythmus (Procopius von Caesarea)*, Groningen

DE LANCKER, H., 1968. *Théodora: impératrice d'Orient*, Paris

DELBRUECK, H., 1913. *Numbers in History*, London

DE ROMILLY, J., 1956. *Histoire et raison chez Thucydide*, Paris

DESANGES, J., 1963. 'Un témoignage peu connu de Procope sur la Numidie vandale et byzantine', *Byzantion* 33, 41-69

DE STE. CROIX, G.E.M., 1981. *The Class Struggle in the Ancient Greek World*, London

DEVREESSE, R., 1940. 'Le christianisme dans la péninsule sinaitique, des origines à l'arrivée des musulmanes', *Revue biblique* 49, 216-20

— 1948. *Essai sur Théodore de Mopsueste, Studi e Testi* 141, Vatican City

DEWING, H., 1910. 'The accentual cursus in Byzantine Greek prose with special reference to Procopius of Caesarea', *Trans. Connecticut Acad. Arts and Sciences* 14, 415-66

DIEHL, C., 1896. *L'Afrique byzantine*, Paris

— 1901. *Justinien et la civilisation byzantine au VIe siècle*, Paris

— 1904. *Théodora: impératrice de Byzance*, 4th ed., Paris

— 1909. *Figures byzantines*, Paris

DIESNER, H.J., 1966. *Fulgentius von Ruspe als Theologe und Kirchenpolitiker*, Berlin

— 1971. 'Eine Thukydides-parallele bei Prokop', *Rheinisches Museum* 114, 93-4

DITTEN, H., 1975. 'Zu Prokops Nachrichten über die deutschen Stämme', *Byzantinoslavica* 36, 1-24

DODDS, E.R., 1965. *Pagan and Christian in an Age of Anxiety*, Oxford

DOWNEY, G.A., 1938a. 'Ephraemius, patriarch of Antioch', *Church History* 7, 367-70

— 1938b. 'Imperial building records in Malalas', *Byzantinische Zeitschrift* 38, 301ff.

— 1939. 'Procopius on Antioch: a study of method in the *De Aedificiis*', *Byzantion* 14, 361-78

— 1940. 'Justinian as Achilles', *Trans. Am. Philol. Association*, 71, 68-78

— 1947. 'The composition of Procopius, *De Aedificiis*', *ibid.*, 78, 171-83

— 1949. 'Paganism and Christianity in Procopius', *Church History* 18, 89-102

— 1950. 'Justinian as builder', *Art Bulletin* 32, 262-6

— 1953a. 'The Persian campaign in Syria in AD 540', *Speculum* 28, 340-8

— 1953b. 'Notes on Procopius, *De Aedificiis* Book I', *Studies presented to David M. Robinson* II, St. Louis, 719ff.

— 1957. (ed.) 'Nikolaus Mesarites: Description of the Church of the Holy Apostles of Constantinople', *Trans. Am. Philosoph. Soc.* 47, 855ff.

— 1958a. 'The Christian schools of Palestine: a chapter in literary history', *Harvard Library Bulletin* 12, 297ff.

— 1958b. 'Justinian's view of Christianity and the Greek classics', *Anglican Theological Review* 40, 13-22

— 1959a. 'Julian and Justinian and the unity of faith and culture', *Church History*, 28, 339-49

— 1959b. *Ekphrasis*, RAC 4, Stuttgart, 921ff.

— 1960. *Constantinople in the Age of Justinian*, Norman, Oklahoma

— 1961. *A History of Antioch in Syria from Seleucia to the Arab Conquest*, Princeton

— 1963. *Gaza in the Early Sixth Century*, Norman, Oklahoma

— 1975. 'Caesarea and the Church', in Fritsch, J., ed., *Studies in the History of Caesarea Maritima*, Bull. Am. Schools Oriental Research 19, Missoula, Montana

DRAKE, H.A., 1976. *In Praise of Constantine*, Berkeley

DRIJVERS, H.J.W., 1977. 'Hatra, Palmyra und Edessa', *Aufstieg und Niedergang der römischen Welt* II.8, Berlin, 863-906

DURLIAT, J., 1981. *Les dédicaces d'ouvrage de defense dans l'Afrique byzantine*, Coll. de l'école française de Rome 49

DUVAL, N., 1981. 'Comment distinguer les inscriptions byzantines d'Afrique?' *Byzantion* 51, 511-32

— 1972. 'Etudes d'architecture chrétienne nord-africaine', *Mélanges de l'école française de Rome* 84, 107ff.

DUVAL, Y., 1970. 'La Maurétanie sitifienne à l'époque byzantine', *Latomus* 29, 157-61

— 1982. *Loca Sanctorum Africae. Le culte des martyres en Afrique du IVe au VIIe siècle*, Paris, 2 vols

DVORNIK, F., 1966. *Early Christian and Byzantine Political Philosophy*, Washington D.C., 2 vols

ECKHARDT, H., 1891. *De Anecdotis Procopii Caesariensis*, Diss. Regimonti

— 1864. *Über Procop und Agathias als Quellenschrifter für den Gothenkrieg*, Progr. Königsberg in Pr.

ELFERINK, M.A., 1967. *'Tychê* et Dieu chez Procope de Césarée', *Acta Classica* 10, 111-34

EMMETT, ALANNA, 1981. 'Introductions and Conclusions to Digressions in Ammianus Marcellinus', *Museum Philologicum Londiniense* 5

— 1983. 'The digressions in the lost books of Ammianus Marcellinus', in Croke and Emmett 1983, 42-53

— forthcoming. 'Digressions in Procopius'

ENGELHARDT, I., 1974. *Mission und Politik in Byzanz. Ein Beitrag zur Strukturanalyse byzantinischer Mission zur Zeit Justins und Justinians*, Miscellanea Byzantina Monacensia 19, Munich

ENNABLI, L., 1975. *Les inscriptions funéraires chrétiennes de la Basilique dite de Sainte-Monique à Carthage*, Tunis

ENSSLIN, W., 1949. *Das Symmachus Historia Romana als Quelle für Jordanes*, Sitz. der bayer. Akad. der Wiss., philol.-hist. kl. 1948, Munich

EVANS, D., 1970. *Leontius of Byzantium*, Dumbarton Oaks Studies 13, Washington D.C.

EVANS, E.C., 1935. 'Physical descriptions of personal appearance in history and biography', *Harvard Studies in Class. Philology* 46, 44-81

EVANS, J.A.S., 1968. 'Procopius of Caesarea and the Emperor Justinian', *Papers of the Canadian Historical Association*, 126-39

— 1969. 'The dates of the *Anecdota* and the *De Aedificiis* of Procopius', *Classical Philology* 64, 29-30

— 1971. 'Christianity and paganism in Procopius of Caesarea', *Greek, Roman and Byzantine Studies* 12, 81ff.

— 1972. *Procopius*, New York

— 1976. 'The attitudes of the secular historians of the age of Justinian towards the classical past', *Traditio* 32, 753-58

EVERT-KAPPESOWA, 1964. 'Antonina et Bélisaire', in J. Irmscher, ed., *Byzantinische Beiträge*, Berlin, 1964, 55-72

FATOUROS, G., 1980. 'Zur Prokop-Biographie', *Klio* 62, 517-23

FENTRESS, E.W.,B., 1979. *Numidia and the Roman Army: Social, Military and*

Economic Aspects of the Frontier Zone, Oxford, British Archeological Reports 53

FIRSOV, L.V., 1979. 'O polozhenii strany Dori v Tavrike', *Viz. Vremennik* 40, 104-13

FISHER, ELIZABETH A., 1978. 'Theodora and Antonina in the *Historia Arcana:* history and/or fiction?', *Arethusa* 11, 253-79 (= J. Peradotto and J.P. Sullivan, eds., *Women in the Ancient World. The Arethusa Papers*, Albany, New York, 1984, 287-313)

FITTON, J., 1976. 'The death of Theodora', *Byzantion* 46, 119ff.

FORSYTH, G.H., 1968. 'The Monastery of St. Catherine at Mt. Sinai – the church and fortress of Justinian', *Dumbarton Oaks Papers* 22, 1-19

FOSS, CLIVE, 1976. *Byzantine and Turkish Sardis*, Cambridge, Mass.

FOTIOU, A.S., 1981. 'Dicaearchus and the mixed constitution in sixth-century Byzantium: new evidence from a treatise on "Political Science" ', *Byzantion* 51, 533-47

FRANTZ, ALISON, 1965. 'From paganism to Christianity in the temples of Athens', *Dumbarton Oaks Papers* 19, 185-206

— 1975. 'Pagan philosophers in Christian Athens', *Proc. Am. Philosophical Society* 119, 29-38

FREND, W.H.C., 1972. *The Rise of the Monophysite Movement*, Cambridge

— 1973a. 'Old and New Rome in the age of Justinian', in D. Baker, ed., *Relations between East and West in the Middle Ages*, Edinburgh, 11-28

— 1973b. 'Severus of Antioch and the origins of the Monophysite hierarchy', *Orientalia Christiana Analecta* 195, 261-75

— 1975a. 'The mission to Nubia: an episode in the struggle for power in sixth-century Byzantium', *Travaux du Centre d'archéologie méditerranéenne de l'Académie polonaise des Sciences* 16, *Études de Travaux* 8, Warsaw, 10-16

— 1975b. 'Recently discovered materials for writing the history of Christian Nubia', *Studies in Church History* 11, 19-30

— 1976a. 'The monks and the survival of the East Roman Empire in the fifth century', *Past and Present* 54, 19-29

— 1976b. 'The early Christian church in Carthage', *University of Michigan, Excavations at Carthage III*, Ann Arbor, 21-40

— 1982. 'The North African cult of martyrs', *Jenseitsvoorstellungen in Antike und Christentum, Gedenkschrift für Alfred Stüber*, Ergänzungsband 9, *Jahrb. f. Antike und Christentum*, 154-62

FRIEDLÄNDER, P., 1912. *Johannes von Gaza und Paulos Silentiarios*, Leipzig

FULFORD, M., 1979. 'Pottery production and trade at the end of Roman Britain: the case against continuity', in Casey 1979, 120-32

GABBA, E., 1981. 'True history and false history in classical antiquity', *Journal of Roman Studies* 71, 50-62

GANTAR, K., 1961. 'Kaiser Justinian als kopfloser Dämon', *Byzantinische Zeitschrift* 54, 1ff.

— 1962a. 'Kaiser Iustinian 'jenem Herbstern gleich'. Bemerkungen zu Prokops *Aed.* I.2.10', *Museum Helveticum* 19, 194-6

1962b. 'Prokops Schaustellung der Tapferkeit', *Živa Antika* 11, 283-6

GAUTIER, E.F., 1927. *L'Islamisation de l'Afrique du Nord. Les siècles obscurs du Maghreb*, Paris

GEANOKOPLOS, DD., 1966. 'Church building and Caesaropapism, AD 312-565', *Greek, Roman and Byzantine Studies* 7, 167-86

— 1976. *Interaction of 'Sibling' Byzantine and Western Cultures in the Middle Ages and Italian Renaissance (330-1600)*, Newhaven and London

GERO, S., 1973. *Byzantine Iconoclasm in the Reign of Leo III,* Corpus Scriptorum Christianorum Orientalium 346, Subs. 41, Louvain

GEROSTERGIOS, A., 1982. *Justinian the Great, the Emperor and Saint,* Belmont, Mass.

GEYER, P. *et al.,* 1965. *Itineraria et alia geographica,* Corpus Christianorum, ser. lat. 175, Turnhout

GIBBON, E., *Decline and Fall of the Roman Empire,* ed. J.B. Bury, 7 vols, London, 2nd ed., 1897-1902

GICHON, S., 1961, 'Roman frontier cities in the Negev', *Acts of the Sixth International Congress of Limes Studies,* Zagreb, 195-207

GOFFART, W., 1980. *Barbarians and Romans, AD 418-584,* Princeton

GOODCHILD, R.G., 1951. 'Boreum of Cyrenaica', *Journal of Roman Studies* 41, 11ff.

GOODCHILD, R., 1976. 'Byzantine, Berbers and Arabs in seventh-century Libya', in Joyce Reynolds, ed., *Libyan Studies,* London, 255-68 (= *Antiquity* 41, 1967)

GOODCHILD, R.G. and WARD PERKINS, J.B., 1953. 'Christian antiquities of Tripolitania', *Archaeologia* 95, 1ff.

GORDON, C.D., 1959. 'Procopius and Justinian's financial policies', *Phoenix* 13, 23ff.

GRABAR, A., 1939. *L'Empereur dans l'art byzantin,* Paris

— 1948. 'Les monuments de Tsaritchin Grad et Justiniana Prima', *Cahiers archéologiques* 3, 49-63

GRAVES, ROBERT, 1938. *Count Belisarius,* London

GRIERSON, P., 1962. 'The tombs and obits of the Byzantine emperors (337-1042)', *Dumbarton Oaks Papers* 16, 1ff.

GRIMBERT, E., 1928. *Theodora. Die Tänzerin auf dem Kaiserthron,* Munich

GRIFFTH, SIDNEY, 1982. 'Eutychius of Alexandria on the Emperor Theophilus and iconoclasm in Byzantium: a tenth-century moment in Christian apologetics in Arabic', *Byzantion* 52, 154-90

GROS, P., 1976. *Aurea Templa: Recherches sur l'architecture religieuse de Rome à l'époque d'Auguste,* Bibl. des écoles françaises d'Athènes et de Rome 31, Rome

GROSDIDIER DE MATONS, J., 1977. *Romanos le mélode et les origines de la poésie religieuse à Byzance,* Paris

GUILLAND, R., 1953. 'Vénalité et favoritisme en Byzance', *Rev. des ét. byzantines* 10, 35-56

GUILLAUMONT, A., 1969-70. 'Justinien et l'église de Perse', *Dumbarton Oaks Papers* 23-4, 41-66

GUTWEIN, K., 1981. *Third Palestine: a Regional Study in Byzantine Urbanization,* Washington D.C.

HANNESTAD, K., 1960. 'Les forces militaires d'après la guerre gothique de Procope', *Classica et Medievalia* 21, 136-83

HANSON, R.P.C., 1979. 'The significance of the doctrine of the last things for Christian belief', *Bull. John Rylands Library* 62, 115-31

HARDY, E.R., 1969. 'The Egyptian policy of Justinian', *Dumbarton Oaks Papers* 22, 36ff.

HARRISON, R.M., 1965. 'The Church of St. Polyeuktos at Constantinople', *Akten des VII Internationalen Kongress für christliche Archäologie,* Trier, 543ff.

HARVEY, SUSAN ASHBROOK, 1977. 'The politicisation of the Byzantine saint', in S. Hackel, ed., *The Byzantine Saint,* Birmingham, 37-42

HARVEY, W. *et al.,* 1910. *The Church of the Nativity at Bethlehem,* Oxford

HAURY, J., 1891. *Procopiana,* Progr. Augsburg

— 1896. *Zur Beurteilung des Geschichtschreibers Procopius von Caesarea*, Munich
— 1900. 'Johannes Malalas identisch mit dem Patriarchen Johannes Scholastikos?', *Byzantinische Zeitschrift* 9, 337-56
— 1934. 'Zu Prokops Geheimgeschichte', *ibid.* 34, 10-14
— 1936. 'Prokop verweist auf seine *Anekdota*', *ibid.* 36, 1-4
HEAD, C., 1980. 'Physical descriptions of emperors in Byzantine historical writing', *Byzantion* 50, 226-40
HENRY, P., 1967. 'A mirror for Justinian: the *Ekthesis* of Agapetus Diaconus', *Greek, Roman and Byzantine Studies*, 8, 281-308
HODDINOTT, R.F., 1963. *Early Byzantine Churches in Macedonia and Serbia*, London
— 1975. *Bulgaria in Antiquity*, London
HOHLFELDER, R., 1977. 'The trans-Isthmian walls in the age of Justinian', *Greek, Roman and Byzantine Studies* 18, 173-9
— 1982. 'Byzantine coin finds from Caesarea Maritima: the 1981 underwater excavations', *Eighth Annual Byzantine Studies Conference*, Abstracts, Chicago, 18-19
HOLMES, W.G., 1912. *The Age of Justinian and Theodora*, 2 vols, London
HOLUM, K., 1983. *Theodosian Empresses*, Berkeley
HOMES DUDDEN, F., 1905. *Gregory the Great*
HONIGMANN, E., 1951. *Evéques et Evêchés monophysites d'Asie antérieure au VIe siècle*, Corpus Scriptorum Christianorum Orientalium subs. 2, Louvain
HONORÉ, TONY, 1978. *Tribonian*, London
HUNGER, H., 1964. *Proöimion. Elemente der byzantinische Kaiseridee in der Arengen der Urkunden*, Wiener Byzantinische Studien I, Vienna
— 1969-70. 'On the imitation (*mimêsis*) of antiquity in Byzantine literature', *Dumbarton Oaks Papers* 23-4, 15-38
— 1978. *Die hochsprachliche profane Literatur der Byzantiner*, 2 vols, Munich
HUNTER, V., 1973. *Thucydides the Artful Reporter*, Toronto
HURST, H., 1977. 'Excavations at Carthage 1976: Third Interim Report', *Antiquaries Journal* 57, 256ff.
HURST, H. et al. 1984. *Excavations at Carthage. The British Mission I. The Avenue du President Habib Bourguiba, Salammbo*, Sheffield, 2 vols
IRMSCHER, J., 1965. 'Die poetische Ekphrasis als Zeugnis Justinianischer Kulturpolitik', *Wiss. Zeitschrift Univ. Jena, Gesellschaft und Sprachwissenschaft* 1-14, 79-87
— 1976. 'Justinianbild und Justiniankritik in frühen Byzanz', H. Köpstein and F. Winkelmann (eds.), *Studien zum 7. Jahrhundert in Byzanz*, Berlin, 131-42
— 1977. 'Justinian als Bauherr in der sicht der Literatur seine Epoche', *Klio* 59, 225-9
JANIN, R., 1969. *La géographie ecclésiastique de l'empire byzantin I.3. Les églises et les monastères*, 2nd ed., Paris
JOHNSON, S., 1980. *Later Roman Britain*, London
JONES, A.H.M., 1962. 'The constitutional position of Odoacer and Theoderic', *Journal of Roman Studies* 52, 126-30
— 1964. *The Later Roman Empire: a Social and Economic Survey*, 2 vols, Oxford
JUNG, J., 1883. 'Geographisch-historischen bei Procopius von Caesarea', *Wiener Studien* 5, 85-115
KADMAN, L., 1957. *The Coins of Caesarea Maritima*, Jerusalem, Corpus Nummorum Palaestinensium 2
KAEGI JR., W.E., 1965. 'Arianism and the Byzantine army in Africa, 533-45',

Traditio 21, 23-53

— 1968. *Byzantium and the Decline of Rome*, Princeton

KAWAR, I., 1957a. 'Procopius and Arethas', *Byzantinische Zeitschrift* 50, 39ff., 362ff. (See also SHAHID).

— 1957b. 'Procopius on the Ghassanids', *Journal of the American Oriental Society* 77, 79-87

KENNEDY, GEORGE A., 1983. *Greek Rhetoric under Christian Emperors*, Princeton

KIHN, H., 1880. *Theodor von Mopsuestia und Junilus Africanus als Exegeten*, Freibourg-im-Breslau

KIRCHNER, K., 1887. *Bemerkungen zu Prokops Darstellung der Perserkrieg des Anastasios, Justin und Justinian von 502 bis 532*, Progr. Wismar

KIRSTEN, E., 1959. 'Edessa', *Reallexikon für Antike und Christentum* IV, 552-97

— 1963. 'Edessa. Eine römische Grenzstadt des 4 bis 6 Jahrhunderts im Orient', *Jarhb. für Antike und Christentum* 6, 144-72

KIRWAN, L.P., 1966. 'Prelude to Nubian Christianity', *Mélanges offerts à K. Michalowski*, Warsaw, 121-8

KITZINGER, E., 1954. 'The cult of images in the period before Iconoclasm', *Dumbarton Oaks Papers* 8, 85-150

— 1958. 'Byzantine art in the period between Justinian and Iconoclasm', *Berichte zum XI Internationalen Byzantinisten-Kongress*, Munich, IV.1

— 1977. *Byzantine Art in the Making*, Cambridge, Mass.

KÖRBS, O., 1913. *Untersuchungen zur ostgotischen Geschichte*, Diss. Jena

KRAUTHEIMER, R., 1974. 'Again Saints Sergius and Bacchus at Constantinople', *Jahrb. f. österr. Byzantinistik* 23, 251-3

— 1980. *Rome. Profile of a City, 312-1308*, Princeton

KUMANIECKI, K., 1927. 'Zu Prokops *Anecdota*', *Byzantinische Zeitschrift* 27, 19-21

KUSTAS, G.A., 1973. *Studies in Byzantine Rhetoric*, Analecta Blatadon 17, Thessaloniki

LADNER, G., 1959. *The Idea of Reform*, Cambridge, Mass.

LAMB, H., 1952. *Theodora and the Emperor. The Drama of Justinian*, Garden City

LAMMA, P., 1950. *Ricerche sulla storie e la cultura del VI⁰ secolo*, Brescia

LAPEYRE, G.G., 1929a. *Vie de Saint Fulgence de Ruspe*, Paris

— 1929b. *Saint Fulgence de Ruspe*, Paris

LAVIN, I., 1962. 'The House of the Lord', *Art Bulletin* 44, 1-27

LEMERLE, P., 1971. *Le premier humanisme byzantin*, Paris

LEVINE, LEE I., 1975. *Caesarea under Roman Rule*, Leiden

LIEBERICH, H., 1900. *Studien zu den Proömien in der griechischen und byzantinischen Geschichtschreibung* II, Progr. Munich

LIEBESCHUETZ, J.H.W.G., 1977. 'The defences of Syria in the sixth century', *Studien zu den Militärgrenzen Roms II*, Vorträge des 10. Internationalen Limeskongress in der Germania Inferior, Köln, 487-99

— 1978. 'Epigraphic Evidence on the Christianisation of Syria', *Akten des XI Internationalen Limeskongress*, Budapest, 485-508

— 1981. 'Problems arising from the Conversion of Syria', *Studies in Church History* 16, 17-24

LITTMANN, R.J. and M.L., 1973. 'The Athenian plague: smallpox', *Trans. Am. Philol. Ass.* 100, 261-75

LLEWELLYN, P., 1970. *Rome in the Dark Ages*, London

LOT, F., 1930 'La conquête du pays d'entre Seine-et-Loire par les Francs', *Revue historique* 165, 241-53

LYNCH, J.P., 1972. *Aristotle's School: a Study of a Greek Educational Institution*, Berkeley

MACCORMACK, SABINE, 1974. 'The Latin prose panegyrics', in T.A. Dorey, ed., *Silver Latin II, Empire and Aftermath*, London, 143-205

— 1981. *Art and Ceremony in Late Antiquity*, Berkeley

— 1982. 'Christ and empire, time and ceremonial in sixth-century Byzantium and beyond', *Byzantion* 52, 287-309

MACKAY, P.A., 1963. 'Procopius' *De Aedificiis* and the topography of Thermopylae', *Am. Journal of Archeology* 67, 241ff.

MCCAIL, R.S., 1971. 'The erotic and ascetic poetry of Agathias Scholasticus', *Byzantion* 41, 205-67

MCCRINDLE, J.W., 1897. *The Christian Topography of Cosmas, an Egyptian Monk*, London

MCNEILL, W.H., 1977. *Plagues and Peoples*, Oxford

MCVEY, KATHLEEN, 1983. 'The domed church as microcosm: literary roots of an architectural symbol', *Dumbarton Oaks Papers* 37, 91-121

MAAS, M., 1982. *Innovation and Restoration in Justinianic Constantinople*, Diss. Berkeley

MADDEN, J.A., 1977. 'Macedonius Consul and Christianity', *Mnemosyne* 30, 153-9

MAHON, Lord, 1829. *La Vie de Bélisaire*, London

MANGO, C., 1959. *The Brazen House: a Study of the Vestibule of the Imperial Palace of Constantinople*, Arkaeologisk-kunsthistoriske Meddeleser Dan. Vid. Selsk. 4.4, Copenhagen

— 1962. 'Antique statuary and the Byzantine beholder', *Dumbarton Oaks Papers* 17, 55-75

— 1972a. *The Art of the Byzantine Empire 312-1453*, Englewood Cliffs, N.J.

— 1972b. 'The Church of Saints Sergius and Bacchus at Constantinople and the alleged tradition of octagonal palace churches', *Jahrb. für österr. Byzantinistik* 21, 189-93

— 1975a. *Byzantine Literature as a Distorting Mirror*, Inaugural Lecture, Oxford

— 1975b. 'The Church of Sts. Sergius and Bacchus once again', *Byzantinische Zeitschrift* 68, 385-92

— 1976. *Byzantine Architecture*, Eng. trans., New York

MANGO, C. and ŠEVČENKO, I., 1961. 'Remains of the Church of St. Polyeuktos at Constantinople', *Dumbarton Oaks Papers* 15, 243ff.

MASEFIELD, J., 1940. *Basilissa: a Tale of the Empress Theodora*, London

MASLEV, S., 1966. 'Die Staatsrechtliche Stellung der byzantinischer Kaiserinnen', *Byzantinoslavica* 27, 308-43

MATHEW, G., 1963. *Byzantine Aesthetics*, London

MATHEWS, T.F., 1971. *The Early Churches of Constantinople*, University Park, Pa.

— 1976. *The Byzantine Churches of Istanbul*, University Park, Pa.

MATTHEWS, JOHN, 1981. 'Anicius Manlius Severinus Boethius', in M. Gibson, ed., *Boethius. His Life, Thought and Influence* 15-43

MAX, G.E., 1981. 'Procopius's portrait of the Emperor Majorian: history and historiography', *Byzantinische Zeitschrift* 74, 1-6

MAYERSON, P., 1963. 'The desert of Southern Palestine according to Byzantine sources', *Proc. Am. Philosoph. Soc.* 107, 160-72

— 1964. 'The first Muslim attacks on southern Palestine (AD 633-634), *Trans. Am Philol. Ass.* 95, 155-99

— 1978. 'Procopius or Eutychius on the construction of the monastery at Mount Sinai: which is the more reliable source?', *Bull. Am. Schools Oriental Research* 230, 33-8

MAZZARINO, S., 1966. *The End of the Ancient World*, Eng. trans. London

MAZZUCCHI, C., 1978. 'Per una rilettura del Palinseto Vaticano 'Sulla scienza politica' del tempo di Giustiniano', in G. Archi, ed., *L'Imperatore Giustiniano, Storia e Mito*, Milan, 237-47

— 1982. *Menae Patricii cum Thomae referendario, De Scientia politica Dialogus*, Univ. Cattolicà di Milano, Scienze filologiche e letteratura 23, Milan

MILIK, J., 1960-1. 'La topographie de Jérusalem vers la fin de l'époque byzantine', *Mélanges de l'Université Saint-Joseph* 37, 145-51

MOMIGLIANO, A., 1955. 'Cassiodorus and the Italian culture of his time', *Proceedings of the British Academy* 41, 207-45

— 1956. 'Gli Anicii e la storiografia latina del VI secolo dopo Cristo', *Entretiens Hardt* 4, 249-90

— 1963. 'Pagan and Christian historiography in the fourth century AD', in Momigliano, ed., *The Conflict between Paganism and Christianity in the Fourth Century, London* 79-99

— 1971. 'Popular religious beliefs and the late Roman historians', *Studies in Church History* 8, 1ff.

— 1973. 'La caduta senza rumore di un impero nel 476 d.c.', *Rivista storica italiana* 85, 5-21

MOORHEAD, J., 1978. 'Boethius and Romans in Ostrogothic service', *Historia* 27, 604-12

— 1983. 'Italian loyalties during Justinian's Gothic war', *Byzantion* 53, 575-96

MUNDELL, M., 1975. 'A sixth-century funerary relief from Dara in Mesopotamia', *Jahrb. der österr. byz. Gesellschaft* 24, 209-27

— 1977. 'Monophysite church decoration', in A.A. Bryer and J. Herrin, eds., *Iconoclasm*, Birmingham, 59-74

NAGY, T., 1967. 'Reoccupation of Pannonia from the Huns in 427. Did Jordanes use the *Chronicle* of Marcellinus at the writing of the *Getica*?', *Acta Acad. Hungar.* 15, 159-86

NANDRIS, J.G., 1980. 'The Djebeliyeh of Mount Sinai – ethnohistorical study of the Thracian affinities of an isolate', *Proc. III Weltkongress für Thrakologie*, Vienna, 2-6 June 1980

— 1981. 'The role of "Vlah" and its rulers on Athos and Sinai', *Rev. des ét. sud-est européennes* 19, 605-10

— forthcoming. 'The Jebeliyeh of Mount Sinai and the land of Vlah', *Qedem*

NELSON, J., 1976. 'Symbols in context', *Studies in Church History* 13, 97-120

NISBET, R.G.M., 1961. *M. Tulli Ciceronis in L. Calpurniam Pisonem oratio*, ed. with text, introduction and commentary, Oxford

O'DONNELL, J.J., 1979. *Cassiodorus*, Berkeley

— 1981. 'Liberius the Patrician', *Traditio* 37, 31-72

— 1982. 'The aims of Jordanes', *Historia* 31, 223-40

OLECK, JACK, 1971. *Theodora*, London

OSTROGORSKY, G., 1956. 'The Byzantine Empire and the hierarchical world order', *Slavonic and East European Review* 35, 1-14

PASCHOUD, F., 1975. *Cinq Etudes sur Zosime*, Paris

PATLAGEAN, E., 1968. 'A Byzance: ancienne hagiographie et histoire sociale', *Annales E.S.C.* 23, 106-26

— 1977. *Pauvreté économique et pauvreté sociale à Byzance, 4ᵉ-7ᵉ siècles*, Paris

PEKKANEN, T., 1964. 'Procopius and the *Periplus* of Arrian', *Eranos* 42, 40-51

PERRIN-HENRY, M., 1980. 'La place des listes toponymiques dans l'organisation du livre IV des *Edifices* de Procope', *Geographica Byzantina*, Byzantina Sorboniensia 3, 93-106

PERTUSI, A., 1968. 'I principi fondamentali della concezione del potere a Bisanzio. Per un commento sul dialogo "Sulla scienza politica" attribuito a Pietro Patrizio (secolo VI)', *Boll. del Ist. Storico Italiano Muratoriano per il Medio Evo* 80, 1-23

PEWESIN, W., 1937. *Imperium, Ecclesia Universalis, Rom. Der Kampf der afrikanischen Kirche um die Mitte des 6. Jahrhunderts*, Stuttgart

PLUMLEY, J. MARTIN, 1976. 'An uncial text of St. Mark in Greek from Nubia', *Journal of Theological Studies* 27, 34ff.

POULTER, A.G., 1983. *Ancient Bulgaria*, 2 vols, Nottingham

PRAECHTER, K., 1900. 'Zum Maischen anonymous *peri politikês epistêmês*', *Byzantinische Zeitschrift* 9, 621-32

PRINGLE, DENYS, 1981. *The Defences of Byzantine Africa from Justinian to the Arab Conquest*, 2 vols, Oxford, British Archeological Reports 99

PÜLHORN, W., 1977. See VEH, 1977

REECE, R., 1980. 'Town and country: the end of Roman Britain', *World Archeology* 12, 77-92

REYNOLDS, SUSAN, 1983. 'Medieval "Origines Gentium" and the community of the realm', *History* 68, 375-90

RINGEL, J., 1975. *Césarée de Palestine. Etude historique et archéologique*, Strasbourg

ROQUES, R., 1954. *L'Univers dionysien*, Paris

RUBIN, B., 1951. 'Der Fürst der Dämonen', *Byzantinische Zeitschrift* 44, 469-81

— 1953. 'Zur Kaiserkritik Ostroms', *Studi bizantini e neoellenici* 7, 453ff.

— 1954. *Prokopios von Kaisareia*, Stuttgart (= Pauly-Wissowa, *RE* 23.1.273-599, 1957)

— 1960. *Das Zeitalter Iustinians* I, Berlin

RUNCIMAN, S., 1931. 'Some remarks on the image of Edessa', *Cambridge Historical Journal* 3, 238-52

— 1977. *The Byzantine Theocracy*, Cambridge

RYCKMANS, J., 1956. *La Persécution des chrétiens himyarites au VIe siècle*, Istanbul

— 1964. 'Le Christianisme en Arabie du Sud préislamique', *L'Oriente cristiano nelle storie della civiltà*, Rome, 413-53

SARTRE, M., 1982. *Trois Études sur l'Arabie romaine et byzantine*, Brussels, Collection Latomus 178

SAUCIUC-SAVEANU, T., 1964. 'Die Charaktisierung des Kaisers Trajan von Prokopios aus Cäsarea', *Rev. des et. sud-est europ.* 2, 547-52

SCAVONE, D.C., 1970. 'Zosimus and his historical models', *Greek, Roman and Byzantine Studies* 11, 56-67

SCHEMMEL, F., 1925. 'Die Schule von Caesarea in Palästina', *Philol. Wochenschrift* 46, 1277-80

SCHINDLER, K.-H., 1966. *Justinians Haltung zur Klassik*, Cologne and Graz

SCHNAYDER, J., 1950. *De periegetarum Graecorum reliquiis*, Lodz

SCHULZ, A., 1871. *Procopius, de bello Vandalico*, Progr. Gotha

SCOTT, R., 1981a. 'The classical tradition in Byzantine historiography', in M. Mullett and R. Scott, eds., *Byzantium and the Classical Tradition*, Birmingham, 61-74

— 1981b. 'Malalas and Justinian's codification', in E. and M. Jeffreys and Ann Moffatt, *Byzantine Papers*, Canberra, 12-31

— forthcoming. 'Malalas, the *Secret History* and Justinian's propaganda'
— forthcoming. 'Justinian's coinage and Easter reforms and the date of the *Secret History*'
SCHUBART, W., 1943. *Justinian und Theodora*, Munich
SCHWARTZ, E., 1939. *Kyrillos von Skythopolis*, Leipzig (Texte und Untersuchungen 49.2)
— 1973. *Drei dogmatische Schriften Iustinians*, M. Amelotti, R. Abertella, L. Migliardi, *Legum Iustiniani imperatoris vocabularium*, subs. II, 2nd ed., Milan
SCHWYZER, E., 1914. 'Die sprachlichen Interessen Prokops von Caesarea', *Festgabe für H. Blümner*, Zurich, 303-27
SEGAL, J.B., 1955. 'Mesopotamian communities from Julian to the rise of Islam', *Proceedings of the British Academy* 41, 109-39
— 1970. *Edessa, the 'Blessed City'*, Oxford
SEIBER, JULIA, 1977. *Early Byzantine Saints*, Oxford, *British Archeological Reports, supp. ser.* 37
ŠEVČENKO, I., 1966. 'The early period of the Sinai monastery in the light of its inscriptions', *Dumbarton Oaks Papers* 20, 255-64
— 1978. 'Agapetus East and West: the fate of a Byzantine 'Mirror of Princes'', *Rev. des ét sud-est. europ.* 16, 3-44
— 1981. 'Levels of style in Byzantine prose', *Jahrb. der österr. Byzantinistik* 31, 289-312
SHAHID, I., 1959. 'The patriciate of Arethas', *Byzantinische Zeitschrift* 52, 321-43
— 1964. 'Byzantino-Arabica: the conference of Ramla, AD 524', *Journal of Near Eastern Studies* 23, 115-31
— 1970. *Cambridge History of Islam* I, 3-29
— 1971a. 'Procopius and Arethas again', *Byzantion* 41, 313-38
— 1971b. *The Martyrs of Najran*, Subsidia Hagiographica 49, Brussels
— 1979. 'Byzantium in South Arabia', *Dumbarton Oaks Papers* 33, 23-94
SHELTON, KATHLEEN, 1981. *The Esquiline Treasure*, London
SKOK, P., 1935. 'De l'importance des listes toponomastiques chez Procope pour la latinité balkanique', *Bull. de l'Inst. archéol. Bulgare* IX, 161ff.
SOLOMONIK, E.I., and DOMBROVSKY, O.I., 1968. 'O lokalizatsii strany Dori', *Arkheologicheskie issledovaniya srednevekovogo Kryma*, Kiev, 11-44
SORABJI, R., 1983. *Time, Creation and the Continuum: theories in antiquity and the early middle ages*, London
SOYTER, G., 1951. 'Die Glaubwürdigkeit des Geschichtsschreibers Prokopios von Kaisarea', *Byzantinische Zeitschrift* 44, 541ff.
— 1939. 'Prokop als Geschichtsschreiber des Vandalen- und Gotenkrieges', *Neue Jahrbücher f. Antike und deutsche Bildung* 2, 97-108
STADELMANN, H., 1926. *Theodora von Byzanz*, Dresden
STEIN, E., 1949. *Histoire du Bas-Empire* II, publ. J.-R. Palanque, Amsterdam
SVENNUNG, J., 1967. *Jordanes und Scandia*. Skrifter utgivna av Kungl. Humanistica Vetenskapssamfundet I, Uppsala, 44.2a, Stockholm
TCHALENKO, G., 1953-58. *Villages antiques de la Syrie du Nord,* 3 vols, Paris
TEALL, J.L., 1965. 'The barbarians in Justinian's armies', *Speculum* 40, 294-322
TEUFFEL, W.S., 1871. *Studien und Charakteristiken*, Leipzig, 191-236
THOMPSON, E.A., 1977. 'Britain, AD 406-410', *Britannia* 8, 303-18
— 1979. 'Gildas and the history of Britain', *ibid.*, 10, 203-26
— 1980. 'Procopius on Brittia and Britannia', *Classical Quarterly* 30, 498-507
— 1982a. 'Zosimus 6.10.2 and the letters of Honorius', *ibid.*, 32, 445-62
— 1982b. *Romans and Barbarians: the decline of the Western Empire*, Maidson,

Wisconsin

THOMPSON, HOMER A., 1959. 'Athenian twilight, AD 267-600', *Journal of Roman Studies* 49, 61-72

THURMAN, W.S., 1968. 'How Justinian I sought to handle the problems of religious dissent', *Greek Orthodox Theological Review* 13, 15-40

TINNEFELD, F., 1971. *Kategorien der Kaiserkritik in der byzantinischen Historiographie von Prokop bis Niketas Choniates*, Munich

TOPPING, E. CATAFYGIOTU, 1977. 'Romanos, on the entry into Jerusalem: a Basilikos Logos', *Byzantion* 47, 65-91

— 1978. 'On earthquakes and fires', *Byzantinische Zeitschrift* 71, 22-35

TOUMANOFF, C., 1963. *Studies in Christian Caucasian History*, Washington, D.C.

TRICCA, A., 1915. 'Evagrio e la sua fonte più importante Procopio', *Roma e l'Oriente* 9, 102-11, 185-201, 283-302; 10, 51-62, 129-45

TROUSSET, P., 1974. *Recherches sur le limes Tripolitanus du Chott el-Djerid à la frontière Tuniso-Libyenne*, Coll. d'ét. d'antiquités africaines, Aix-en-Provence, Paris

TRYPANIS, C.A., 1968. *Fourteen Early Byzantine Cantica*, Wiener byzantinischer Studien 14, Vienna

TSAFRIR, Y., 1978. 'St. Catherine's Monastery in Sinai: Drawings by I. Dunayevsky', *Israel Exploration Journal* 28, 218-29

TSIRPANLIS, C.N., 1974. 'John Lydos on the imperial administration', *Byzantion* 44, 479ff.

UDAL'COVA, Z.V., 1965. 'La chronique de Jean Malalas dans la Russie de Kiev', *Byzantion* 35, 575-91

— 1972. 'Le monde vu par les historiens byzantins du IVe au VIIe siècles', *Byzantinoslavica* 193ff.

— 1974. *Ideino-politicheskaya bor'ba v rannei Vizantii po dannym istorikov IV-VII vv.*, Moscow

ULLMANN, W., 1966. *Principles of Government and Politics in the Middle Ages*, 2nd ed., London

UNDERHILL, CLARA, 1932. *Theodora, the Courtesan of Constantinople*, New York

URE, P.N., 1951. *Justinian and his Age*, Harmondsworth

VALDENBERG, V., 1925. 'Les idées politiques dans les fragments attribuées à Pierre le Patrice', *Byzantion* 2, 55-76

VANDERCOOK, J.W., 1940. *Empress of the Dusk. A Life of Theodora of Byzantium*, New York

VARADY, L., 1978. *Die Auflösung des Altertums*, Budapest

VEH, O., 1950-51. *Zur Geschichtschreibung und Weltauffassung des Prokop von Caesarea* I, Wiss. Beilage z. Jahresbericht 1950-51 des Gymnasiums Bayreuth

— 1951-52. id., II

— 1961-77. *Procopii Opera*, German translation, Munich (*De Aedificiis* 1977, with commentary by W. Pülhorn)

VEIMARN, E.V., 1980. 'Ot kogo mogli zashchishcnat' gotov v Krymu 'dlinnie steny' Prokopiya?', *Antichnye traditsii i vizantiiskie realii*, Sverdlovsk, 19-33

VELKOV, V., 1958. 'La construction en Thrace à l'époque du Bas-Empire', *Archeologia* 10, 124ff.

— 1977. *Cities in Thrace and Dacia in Late Antiquity*, Amsterdam

— 1983. 'La Thrace et la Moésie inférieure pendant l'époque de la Basse Antiquité (IV-VI ss.)', in Poulter 1983, 177-93

VEYNE, P., 1981. 'Clientèle et corruption au service de l'Etat: la vénalité des offices dans la Bas-Empire romain', *Annales ESC* 36, 339-61

VINCENT, L.H. and ABEL, F.M., 1914. *Bethléem. La Sanctuaire de la Nativite*, Paris
— 1926. *Jérusalem Nouvelle*, 2 vols, Paris
VOLBACH, W.F., 1962. *Early Christian Art*, New York
VÖÖBUS, A., 1958. *Literary Critical and Historical Studies in Ephrem the Syrian*, Stockholm
WAGNER, N., 1967. *Getica: Untersuchungen zum Leben des Jordanes und zur frühen Geschichte der Gothen*, Berlin
WARD, BENEDICTA, SLG, 1980. *The Lives of the Desert Fathers*, London and Oxford
WARD, J.O., 1968. 'Procopius' "Bellum Gothicum" II.6.28. The problem of contacts between Justinian I and Britain', *Byzantion* 38, 460ff.
WEITZMANN, K., 1976. *The Monastery of Saint Catherine at Mount Sinai: the Icons, I. From the Sixth to the Tenth Centuries*, Princeton
— 1979. *The Age of Spirituality. Late Antique and Early Christian Art. Catalogue of the Exhibition at the Metropolitan Museum of Art, Nov. 19, 1977 through Feb. 12, 1978*, New York
WELLAND, J., 1966. *You with the roses – what are you selling?* London
WELSBY, DEREK A., 1982. *The Roman Military Defence of the British Province in its Later Phases*, Oxford, British Archeological Reports
WES, M.A., 1967. *Das Ende des Kaisertums im Westen des römischen Reichs*, The Hague
WHITBY, L.M., 1983. 'Theophanes' chronicle source for the reigns of Justin II, Tiberius and Maurice' (AD 565-602)', *Byzantion* 53, 312-45
— 1982. 'Theophylact's knowledge of languages', *Byzantion* 52, 425-8
WICKHAM, C., 1981. *Early Medieval Italy*, London
WILKINSON, J., 1971. *Egeria's Travels*, London
WILLIAMSON, G.A., 1966. *Procopius. The Secret History* (trans.), Harmondsworth
WILSON, N.G., 1983. *Scholars of Byzantium*, London
WINDSTEDT, E.O., 1909. *The Christian Topography of Cosmas Indicopleustes*, Cambridge
WIRTH, G., 1964. 'Mutmassungen zum Text von Prokops Gotenkrieg', *Helikon* 4, 153ff.
WOLSKA, W., 1962. *La Topographie chrétienne de Cosmas Indicopleustes. Topographie et science au VIᵉ siècle*, Paris
WOOD,, IAN, 1984. 'The end of Roman Britain: continental evidence and parallels', in D.N. Dumville and M. Lapidge, eds., *Gildas: New Approaches*, Woodbridge, 1-25
WORTLEY, J., 1980. 'The legend of the Emperor Maurice', *Actes du XVᵉ Congrès international d'ét. byz.*, Athens, 382-91
YAKOBSON, A.L., 1964. *Srednevekovy Krym*, Moscow-Leningrad
ZACOS, G. and VEGLERY, A., 1972. *Byzantine Lead Seals* I, Basel
ZIEGLER, P., 1969. *The Black Death*, London

Index

1. General

2. Passages cited

(page references to this book are in bold type)

Persian Wars I

1.1: **5**
1.2: **207, 249**
1.3: **135**
1.5: **37**
1.16: **37**
2.1f.: **153**
2.2: **37**
2.6: **154**
3.1-4.35: **154**
3.2-7: **218, 219**
5: **155**
5.30: **240**
6: **155**
6.15, 19: **240**
7.5: **30, 115**
7.7: **61**
7.22: **30, 96, 128**
7.23: **115**
8: **156**
8.5: **240**
8-9: **154**
9: **156**
10: **156**
10.1-12: **216, 232**
10.9: **153**
11.6f.: **153**
11.12: **231**
12-22: **136**
12.1-19: **156**
12.2-5: **122, 216**
12.8: **123**
12.24: **135**
13.5-8: **157**
13.9f.: **107, 157**
13.12f.: **146**
14.1-12, 13-27: **146**
15.3: **240**
15.20-5: **216**
16.1: **239**
17.17: **125**
17.40: **240**
17.47, 48: **125**
18: **146, 157-8**
18.36-7: **125**
18.38: **239, 240**
19-20: **121, 147**
19.17f.: **96**
20.10: **240**
21.2: **158**
23.1: **143, 158, 162, 163**
23.24: **156**
24: **64, 65, 76, 143, 144, 166-7**

24.6: **241**
24.8: **227**
24.12: **231**
24.16: **231**
24.18: **240, 243**
24.32: **69**
24.33f.: **69**
24.37: **69**
25: **51, 69, 159**
25.9: **231**
25.11: **188**
25.43: **236**
26: **159**

Persian Wars II

2.4f.: **149**
2.6: **143**
2.14: **38**
3.32-53: **149**
4.11: **220**
4.17f.: **113**
5.14-27, 28: **163**
5.28: **129**
6.7: **227**
7.16, 8.17: **164**
8.14: **119**
8.17-19, 25-9: **165**
8.35: **232**
9.8f.: **143, 165, 239**
10.1: **30, 117, 145**
10.4: **29, 117, 145**
10.13, 14: **239**
11.14f.: **30**
11.26: **239**
11.28: **114**
11.31f.: **163**
11.32f.: **75, 129**
12.6-30: **116, 164, 231**
12.22: **92**
13.22: **119**
15.6-9: **122**
16-19: **160**
18.5f.: **149**
19.14: **130**
19.26: **125**
20.1, 8: **163**
20.16: **30**
20.20: **161**
22.1-5: **40, 153, 234**
22.2: **29, 166, 167-8**
22.9: **8, 41, 49, 135, 163**

22.10: **56**
22.22f., 29f.: **41**
23.3f.: **41**
23.5-13: **128**
23.12f.: **41**
23.14-16: **41, 128**
23.17-21: **42**
24.1: **42**
24.2: **169**
26: **160, 231**
26-7: **117, 164**
29.14-26: **216**
30: **157, 169**
30.17: **150**
30.49: **70**

Vandal Wars I

1.1-4: **207, 208f.**
1.1-9: **171**
2.2-6: **218**
2.31f.: **213**
4.9: **30**
4.20: **118**
4.24: **209**
6.26: **36**
8.25f.: **40**
9.12-16: **113**
9.25: **158, 173**
10.1f.: **114, 173**
10.7-21: **173**
12.1-2: **173**
12.2-3: **70, 114, 135**
12.13: **113**
13.3: **135**
13.24: **70**
14.1-3: **173**
14.3-4, 7-13, 15: **135, 173**
15.35: **135**
16.2f., 9f.: **62**
16.9-11: **185**
16.13: **149**
16.14: **113**
17.6: **174**
18.2: **118, 174**
19: **136**
19.6: **113**
19.11: **70**
19.25: **118, 174**
20.1: **70, 166, 174**
20.18-20: **185**
20.19f.: **62, 174**